AF615007

2491 X

FIFTH GENERATION WAFER ARCHITECTURE

FIFTH GENERATION WAFER ARCHITECTURE

MALCOLM J. SHUTE
Microelectronics Centre,
Middlesex Polytechnic, London

PRENTICE HALL
NEW YORK LONDON TORONTO SYDNEY TOKYO

First published 1988 by
Prentice Hall International (UK) Ltd,
66 Wood Lane End, Hemel Hempstead,
Hertfordshire, HP2 4RG
A division of
Simon & Schuster International Group

© 1988 Prentice Hall International (UK) Ltd

All rights reserved.
No part of this publication may be reproduced, stored in a retrieval system, or transmitted, in any form or by any means, electronic, mechanical, photocopying, recording or otherwise, without the prior permission, in writing, from the publisher.
For permission within the United States of America contact Prentice Hall Inc., Englewood Cliffs, NJ 07632.

Printed and bound in Great Britain at
the University Press, Cambridge

Library of Congress Cataloging-in-Publication Data

Shute, Malcolm J., 1955–
Fifth generation wafer architecture/by Malcolm J. Shute. p. cm.
Bibliography: p.
Includes index.
ISBN 0-13-314238-8
1. Fifth generation computers. 2. Computer architecture. 3. Integrated circuits—Design and construction. I. Title.
QA76.85. S58 1988
004. 16–dc 19 87-27313

British Library Cataloguing in Publication Data

Shute, Malcolm J.
Fifth generation wafer architecture.
1. Computer architecture
I. Title
004.2′1 QA76.9.A73

ISBN 0-13-314238-8

1 2 3 4 5 91 90 89 88 87

ISBN 0-13-314238-8

24/9

Remembering Gran and Grandpa,
whose inspired purchase (Hellyer 1971)
started me along this path

CONTENTS

PREFACE

This volume explores the possible realisation of fifth generation computer architectures through wafer scale integration. It looks at architectural considerations, and designs for fifth generation, non-von-Neumann computer architectures. It also considers fault tolerance, failure tolerance, reconfiguration and wafer scale integration.

As integrated circuit technology improves, the demands on it increase too. Invariably, as hardware is developed for one application, such as a computer architecture, the demands for more functionality, and a consequential proliferation of its components, promptly follow.

Present technology now allows the fabrication of circuits with more than 100 000 transistors per die. Future systems will require even more than this, but how can these circuits be fabricated, given that present technology is stretched nearly to the limit? How can they be designed, given that present designs are already more complicated than the combined road, rail, electricity, gas, water and telephone layouts of a major city? What principles of operation will be employed, given that the current ones now show severe signs of limitation?

This book sets out to answer these questions. It describes a number of the techniques and problems of building the largest single chip computers possible, namely those which occupy an entire wafer of semiconductor. It necessarily spans the many subject areas which influence computer design, in particular those of computer science, suggesting that which is desirable in a computer, and those of microelectronics, indicating that which is possible in a computer.

The skills of the computer engineer will be in great demand to design new architectures for the future breeds of supercomputer. The exciting prospect of finding a successor to a system which has not been surpassed in forty years is now realistic.

The academic study of this subject seems to be polarised into two classes of department: those which study computing, and those which study electronic engineering. However, this book is neither a computer science text, nor one for microelectronics, though both areas are introduced here. Instead, it reports on some exciting research work from various sources around the world which is relevant to computer engineering and computer architecture design.

Although the work which is reported here is currently the subject of research, this book has been written with Master's level teaching in mind. Some of the introductory material is included simply because it is useful to have a basic introduction included in the one text rather than be constantly referred elsewhere. Ample references are given though for further reading.

ACKNOWLEDGMENTS

Firstly, I would like to thank Dr Paul Kelly who, with his amazing library of up-to-date papers and proceedings and his breadth of understanding in a vast spectrum of studies, has contributed more than significantly to the writing of this book.

I am very grateful to: everyone working on the Alvey Cobweb (Alv/IKBS/064/150) project. Professor Peter Osmon and Dr Chris Hankin have been close friends of mine since the beginnings of my postgraduate studies, and have been a constant source of encouragement, and learning. Notably, they have contributed to the computer science side of the work which is reported here, in Chapters 2 and 3.

Indeed, I am doubly indebted to Chris Hankin, and also to Andrew McCabe, both of whom gave me the highly critical, yet encouraging reviews which an earlier draft of this book needed. I am also very grateful to Drs Chris Jesshope and Tony Ambler, both of whom gave similarly constructive critisms of an even earlier draft.

From the Alvey Wafer Scale Integration project (Alv/Prj/Arch/073) I would like to thank Dr Geoff Sumerling, and Dr Russell Aubusson for their contributions to my general understanding of wafer scale integration; Dr Will Moore for his help with the performance and economics of water scale integration; Professor Mike Lea and Steve Clarke for their frequent seminars, discussions and reports on many aspects of wafer scale integration; Andrew McCabe for his contributions in systolic array and photolithography discussions; Ken Warren for his contributions to my discussion of electrical design issues; Richard Illman who helped me to understand some of the issues of built-in self test and electronic computer-aided design; Ray McKirdy for his help with my discussion of the physical design issues of wafer scale packaging; and each of the group leaders, whose reports I have used as the basis for Chapters 7 and 8.

The help given by my collegues at Middlesex Polytechnic has been invaluable, notably that from: Richard Bayford for his suggestions on the systolic array and built-in self-test sections; Kevin Johnstone for his comments on the electrical design issues sections; Keith Pitt for his contributions to the section on packaging; John White for his help with aspects of ion implantation; Dave Court for his general comments about microelectronics fabrication; Dick Gledhill for his critical comments on the final draft; Dr Richard Seals and Ray Ruocco for their many helpful suggestions concerning the presentation of Chapters 2 and 3. Thank you too, to Linda Moore and her long-suffering team of computer operation and reception staff who bore with me during the writing stages of the lecture notes which finally lead to this book.

I also acknowledge the funding which is provided by Middlesex Polytechnic, and the Alvey directorate of Great Britain, particularly on the above-mentioned Cobweb and WSI projects, which have enabled me to conduct this work. In particular, I thank Professors John Butcher and Frank Tye for securing the research post at the polytechnic. Most of all, I would like to thank Alan Bagshaw of the Alvey directorate for his tremendous support.

In addition, I thank Simon Peyton Jones and Chris Clack for many productive conversations, and Professor Ronan Sleep, also Professors John Darlington and John Gurd, respectively, for their discussions on the Flagship and Manchester University Dataflow projects. Also thanks go to Leon Bentley for suggestions during the writing of the sections on rotary switch replication, and mechanical antifuses; Dr Mary Sheeran for the sections on μFP; Hugh Glaser for discussions on the historical aspects of computing; Dr P.K. Chaturvedi for his comments about WSI packaging; Ruben Ashkenasy for discussions on direct-write photolithography; and Paul Anderson for his comments and suggestions in review of Chapters 2 and 3.

The author is indebted to Glen Murray for his continual help and advice during the preparation of this text, and for his work in finding the highly constructive reviewers of the early manuscripts; also to Glynice Smith, who provided much guidance on my writing style; and, of course, also to all of my friends and relations, especially Mum, Dad, Jancis and John, for putting up with me during the final stages of the writing.

GLOBALLY RESERVED NAMES

A number of terms are used consistently throughout this book. These are listed here, along with a brief definition. Fuller definitions can be found in the glossary at the back of the book, and in the text, mainly on pages 125–35.

a	area of cell	A	area of device
δa	area of fault/failure tolerant overhead per circuit	δA	area of non fault/failure tolerant overhead per device
$\mathbf{a}$	area of circuit with fault/failure tolerance logic	A'	area of complete fault/failure tolerant device
b	reliability of cell	B	reliability of device
δb	reliability of failure tolerant overhead per circuit	δB	reliability of non failure tolerant overhead per device
$\mathbf{b}$	reliability of circuit with failure tolerance logic	B'	reliability of complete failure tolerant device
c	number of cells needed	C	number of cells fabricated
$\mathbf{c}$	number of cells per circuit		
d	diameter of water	D	fault density
δd	unusable margin round wafer		
d'	usable diameter of wafer		
		F	number of faults/failures tolerated by device
h	harvest of cells	H	harvest of devices
j	an integer		
k	an integer	K	number of faults/failures to kill the device
m	number of rows of cells needed	M	number of rows fabricated
n	number of columns of cells needed	N	number of columns fabricated
p	a probability ($0 \leq p \leq 1$)		
r	distance from centre of wafer	R	replication factor
s	number of sides on a cell	S	speed ratio
t	time		
v	yield of circuits	V	yield of fault/failure tolerant devices
		W	usable area of wafer
y	yield of cells	Y	yield of devices

- $\mathbf{y}$ yield of circuits with fault/failure tolerance logic
- z number of test processors per device
- Y' yield of fault/failure tolerant devices

- α fault clustering factor
- θ angle relative to the major water flat
- $\varkappa$ transistor
- λ unit length in circuit layout
- σ standard deviation
- τ transistor switching time

- *crop* number of working devices obtained per wafer
- *crop'* number of working fault/failure tolerant devices obtained per wafer
- *num* number of devices fabricated per wafer
- *rca* relative cell area
- *rco* relative cell overhead
- *rda* relative device area
- *rdo* relative device overhead
- *rpa* relative processor area
- *rpo* relative processor overhead
- *TC* test coverage
- *TQ* test quality

1

FIFTH GENERATION COMPUTING BACKGROUND

Digital electronic computer design has been an engaging subject for forty years. In this time, some five orders of magnitude of improvement of performance have been attained, but solely through trimming the original design to its present highly honed state. There is no doubt that further improvement of performance is needed, but this cannot be expected to be achieved by mere tuning of the current design any further. As a result, radically new types of computer are being investigated by research groups throughout the world, and this book reports on some of the implications of this work. A study is made of some possible applications in which these machines might be used, programmed and implemented. Necessarily, some degree of conjecture is involved, along with a backward glance at how the predecessors are used, programmed and implemented. The latter is necessary in order to understand why certain techniques and styles are still adopted, and others have been modified or dropped in the light of the lessons of the past.

Over recent decades, many lessons have been learned. Not least, there is a striking similarity between many of the problems and their possible solutions which are found in electronic engineering and computer programming. Both disciplines have learned that the design task becomes very much easier if the system is *hierarchical*, highly *regular* and highly *modular*. They have also learned how efficiency of the final product benefits from the use of *local*, highly *parallel* interconnections within the regular arrangement of modules. However, it is critical that the right *granularity* be found in all cases, and at *all* levels of detail. In other words, the modules must neither be too small and plentiful, nor too large and scarce; similarly, communications should involve messages which are neither too short and prolific, nor too long and infrequent (Figure 1.1).

From the hardware end, computer architects want programming languages which make efficient use of their hardware primitives. From the software end, functional language designers want new computer architectures which support their ideas

Parallel interconnectivity
Local interconnectivity
High modularity
High regularity
Optimum granularity

FIGURE 1.1 *Recurring themes*

efficiently. In a third corner, computer engineers need computer-aided design programs to describe the structures which they intend to implement (Ullman 1984, Sheeran 1985). There are, therefore, many lessons which each group can learn from the others, and much virtue in a closer co-operation between the disciplines to solve the imminent problems in computer design. Since this idea is so central to the aim of this book, the common themes, as listed above, are repeated in Figure 1.1. They will appear many times in this text, even across many subject boundaries. The computer architect must be on the alert for this sort of commonality, and ready to exploit it at all times.

This book concentrates on two seemingly unrelated ideas, namely functional language programming, and wafer scale integration (WSI), and uses them to illustrate the common points of computer science and microelectronics. It does not matter whether WSI ever becomes economically viable. It is not certain even that functional programming will become economic. What is important is that the techniques which are eventually adopted will bear the same sort of interrelationships. Functional language programming and WSI are therefore used here merely as the vehicles with which to illustrate, to catalogue and to classify the points which are made in this book.

A summary is given in the next section (Section 1.1) of the aims and concerns of the fifth generation programme. This helps to set the context: the goals towards which the computer engineering ideas of this book hope to contribute, at least in some small way. The section after (Section 1.2) describes the ideas on which the new architectures must be built if forty years of work and lessons are not to be ignored.

1.1 BACKGROUND STUDY OF FIFTH GENERATION COMPUTING

The fifth generation programme was initiated by the Japanese in 1981 (Simons 1983) to develop computer systems which are faster, more reliable and more intelligent than those of the present, and was scheduled, rather optimistically, for completion in 1991. Western countries, perceiving an imminent domination by the Japanese, followed with their own initiatives. Respectively, they are Alvey (in the UK), ESPRIT (in the EEC), DARPA and MCC (both in the USA). Along with the Japanese ICOT programme, they can be grouped collectively under the 'fifth generation' label.

1.1.1 Targets and requirements

As technology develops and allows new heights in performance to be achieved, such as an increased execution speed from computers, Parkinson's law suggests that the demands on the system grow to absorb the extra capacity, for example more load is placed on the faster computers. Thus, despite the improvements in performance, there is an ever-pressing requirement for more.

Also, humankind is becoming increasingly aware of the limits of the planet's resources. Computers, which have proved useful in combating inefficiency in manufacturing industry, are now required to do the same for the extraction, farming and service industries, by the provision of more accurate and timely information. As well as helping in conservation, computers might also help in the search for new sources of energy and raw materials.

Computers might also be used to tackle the new problems which are faced by society: problems which have been, to some extent, caused by computer automation in the past. The development of *user-friendly* interfaces will make computers easier and more enjoyable to use, and demanding less specialist skills, so enabling the vast pool of unemployment to be matched to the equally vast mountain of available work.

In order for fifth generation computers to support this fast, intelligent, informative, likeable software, they must be very much faster than those of the present. It is estimated that computers will need to attain speeds of between 10^8 and 10^9 logical inferences per second (lips). The unit of work, known as a *logical inference*, can be compared to the more usual measure on conventional computers: one million inferences per second (1 Mlips) is roughly equivalent to a hundred million conventional instruction cycles per second (100 Mips). Between 100 Mlips and 1 Glips therefore, is equivalent to a conventional computer running at a speed between 10^4 and 10^5 Mips, that is between 10 and 100 Gips. This is about two orders of magnitude greater than can be achieved by contemporary computers. Logically, it is necessary only to make bigger, more ambitious versions of the computers which are already in existence. There is a problem even with conventional computers, though, known as the *von Neumann bottleneck* (Backus 1978), which manifests itself in two major ways. Firstly, it takes programmers a long time to write, and later to upgrade, today's programs so that they work, that is there is a bottleneck between program conception and program run. Secondly, it takes a long time for today's computers to execute today's program, that is there is a bottleneck between the input of data and results filtering out in return.

To say 'so that they work' is not as redundant as it sounds. Many of the programs that are around today, for instance in air traffic control, and missile defence systems, are so complicated that they have never been fully tested. They have been tested only for a statistical sample of cases. No one knows whether they still contain errors which will take effect only under certain extremely rare circumstances. A graphic example was provided by the British Stock Exchange in October 1986 when its new computer system was first brought into operation after years of careful planning.

This experience should set alarm bells ringing in the minds of those who design energy efficient passenger aircraft which cannot be flown without computer intervention, and in the minds of those administrators who are confidently pouring funds into the Strategic Defense Initiative.

The problems of excessive program development time, and excessive program execution time, are not just technical concerns. Time is involved, and time is money. Industry is therefore serious in its quest for solutions to the problem of the von Neumann bottleneck.

Like the previous generations, the fifth will not evolve gradually, but through a sudden major advance (Simons 1983). In the past, this has been achieved solely through the development of improved hardware technology, as charted in Figure 1.2. The first computers and calculators were mechanical, relying on the positions and velocities of levers and wheels, man's oldest inventions, to represent numbers. Electronics provided the first major improvement, in the form of thermionic valves, making implementation practicable. Successive improvements have been obtained by the adoption of semiconductors instead, first using discrete germanium transistors, and then by the use of silicon. Then came the rapid succession of circuit integration from small scale integration (SSI) to the present very large scale integration (VLSI).

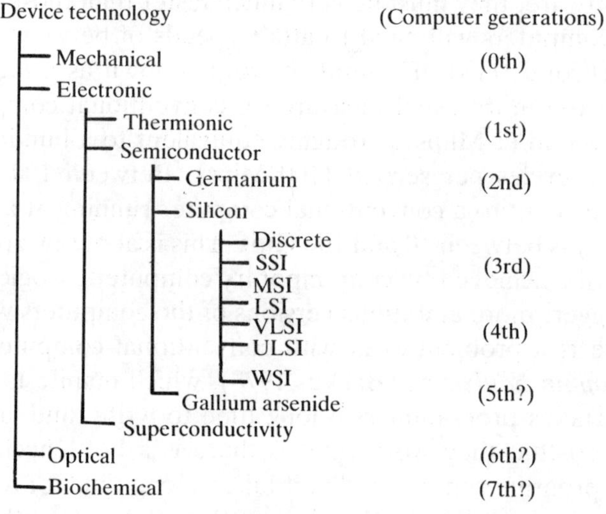

FIGURE 1.2 *Device technology*

Commentators on future technology point variously to different technological improvements for the next generation. Some suggest that ultra large scale integration (ULSI) is the next step after VLSI; others that full-blown WSI would be better. Yet others have suggested (Yuba and Kashiwagi 1987) that silicon ought now to be superseded by gallium arsenide, and others that superconducting devices, such as Josephson junctions, might be used in place of semiconductors.

Looking further ahead, it has been suggested that electronic circuits might be replaced by the use of optical-switching logic (*Economist* 1986), and that biochemical devices offer the ultimate means of mimicking some of the desirable properties of the mammalian brain. However, work on these proposals is still in its infancy and will not be considered further here. Instead, WSI has been assumed throughout this text, provided that it is understood that much of what is stated for this technology is equally applicable to ULSI, and some of the others too.

Unlike the previous four generations, the fifth cannot depend so heavily on advances in hardware technology alone since many fundamental limits are now nearly reached. Instead, hope must be placed on the combined advances in virtually every other human discipline (Simons 1983). Figure 1.3 suggests some areas of study which might have a direct effect on improving program development and execution. The studies are complementary, and progress in the various disciplines is iterative with that in others. For example, advances in psychology suggest possible future lines of enquiry in artificial intelligence, which in turn gives new insight into the behaviour of the animal mind.

Since the aim is to design and to build computers which are faster, more reliable and more intelligent than present ones, the temptation is constantly to look at the mammalian brain for clues as to how it achieves the same goals. However, the aim is not merely to imitate the brain; it would be pointless to invent a machine whose skills are already available in great quantitity. The machine must complement the strengths of human beings, to do things which humans are poor at doing. However, designers are still free to extract as many good characteristics as they can to achieve their ends.

Computer engineering	→ New architectures
Computer science	→ Efficient programming
Control theory	→ Robotics
Data communications	→ Multiprocessor design
Cognitive science	→ Artificial intelligence
Linguistics and psychology	→ Speech understanding

FIGURE 1.3 *Some of the diverse influences on fifth generation design*

As an aside, some suggest that there will be an increasing rôle for the arts too, not to help in the quest for fifth generation computing, but to compensate for the detrimental effects of its success. Computer command languages will continue to become more abstract with each passing generation, until at last they resemble natural language. This seems to be desirable, and certainly it is inevitable. However, consider the position in the 1990s, during the transition between the 'cp/usr/fred/a.out objs/go' conversations of the present day, and the verbal dialogues of 2001 (Clarke 1968). Natural language tends to be verbose, ambiguous, capable of great abuse which is made tolerable in society by the human listeners' ability to understand even the most malformed and grammatically incorrect of sentences.

Used as a computer language, therefore, it is cumbersome, error prone (where the machine misunderstands the user's intention) and currently quite impracticable. The language which is used must, therefore, be a highly restricted and formalised subset of the English language. It will, though, be used each and every day by a vast portion of society. This was precisely the intention: to promote the use of computers by all. But what will happen to normal human conversation during this period? Surely, everyone will become accustomed to conversing in restricted English, and will continue to use it even when socialising. The arts will be needed to ensure that social communication is injected with a richness which will, by necessity, be lacking from machine communication.

1.1.2 The new study areas

From Figure 1.3 it is clear that fifth generation computing studies span many subjects. It is useful, therefore, to identify some new divisions into which the work can be grouped. The languages and media with which data and instructions are communicated to the computer, and with which results are returned, can be grouped under the title of *man–machine interfaces* (MMI). The programs which will be run on the new computers centre on those which are classed as *intelligent knowledge-based systems* (IKBS). The environment in which programs are developed, such as operating systems and editors, is covered by the *software engineering* (SE) title. *Architecture* covers the design of computer hardware, and *microelectronics* covers the technology which will be used to implement them. Each of these titles is now taken in turn for further discussion.

Man–machine interfaces

Much of the computer's processing capacity will be used to make the computer user-friendly: to accept natural language as an input/output medium, and generally to make use of the computer more palatable to the novice. It could be argued that there will always be a pool of experienced users who would prefer to sacrifice some of this friendliness for extra raw power, and there is no reason why this should not be possible. However, the ability to process natural language is more important than merely as a means of communication. Much of human thought is dependent on the way in which meaning is mapped into the language (Hofstadter 1980); computers must have access to this information too.

Speech synthesis and graphics output are now becoming viable, relying in no small way on the superior abilities of the human to interpret the crude output which is produced. For input, too, voice recognition and natural language analysis are possible, provided that the vocabulary is relatively small and predetermined. Digitisers, the traditional method for diagram input, will increasingly give way to television cameras, with the added impetus that similar technology is needed for reading signatures and handwritten text, and for robot vision.

Intelligent knowledge-based systems

Present generations of computers are used for *data processing*, but the fifth will be used for *information processing*. Computer memory is usually likened to an array of pigeon-holes, each slot having an address, and able to store one item. On present day computers, the contents are limited to simple binary integers, of some arbitrarily short size. Most problems can be tackled using this simple structure, but it is far from convenient. Programming languages provide an interface which allows us to 'simulate' more elaborate types of memory. For instance, assembler languages allow the memory to be treated as though it could store decimal integers, with symbolic names used to represent abstract objects. High level languages, such as Pascal, allow memory to be visualised as if it could represent some arbitrary mixture of integers, fractional numbers, textual characters, colours, days of the week. They also allow the specification of quite complicated structures to represent abstract ideas. Very high level languages, like Prolog, carry the structuring idea further, and allow memory to be visualised as an array of slots, each capable of holding arbitrary-sized objects. To illustrate the power of expression which this allows, consider an address book; superficially, it appears to have the same structure as computer memory, in that it consists of a large number of identical slots, but each of these can contain different numbers of different length fields for forenames, surname, house number, street, town, etc.

The efficient representation and storage of information as a body of *knowledge* is not sufficient. The new machines will have to be able to learn, that is to extract new information, if they are to improve on the programs which already exist. They will need to incorporate new information which neither conflicts with nor contradicts existing knowledge. Many books, including this one, assume that this is best achieved for the present by the use of *formal logic*. Ironically though one of its major strengths, the fact that all of its results are guaranteed to be correct, is its final downfall. Pattern matching has long been recognised as being of importance to the support of this logic, but there is a need to recognise patterns using only incomplete information, and in the *heuristic* process of drawing analogies. As well as there being a case for using *fuzzy* logic, able to deal with probablistic statements, and uncertainties, there is a need to use *non-monotonic logic*, which is able to withdraw conclusions in the light of new evidence (Simons 1983). Moreover, mechanically applied formal logic has been shown, by Gödel, Turing and other philosophers, to be completely inadequate for representing intelligent behaviour (Hofstadter 1980).

One application which will greatly benefit from achievements in the IKBS area is that of *expert systems*. These are machines which are able to provide specialist knowledge where it is in short supply. For instance, in local hospitals, which though having good teams of doctors who are able to treat the most commonly occurring complaints, cannot provide a whole complement of specialists in all of the tropical diseases, rare neural conditions, etc. Alternatively, an overstretched surgery might be able to entrust the treatment of routine ailments to nurses, with their skills augmented by an expert system, so freeing the doctors to deal with what, to them, are the more interesting, rarer complaints. Moreover, a machine expert might even perform better than a human, for instance in medicine, where the human expert can easily be guilty of avoiding making decisions at the right time, owing to fears concerning the magnitude of the decision, and through not necessarily conscious personal or career-motivated bias.

Software engineering

Programming languages form part of the environment in which programming ideas are conveyed to the machine. These, as has already been implied, must be improved to facilitate the ease of expression of abstract ideas. Moreover, other parts of the design environment must be enhanced too. For instance, operating systems need to be made more powerful, dealing with more complex resources, such as parallelism, networks and information stores (knowledge bases). Their command languages have to reflect this, which is where the use of natural language and graphical input and output are most likely to make an immediate impact. Even the task of editing, which seems to occupy so much of the average programmer's time, will need to see significant improvement. Screen editors are gradually replacing line editors, but eventually these too will give way to the use of graphical and natural language editors. As well as needing new programs to aid the design of software, new electronics computer-aided design (ECAD) programs are necessary to design the new hardware, and the new computers must have new ECAD tools written for them, in order to design succeeding machines.

The integrated programming systems environment (IPSE) will be one product of software engineering, producing systems in which the same commands and data structures are applicable to programs, directories and text files. The Occam/Transputer environment is perhaps one early example of this. Such systems must be more helpful than those of present, explaining to the novice how to use them and offering meaningful diagnostics when things go wrong.

Architectures

Computer scientists, notably Backus (1978), have suggested that excessively long program development times, and bug-ridden programs, are largely attributable to the use of inelegant programming languages. Program development time would be greatly reduced if programmers used declarative languages, such as Miranda (Turner 1985), in preference to imperative ones, such as Fortran and Pascal. However, present day implementations are inefficient at executing programs which are written in declarative programming languages. Computer scientists therefore urge the design of computers which allow for the efficient implementation of these languages.

Computer programmers have suggested that execution times might be diminished by the exploitation of parallelism. Many parts of programs can be executed concurrently, neither interfering with nor being influenced by other parts. This implies the use of multiprocessor computers: computers in which each autonomous part of the program can be executed on its own processor. However, there are still few successful multiprocessor designs for general purpose computation.

Lastly, electronics engineers have observed that hardware is extremely cheap, and that it will soon be possible to fabricate circuits containing millions of transistors. However, there seems little point in doing so if most of the transistors are going to remain idle for the majority of the time. They therefore urge the design of computers which will make more effective use of the available hardware.

Designers have attempted to use multiple conventional processors connected in various configurations. Many have had some degree of success, especially when used in specialised applications. However, the immense problems which are involved in programming such networks of relatively conventional processors has led many researchers around the world to work on new computer architectures. Many have strayed away from the idea of connecting several conventional computers together in a network and then somehow arranging for them to be synchronised. Instead, they have completely thrown off the von Neumann style of execution model, and are working on new models. However, many execution models, alternatives to von Neumann's arrangement, are useful only for certain parts of the computation; for example they might be excellent for arithmetic execution but incapable of arranging for input/output to work efficiently. These are not adequate as replacements for the von Neumann model. The new model must be at least as universally applicable as the old. None has as yet arisen which meets this exacting criterion, and hence few machines are available that employ such modes of execution.

Microelectronics

Prior to the invention of the integrated circuit (IC) *circa* 1958, transistors were fabricated on wafers of silicon, only to be separated and packaged individually. Circuits were constructed by connecting transistors together on printing circuit boards. Because of their reduced size, weight, power requirements and heat dissipation, and their increased operation speeds, communication speeds and connection reliability (Sze 1983), integrated circuits appeared attractive to the space and defence programmes. Once the techniques had been developed, they then appeared attractive for commercial applications too, with the added advantage of faster, and hence cheaper, assembly times.

At first, only a few transistors were involved in each integrated circuit, using technology which was referred to, retrospectively, as small scale integration. However, the advantages listed above are still valid. There is therefore an ever-present drive for more circuit connections to be made on the silicon, and hence for more transistors to be included in each circuit. Thus, there has been a development, as traced in Figure 1.4, through medium scale integration (MSI), to large scale integration (LSI), and now to VLSI.

Rent's rule (Landman and Russo 1971) indicates that on average, for a module which contains a given number of 'randomly' connected transistors, $\varkappa$, the number of external connections is given by:

$$\text{connections} = 2.5\varkappa^{0.61}$$

When the modules are fabricated on a single piece of semiconductor, this inter-

SSI	2 –	100 transistors
MSI	100 –	1 000 transistors
LSI	1 000 –	50 000 transistors
VLSI	50 000 –	500 000 transistors
ULSI	500 000 –	5 000 000 transistors
SLSI	5 000 000 –	50 000 000 transistors
ELSI	50 000 000 –	500 000 000 transistors

FIGURE 1.4 *Spectrum of integration*

connection demand can be met easily without being bounded by the limit on the pin count which is incurred by separate integrated circuit module versions of the same system. There is every reason to suppose that the drive will continue, and more transistors will be required per circuit. Adopting some terminology from the radio frequency band names, future integration could, therefore, proceed to ultra (ULSI), super (SLSI), and extremely large scale integration (ELSI).

Increases in the transistor count have been achieved to date by reducing the dimensions of each transistor, and by using more densely packing design styles. For some time, according to Moore's law, circuit complexity, as measured by the transistor count, has been quadrupling every four years, and the linear dimensions of the circuit elements have been halving in the same time. More transistors, therefore, fit into roughly the same area, and so the area of the average die has increased by little more than an order of magnitude in the forty years since the invention of the transistor. However, there are signs that further improvements will be less forthcoming this way. The active regions of transistors are now so small that they contain about a hundred doping atoms; if they are made much smaller than this they will cease to operate properly as transistors (Barker 1986). Therefore, subsequent increases in the transistor count will be achieved by corresponding increases in the area of the final device (Moore 1986a).

However, using conventional techniques, the presence of a single fault in a circuit is enough to render the circuit unusable. The proportion which work, relative to the total number fabricated, is called the *yield*. Simplistically it can be modelled by Poisson statistics (Stapper and Rosner 1982):

$$Y = e^{-DA}$$

where D is fault density (typically 0.05/mm^2) and A is area of the circuit. This exponential law means that it is not realistic even to contemplate an ULSI or wafer scale circuit without rerorting to the use of fault or failure tolerance.

Wafer scale integration is not part of the series which is traced in Figure 1.4. It is a particular group of techniques, not a measure of device complexity. A 50-transistor device occupying a 25 mm diameter water, for instance, would be an example both of SSI and of WSI. However, WSI (Butcher 1984) normally implies a state-of-the-art wafer, which might be 150 mm in diameter, used to fabricate a single device at state-of-the-art packing densities, such as 5 000 transistors/mm^2. Once this has become practicable, the drive will continue for further increases in device area, achieved by increasing the diameter of the wafer. Already industry is experimenting with 200 mm diameter wafers, and so devices constructed from 150 million transistors suddenly become feasible.

Of the applications which have been proposed to demonstrate the feasibility of WSI (Jesshope and Moore 1986), one interesting idea is to use it for artificial vision systems; not only would the wafer perform the light sensing, using an array of photo-detectors, but it would also perform much of the image processing *in situ*. Similarly, a graphics display could be fabricated from a wafer which was covered with light-emitting cells, along with the circuitry for performing the graphics work. But by far the most interesting application, at least from the author's point of view, is the prospect of constructing an entire multiprocessor *supercomputer on a wafer*. For this reason, the operation of the conventional computer is briefly described next, as the foundation on which the descriptions of newer designs can be built.

1.2 COMPUTER ARCHITECTURE: THE CONVENTIONAL MODEL

To the user, the digital electronic computer is a black box, a filter into which data and problems are entered, and from which results are expected in return. To a large extent, the user does not care how the data and problems are converted into the results, so long as it happens, happens quickly and happens correctly. The rate of conversion is the computer's throughput, as discussed in Chapters 3 and 4, and is inversely proportional to the program execution time. Another important measure (Chapter 2) is the programmer's throughput, which is the rate at which the computer can be (re)programmed, and is inversely proportional to the program development time. These, of course, are the two aspects of the von Neumann bottleneck.

Like its analogue audio counterpart, the digital electronic computer filter needs control information, but instead of needing to vary the gains of amplifiers according to switch and potentiometer settings on the front panel, the computer needs to insert and to remove adders, multipliers, etc. into the paths of the incoming digital data. Again, switches could be provided on the front panel, one for each step in the filtering process, but the complexity of most programs would require the provision of several thousand switches. Instead, only a few switches are provided, along with a memory unit to remember the switch settings which are keyed in, a few at a time, before the program is started. The computer therefore refers to the memory for its control information, instead of directly to the front panel.

When digital electronic computers were first developed, the patterns of bits which made up the program and data were entered in precisely this way. Understandably, this is a very slow and tedious process. More importantly, it is highly prone to error, with very few aids to help locate these *bugs* when they occur. Figure 1.5 shows a column of binary numbers, but who can say what this program does, or whether there are any errors in the list?

```
0001010111110111
0000000000000000
0000000001011100
0001010111110111
0000000001010110
0000000001010100
0001111111110111
0000000001010000
0000000001001010
0110010111110111
0000000000000001
0000000001001000
0001111111110111
0000000001000100
0000000001000000
0010110111110111
0000000000111010
0000000000111010
0000011100001111
1110010111110111
0000000000000001
0000000000110100
0001110111111111
0000000000101110
0000000000101110
0110010111110111
0000000000000001
0000000000101000
0001110111111111
0000000000100000
0000000000100100
0001010111110111
0000000000000001
0000000000011110
0010110111010111
0000000000011000
0000000001011100
0000010111100000
0010110111010111
0000000000010010
0000000000000001
0000001111010110
0000000000000000
0000110000001110
0000110000010110
0001110100001110
0000000000000000
0000000000000000
0000000000000000
0000000000000000
```

FIGURE 1.5 *Representation of a program expressed in binary code*

The computer can be divided into three major components (Hamacher *et al.* 1984): the central processor unit (CPU), the memory (MEM) and the input and output controller (IOC). This is depicted in Figure 1.6. The three units are linked together by three *buses*: the data bus, the address bus and the control bus.

In the true spirit of top-down design (Glaser *et al.* 1984), these components are now selected, one at a time, for further study. Sections 1.2.1 and 1.2.2 conduct this exercise for the CPU and the memory respectively. Section 1.2.3 summarises the operation of the complete computer, executing a simple program, and Section 1.2.4 concludes this section by characterising the major properties which this type of machine exhibits.

1.2.1 The central processor unit

Figure 1.7 shows the CPU broken into two major components: the arithmetic and logic unit (ALU), and the control unit (CNTL). The former performs the arithmetic functions, whilst the latter controls the entire computer, including the ALU.

Each of these units might have a special register associated with it: the accumulator (ACC) for the arithmetic and logic unit, and the program counter (PC) for the control unit (Figure 1.7). The accumulator is a simple block of storage elements for intermediate results during a calculation. The program counter is another block of storage elements which is used for holding an address (the numerical position of a required location in the memory, as described next).

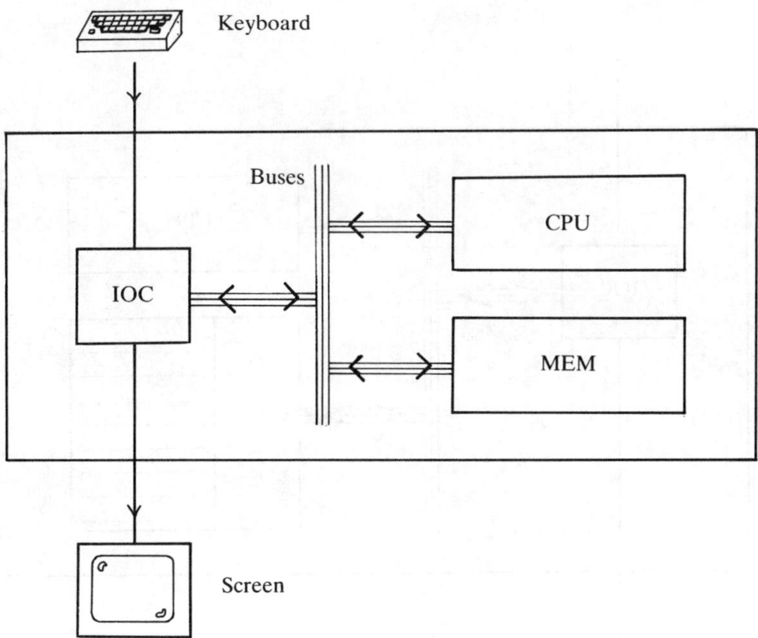

FIGURE 1.6 *Major components of a conventional computer*

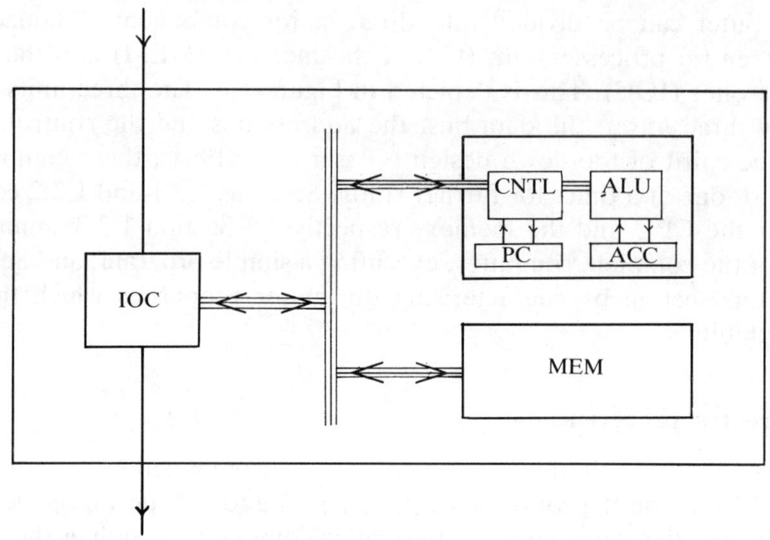

FIGURE 1.7 *Focusing on the major components of the CPU*

1.2.2 The memory

Figure 1.8 shows how the memory block can be subdivided into a block of logic called 'address decode', and a (large) number of memory locations, called *words*. Generally, the processor needs to select words in some arbitrary order, and hence

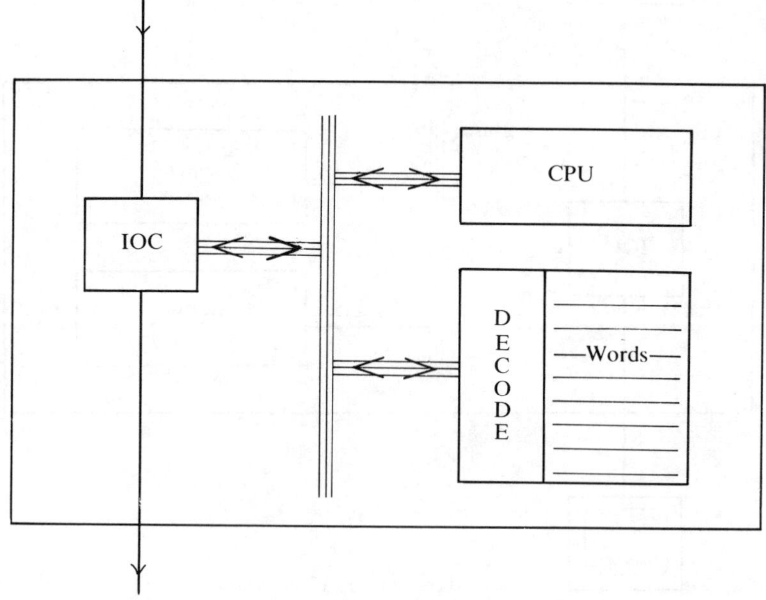

FIGURE 1.8 *Focusing on the major components of the memory*

the type of memory which is implemented is usually known as *random access memory* (RAM).

Since the memory and similar structures feature heavily in later chapters, time will be spent now to consider its construction in greater detail. Thus, the blocks can be subdivided, and viewed as a large vector of registers, or alternatively as a large two-dimensional grid of storage elements. In Figure 1.9, eight four-bit words are shown, although in practice one would expect memory to be much larger than this.

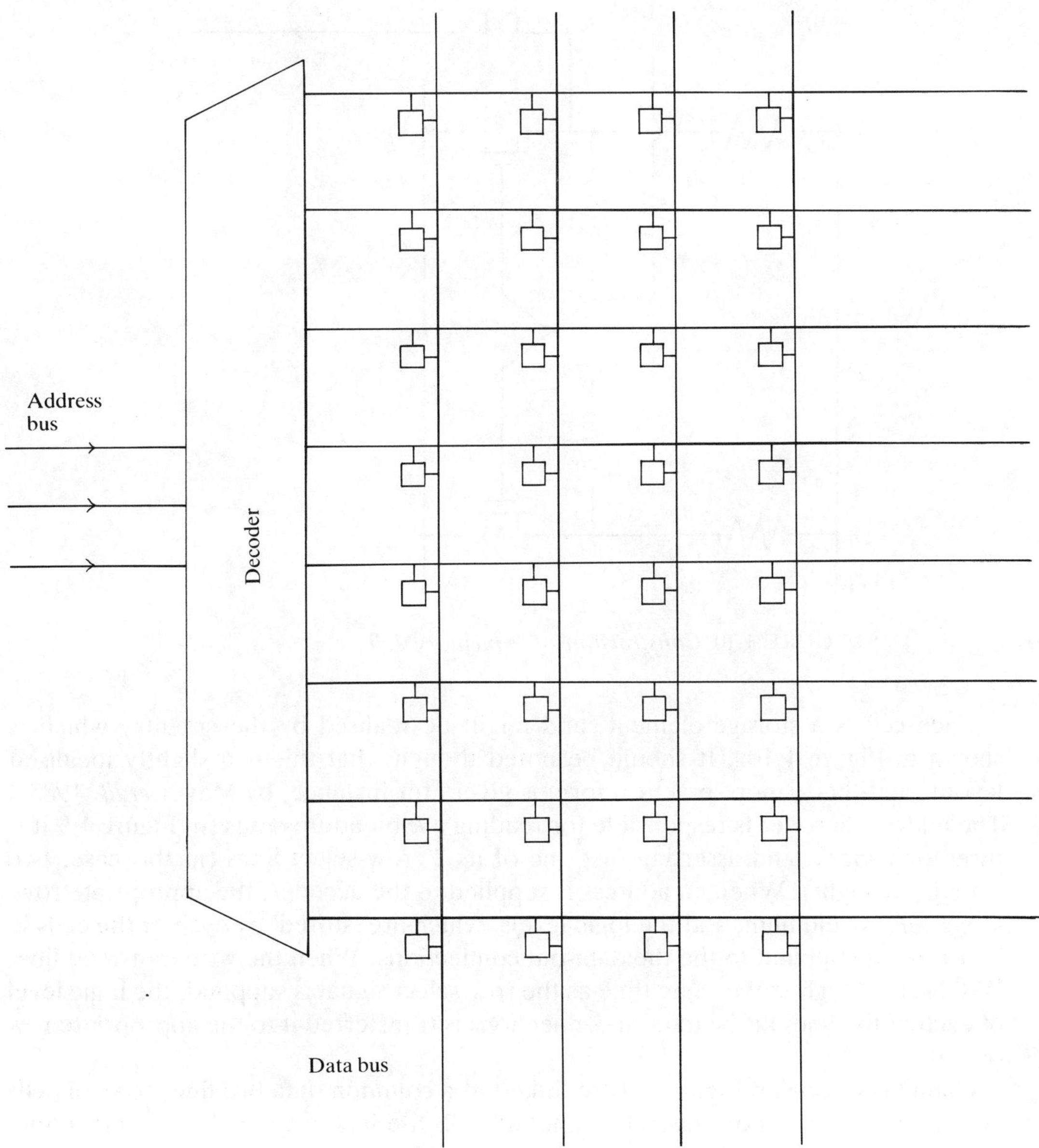

FIGURE 1.9 *Schematic representation of an 8 by 4 memory*

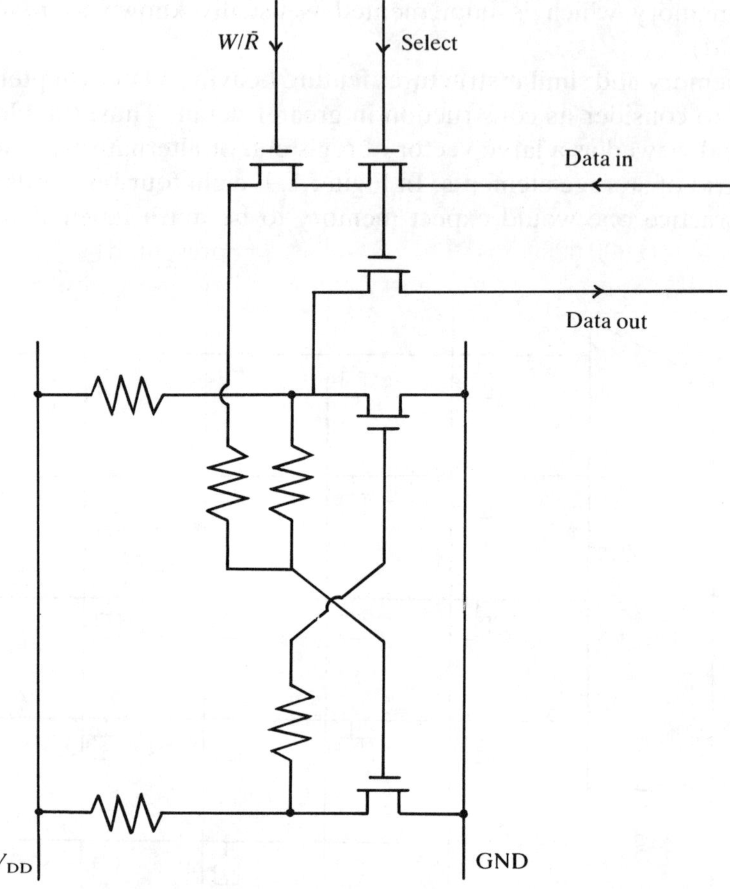

FIGURE 1.10 *Construction of a memory cell*

Each cell is a storage element, and might be realised by the circuitry which is shown in Figure 1.10. (It should be noted though, that this is a slightly idealised layout, and that a more practical form is given, for instance, by Mavor *et al.* 1983.) The address decoder is responsible for reading a *k*-bit address bus (in Figure 1.9 it is three bits wide), and asserting just one of its 2^k row-select lines (in this case, two cubed, i.e. eight). When an address is supplied to the decoder, the appropriate row-select line is held high, and the logic levels, which are 'stored' by each of the cells in that row, are applied to the the data-out connections. When the write/not-read line, W/$\overline{\text{R}}$, is held high at the same time as the row-select signal is supplied, the logic level of each of the lines at the data-in connections is transferred into the appropriate row of cells.

Columns of cells in Figure 1.9 are linked to a common data bus line; rows of cells are linked to a common row-select line; all cells are linked to the W/$\overline{\text{R}}$ control line, and to the power supplies. The properties of this arrangement of memory have a pervasive effect on the behaviour of the computers which use it, as is described next.

1.2.3 Instruction execution

The operation of the complete machine is illustrated by way of an example: that of a (very simple) program running on an (extremely simple) computer, Figure 1.11.

The contents of memory can be partly data, and partly program. The example in Figure 1.11 depicts a memory which contains sufficient program instructions and data to compute the value of '77 minus 35'. (In order to abbreviate the diagram, the binary pattern '0100 0000 0000 0101', for example, is represented as '4005'. By taking the 16 binary digits in groups of four, they can be represented using four digits, as summarised in Figure 1.12. This is only a notation; the memory, of course, contains the appropriate 16 bits.)

The CPU repeatedly runs through a fixed, fairly short, cycle of operations, called the *instruction cycle*. This is typically as listed in Figure 1.13.

The initial contents of memory are as listed in Figure 1.14. Assume that when the computer is started up both PC and ACC contain zero. Assume also that program instructions are made up from four digits, for example 4005, and that the first digit is the operation code, or *op-code*, and that the other three digits form the *operand address*. The significance of this is explained next.

Referring to the instruction cycle, as given in Figure 1.13, the first action is for the contents of PC, that is 000, to be sent along the address bus to the address decoder. The memory responds to this by sending the contents of location 000, that is 4005, in reply. These are sent along the data bus, and are received by the CPU. Next, the contents of PC are incremented to 001.

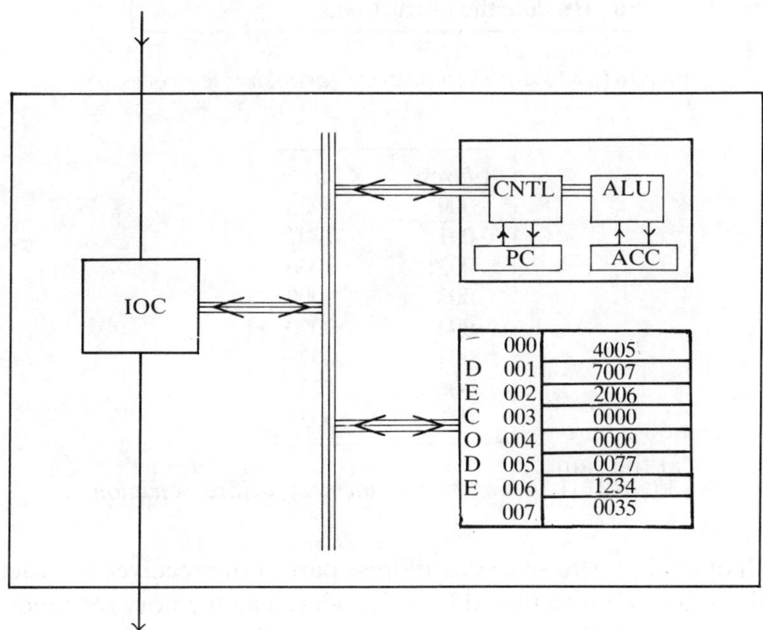

FIGURE 1.11 *A simple computer running a simple program*

Binary	*Hexadecimal*
0000	0
0001	1
0010	2
0011	3
0100	4
0101	5
0110	6
0111	7
1000	8
1001	9
1010	A
1011	B
1100	C
1101	D
1110	E
1111	F

FIGURE 1.12 *The translation between binary and hexadecimal numbers*

1. Send contents of PC to address decoder.
2. Receive instruction from memory.
3. Increment contents of PC.
4. Send address of data to address decoder.
5. Receive data from memory.
6. Execute the instruction.

FIGURE 1.13 *Instruction cycle for a simple processor*

Address	*Contents*
000	4005
001	7007
002	2006
003	0000
004	0000
005	0077
006	1234
007	0035

FIGURE 1.14 *Contents of memory before execution*

The fourth operation is to send the address part of the received instruction, that is 005, along the address bus to the address decoder. The memory responds by sending the contents of location 005, that is 0077, in reply. These too are sent back along the data bus, and are received by the CPU. Lastly, the instruction is executed. From the

Instruction op-code	*Meaning*
0	Halt the computer
2	Store contents of ACC in memory
4	Load data into ACC
6	Add data to ACC
7	Subtract data from ACC

FIGURE 1.15 *Instruction set of the simple processor*

table in Figure 1.15, it can be seen that the 4 of the original instruction 4005 means 'Load data into accumulator'. Thus ACC now contains 0077.

The first cycle is now complete, and the second one is begun. Now, PC contains 001, so it is the value 7007 which is received as the next instruction, and PC is incremented to 002. The address part, 007, causes 0035 to be received as the data, and so 0035 is subtracted from the contents of ACC, because of the meaning of the first 7 in the instruction. Thus ACC now contains 0042.

In the third cycle, 002 is sent by the PC, 2006 is received as the next instruction, and PC is incremented to 003. The address 006 is sent to the memory and, although 1234 is received as the data, nothing happens to it because the processor finds that the meaning of the 2 in the instruction is to store the contents of ACC in the memory. So the execute part of this cycle involves sending 0042 along the data bus to the memory. Since this value is sent along as data, and not as an address as has previously been the case, the memory then stores it, in this case at location 006 since this is the address which is still supplied by the address bus.

In the fourth cycle, 003 is sent to the memory, 0000 is received and PC is incremented to 004. 000 is sent as an address, and 4005 is received as data, but again this is wasted effort in this case because the execute phase of the cycle finds that the meaning of the first 0 of the instruction is to halt the computer. The programmer, on noticing that the program has terminated, looks in the memory, Figure 1.16, to find the answers that the program has computed. In this case, he would have to remember that he had written his program to store the result of the computation in memory location 006.

Address	*Contents*
000	4005
001	7007
002	2006
003	0000
004	0000
005	0077
006	0042
007	0035

FIGURE 1.16 *Contents of memory after execution*

1.2.4 Characteristics

A number of general characteristics are apparent from the preceding section: properties which are exhibited by virtually every computer in use today. Most importantly, each memory location can hold just one fixed length integer, usually represented in base 2. The *memory-write* operation destroys the previous contents of the location; but the *memory-read* operation is non-destructive.

Each memory location has an *address* which is represented as another fixed length integer. They can be accessed only one at a time.

The CPU has *registers*, each with properties similar to the individual locations in memory. In particular, they each can store a single fixed length integer, and have the same properties of destructive write and non-destructive read.

The CPU runs repeatedly through its *instruction cycles*. This keeps the buses in heavy demand for most of the time. An address integer is sent to the memory, and the memory sends the integer contents of that location in reply. Sometimes new contents are sent to the memory to overwrite the old ones.

The CPU treats integers variously as executable instructions, addresses or data. This interpretation depends on context, mainly on what part of the instruction cycle is being obyed when the integer is read into the processor.

The next chapter demonstrates how each of these properties of computer hardware has an identifiable effect on the appearance of programming languages, to the extent that hardware design decisions made forty years ago still affect the style of program writing today.

1.3 SUMMARY AND ORGANISATION OF THE BOOK

This book is about possible future computer design, programming and implementation. It uses functional language programming as the vehicle for describing desirable attributes in the programming style, and WSI as a vehicle for describing some representative properties of hardware design. In each of these areas, the designer should be constantly on the alert for methods for imposing modularity, regularity and parallelism on the system. The organisation of this book is summarised in Figure 1.17.

Within this structure, this book highlights certain ideas, and trends, dealing in generalities in preference to details. For this reason, many of the programming examples have taken liberties with the programming languages which they use. Integer and floating-point arithmetic have been mixed, user-defined names have been made longer than are normally allowed in some language implementations and the names of some of the primitives have been altered in places too. For the purposes of the illustrations in this text, this disregard for implementation detail is considered to be well justified.

On the hardware side, although the words ‘silicon’ and ‘wafer scale integration’

Chapter		
1	Summary	– Introductory
2	Granularity and design	– Software
3	Software concerns	
4	Logical realisation	– Software (computer architecture)
5	Fault and failure tolerance	
6	Logical realisation	– Hardware
7	Hardware concerns	
8	Granularity and design	– Hardware
9	Summary	– Conclusive

FIGURE 1.17 *Structure of this book*

are used frequently, the techniques are not dependent in any major way on any particular technology. Any semiconductor material could be used, and many of the techniques are appropriate even using some of the other technologies which are mentioned in Figure 1.2.

This book describes the design of new computer architecture using a top-down design style: first in terms of the programming languages which it must support, then in terms of successively lower layers of architectural detail, and finally a description of some of the circuit elements which will be needed to implement it. Chapter 2, therefore, commences the process with a brief review of the styles of computer programming languages.

1.4 EXERCISES

1.1 If the processor in section 1.2.3 were to run the program listed in Figure 1.18, what would be the contents of the memory when the computer halted?

Address	*Contents*
000	4007
001	2006
002	6005
003	2005
004	0000
005	0034
006	0023
007	0012

FIGURE 1.18 *Contents of memory before execution*

1.2 How many data and address transfers are made along the buses during the execution of the program in Figure 1.18?

2

EXPRESSING IDEAS TO THE COMPUTER

Computer programming languages have been around for about forty years but, even so, they could be considered to have been developed almost as an after-thought. The hardware was designed first after the Second World War, and gradually the need for efficient methods of programming it was recognised. Figure 2.1 shows a possible taxonomy of the programming languages that have been developed since then, along with some common examples.

The left to right progression between the classes of programming language can be viewed historically as the desire to make the computer do more of the programming work (Barron 1977). Programming a computer is a major task, and the more that the computer can do to help the programmer the better. Programs will be developed faster, and with fewer *bugs*, because the programmer is free to express the program in a way which is convenient to him, and it is left to the computer to convert the representation into a form which is convenient to it. Thus programs become cheaper to develop, and reliability is enhanced. This chapter traces the development of current computer programming ideas through the use of numerous illustrations, culminating in the declarative languages.

Computer programming languages are called *languages* because their purpose is 'to convey meaning' (i.e. to carry *semantics*). The computer is a machine; the programmer wants to make it do something. Language, in this case a programming language, is the means whereby such intentions can be articulated. Once expressed, though, programs serve three audiences. The first is of course the computer. The second is the programmer who, when setting out to write a program, might not at first have any clear idea of what to write. Having jotted down the first ideas, the problem usually becomes much clearer, and the programmer is able to fill in a little more of the detail. This, in turn, makes the situation clearer still, and yet more detail can be resolved. Thus programming is an incremental, iterative process. The programmer must be able to read and to understand readily the parts of the program which he has already written, especially if he is to modify parts which were written several months earlier.

The third audience is the 'group'. The programmer might be working on develop-

Computer programming languages

- Imperative
  - Unstructured: Assembler, Fortran, Cobol, Basic, Forth
  - Structured: Algol-68, Pascal, C, BCPL, Ada, Modula2, occam
- Declarative
  - Functional: Pure-Lisp, Hope, KRC, SASL, ML, FFP, Sugar, Miranda
  - Logic: Pure-Prolog

FIGURE 2.1 *Taxonomy of programming languages*

ing a very large program as part of a team, whose members must be able to understand each others' programs in sufficient detail. Alternatively, a valuable program might need to be modified at a later date by a programmer who is not the original creator. He too must be able to read and to understand the workings of the program as it stands. Thus, not only is computer programming a technical activity, the means by which human operators can control a machine to perform a given job, but in recent years it has been recognised to be almost an artistic activity (Touretzky 1984), a means of expression whereby the creator can convey his ideas to other observers. Admittedly though, this has been generally for the pragmatic reasons of efficiency, rather than for the artistic ones of beauty and elegance for its own sake and, in common with other technical communication, it is generally not applicable for making introspective statements about human emotions (Kapp 1957).

It is generally assumed that there are two levels of programming language: high and low. This, conceptually at least, is true. High level languages facilitate *abstraction*, the ability to express ideas in an abstract fashion, so releasing the programmer from having to worry about the details of the problem. In reality, however, there have been so many thousands of languages developed, each with different powers of expression, that they can be considered to fit into a continuum of levels.

In the drive to produce higher levels of langugage, two major classes have emerged. The imperative languages are engineering driven, whilst the declarative languages are mathematics driven, the bases for the functional (applicative) and logic language being *lambda* and *predicate calculi* respectively. Imperative languages were developed to map easily on to the early computers, and thus to express ideas in a way which is tailored to the machine design. Declarative languages are tailored more to suit the expression of human ideas, and so can be considered to be higher level languages.

Since computer programming involves the articulation of the programmer's ideas in an unambiguous form, the computer programmer must be provided with tools which are powerful, usable and clear for the purpose of expressing these ideas. It is apparent that sitting in front of a computer, operating switches according to a long sequence of ones and zeros is far from ideal. The next sections therefore trace the progress which has been made to rectify this situation; the headings used are plotted in Figure 2.2.

Programming in binary object code was mentioned briefly in the previous chapter. Section 2.1 describes the improvements which are made possible by the use of decimal, octal and hexadecimal assemblers. Section 2.2 describes the further improvements which symbolic assemblers made possible. The development of high level language compilers is described in Section 2.3, and their further improvement through the use of structured languages in Section 2.4. Section 2.5 completes the progression, as it has been realised to date, by describing the use of some functional languages.

2.1 DECIMAL, OCTAL AND HEXADECIMAL ASSEMBLERS

Human beings are very poor at manipulating anything as featureless as binary numbers, but are very good at manipulating symbols. Even numbers represented in base 16 have slightly more 'texture' and compactness, and so are easier to handle than those in base 2. The conversion between the two notations can be automated, and performed by a computer program. The hexadecimal numbers are read from the keyboard, and translated into the appropriate binary numbers, which in turn are then loaded into memory. Such a program is known as a hexadecimal *assembler*, and simply takes each digit which it receives and outputs the corresponding four binary digits, as defined in Figure 1.12.

Octal and decimal assemblers also exist, and work in precisely the same way, taking their input in the form of base 8 or base 10 numbers respectively, and using them to generate the appropriate base 2 output. Figure 2.3 shows an example of input to an octal assembler. The output is the list which is given in Figure 1.5.

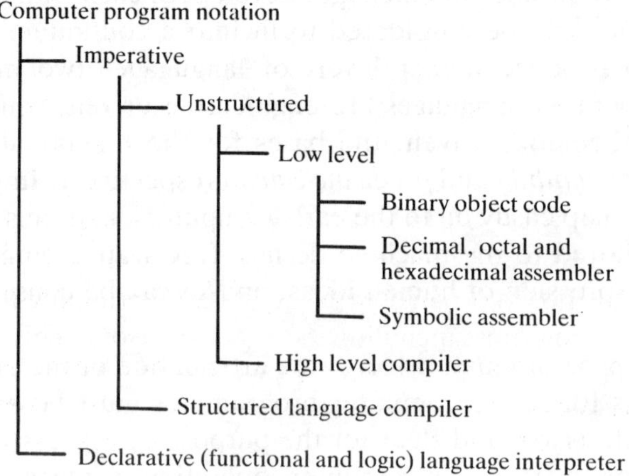

FIGURE 2.2 *Progression of program notations*

```
012767,000000,000134,012767,000126,000124,017767,000120,
000112,062767,000001,000110,017767,000104,000100,026767,
000072,000072,003417,162767,000001,000064,016777,000056,
000056,062767,000001,000050,016777,000040,000044,012767,
000001,000036,026727,000030,000134,002740,026727,000022,
000001,001726,000000,006016,003026,016416,000000,000000,
000000,000000.
```

FIGURE 2.3 *Example of octal code*

In principle, the *source code* from Figure 2.3 could be inserted into a computer which is devoted to converting octal to binary (Figure 2.4), with the output then loaded into a second computer's memory where it is run. In practice, the two operations tend to be performed on the same computer. The source text is inserted, converted to binary and stored somewhere convenient, in disk memory usually. From there, it can be read back later into the computer's memory, and executed.

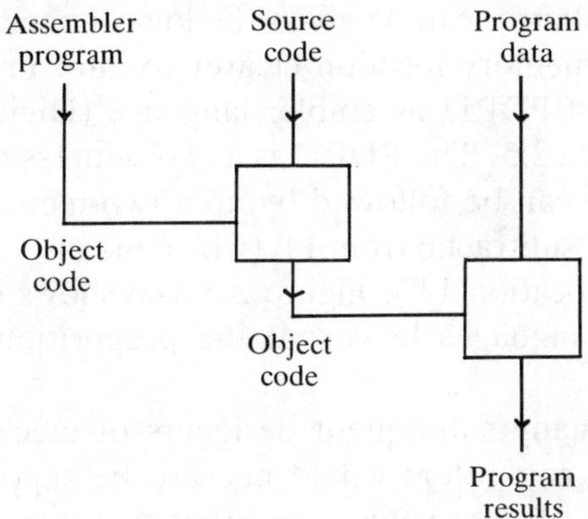

FIGURE 2.4 *A computer represented as a programmable filter*

Thus, there are three programs in Figure 2.4: the source program is the one which is understood by the human programmer, the object program is the one which is generated, and the assembler program is the one which is already understood by the computer because it is already expressed in object code.

At first, the assembler program would probably have to be loaded into the computer by way of the front panel switches; but once running it would be available to help write other programs, including its own successors. This process is known as *bootstrapping*. The usual analogy is with workshop or even prehistoric tools: once the primitive flint tools have been used to hammer iron ones into shape, these iron tools become available for constructing even more elaborate ones. Assemblers are tools, or *system utilities*, which help in the process of writing programs and form part of the programming systems environment.

2.2 SYMBOLIC ASSEMBLERS

The next improvement was made through the development of symbolic assemblers. These allow programs to be typed as a series of named instructions (mnemonics), rather than as amorphous lists of numbers (object code).

The style adopted was heavily influenced by the organisation of the underlying machine, where each instruction tends to be like an imperative command in English. Instructions consist of a verb followed by a noun, where the verb is chosen from the processor's instruction set and the noun is the address of a location of memory, or a register. Thus the following style is typical:

```
LOAD        5
SUBTRACT    7
STORE       6
JUMPTO      4
```

Further developments allowed memory addresses to be given logical names in place of their physically numbered address. A memory location to hold the value of a numerical count, for instance, can be given the logical name 'counter', so making the intended use of this memory location clearer to later programmers.

An abridged example of PDP11 assembler language (Digital 1974, Hamacher *et al.* 1984) is shown in Figure 2.5. The PDP11 is a two-address machine, which means that each imperative verb can be followed by up a two-memory location nouns, as for example in the phrase 'subtract 6 from 14' (which means 'subtract the contents of location 6 from those of location 14'). Figure 2.5 also shows how, to economise on typing, most assembler languages leave out the prepositions and abbreviate the verbs.

Babbage (1837), and many subsequent designers of mechanical and electronic computers, assumed that computers would need to be supplied with a stream of instructions and a stream of data values, and that these are most easily provided from two separate sources (such as from punched card readers). Von Neumann's innovation, that of the *stored program*, was to store and supply data and programs in a single memory unit. Consequently, von Neumann assemblers must contain facilities for specifying data and instructions in one unified language. These facets are described in the following two sections.

2.2.1 Data structures

Data can be represented in many forms, some of which are more expressive than others. Usually in assembler programming languages only the most elementary of data forms are provided, ones which have very little internal structure. Indeed, there is generally only one type of data structure on a machine of this type; in the case of the PDP11, each address in the memory vector can store one 16-bit word of information, which can be used to represent a single binary integer. Some computers also

```
; Program to Sort a List of
; Numbers into Ascending Order
Start:  MOV   #0, Sorting
        MOV   #Vector, Pointer
Loop:   MOV   @Pointer, Firstvalue
        ADD   #1, Pointer
        MOV   @Pointer, Secondvalue
        CMP   Firstvalue, Secondvalue
        BLE   Label
        SUB   #1, Pointer
        MOV   Secondvalue, @Pointer
        ADD   #1, Pointer
        MOV   Firstvalue, @Pointer
        MOV   #1, Sorting
Label:  CMP   Pointer, #Vecend
        BLT   Loop
        CMP   Sorting, #1
        BEQ   Start
        HLT

Vector: BYTE 14, 16, 6, 26, 35, 16
Vecend:

Firstvalue:   0
Secondvalue:  0
Pointer:      0
Sorting:      0
.END
```

FIGURE 2.5 *Abridged PDP11 assembler program to sort a list of numbers*

provide special registers for small scale data storage but, semantically, registers are just extra cells of memory which are especially convenient, fast and efficient to access.

The meaning of an integer depends on its context. Even the meaning of the noun integers in the instructions depends on the *addressing mode*. The simple machine of Figure 1.11 has only one addressing mode, but the PDP11 has many, of which three are illustrated in Figure 2.5. Direct addressing is described at the beginning of Section 2.2, and is illustrated by the instruction:

CMP Firstvalue, Secondvalue

Literal addressing allows the noun to be used as a constant, for example:

ADD #1, Pointer

causes the contents of 'Pointer' (direct addressing) to be incremented by the constant '1' (literal addressing), and similarly the instruction:

MOV #Vector, Pointer

causes the address of 'Vector', which is a constant, to be copied to be the new contents of 'Pointer' (direct addressing again). Lastly, the instruction:

MOV @Pointer, Firstvalue

indicates that the contents of 'Pointer' constitute an address, and it is the contents of the location at this address (indirect addressing) which are to be copied as the new contents of 'Firstvalue' (direct addressing).

One important property of integer memory locations is common to all conventional computers: they support non-destructive read, and destructive write operations. The value which is stored in any given memory cell can be read repeatedly and indefinitely; however, when a new value is written into a cell the old value is completely destroyed. This property is exhibited not only by the MOV instruction, the instruction which reads one cell and copies the contents into another, but also by each of the arithmetic and logic instructions. For instance, the ADD instruction not only adds the contents of the two named cells together, but overwrites the second of them with the result.

Another property, which stems from the von Neumann concept for the stored program, means that instructions are treated like integers. In this way, they can be held alongside their data in the same memory vector. This has the benefit of making it easier to write programs which produce program code as their output; for instance assemblers make use of this property. The disadvantage is that instructions and data are indistinguishable, with few safeguards to prevent the inadvertent manipulation of instructions as integer data, or the inadvertent execution of data as if it were a valid program.

Just as the integer locations of memory can be used to store program instructions, so too can they be used to store memory addresses (pointers) and alphabetic characters. By using more than one memory location at a time, fractional numbers also can be represented. As before, though, this is only through a convention which is established by the programmer, and determinable only by context. There is nothing in the contents of an area of memory that directly indicates which of the above types of data is stored in each location, nor is there anything to prevent a run-away program from wrongly treating any of the above objects as integers, program instructions or pointers.

2.2.2 Control structures

As another consequence of von Neumann's model of the stored program, picking instructions out of memory for execution is little different from picking integers out of memory for arithmetic manipulation. The program counter is simply a register, or a memory location since the two are semantically equivalent, which contains the address of the next integer (instruction) that is to be fetched and executed. Normally, one instruction after another is executed in direct sequence, and is achieved by incrementing the contents of the program counter each time. A jump in the flow of control through the program can be achieved by assigning a new value into the program counter. Since an address is itself an integer, this can be implemented by the use of a MOV or ADD instruction. This is so common an operation, though, that special branch instructions are provided to achieve the same effect more efficiently. The point is still valid though: the branch, jump or GOTO is a special case of the assignment (destructive write) operation.

Conditional execution is usually supported by the provision of conditional jump instructions. On the PDP11 (Figure 2.5) the effects of two instructions are combined; for example CMP compares the contents of two data locations, and the conditional branch instruction takes or ignores the branch accordingly. For instance BLE will take the branch if the contents of the first location are less than or equal to those of the second, and will ignore it otherwise. Similarly, BEQ will take the branch only if the contents of the two locations are equal.

Programming with symbolic assembler languages is significantly more abstract, involving less detail, than programming directly in object code. However, the programmer is still forced to think very much in terms of the machine's internal operations and its instruction cycle. The next jump in power of expression was made with the development of high level computer languages, and is described next.

2.3 COMPILERS

Fortran (Day 1974) and Cobol (Parkin 1982) allow complex ideas to be expressed simply: the former for scientific and numerical calculations, and the latter for commercial and business tabulation. For instance the expression −B+sqrt(B*B−4*A*C) can be typed directly in Fortran, instead of as a sequence of low level machine instructions. This expresses the programmer's intention more clearly: that of wanting to evaluate the given expression, rather than wanting to embark upon some sequence of data manipulations between memory and registers. The sequence of data manipulations still occurs; however, the programmer need not be aware of it but only the final result.

As with the assembler, the text is read as data by a program, the output of which is a sequence of executable binary digits and data. Such a program is called a *compiler*, and is another example of a system utility. The distinction between assemblers and compilers is that the former tend to produce a few binary numbers of object code for each statement of the source program that they read, whereas the latter can accept arbitrarily complicated expressions and produce correspondingly large streams of binary numbers.

Important characteristics of languages like Fortran are the presence of assignment operators and GOTO statements. High level languages try to free the programmer from the details of the operation of the underlying machine, but the characteristics of the machine are inscribed indelibly in the language. Fortran's assignment operator '=' is an indication that the machine is able to perform destructive write operations easily. Fortran's GOTO statement is an indication that the machine is able to perform program branches, or jumps, effectively.

As with assemblers, compilers must provide facilities for declaring data and control structures. These are taken in turn, in the next two subsections.

2.3.1 Data structures

In high level languages, it is recognised that programs need to handle many types of data, and that it is convenient to be able to distinguish the different types explicitly. Thus Fortran allows named memory locations (variables) to be specified of type 'integer', 'real' and 'logical' in which to store respectively integers, floating-point (fractional) numbers and logical (boolean) values.

The other major data type which languages like Fortran introduce is that of the array. The mathematical notation of the vector, the matrix and the multidimensional array are each extensively used in scientific applications, and can be represented directly using this structure.

2.3.2 Control structures

The two most important control structures in Fortran are GOTO and IF. The GOTO is the high level version of the jump or branch, commanding a jump to a labelled statement, rather than to a physically named address in memory. The IF is a high level version of the condition testing in assembler languages. In both cases, Fortran releases the programmer from much of the detail which would be otherwise involved.

Another area where the high level language helps the programmer is through the ability to define modules, with all of the advantages of modularisation that this introduces; sections of the program can be broken off, packaged into modules and worked on separately, so easing the problem of writing, and of reading them at a later date. However, it needs some discipline on the part of the programmer, one which Fortran does not enforce itself, to provide a clean interface between the modules. The programmer is free to fritter away the above advantages, and to produce a very tangled set of interactions between the modules. In particular, many programmers tend to use the Fortran COMMON statement to declare globally accessible variables, and to use these to exchange values between the modules when the use of some well-chosen function definitions would be greatly more preferable.

There are two types of subprogram module in Fortran: *subroutines* and *functions*. Since the latter are so important to later discussion, they are described next in greater detail.

2.3.3 Functions

In general, functions have a name, plus an arbitrary number of inputs (arguments), and they return a single value as a result. In mathematics, and most programming languages, function applications are specified in the following syntactic form:

functionname (arg1, arg2, arg3, . . . , argn)

Figure 2.6 shows an example of function usage in Fortran. It shows a user-defined function called 'filt', which is to be applied twice, using different parameters each time.

```
value1 = filt ( 3, 0.25 )
value2 = filt ( 3, 0.5 )
PRINT valuel, value2
STOP
END
```

FIGURE 2.6 *Function application in Fortran*

Figure 2.7 shows how the programmer might wish to define the function to perform some specific arithmetic operations on its arguments, 'k' and 'x'.

```
FUNCTION filt ( k, x )
filt = sin(x) + (1+k)*cos(x)
RETURN
END
```

FIGURE 2.7 *Function definition in Fortran*

Due to the background of mathematics in program design, the word 'function' has taken on a mixture of meanings drawn from both computer programming and mathematics. To the mathematician, 'factorial (3)' *is* 6. It is identically equal. By a property which is known as *referential transparency*, anywhere that one can go the other could be used to replace it. To the computer programmer though, 'factorial (3)' *returns the value* 6. This implies unidirectional conversion, and the passage of an arbitrary but significant duration of time, a delay, caused by instruction execution. To say 'hexagonsides = factorial (3)' instead of 'hexagonsides = 6', is somewhat pointless and misleading, but is nevertheless mathematically valid. The two phrases have the same semantics, but not the same operational characteristics, since the former will introduce a longer execution time delay than the latter. Similarly, the following two expressions are equivalent, but the former will normally take longer to compute than the latter, for large values of k.

$$\sum_{j=1}^{k} j = \frac{k(k+1)}{2}$$

Another example is depicted in Appendix 2, where different representations have implications not only on the execution time, but also on the accuracy of the numerical result which is returned.

Functions in imperative languages are also significantly different from mathematical functions because of the possibility of *side effects*. For example, the definition in Figure 2.7, in addition to computing the arithmetic expression, could have arranged for messages to be printed on the user's screen, for instance, or for values of variables in other modules to be changed. These are both unsound operations for a function to be allowed to perform.

In imperative languages, where programs command the computer to do things in a given sequence, the subprograms are inevitably constructed in the same style. Fortran's subroutines are literally 'little programs' which have been broken off from the main program as separate modules. Fortran's functions are implemented merely as extensions of this idea, and are, in effect, subroutines which are allowed to return a result, as well as to execute a miniature program.

This less than perfect method of implementing functions has now been recognised to be a serious impediment to the design of working programs. However, before this was recognised language designers attempted to reduce program development time by matching the human programmer's expressive needs more exactly through the provision of more complex facilities. This led to the design of the so-called structured programming languages, as described next.

2.4 *STRUCTURED IMPERATIVE LANGUAGES*

The development of the unstructured high level languages from assembler languages allowed an order of magnitude improvement to be achieved in the throughput of a typical computer programmer. However, Parkinson's law applies, as always, and increased throughput is followed by increased demands for more program complexity. Further aids are needed therefore to help the programmer.

The designers of Cobol recognised that human problems rarely consist solely of integers, continuous numbers and boolean values. It is true that these can be used to tackle most problems, but normally information is more complicated than this. Meanwhile, the designers of Fortran recognised that expressive arithmetic and control structures were necessary for tackling scientific problems. The structured programming languages, in part, set out to unify the facilities of these two seminal languages. In addition, the designers of the new languages took the opportunity to observe that, though the computers and languages were supposed to imitate mathematical operations, they were far from perfect. The semantics, and more importantly the effect on program productivity, maintainability and readability, of the assignment statement (and hence also of the GOTO statement since this is a special case of assignment) proved to be one of the greatest impediments. The new languages were therefore proposed to go some way to rectifying the situation through the provision of better control structures. However, as mentioned above, the new languages also provide better facilities for specifying data structures, and these are described next.

2.4.1 Data structures

The new programming languages provide a richer menu of data types for their variables. Not only are new primitive types provided, such as the textual characters which can be stored in variables of type 'char', but the user is able to define his own types. Thus types like 'monthsofyear', 'daysofweek' and 'colour' can be defined, as shown in Figure 2.8.

```
TYPE monthsofyear = (January, February, March, April, May, June, July, August,
                     September, October, November, December);
     daysofweek = (Sunday, Monday, Tuesday, Wednesday, Thursday, Friday,
                   Saturday);
     colour = (Red, Orange, Yellow, Green, Cyan, Blue, Violet);
```

FIGURE 2.8 *Declaring new data types in Pascal*

Fortran allows arrays to be declared. These are regular structures, all of whose elements have the same data type. Often it is necessary to represent information whose components are each of different types. This is achieved in Pascal by use of the *record*, an example of which in Figure 2.9 depicts the declaration of a new type for the representation of calendar dates.

```
TYPE date = RECORD
              day : daysofweek;
              number : integer;
              month : monthsofyear;
              year : integer;
            END;
VAR today, tomorrow, yesterday : date;
```

FIGURE 2.9 *A user-defined record*

The variables 'today', 'tomorrow' and 'yesterday' are declared to be of type 'date', each one having subcomponents to hold the name of the day, the number in the month, the name of the month, and the year. The syntax for accessing these subcomponents is particularly simple, for example 'today.month', 'yesterday. number' and 'tomorrow.year'.

2.4.2 Control structures

As well as providing a richer choice of data structures, the new programming languages also provide a richer selection of control structures. Many of these owe their origins, perhaps, to a lesson which was learned from Fortran. The DO structure was originally provided to improve execution efficiency, and was included in the language despite the fact that the same effect could be achieved using a combination of an IF, a GOTO and two assignment statements. However, it also proved to be elegant at expressing a particularly useful operation, and showed that certain ideas could be expressed without recourse to using the now infamous GOTO. To observe how this idea can be extended, consider next the example fragment of Fortran program which is shown in Figure 2.10.

```
      IF ( x .LE. y ) GOTO 20
        maximum = x
        minmum = y
20 CONTINUE
```

FIGURE 2.10 *Fragment of Fortran code*

The conditional expression in the IF statement is the reverse of the one which is required for the statements which immediately follow it to be executed. Instead, it is more natural to specify when the given piece of code is to be executed. This is depicted in Figure 2.11.

```
IF ( x > y ) THEN BEGIN
  maximum := x;
  minimum := y;
END;
```

FIGURE 2.11 *Fragment of Pascal code*

This change looks minor, but when it occurs in a large program the simplification can be quite dramatic. The programmer's intention is stated explicitly, thus freeing him to think about the problem rather than the detailed meaning of the program as written so far. It is made possible by the invention of the *block*, which generally consists of any number of statements surrounded by bracketing words, such as BEGIN and END.

Another example of a typical use of GOTOs in Fortran is shown in Figure 2.12. Again, it is fairly obvious what is happening in this short example. However, the explicit message which is conveyed in Figure 2.13 is to be preferred for programs of any useful complexity.

```
   x = 3.0
30 delta = ( x*x - 10.0 ) / ( 2.0 * x )
   x = x - delta
   IF ( delta .GE. 0.0001 ) GOTO 30
```

FIGURE 2.12 *A fragment of Fortran code*

```
x := 3.0;
REPEAT
  delta := ( x*x - 10.0 ) / (2.0*x );
  x := x - delta;
UNTIL delta < 0.0001;
```

FIGURE 2.13 *A fragment of Pascal code*

In both of these cases, the more expressive control structures of the new language manage to avoid any use of a GOTO statement. These are only two of the many control structures which are provided by languages such as Pascal (Jensen and Wirth 1975, Wilson and Addyman 1982).

The GOTO statement, in combination with the IF statement, is very flexible. These two statement types in Fortran can be used to achieve the same effect that a language like Pascal achieves through the provision of the statement types IF, WHILE, REPEAT and CASE. Fortran therefore appears to be more economical, and can produce programs which run faster and which occupy less computer memory. However, the use of the control structures of the structured languages make the program clearer and hence faster to develop. For a good programmer who controls his use of the GOTO statement, the benefit of using languages like Pascal is only marginal. However, the world is not full of good programmers. The GOTO is so flexible that its power can be abused very easily, usually through a well-intentioned attempt at reducing the program size and execution time. It allows any program to execute any part of memory, regardless of whether it is sensible to do so or not. GOTOs can cause execution to jump suddenly into the middle of a deep nesting of loops, into the middle of a function or subroutine, into someone else's program, or into a block of data. Consider an attempt to prove anything mathematically useful about the short Fortran program in Figure 2.14. (Though this is a contrived example for illustrative purposes, the author has seen commercial programs in which the writers have used a GOTO to jump out of one deep nesting of loops into the middle of another, so the illustration in Figure 2.14 is tame rather than exaggerated.)

Compilers can be made to check for this sort of abuse, but languages like Algol-68, Pascal, Modula2, Ada, C and BCPL have shown that this can be made unnecessary simply by discouraging the use of the GOTO altogether. They provide

```
C Program to read in a 20 by 20 array of real numbers,
C to multiply elements mat (1,1) through to mat (6,13)
C by 2, to multiply elements mat (6,14) through to
C mat (15,2) by 4, and then to output the results.

        DIMENSION mat (20,20)
        LOGICAL more

        more=.TRUE.
        READ mat
        DO 30 i=1,20
            DO 20 j=1,20
10                  mat (i,j)=mat (i,j) *2.0
                    IF ((i.EQ.15) .AND. (j.EQ.2)) GOTO 40
20          CONTINUE
30      CONTINUE
40      IF ( .NOT. more) GOTO 50
        i=6
        j=14
        more=.FALSE.
        GOTO 10
50      PRINT mat
        STOP
        END
```

FIGURE 2.14 *A tangled Fortran program*

constructs that are powerful enough to allow the programmer to perform all reasonable actions, such as iteration and conditional execution of blocks of code, without the power to perform less sensible actions. The programmer's loops and conditionally executed blocks of program are converted into machine instructions by the compiler, complete with jumps and branches, but the programmer can be quite oblivious of their existence. Although the new languages generally still provide GOTO facilities, the majority of programs can avoid any recourse to using them, and the programmer is given every encouragement to avoid them.

Further to this argument, programmers can be greatly helped by the use of pedantic compilers which complain even at the least important of syntax errors. It has been estimated that three-quarters of programming errors are syntactic. Although it is irritating whilst the compiler is picking them up, it is far better that it does so rather than make (incorrect) assumptions about what the programmer really meant by a certain ambiguous statement, and then leave the programmer to locate these errors laboriously at run-time. For this reason, *strong type-checking* compilers, like those of Pascal, are to be preferred to the optionally *weak type-checking* ones for C (Kernighan and Ritchie 1978) whenever the application does not need the extra power which, admittedly, the weak-type checking compilers allow.

2.4.3 Functions

Subroutines, or *procedures* as they are also known, and functions are still represented as miniprograms. However, certain aspects of their use are made more formal and more expressive. This is described next.

The most important contributions which these newer languages made to function evaluation are all concerned with the handling of local variables. Fortran has only one mechanism for passing parameters, that of *call-by-reference*, the details of which are normally hidden from the programmer. When a main program calls a function, or a subroutine, the subprogram is provided with the addresses of its parameters, not the values themselves. Of course, the subprogram mechanism is implemented so that arguments are properly dereferenced and the appropriate values are obtained. A more obvious way to think of parameter-passing, though, is through the *call-by-value* mechanism, in which the values of the parameters, rather than their addresses in memory, are transferred directly to the subprogram. When subprogram arguments are used in a read-only fashion there is little difference between the two mechanisms, as far as the programmer is concerned. One difference becomes apparent, though, when the subprogram changes the values which are stored in some of its arguments. To illustrate this, consider the Pascal example of Figure 2.15.

```
PROGRAM example:

VAR vector : ARRAY [1..2] OF real;
    i : integer;

FUNCTION munge ( cell : real ) : real;
BEGIN
   cell := 23.0;
   i := 1;
   munge := cell;
END;

BEGIN
   vector[1] := 12.0; vector[2] := 17.0;
   i := 2;
   write ( munge ( vector[i] ) );
   writeln( vector[1], vector[2] );
END.
```

FIGURE 2.15 *A program to illustrate parameter passing*

If Pascal had, like Fortran, adopted a call-by-reference parameter-passing mechanism, the output of this program would be:

23.0 12.0 23.0

Writing to the variable called 'cell' would be the same as writing to the memory location whose address is that of the second element of the array, 'vector[2]'. Normally though, Pascal uses a call-by-value mechanism, so the program output is:

23.0 12.0 17.0

Only the contents of the local variable called 'cell', which were previously 17.0, are changed. However, although this is generally the more natural way to think of parameter-passing, there are times when call-by-reference is useful, mostly for reasons of execution efficiency. For instance, it is quicker to copy the address of a large array and to pass that as a parameter than it is to transfer every value of every element from the array into a local copy. Consequently, Pascal provides optional facilities for specifying the use of either mechanism.

Scoping (Burge 1975) is the next facility which these languages provide, making use of the property that not all variables, functions and procedures need be accessed by all subprograms. The rules governing which ones can be accessed are very strict but are very easy to use, in essence limiting variables to be used only by the subprogram in which they are defined, and by any subprograms which are defined within it. This facility is a further aid to help the programmer understand his program.

Lastly, the power of supporting recursion was recognised by the designers of these languages. The details of this can be best described by considering an example. Suppose for instance, that the intention is to write a function to compute factorial. An informal specification might be: 'factorial (n) is the result of multiplying all the integers from n down to 1'. This leads to the design of the iterative loop of Figure 2.16.

```
FUNCTION factorial ( n : integer ) : integer;
VAR answer, i : integer;
BEGIN
  answer := 1;
  FOR i := n DOWNTO 1 DO answer := answer * i;
  factorial := answer;
END;
```

FIGURE 2.16 *Iterative style definition of 'factorial (n)'*

There is an alternative style which is often useful, in which the definition might become: 'factorial(n) is the result of multiplying factorial($n-1$) by n, where factorial (1) is defined to be 1'. Although this is a longer definition, each of its component clauses turns out to be very much simpler. This uses recursion: the act of defining a function in terms of itself. The boundary condition, 'where factorial(1) is defined to be 1', ensures that the recursion terminates for all positive values of n. Figure 2.17 shows how much more compact this type of definition can be.

```
FUNCTION factorial ( n : integer ) : integer;
BEGIN
  IF n = 1 THEN factorial := 1
           ELSE factorial := factorial(n − 1) * n;
END;
```

FIGURE 2.17 *Recursive style definition of 'factorial (n)'*

When this function is to be evaluated, for instance to compute the value of 'factorial(4)', it is evaluated with *n* set to the value 4. It then recurses, requesting the value of 'factorial(3)'. Recursion involves making new copies of all of the local variables (Abelson and Sussman 1985), so a completely new variable called *n* is created, and is used to hold the value 3. The contents of the old variable called *n* are not destroyed, but are merely held in limbo until the result of 'factorial(3)' is returned, and together they can be used in the multiplication.

Since Figure 2.17 demonstrates that iterative loops can be avoided simply by replacing them with recursive function calls, it is tempting to think that iterative looping could be dispensed with altogether. This is one of the characteristics of programming in declarative languages, as described next.

2.5 DECLARATIVE LANGUAGES

The next improvement in programming style was made possible by observing that the assignment statement was almost as bad as the GOTO. The assignment statement's origins lie in the fact that most computers provide facilities for destructively writing new values into memory locations. However, assignment is a very unmathematical thing to do, as it destroys the referential transparency of the statements and expressions in the program. Fortran even confuses the notion of assignment with that of equality, allowing such mathematical nonsense as $N = N + 1$.

Just as the move from unstructured to structured imperative programming languages was motivated largely by a desire to avoid use of the troublesome GOTO statement, or its equivalent, so declarative languages do without the equally troublesome assignment statement (MOV etc. in assembler, = in Fortran and := in Pascal). However, before considering the implications of this, the differences between the imperative and declarative programming styles are highlighted.

As the name suggests, programs which are written in imperative languages consist of an ordered sequence of commands. Using the example given by Glaser *et al.* (1984), a program to instruct a robot to build a shed, for example, might appear in the form which is shown in Figure 2.18.

```
Lay the foundation!
Erect the walls!
Put on the roof!
```

FIGURE 2.18 *The imperative style of building a shed*

All of the statements are of an imperative nature, as highlighted by the exclamation marks. This might appear in Pascal or Fortran in the form which is shown in Figure 2.19.

```
lay (foundations);
erect (walls);
puton (roof);
```

FIGURE 2.19 *A Pascal version of the shed-building program*

This is in contrast to programs which are written using declarative languages. As this name suggests, these consist of a collection of factual statements, not necessarily in any particular order. To use the same example again, a declarative program to build a shed might appear as shown in Figure 2.20

```
A shed has a roof, foundations and walls.
The roof is supported by the walls.
The walls are erected on the foundations.
Build a shed!
```

FIGURE 2.20 *The declarative style of building a shed*

The program is marginally longer using the declarative style than it is using the imperative one and, significantly, still contains one imperative statement. However, the programmer has been freed from specifying implementation details; he has not had to think of the order in which to place the statements, nor any of the other details of how to execute them. It is left to the computer to realise that the walls will have to be erected before the roof can be put on, and that the foundations will have to be laid before the walls can be erected. If the statements of the imperative program are shuffled, the robot will still obey them literally, and the shed will not be constructed properly. If, however, the statements of the declarative program are shuffled, the meaning of the program is left unchanged. The style is therefore seen to be a high level one, freeing the programmer to concentrate on the problem rather than on the details of its sequencing.

There are two major subdivisions of declarative language: the functional languages and the logic languages, but only the former are considered here. In these, the function is both the central control and data structure. Programs are composed of function definitions, and the applications of those functions to given values. The next section describes the principles of the functional programming style as if it had been an evolutionary development from high level, structured programming languages.

2.5.1 Data structures

One of the central aims of functional programming languages is that functions should be manipulated like any other item of data. This is an idea which is originally found in the branch of mathematical logic known as *lambda calculus*. In order to develop a programming language along these lines, one might first allow variables of type 'function' to be declared. A pseudo-Pascal version of this might appear as shown in Figure 2.21.

```
PROGRAM example( input, output );

VAR ans, m, n : real;
   filt, fn : function;

BEGIN
   m := (2.6 * 4.3) − (9.78 + 0.9);
   n := m;
   filt := FUNCTION ( k:integer; x:real ) BEGIN
            sin(x) + (1+k) * cos(x)
         END;
   fn := filt;
   ans := fn (3,n);
   writeln ('The answer is', ans);
END.
```

FIGURE 2.21 *A pseudo-Pascal attempt at a functional language*

In Figure 2.21, a function definition assigned to a function variable in the same way that the result of an arithmetic expression is assigned to a numeric variable. Such an object can be manipulated like any other, as for example in the copying process which is involved in assigning the contents of 'filt' to 'fn.'

This is a start, but it has missed one essential property of the mathematics behind it. Although x might be a variable, it can be *instantiated* to (i.e. taken on) only one value. Even when solving:

$$(x - 3)(x - 4) = 0$$

x can take on the value of 3, *or* the value of 4. It does not take on both values: it takes on one of these values *for all time* in that equation. This is opposed to assignment in an imperative language, which is not like mathematical instantiation since a variable can have its value changed during program execution. For example, in the following lines of Fortran:

```
INTEGER ans, x, factorial, fibonacci
x = 3
ans = factorial( x ) + fibonacci( x )
```

there is nothing to stop the programmer writing the definitions of 'factorial' and 'fibonacci' so that they change the values of x. Figure 2.22 demonstrates such as a defintion.

```
   FUNCTION factorial( n )
   factorial = 1
10 factorial = n * factorial
   n = n - 1
   IF( n .GT. 1 ) GOTO 10
   RETURN
   END
```

FIGURE 2.22 *A definition of 'factorial' which changes its argument*

Even in Pascal, whose call-by-value mechanism would ease the problem of Figure 2.22, assignment operations can lead to very serious problems. Consider, for instance, the valid Pascal program which is shown in Figure 2.23. This time, nothing untoward happens to the function argument, but still unexpected results are produced.

```
PROGRAM unclean ( input, output );
VAR a : integer;

FUNCTION factorial ( n : integer ) : integer;
VAR i : integer;
BEGIN
  a := 1;
  FOR i := 1 TO n DO a := a*i;
  fac := a;
END;

BEGIN
  a := 42;
  writeln ( (2*a) + factorial(4) );
  a := 42;
  writeln( factorial(4) + (2*a) );
END.
```

FIGURE 2.23 *An example of an unclean program*

The Pascal program in Figure 2.23 is not semantically clean. One expects that '(2*a)+factorial(4)' will have the same value as 'factorial(4)+(2*a)', that is that the '+' operator will obey the same laws of commutivity in Pascal as it does in mathematics. In Figure 2.23, though, the first 'writeln' prints the value '108', whilst the second prints the value '72'. The solution to the problems that are caused by this abuse appears to be to control the use of variables, as described next.

2.5.2 Control structures

Backus observed that many problems stem from the use of global variables, that is variables whose values can be changed by any function or procedure, and the use of the call-by-reference mechanism. The banishment of these facilities from the language prevents the problems which occur in Figures 2.22 and 2.23, but it does not prevent variables from changing values during the execution of a single procedure. The next step therefore is to ban multiple assignment. A variable can either have one value assigned to it, or none. Second, third and subsequent assignments are illegal, and can generally be detected at compile time.

This one step changes the appearance of the language quite dramatically. Many *single assignment languages* (Welcome and Skedzielewski 1985) do not have a condition IF statement, as in Pascal:

IF x > y THEN maximum := x ELSE maximum := y;

Instead, they use a functional version, an IF expression, as in the line:

maximum := IF x > y THEN × ELSE y;

Also iterative loops are not allowed, and recursive function calls must be used instead.

Like all high level languages, the aim is to simulate a desirable behaviour on computer hardware which does not directly support that behaviour. Thus although single assignment of variables is advantageous to the programmer in the high level language, it cannot be directly supported in the hardware since the computer would very quickly run out of memory locations for variables. Some method must be provided for detecting when a variable has been read for the last time, when its memory location can be re-used to hold a new variable. *Garbage collection*, as it is called, has long been important to imperative environments; to single assignment and declarative environments it is crucial (Hughes 1984).

Having taken each of these steps, and precautions, the idea of assignment now can be dispensed with altogether since, if a variable can take on only one value, it can be treated as a constant. thus 'x=3' is a declaration that 'x' is the name of an integer which has the value of 3, and 'y=2*fac(x)' is a declaration that 'y' has one specifiable value – one which is not yet known, but for which the specification has been provided. Thus the pseudo-Pascal example in Figure 2.21 can be rewritten using Pascal's CONST declaration (Figure 2.24).

```
PROGRAM example ( input, output );
CONST
  m = (2.6*4.3) - (9.78 + 0.9);
  n = m;
  filt = FUNCTION ( k:integer; x:real ) BEGIN
         sin(x) + (1+k)*cos(x)
       END;
  fn = filt;
  ans = fn( 3, n );
BEGIN
  writeln ( 'The answer is ', ans );
END.
```

FIGURE 2.24 *A pseudo-Pascal attempt at a functional language*

The example in Figure 2.24 now looks like a true declarative language; all of the work is performed in the declaration section, and only the commands to print results on the terminal are placed in the imperative section. It is interesting to compare this with the observations which were made about Figure 2.20.

Since all of the work is specified in the declaration section of the pseudo-Pascal program, it will be physically conducted by the compiler. Thus the object code version of the program would do no more than print the final (constant) results. If this minor work too is given to the compiler to perform, then no object code need be produced from the compiler. The program, which is run directly from the source code, is being *interpreted* by the compiler. It is this progression of ideas, facilitated by the fact that declarative languages are generally very simple to implement in this way, which has led to most declarative languages being interpreted instead of compiled (Abelson and Sussman 1985). The advantages of this are discussed in the next chapter.

Having followed this development for pseudo-Pascal, two real functional languages are described. The first (in Section 2.5.3) is the seminal functional language, being only marginally younger than Fortran, whilst the second (in Section 2.5.4) demonstrates some more recent ideas.

2.5.3 High level languages

Because of its age, Lisp (Winston and Horn 1981) was developed before the disadvantages of the imperative programming style were fully appreciated. As a result, many versions of the language have facilities which allow it to be used in an imperative fashion. SET and SETQ are Lisp's equivalent of assignment. Similarly the PROGRAM and GOTO primitives are provided in 'dirty-Lisp'. However, these primitives are gradually being discouraged, and a style which uses 'pure-Lisp' is being adopted in many computer science departments.

One major difference between Lisp and Fortran is that the former is a symbolic language, whereas the latter is numeric. Suppose for example, the aim is to write a program to solve:

$$\sin(x) + 4\cos(x) = 0$$

using the Newton–Raphson successive approximation method (Kreyszig 1972). In Fortran, the programmer writes the loop, like the one found in Figure 2.12, having first differentiated the function with respect to x. In Lisp, the same loop can be written but with the function supplied as a parameter. Not only can the computer preform the substitution and evaluation, but it can perform the differentiation too. This is a more flexible approach, since the Lisp routine will apply the Newton–Raphson method to any function that is supplied at run-time, and it is higher level since the programmer has less work to do. This operation can be achieved in Fortran too since it, too, is a general purpose language, but the final result will be very unwieldy and hence will take a long time to write and to debug.

2.5.4 Very high level languages

Subsequent to Lisp's development, many languages of greater expressivity have been developed. Figure 2.25 shows the program from Figures 2.6 and 2.7 written in a language called 'Sugar' (Glaser *et al.* 1984). The first three lines define functions, and the final two apply them by requesting that their values be printed.

```
filt = [ k, x ] sin(x) + (1+k)*cos(x);
value1 = filt ( 3, 0.25 );
value2 = filt ( 3, 0.5 );
value1?
value2?
```

FIGURE 2.25 *Sugar example*

The syntactic differences are only marginal, and belie the enormous increase in the power of expression which this gives Sugar over Fortran. It is interesting in fact to compare this syntax with one which has been included in Fortran since its earliest days: the facility for in-line function definition which is available for simple functions (Monro 1982) (Figure 2.26).

```
filt( k, x ) = sin(x) + (1+k)*cos(x)
value1 = filt ( 3, 0.25 )
value2 = filt ( 3, 0.5 )
PRINT value1, value2
STOP
END
```

FIGURE 2.26 *Fortran example*

The similarity is only syntactic, and hence very shallow. In Sugar, the function can be subjected to quite complex manipulations. For instance, the function can be copied, as in the expression:

fn = filt;

which means that 'fn' is an identical function, taking two arguments and having the same definition as 'filt'. The function can also be partially evaluated, as shown in the expression:

phfilt = filt(3);

The function 'phfilt' is one which takes just one argument, and has the definition:

phfilt = [x] sin(x) + 4*cos(x);

This ability to evaluate functions partially as the parameters become available is known as *Currying*. The function 'phfilt' is said to be a *Curryed function*, or a *higher order function*. The tremendous power which this makes available (Peyton Jones 1984), cannot be adequately tackled here, other than to say that it has implications on abstraction, economy of expression, and execution efficiency. The second, and third of these can be shown, as in the example in Figure 2.27, whilst the first is illustrated, ironically in the later hardware chapters, where it is first assumed that the fault density function is not dependent on any parameters, but later, more detailed studies require that two parameters be taken into account.

```
filt = [ k, x ] sin(x) + ( 1+k )*cos(x);
phfilt = filt ( 3 );
value1 = phfilt ( 0.25 );
value2 = phfilt ( 0.5 );
value1?
value2?
```

FIGURE 2.27 *Sugar example with higher order functions*

2.6 CONCLUSIONS

Historically, there is a progression of ideas that has led to the development of high level languages, each more capable of expressing programs in a more abstract form than its predecessor. Thus the computer, by running the high level compiler, is given more of the routine work of program writing, so freeing the programmer to concentrate on the creative parts of problem solving. In this, the words of G.W. Leibniz in 1617, justifying the design of his mechanical adding machine, are ever pertinent:

> It is unworthy of excellent men to lose hours like slaves in the labour of calculation which could be safely relegated to anyone else if machines were used.

In the field of computer programming, and computer-aided design too, this advice is taken to the extreme: routine tasks are not even relegated to less skillful human operators, but to the machine itself.

The writing of clear, self-explanatory programs has a direct impact on the ability to write error-free programs quickly. Much progress has been made in this respect by banishing side effects: constructs in the languages whose semantics are far from clear. The move from unstructured to structured imperative languages was made by dispensing with the GOTO statement and replacing it with constructs like WHILE and REPEAT. Facilities were also provided for defining a richer selection of compound and simple data types. The move from imperative to declarative languages was made by dispensing with the assignment operation, and using the ability to define and to apply functions recursively instead. The new constructs are less powerful than the old, in that certain programming operations become very difficult to describe in the new languages. However, these operations are the ones which are associated with bad programming practice, and so their exclusion is an advantage. Paradoxically, the new constructs are also more powerful than the old, in that they more succinctly express the programmer's aims.

High level languages have been developed precisely to enable the expression of abstract ideas. Assuming that this process will continue, the ultimate goal must be to use natural language as the eventual mode of expression. However, declarative programming languages are the best that are available at present. They are semantically clean, having no side effects, and so it is easier to write programs, and to make them work first time. It is also easier to read programs, and to modify them (e.g. to upgrade them). Both of these effects serve to reduce the program development time. Declarative languages are also very powerful despite their simplicity. The same power as a high level imperative language can be achieved with much less complexity, so enabling most declarative languages to be interpreted.

These are the main advantages; the main disadvantage, though, is the prolonged execution time on conventional computers. Imperative languages were tailor made to run on von Neumann machines, and hence they can be made to run very efficiently. Since declarative languages were not tailor made to run on such machines, they tend not to be so efficient, and so there is now a need to design a computer whose design is optimised for running declarative languages.

This is a change of emphasis (Kennaway and Sleep 1984a). Whereas von Neumann machines were designed first, and this led to the design of imperative computer programming languages and thence to a new branch of mathematics, this branch, computer science, is pushing for the design of declarative programming languages and thence to new designs for computers. Chapter 3 commences this process by considering some high level languages, imperative and declarative, which might be suitable for use as the bases for supercomputer instruction sets.

2.7 EXERCISES

2.1 The fibonacci function is defined so that 'fibonacci(n) is the sum of fibonacci($n-1$) and fibonacci($n-2$), where fibonacci(2) = fibonacci(1) = 1'. Design a recursive program which will embody this definition for positive values of n.

2.2 Design an iterative program to embody the definition of fibonacci from question 2.1.

3

BRIDGING THE SOFTWARE GAP

Low level languages are ones in which the statements in the source code bear a simple relationship to the numbers in the object code. All other languages are deemed to be high level, and, for instance, no practical computer exists which can represent a statement like x=(−b+sqrt(b*b−4*a*c))/(2*a) using just one instruction. So, between the high level languages and the target machine code there is a gulf, the *software gap* (Myers 1982), which must be bridged by the compiler. This is the gap between the power of expression of high level source code statements, and that of machine instructions.

The next chapter describes how the gap might be reduced through the design of more powerful instruction sets, supporting carefully chosen languages directly in the hardware. By definition, this process reclassifies previously high level languages into low level ones. This chapter describes (in Section 3.1) some of these, which it might be safest to call 'medium level' languages. Section 3.2 describes a technique for translating high level source code into two of these languages.

3.1 MEDIUM LEVEL LANGUAGES AND INTERPRETATION

In practice, even the seemingly clear-cut definition of high and low level languages is quite vague. Different high level languages have different powers of expression, some of which could therefore be considered to be 'very high level', and others to be 'slightly high level'. At the other extreme, some assembler languages are more powerful than others. This of course means that the computers for which they are targeted are more powerful than others. For instance, the PDP11 computer has a more powerful instruction set than does the Intel 8080. The original definition of a low level language falters when one considers an assembler which takes PDP11 assembler source code and uses it to generate 8080 object code. Such *cross-assemblers* no longer find a simple relationship between source statements and object numbers.

The difference between a compiler and an assembler is simply the level of the source language. Thus a high level language is compiled, whilst a low level language is assembled. To all intents and purposes, the two are otherwise identical. The development of a typical program of either type can be traced as depicted in Figure 3.1.

Programmer has an idea for a program.
→ Programmer uses a terminal and an editor to transfer his ideas into source code.
Programmer uses a compiler to convert the source code into object code.
Programmer runs the object code.
Programmer analyses the results and run-time errors.
← Programmer has ideas for improvements to the program.

FIGURE 3.1 *Development loop for a compiled program*

This is a fairly lengthy process, especially when the programming language is badly chosen, and frequent cycles around the loop are involved. The interpreted languages were originally designed to reduce the development time, though not by reducing the number of cycles around the loop but by reducing the size of the loop. This is described in the next section.

3.1.1 Interpreted languages

Now that hardware is cheap, the availability of large amounts of memory and program execution time have become less of a problem. However, now that salaries are expensive, the length of program development time has increased in importance. Interpreters provide an environment which supports *rapid prototyping*, with a shorter development loop, as shown in Figure 3.2. As each part of the program is written it can be quickly tested, modified and incorporated into the next part of the program which is to be written.

Programmer has an idea for a program.
→ Programmer uses a terminal and an editor to transfer his ideas into source code.
Programmer runs the source code.
Programmer analyses the results and run-time errors.
← Programmer has ideas for improvements to the program.

FIGURE 3.2 *Development loop for an interpreted program*

In addition, by an extension of the *bootstrapping* technique, the implementor needs only to design the very small core of the system. Usually, the system will then read in the majority of its primitives, written in the language itself, from backing store. How much is defined here depends on the system: the user might find that one system provides everything up to floating-point arithmetic primitives, and that another only provides integer addition and subtraction. The beauty of the technique is that, having written the program using a system which has the higher functions defined as primitives, the program can be made to run on the simpler system merely by attaching appropriate definitions for the primitives which are missing.

One example of an interpreted language is Basic. However, if the aim of programming languages is to make the programmer's intention clear to the computer, to the programmer who is writing the code, and to future programmers who wish to modify the program, Basic is an out-and-out failure. Nearly every aspect of the language is ideal for hindering program development. It was created when Fortran was the only alternative in its field, and so, to its credit, Basic was instrumental in pointing out areas in which Fortran was deficient. Since then, other languages, such as Forth (Anderson *et al*. 1984), which is described next, have been developed which also remedy these shortcomings, so the attraction of Basic on technical grounds is no longer present. It can only be its intense marketing which now keeps it going, and the technology entrenchment which has followed.

3.1.2 Unstructured imperative languages

In one respect, Forth is a lower level language than Basic, in that it uses reverse Polish notation: all of the arithmetic operators are postfix, instead of infix. For example, the addition of 2 and 3 is written as '2 3 +' instead of the more usual '2 + 3.' As a more complex example, the expression:

sin(x) + (1 + k)*cos(x)

becomes:

(x sin) ((1 k +) (x cos) *) +

In many respects, though, this is a very clean notation which has allowed the language to provide new facilities, ones which Basic cannot offer, as simple and consistent extensions within the established framework.

In another respect, Forth is definitely higher level than Basic: it allows user-defined names to be of arbitrary length (though sometimes a local maximum is enforced). The ability to choose mnemonics for function and variable names in a language has a great impact on the clarity of the program.

Forth uses structures which are efficient and economical on conventional computers. The stack, for example, has long been recognised as a useful data type by the computer programmer. It is a particular structure of memory cells which allows only restricted access to its individual elements. The usual analogy is with dinner plates in a stack, or carriages shunted into a railway siding; when one is to be removed it is only the most recently added one which can be accessed first. When functions and subroutines are called, it is convenient to store the return address on a stack

(Hamacher *et al.* 1984, Abelson and Sussman 1985); when arithmetic is performed, it is convenient to store intermediate results on a stack. The reverse polish notation which is adopted by Forth is well suited to this style.

One of the many possible implementations for a (hypothetical) floating-point version of a 'pure-Forth' system is described in this section. First though, an example fragment of program code is illustrated:

```
: k 3;
: x 0.5;
x sin 1 k + x cos * + print;
```

The first two lines are definitions, as indicated by the colons, ':'. They are each functions which simply push a constant on to the arithmetic stack. The last line is an application which makes calls on these and other definitions.

This version of Forth works by maintaining four areas, respectively called 'S', 'T', 'M' and 'C'. S is the arithmetic stack, which is assumed to be empty for the moment. T is the symbol table; it maintains a list of the names of the user-defined functions, and the address at which their definitions can be found in memory. M is the memory where the function definitions are held. Lastly, C is the storage space for the statement which is presently being interpreted. Assuming that the definitions of 'k' and 'x' have already been accepted, and that the system is about to evaluate the application line, the state will be as depicted in Figure 3.3.

Execution now proceeds by *popping* (i.e. removing) the first item C, and looking it up in T. In this case x is found to correspond to memory address 1026. The contents of M are examined from that address down to the ';' delimiter; in this case there is only one item, 0.5. In general, and this is an idealised mechanism rather than the one which is normally implemented, the items which are found here are *pushed* (i.e. loaded) on to the top of C. Figure 3.4 shows the new state of the machine, remembering that x has been popped from the top of C.

The second cycle can now begin, and the top item is removed from C. Since it is a constant, it is simply pushed on to S. At the end of the second cycle, the state of the machine is as shown in Figure 3.5.

In the third cycle, the top item is popped from C. Assuming that 'sin' is a primitive

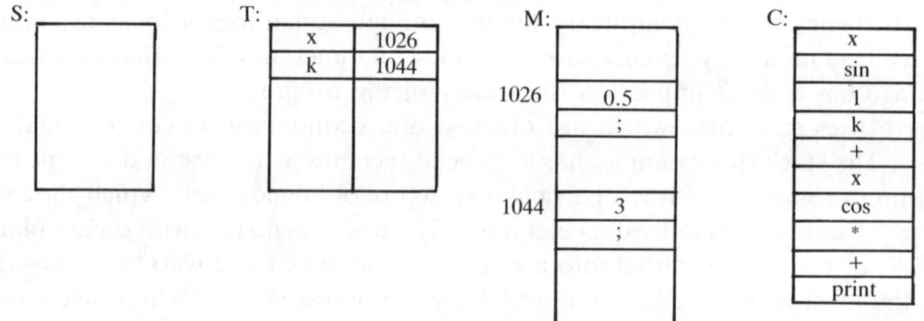

FIGURE 3.3 *State of the system before execution*

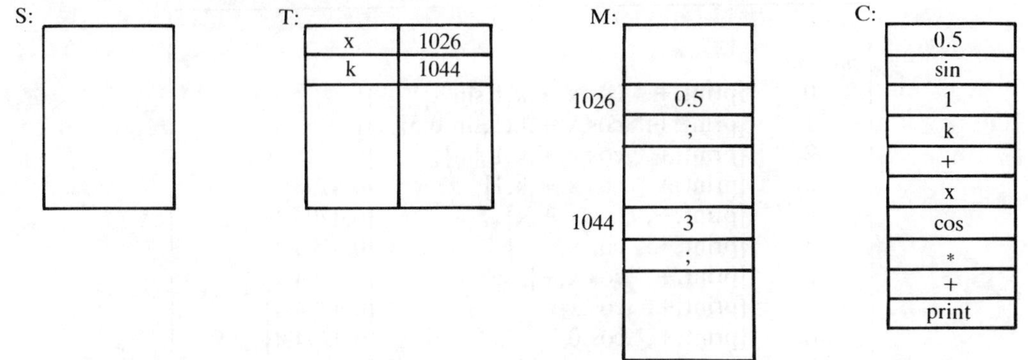

FIGURE 3.4 *State of the system after the first cycle*

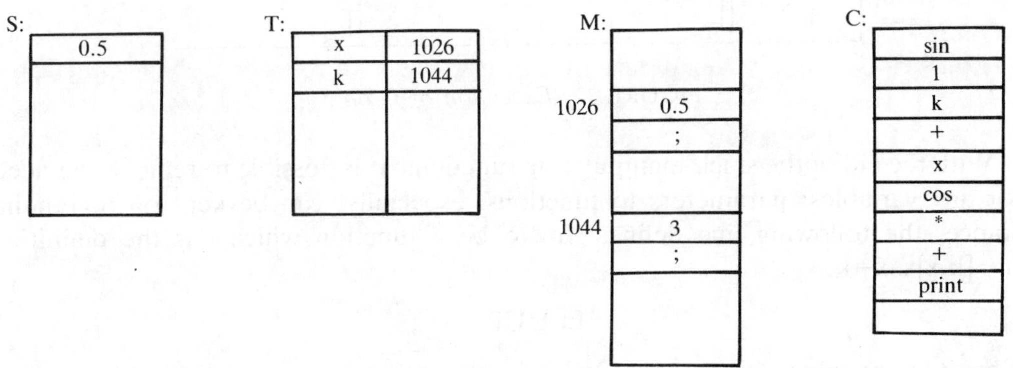

FIGURE 3.5 *State of the system after the second cycle*

operation, which is already defined in this version of Forth, it is applied to the top item on S and the result is written in its place. Rather than redrawing the full diagram with S, T, M and C each time, Figure 3.6 traces the changes which occur in S and C, since these are the only stacks which change in this example. Each stack is depicted with its head at the right.

In cycle 13, the result of the computation is popped from the arithmetic stack, S, and is printed, so leaving S empty again. Since the control stack, C, is also empty, the computation stops.

As well as the arithmetic operators, Forth has a number of primitive functions which move, swap, copy and delete items on the stack. For example, 'DUP' is the function which copies the top item on S. So, in order to computer x*x−k, instead of writing:

x x * k −

one could write:

x DUP * K −

Cycle number	*C*	*S*
0	[print,+.*,cos,x,+,k,1,sin,x]	[]
1	[print,+,*,cos,x,+,k,1,sin,0.5]	[]
2	[print,+,*,cos,x,+,k,1,sin]	[0.5]
3	[print,+,*,cos,x,+,k,1]	[0.4794]
4	[print,+,*,cos,x,+,k]	[0.4794,1]
5	[print,+,*,cos,x,+,3]	[0.4794,1]
6	[print,+,*,cos,x,+]	[0.4794,1,3]
7	[print,+,*,cos,x]	[0.4794,4]
8	[print,+,*,cos,0.5]	[0.4794,4]
9	[print,+,*,cos]	[0.4794,4,0.5]
10	[print,+,*]	[0.4794,4,0.8776]
11	[print,+]	[0.4794,3.5103]
12	[print]	[3.9898]
13	[]	[]

FIGURE 3.6 *Execution of C on S*

With the aid of the stack-manipulating functions, it is possible to remove the need for any variables; parameters to functions, especially, can be kept on S. For instance, the following line defines 'fn' to be a function which has the definition fn=[k,x]x*x−k:

: fn DUP * − ;

Now it is possible to evaluate fn(9,5) using the following code:

9 5 fn ;

This causes the result, 16, to be left on the top of S.

The reader is invited to confirm that the code '9 5 fn' will result in the same final state for the machine as will the code '9 5 DUP * −'. This effect, where the name of the function can be literally replaced by its definition, is paradoxically part of the process of *reduction*, and is encountered again in Section 3.1.4.

Conditional execution is handled in Forth by the IF primitive. The following statement causes 'factorial(x)' or 'fibonacci(x)' to be computed, depending on whether x is less than 8, and the result to be multiplied by two:

x 8 < IF x factorial ELSE x fibonacci THEN 2 * ;

In Section 3.2.3, some new Forth stack-manipulating commands are needed. Assuming that they are not provided as primitives, they can be easily defined by the user, as suggested in Figure 3.7. Commands of the form 'C⟨n⟩' cause the *n*th item on the stack to be copied to the top. So if the stack contains [a,b,c,d,e], where the top of the stack is at the right, then executing C4 causes the stack to become [a,b,c,d,e,b]. Commands of the form 'O⟨n⟩' cause the (*n* + 1)th item on the stack to be brought to the top, that is to jump over *n* items. Thus if the stack contains

```
: NOP ;              (do nothing)

: C1 DUP ;
: C2 OVER ;
: C3 2 PICK ;        (à la Forth-83)
: C4 3 PICK ;

: O1 SWAP ;
: O2 ROT ;
: O3 3 ROLL ;        (à la Forth-83)
: O4 4 ROLL ;

: S1 SWAP ;
: S2 SWAP ROT ROT ;
: S3 ROT 3 ROLL 3 ROLL 3 ROLL ;
: S4 3 ROLL 4 ROLL 4 ROLL 4 ROLL 4 ROLL ;

: D1 DROP ;
: D2 SWAP DROP ;
: D3 ROT DROP ;
: D4 3 ROLL DROP ;
: D5 4 ROLL DROP ;
```

FIGURE 3.7 *Example definitions of NOP, C⟨n⟩, O⟨n⟩, S⟨n⟩ and D⟨n⟩*

[a,b,c,d,e], and O2 is executed, the new stack will contain [a,b,d,e,c]. Commands of the form 'S⟨n⟩' cause the *n*th item on the stack to be swapped with the $(n + 1)$th. If the old stack contains [a,b,c,d,e] and S3 is executed, the new stack will contain [a,c,b,d,e]. Lastly, commands of the form 'D⟨n⟩' cause the *n*th item on the stack to be deleted. Thus if D4 is executed when the stack contains [a,b,c,d,e], the new stack will contain [a,c,d,e].

Before these are put to use, though, the other styles of interpreted language are described. The structured languages, being more complicated than their predecessors, tend to be less appropriate to interpretation, which relies on simplicity of the source language, and so the next section (Section 3.1.3) is necessarily brief. However, the declarative languages take particular pride in their simplicity, and hence are ideal for interpreted implementation. Section 3.1.4 therefore covers one particularly economic style in the same depth as this section does for Forth.

3.1.3 Structured imperative languages

Assembler languages are generally supported only on the machine whose instruction mnemonics they assemble. One of the great advantages of high level languages over the low level ones is that they are machine independent. This means that Pascal programs, for example, are portable to a large number of different computers if each has its own Pascal compiler generating the appropriate object code. However, someone must first write the Pascal compiler and run-time support for each of these machines.

Compilers can be constructed from two major components: the *parser*, which reads in the source program, and the *code generator*, which produces the appropriate object code (Figure 3.8). The first part can be common to all computers since it is the machine independent part of the compiler. It communicates the partially digested source code to the code generator in the form of an *intermediate code*. The introduction of a new computer need only mean the writing of a new code generator. Assuming that the parser is itself written in the intermediate code, it can be merely copied to the new machine. Pascal compilers are generally designed to make full use of this technique. By extending the idea further, and arranging for all compilers to use the same *universal compiler-orientated language* as their intermediate code, the porting of software to new computers becomes even less problematic.

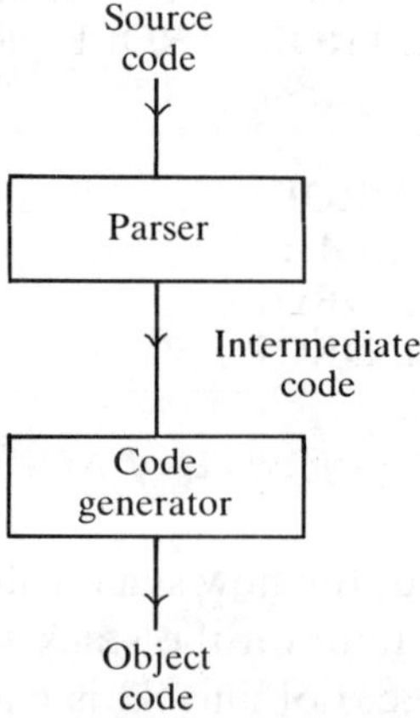

FIGURE 3.8 *Components of a compiler*

The intermediate code, which is known as *P-code*, is well defined, well documented (Welsh and Hay 1986), and is primarily intended as an intermediate code for Pascal compilers. Clearly then, a computer which supports P-code at the assembler level promises to be an excellent machine on which to run Pascal programs.

Quite separately from this, the disadvantage which interpreted languages display is that, because every line of the source code must be *parsed* and interpreted as it is executed, it executes more slowly than does the object code equivalent. One compromise is to develop a program using an interpreter, and then to compile the final release version of the program. Another approach, rather than interpreting the source code each time, is to convert it into some internal format. This is a type of *pseudo-code*: not the true op-code of the host machine, but a type of object code which is easy to generate from the source code, and is easy to interpret while the program is running. The temptation therefore is to consider writing an interpreter which uses a compiler intermediate code as its pseudo-code, and indeed this has been done for P-code.

Occam is another language residing at this level (Jones 1985). Unlike P-code, though, it was designed with the intention that humans should program in it. The occam language is designed to have very tidy mathematical properties, a characteristic which was considered to be particularly important because of the need to describe the vast amounts of parallel activity which are envisaged for large networks of Inmos Transputers. The idea of a computer like the Transputer (Inmos 1985) only being programmable in this language, with no access given to the assembler level microcode, is very attractive.

As a final thought in this section, it is worth thinking back to the description of the Forth system. The symbol table, T, and the memory, M, in this system can be considered to be a single unit, always working together in tandem, providing information about the *environment*, E. When a function is executed on C, it works in an environment which consists of the definitions of whatever variables and functions are available at the time. S is still the arithmetic stack, and C is the control stack – the one which instructs the system what to do next. It is only necessary to have one more stack, a large one called the *dump*, D, which is capable of holding the entire contents of all of the others put together, for the machine to be completely general purpose and capable of handling scoping. Such a theoretical model for a computer, the SECD machine, is described by Landin (1964).

3.1.4 Declarative languages

Combinators, which in many ways can be considered to be a declarative version of Forth, can be used as an intermediate language (Turner 1979). Just as Forth provides primitives for copying, deleting and moving items on a data stack, so combinators allow for copying, deleting and moving elements in function argument lists. Thus, instead of working with an arithmetic stack, S, they perform their work on the control stack, C.

Combinators were invented as a branch of functional logic in the 1920s by Schönfinkel (Curry and Feys 1958). As with Lisp, expressions consist of lists, such as:

(a b c d e f . . .)

though, unlike Lisp, the parentheses are not strictly necessary, but will be continued here. Again, prefix notation is used, thus the above expression indicates that the function 'a' is to be applied to the other arguments. Unlike most other notation, though, combinator functions can be given more arguments than they need, and they will only use those that they do need. For instance, the arithmetic operators each take exactly two arguments, and so the following conversions are possible:

(+ 1 3 d e f . . .) = (4 d e f . . .)
(− 25 9 d e f . . .) = (16 d e f . . .)
(* 5 5 d e f . . .) = (25 d e f . . .)

If more than two arguments are to be processed, they must be represented using separate sub-expressions:

$$(+ (+ 1\ 3)\ 5\ d\ e\ f \ldots) = (+ 4\ 5\ d\ e\ f \ldots) \\ = (9\ d\ e\ f \ldots)$$

The outermost plus operator finds that one of its two arguments is a subexpression, as represented by the nested parentheses, and must be evaluated first. In this way, arbitrarily complex arithmetic expressions can be represented, for instance:

$$(- (* 2.6\ 4.3)\ (+ 9.78\ 0.9)\ d\ e\ f \ldots) \\ = (- 11.18\ 10.68\ d\ e\ f \ldots) \\ = (0.5\ d\ e\ f \ldots)$$

There is an implicit binding from left to right, thus:

$$(a\ b\ c\ d\ e\ f \ldots) = ((((((a\ b)\ c)\ d)\ e)\ f) \ldots)$$

This is why each of the above arithmetic operations works, even in the presence of unnecessary arguments:

$$(+ 1\ 3\ d\ e\ f \ldots) = ((((((+ 1)\ 3)\ d)\ e)\ f) \ldots) \\ = (((((+ 1\ 3)\ d)\ e)\ f) \ldots) \\ = (((((4)\ d)\ e)\ f) \ldots) \\ = (4\ d\ e\ f \ldots)$$

In this process, which is described in Section 2.5.4 as that of Currying (Curry and Feys 1958), the function + is applied to the argument 1 and returns the function (+ 1). This new function, which might, in another example, have been given the name 'increment', can be used like any other. It can be applied to an argument, for instance 3, to return a new function ((+ 1) 3). This new function is synonymous with the function called 4, that is one which takes no arguments, and returns the result 4. Wherever an executable part of a string such as ((+1) 3) appears, it can be validly replaced by the string 4. This process is called *string reduction*, and is almost just a text-editing operation.

As an example of the conventional process of evaluation, consider the following three lines:

```
k = 3 ;
x = 0.5 ;
( print ( + ( sin x ) ( * ( +1 k ) ( cos x ) ) ) )
```

The first two lines are definitions, as indicated by the '=' signs. The last line is an application. The stages in the evaluation of these expressions are traced in Figure 3.9 .

As well as the arithmetic operators, there are structural operators whose job is to shuffle arguments about, in the same way that DUP, SWAP, etc. shuffle arguments about in Forth. First, there is the identity combinator, which is the functional language equivalent to the imperative NOP.

$$(I\ b\ c\ d\ e\ f \ldots) = (b\ c\ d\ e\ f \ldots)$$

```
( print ( + ( sin x ) ( * ( +1k ) ( cos x ) ) ) )
( print ( + ( sin 0.5 ) ( * ( +13 ) ( cos 0.5 ) ) ) )
( print ( + 0.4794 ( * 4 0.8776 ) ) )
( print ( + 0.4794  3.5103 ) )
( print 3.9898 )
()
```

FIGURE 3.9 *Evaluation of an arithmetic expression*

There are combinators for deleting items from the string, just as Forth has instructions for popping items from the stack. G is like DROP or D1, and K is like D2.

(F b c d e f . . .) = (c d e f . . .)
(K b c d e f . . .) = (b d e f . . .)

There are combinators for swapping items about in the string, just as Forth has instructions for swapping items about in the stack. G is like SWAP or S1, and C is like S2.

(G b c d e f . . .) = (c b d e f . . .)
(C b c d e f . . .) = (b d c e f . . .)

There are combinators for copying arguments in the string, just as Forth has instructions for copying items in the stack. V is like DUP or C1.

(V b c d e f . . .) = (b b c d e f . . .)
(W b c d e f . . .) = (b c c d e f . . .)

There are also combinators to perform operations which are not generally needed in Forth. For instance, the construction of combinator subexpressions is akin to the hypothetical creation of new temporary arithmetic stacks in Forth, on which to conduct intermediate work.

(B b c d e f . . .) = (b (c d) e f . . .)
(S b c d e f . . .) = (b d (c d) e f . . .)

Figure 3.10 shows examples of the operation of some of these combinators. The last line shows that any (arbitrarily complex) subexpression behaves as a single object, capable of being copied, deleted or exchanged with another *en masse.*

The combinators C, B and S perform three functions which are very heavily used in computer programs. So significant are these functions that each one has a common variant, respectively called C', B' and S', which are often useful as optimisations.

(C′ b c d e f . . .) = (b (c e) d f . . .)
(B′ b c d e f . . .) = (b c (d e) f . . .)
(S′ b c d e f . . .) = (b (c e) (d e) f . . .)

```
(I 3)             = (3)                   = 3
(K 4 5)           = (4)                   = 4
(S + sq 6)        = ( + 6 ( sq 6 ) )      = ( +6 36 ) = 42
(B sin cos 1)     = ( sin ( cos 1 ) )     = 0.5144
(C - 14 23)       = ( -23 14 )            = 9
(W * (+ 2 3)) = ( * (+ 2 3) (+ 2 3) = ( * 5 5 ) = 25
```

FIGURE 3.10 *Some simple examples*

There is also a conditional operator IF which causes the first and third arguments to be deleted when the first is 'true', and causes the first and second arguments to be deleted otherwise.

```
(IF b c d e f ... ) = ( c e f ... ) when b = true
                      ( d e f ... ) when b = false
```

For example:

```
( *( IF ( < x 8 ) ( factorial x ) ( fibonacci x ) ) 2 ) where x=4
   = ( *( factorial 4 ) 2 ) = 48
```

The expression (S′ * I I), which can be studied in isolation because of its Currying property, behaves as a function that takes a single numerical argument, and returns its square. Thus (S′ * I I) can be given the name 'sq', and used in further function applications. Figure 3.11 shows the process of substituting a function definition where it is referenced.

```
( sq 5 )        where sq = ( S′ * I I )
= ( ( S′ * I I ) 5 )
= ( S′ * I I 5 )
= ( * ( I 5 ) ( I 5 ) )
= ( * 5 5 )
=25
```

FIGURE 3.11 *An example of function definition and application*

Figure 3.12 shows a more complex example. The function 'sumsq' takes two numeric arguments and returns the result of computing the sum of their squares. In this, the simpler equivalent definition sq=(W *) is used.

Thus combinators, in common with Forth's primitives, are extremely simple and yet are capable of expressing arbitrarily complex computer programming ideas. The next chapter considers the possibility of designing computers which use these representations in their instruction sets. The next section (3.2), therefore, contemplates the feasibility of designing compilers which can generate the object codes for these machines.

```
(sumsq 3 4)
   where sumsq=(C(BS(BK(B+sq)))sq)
   and   sq   =(W*)
=((C(BS(BK(B+sq)))sq)3 4)
=(C(BS(BK(B+sq)))sq 3 4)
=((BS(BK(B+sq)))3 sq 4)
=(BS(BK(B+sq))3 sq 4)
=(S((BK(B+sq))3)sq 4)
=(((BK(B+sq))3)4(sq 4))
=((BK(B+sq))3 4((W*)4))
=(BK(B+sq)3 4(W*4))
=(K((B+sq)3)4(*4 4))
=(((B+sq)3)16)
=((B+sq 3)16)
=(B+sq 3 16)
=(+(sq 3)16)
=(+((W*)3)16)
=(+(W*3)16)
=(+(*3 3)16)
=(+9 16)
=25
```

FIGURE 3.12 *A more complex example*

3.2 PROGRAM COMPILATION AND THE EXECUTION MODEL

The subject of compilation is vast, well researched (Aho and Ullman 1977) and far beyond the scope of this chapter. However, one small aspect of one possible compiler technique is worth describing here. Figure 3.8 depicts the parser as one of the main components of the compiler. It is needed, too, when implementing interpreters, and so the discussion in these sections is relevant to the support of Forth, P-code and declarative languages. Its output might be required in a one-dimensional format, for example for use as object code or pseudo-code. Sections 3.2.1 and 3.2.2 investigate some useful techniques for achieving this, whilst Sections 3.2.3 and 3.2.4 apply them to the production of Forth and combinator code respectively.

3.2.1 Building a syntax tree

The process starts with the entry of the expression in a high level language, typed in as a string of characters. For instance, using the following expression as an example:

```
filt = sin(x) + (1+k)*cos(x);
```

The expression to the right of the '=' sign is scanned from left to right, and used to build up a syntax tree. In this process, each *symbol* in the original text is allocated to a node on the tree. As well as having a name, like '+', '*', filt, 'sin', 'cos', 'x', and 'k', each symbol also has a precedence, as listed perhaps in Figure 3.13.

+	has a precedence of	1
−	has a precedence of	1
*	has a precedence of	2
/	has a precedence of	2
^	has a precedence of	3
numbers	have a precedence of	4
names	have a precedence of	4
(	causes the precedence to increase by	5
)	causes the precedence to decrease by	5

FIGURE 3.13 *List of precedence values*

The stages in the building of the syntax tree are depicted in Figure 3.15 for the expression which is given above. It commences by taking the first symbol, 'sin', and placing it on the tree. The rules for governing the subsequent actions in the construction process are then as listed in Figure 3.14, or as embodied by the Pascal program in Appendix 3.

1. Get the next symbol.
2. Compute its precedence value.
3. Scan down the right-hand spine of the tree until a symbol is found with a higher (or equal) precedence value than that of the new symbol.
4. Snap the branch immediately in front of the symbol whose precedence is higher or equal.
5. Graft the new symbol on to what remains of the right-hand spine of the tree.
6. Graft the snapped-off portion of tree to the left of the new symbol.

FIGURE 3.14 *Inserting a new symbol in the syntax tree*

In the example, the next symbol is 'x', and has a higher precedence, 9, than 'sin' because it is inside a set of parentheses. It is placed below 'sin', and to the right. The next symbol is '+', which has a lower precedence, 1, then either 'sin' or 'x', and so must be placed above them both. The displaced subtree is therefore joined on as a left branch of the new node. Since only the rightmost subtree is being scanned, the next symbol is only compared with the node containing '+'. Since '1' has a higher precedence, 9, than '+', it is appended as a right branch. The next symbol, '+', has a higher precedence, 6, than the previous '+', 1, due to the parentheses, but a lower one than the '1'. It must therefore be inserted between them, with '1' displaced to the new left subtree.

The next symbol, 'k', can only have its precedence compared against the two '+'

nodes. It has a higher precedence, 9, than either, and so is appended as a new right subtree. The final diagram, Figure 3.15i, represents the complete syntax tree for the original expression.

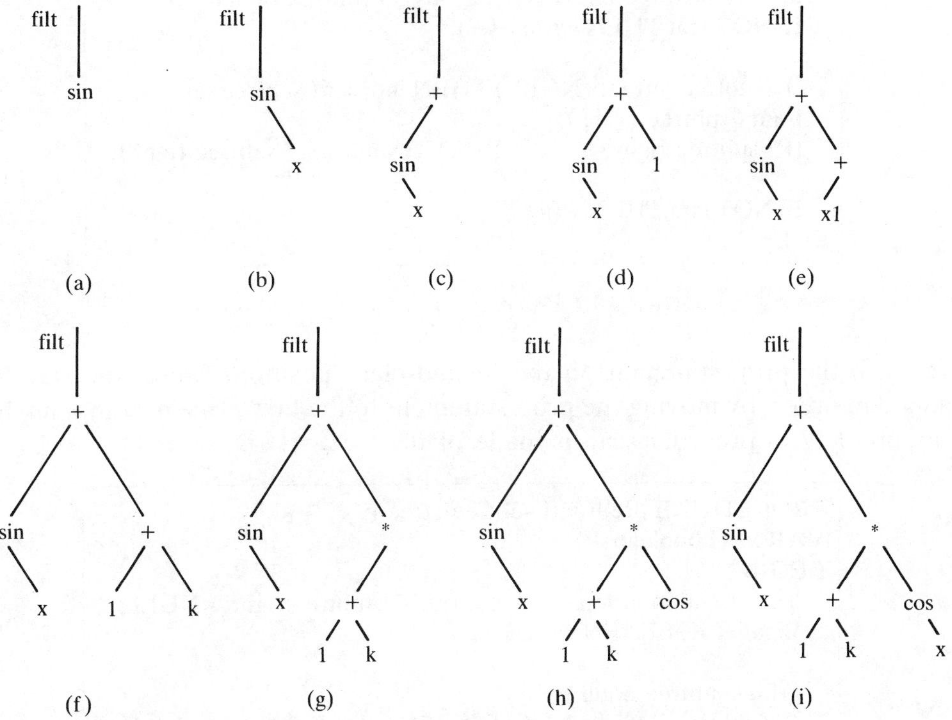

FIGURE 3.15 *Building the syntax tree for sin(x) + (1 + k) * cos(x)*

3.2.2 Reading a syntax tree

The syntax tree is a very powerful representation. To illustrate this, first consider the procedure which is defined in Figure 3.16, and a subsequent call on 'inorder (filt)'.

By applying this to the tree which was developed in Figure 3.15, the following text is obtained:

((sin x) + ((1 + k) * (cos x)))

This is not identical to the original source code, but the differences are only in the distribution of parentheses, and the information content is otherwise identical. This indicates that the tree representation is equivalent to the original source code, and that either can be regenerated from the other.

Having been assured of this important property, two further procedures can be investigated. Figure 3.16 shows that the heart of the procedure consists of three statements: one which recurses down the left subtree, one which prints the value of the node, and one which recurses down the right subtree. The procedure in Figure

```
PROCEDURE inorder( subtree : tree );
VAR leaf : boolean;
BEGIN
  leaf := ( subtree.left = NULL )AND ( subtree.right = NULL );
  IF NOT leaf THEN write ('( ' );

  IF (subtree.left <> NULL) THEN inorder ( subtree.left );
  print ( subtree.node );
  IF ( subtree.right <> NULL ) THEN inorder ( subtree.right );

  IF NOT leaf THEN write ( ' )' );
END;
```

FIGURE 3.16 *Procedure to scan a tree inorder*

3.16, with the print statement in the second-place position, causes the tree to be scanned in order; by moving the print statement to the first-place position, as shown in Figure 3.17, a preorder scan is made of the tree.

```
PROCEDURE preorder( subtree : tree );
VAR leaf : boolean;
BEGIN
  leaf := ( subtree.left = NULL )AND( subtree.right = NULL );
  IF NOT leaf THEN write ( '( ' );

  print ( subtree.node );
  IF ( subtree.left <> NULL ) THEN preorder ( subtree.left );
  IF ( subtree.right <> NULL ) THEN preorder ( subtree.right );

  IF NOT leaf THEN write ( ' ) ' );
END;
```

FIGURE 3.17 *Procedure to scan a tree preorder*

When the procedure in Figure 3.17 is called, as in 'preorder (filt)', the following text is generated.

(+ (sin x) (* (+ 1 k) (cos x)))

The process of building the tree, and then scanning it preorder, has succeeded in translating the original source code, which used conventional infix notation, into the equivalent prefix notation code. The word 'equivalent' can be used because, once again, no information has been lost. This procedure is therefore a major step in the process of translating from conventionally notated languages into Lisp.

The last alternative is to move the print statement to the third place position, as depicted in Figure 3.18. By applying the procedure to the original syntax tree, as in 'postorder (filt)', the following text is generated:

((x sin) ((1 k +) (x cos)*) +)

Now the original source code, using infix notation, has been converted into the equivalent expression using postfix notation. This is a major step in the conversion from conventional notation to Forth, as is described next.

```
PROCEDURE postorder( subtree: tree );
VAR leaf : boolean;
BEGIN
  leaf := ( subtree.left = NULL )AND( subtree.right = NULL );
  If NOT leaf THEN write( '(' );

  IF( subtree.left <> NULL ) THEN postorder( subtree.left );
  IF( subtree.right <> NULL ) THEN postorder( subtree.right );
  print( subtree.node );

  IF NOT leaf THEN write( ')' );
END;
```

FIGURE 3.18 *Procedure to scan a tree postorder*

3.2.3 Compiling to Forth

Postfix notation, which is also known as reverse-Polish notation, will be familiar to those who have used Forth, or who owned some of the early electronic calculators. For this, the structuring information, which is given by the parentheses, is usually redundant since it is already given by context, in that 'sin', 'cos', '*' and '+' can only take a known number of arguments. This gives rise to the following abbreviated form of the text:

x sin 1 k + x cos * +

This expression, when executed in Forth, causes the appropriate values to be pushed and manipulated on the arithmetic stack, S, and the final result to be left on the top of S at the end. This is illustrated in Figure 3.6.

Suppose now that the following program is to be converted into Forth.

```
filt = [ k, x ] sin(x) + (1+k)*cos(x);
print( filt( 3, 0.5 ) );
```

Since Forth is a stack-based language, it is possible to remove all references to local variables from the function definitions. In order to do this, it is useful to return to the syntax tree, and to annotate it as shown in Figure 3.19.

The arcs of the tree are first labelled with information about the contents of the arithmetic stack. The input stack at the root contains [k,x]. Annotations are placed on the descendant branches, specifying which of the stack values are required by the respective subtrees. In the example, the right subtree requires both [k,x], but the left

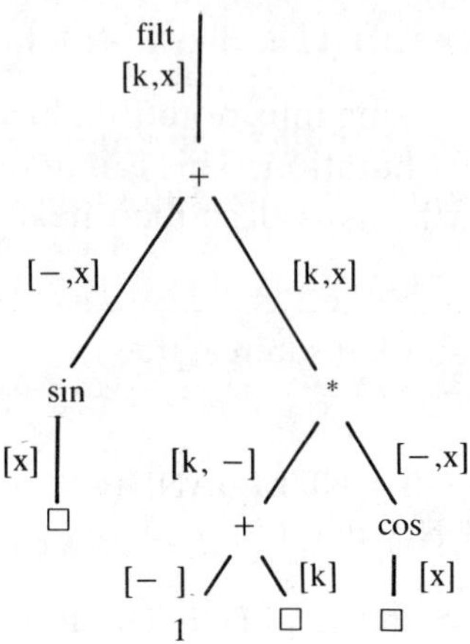

FIGURE 3.19 *Annotating the syntax tree*

subtree only requires 'x', so it depicts the 'k' position as being blocked, [−,x]. From that point on, in the left subtree there is only one item on the stack, so the annotation on successive subbranches can be either [x] or [−]; in the event, [x] is used. Figure 3.19 shows this process completed, with all references to local variables in the tree replaced by the □ symbol to indicate that they have been successfully removed.

Now the tree is re-annotated. The left branches are each given as many 'C⟨n⟩' symbols as there are items, *n*, on the stack. Thus [x] indicates 'C1', [k,x] indicates 'C2 C2', and [a,b,−,d,e,−] indicates 'C6 C6 C6 C6 C6 C6', independently of the fact that some of the stack items have been blocked. The process is then repeated on the right-hand branches using *n* occurrences of 'O⟨n⟩'. When there is only one subtree

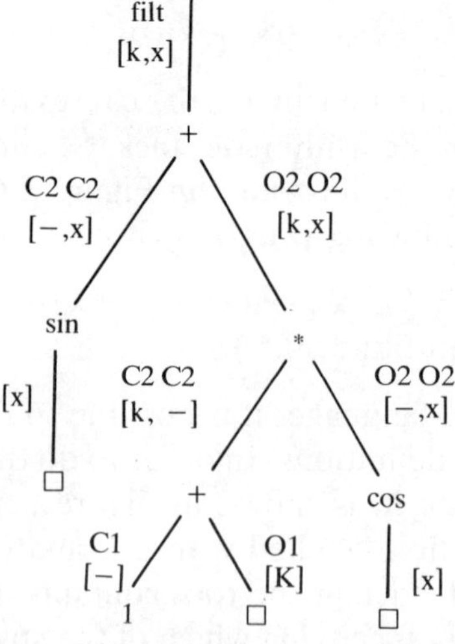

FIGURE 3.20 *Second annotation of the syntax tree*

there are no changes to be made to the stack's structure, so no new annotations are introduced. The result is depicted in Figure 3.20.

The tree is re-annotated one last time, scanning the stack information on each arc from left to right, and replacing it by the same number of 'D⟨n⟩' symbols as there are blocked items on the stack. The value of *n* is calculated by counting from the right, thus [a,b,−,d,e,−] would be replaced by 'D4 D1'. The result of this operation is depicted in Figure 3.21.

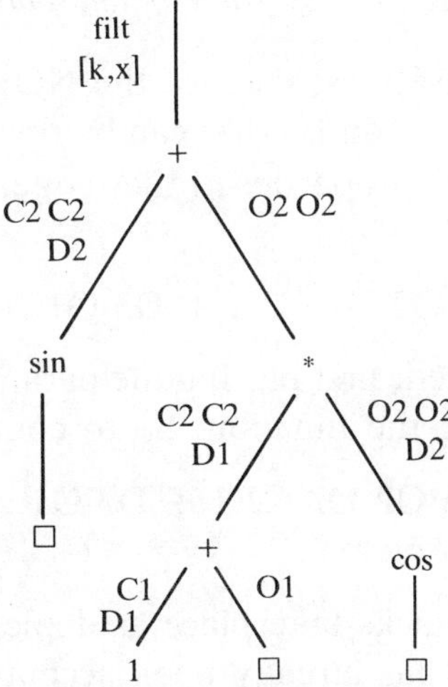

FIGURE 3.21 *Third annotation of the syntax tree*

Now the tree is walked postorder, using a modified version of the procedure, as shown in Figure 3.22. This procedure ensures that the extra symbols, which are carried by the arcs, are generated as output too.

```
PROCEDURE postorder( subtree : tree );
BEGIN
   print( subtree.arc );
   IF( subtree.left <> NULL ) THEN postorder( subtree.left );
   IF( subtree.right <> NULL ) THEN postorder( subtree.right );
   print( subtree.node );
END;
```

FIGURE 3.22 *Procedure to scan a tree postorder*

This generates the following code:

C2 C2 D2 □ sin O2 O2 C2 C2 D1 C1 D1 1 O1 □ + O2 O2 D2 □ cos * +

where the symbol '□', that is NOP, has been used to denote that a reference to a variable has been removed. The above string is a valid Forth expression, capable of being executed. However, before testing it with some parameters, the code can be optimised a little, according to the rewrite rules which are summarised in Figure 3.23.

Initial string	*Optimised strings*			
	$m < n-1$	$m = n-1$	$n = 1$	$m \geqslant n \geqslant 2$
$C\langle m\rangle\ D\langle n\rangle$	$D\langle n-1\rangle\ C\langle m\rangle$	$O\langle m-1\rangle$	NOP	$D\langle n-1\rangle\ C\langle m-1\rangle$
$O\langle m\rangle\ D\langle n\rangle$	$D\langle n\rangle\ O\langle m\rangle$	$D\langle n-1\rangle\ O\langle m-1\rangle$	$D\langle m+1\rangle$	$D\langle n-1\rangle\ O\langle m-1\rangle$

FIGURE 3.23 *Some optimisations*

In addition to these optimisations, each of the NOPs can be omitted since they literally 'do nothing', and 'O1 +' and 'O1 *' can be rewritten respectively as '+' and '*' because of the commutative properties of these operators. The code for 'filt' now becomes:

C1 sin O2 O2 C2 1 + D3 O1 cos * +

This last version can be tested, first placing the parameters in the correct order on the stack, and then by calling the function. So to confirm that it works, consider:

```
: filt C1 sin O2 O2 C2 1 + D3 O1 cos * + ;
3 0.5 filt print ;
```

The actions on the C and S stacks take place as depicted in Figure 3.24, assuming that the definition statement has already been accepted, and that the application statement is about to be executed. (It should be emphasised though that Figure 3.24 does not represent a formal proof that the program is correct, but just a confirmatory check.)

C	*S*
[print,filt,0.5,3]	[]
[print,filt,0.5]	[3]
[print,filt]	[3,0.5]
[print,+,*,cos,O1,D3,+,1,C2,O2,O2,sin,C1]	[3,0.5]
[print,+,*,cos,O1,D3,+,1,C2,O2,O2,sin]	[3,0.5,0.5]
[print,+,*,cos,O1,D3,+,1,C2,O2,O2]	[3,0.5,0.4794]
[print,+,*,cos,O1,D3,+,1,C2,O2]	[0.5,0.4794,3]
[print,+,*,cos,O1,D3,+,1,C2]	[0.4794,3,0.5]
[print,+,*,cos,O1,D3,+,1]	[0.4794,3,0.5,3]
[print,+,*,cos,O1,D3,+]	[0.4794,3,0.5,3,1]
[print,+,*,cos,O1,D3]	[0.4794,3,0.5,4]
[print,+,*,cos,O1]	[0.4794,0.5,4]
[print,+,*,cos]	[0.4794,4,0.5]
[print,+,*]	[0.4794,4,0.8776]
[print,+]	[0.4794,3.5103]
[print]	[3.9896]
[]	[]

FIGURE 3.24 *The evaluation of 'filt'*

The next section is a repeat of this one, but using combinator code as the target representation. Like the method of compiling to Forth, it involves annotating a syntax tree, with the aim of removing all references to the named arguments. The procedure turns out to be very much simpler, though, because combinators are not restricted to performing arithmetic operations only at the head of the stack.

3.2.4 Compiling to combinators

Very simple methods exist for compiling functions into the combinators S, K and I (Curry and Feys 1958). This text, though, compiles to the combinators S′, C′, B′, B and I (Kennaway and Sleep 1984a) by taking each of the arguments in turn, working from right to left, and using them to annotate the syntax tree with 'signposts', or *directors*. These are arrows which indicate which of the subtrees need to use the given argument. '↙' is used to indicate that the argument is used in the left branch only, '↘' for the right branch only, '↙↘' indicates its use in both branches, and '↓' indicates that there is only one branch and that the argument is used there. Whenever bound variables, that is those which are named as arguments in the function, are removed, they are each replaced by a '□'. When a director is placed on a node which already bears an earlier director, parentheses are used to enforce a right-to-left binding, so overriding the normal left-to-right binding. For the example which is used in Section 3.2.3, there are two arguments to the function, so the annotation of the tree, Figure 3.25, takes place in two stages.

The tree, Figure 3.25(c), is now scanned preorder to read off the appropriate combinator string:

$$\begin{aligned}\text{filt} = (&\searrow (\swarrow\!\!\searrow +)(\downarrow \sin \square)\\ &(\swarrow (\searrow *)(\swarrow + \square\ 1)(\downarrow \cos \square)))\end{aligned}$$

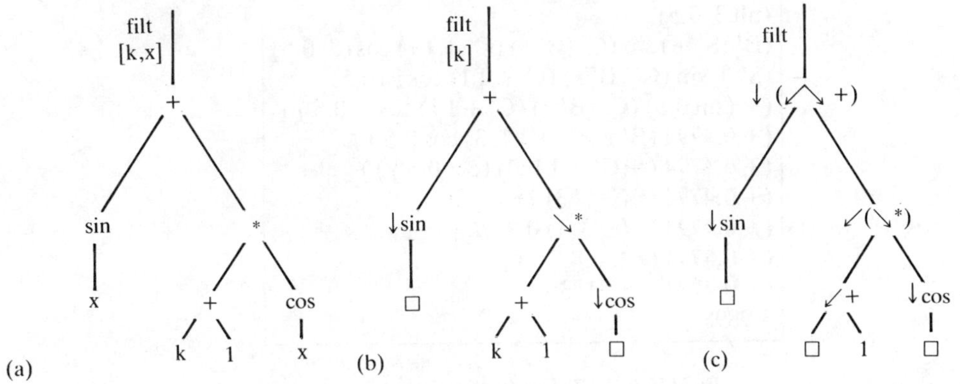

FIGURE 3.25 *Annotating the syntax tree with directors*

It is now only necessary to note that '↘' is the B′ combinator, '↙' is C′, '↙↘' is S′, '↓' is B, and '□' is I. Thus the code becomes:

filt = (B′ (S′+) (B sin I)
(C′ (B′ ∗) (C′ + I 1) (B cos I)))

Although 'I' acts as a NOP, it cannot be removed. Unlike the Forth system where NOP indicates that nothing is to be done to the arithmetic stack, S, the combinator system performs its arithmetic work on the control stack, C. It uses the I combinator as a place marker, conveying certain structural information. However, there are other optimisations which can be made, as summarised in Figure 3.26.

```
B  x I   → x
S  x I   → W x
C′ I     → C
C′ x I   → C x
B′ I     → B
B′ x y I → x y
S′ I     → S
S′ x I   → S x
S′ x I I → W x
```

FIGURE 3.26 *Simple optimisations*

Thus the code becomes:

filt = (B′ (S′ +) sin (C′ (B′ ∗) (C′ + I 1) cos))

To confirm that it works, consider the effect of demanding the result of:

filt 3 0.5 ?

The history of the ensuing computation is traced in Figure 3.27.

```
(filt 3 0.5)
(B′ (S′ +) sin (C′ (B′ ∗) (C′ + I 1) cos) 3 0.5)
(S′ + sin (C′ (B′ ∗) (C′ + I 1) cos 3) 0.5)
(+ (sin 0.5) (C′ (B′ ∗) (C′ + I 1) cos 3 0.5 ) )
(+ 0.4794 (B′ ∗ (C′ + I 1 3) cos 0.5 ) )
(+ 0.4794 (∗ (C′ + I 1 3) (cos 0.5 ) ) )
(+ 0.4794 (∗ (+ (I 3) 1) 0.8776 ) )
(+ 0.4794 (∗ (+ 3 1) 0.8776 ) )
(+ 0.4794 (∗ 4 0.8776 ) )
(+ 0.4794 + 3.5103 )
3.9898
```

FIGURE 3.27 *Evaluation of 'filt'*

This short text cannot hope to cover all of this area, and the interested reader is referred to more complete works (Peyton Jones 1987). One area which has not been fully covered is that of removing all of the variables. In the above, the bound variables (arguments) 'k' and 'x', were removed, but the removal of the potentially more troublesome free variables (the global variables) has not been shown. To achieve this, special infix 'is applied to' operators, '@', are inserted between every symbol, thus:

filt = (B′ @ (S′ @+) @ sin @ (C′ @ (B′ @ *) @ (C′ @ + @ I @ 1) @ cos))

and a second syntax tree is constructed. This places such variables as 'sin' and 'cos' at the leaves ready for removal in the same way as before. This then means that the definitions of these functions must be passed as extra parameters when the function is applied. However, there are problems with recursive function definitions, and this leads to the introduction of a new combinator, Y, which is analogous to the RECURSE or SELF functions of Forth, and for which an excellent treatment is given by Burge (1975).

The removal of function names can be taken to extremes. All of the combinators can be replaced by definitions involving only S and K. Similarly, the symbols '+' and '*' are no more than the names of the plus and multiply functions. If these are not supplied as primitives, these too can be removed, and the appropriate definitions passed as parameters to the function. Moreover numbers, like '3', are functions which take no parameters, and always return the same result. The nineteenth-century mathematician, Peano, showed that integers, and hence floating-point numbers too, are only the external names of functions whose definitions can be supplied separately. These representations, involving the use of the functions 'successor' and 'zero', might be very desirable to the purist, the mathematician and the computer scientist, but would be disastrous as far as the computer engineer is concerned, in terms of both memory demands and execution speed. They are too fine a grain of representation. Consequently, numeric constants and arithmetic operators are generally provided as primitive functions.

This book must now turn from its brief look at compilation. Instead, attention is turned to some of the evaluation mechanisms which can be chosen for the execution of computer programs.

3.2.5 Evaluation mechanisms

Just as imperative languages use a variety of parameter-passing mechanisms, so too do functional languages. *Applicative order reduction* is very similar to the imperative language call-by-value mechanism (Section 2.4.3) in that every parameter in function applications is fully evaluated and the final values are passed to the function, which can then start executing. This is a fairly efficient mechanism, in that it only causes each parameter to be executed exactly once, regardless of the number of references which are made to its value within the function definition. However, this is not efficient enough for computer programmers who, with their taste for new, powerfully expressive notations, wish to represent infinite data structures in their programs (Abelson and Sussman 1985). For instance, they might want to represent the set of all even numbers, or the set of all prime numbers. So a better mechanism is required: one which does not evaluate its parameters completely until required.

There is a third mechanism, *call-by-name*, which is rarely seen in imperative languages. In this, functions are given the unevaluated parameters directly as they appear at the point of function application. The program in Figure 2.15 would print the results '12.0 12.0 23.0' since the value which 'munge' returns is called 'vector [i]', and its evaluation, including that of the index *i*, is deferred until it is needed in the assignment statement. *Normal order reduction* is the declarative version of this, which would not permit the side effect of the change which occurs to the value of a[1] for instance. It is normally implemented by evaluating only the leftmost operator in a prefix expression. This relies on the Currying property, in which it is meaningful to evaluate functions without fully knowing their parameters. The other, non-leftmost expressions are eventually triggered when a *strict function*, such as an arithmetic operator, is found in the leftmost position. Since such functions cannot complete their execution until they have been given concrete, numeric values for their parameters, it is considered safe to proceed immediately with their evaluation. Figure 3.27 depicts most of these points.

The particular version of reduction mechanism which has been described so far is *string reduction*. This is a particularly useful mechanism for supporting Curryed function evaluation and normal order reduction. In this, a string of symbols is taken, and is reduced to an equivalent string. Thus,

(sq (+ 2 3))

is reduced to:

(sq 5)

since the string '(+2 3) can be replaced by the equivalent string '5'. This can be further reduced to:

(S′ * I I 5)

since the string 'sq' can be replaced by the string '(S′ * I I).' This process is called *reduction*, not because the string always grows shorter, which clearly is not always the case, but because its component parts become simpler. In the example, instead of involving the user-defined symbol 'sq', the string now only contains primitive combinators, arithmetic operators and integers.

With string reduction, code is copied each time it is needed. For example, the function definition:

double = [f] f+f

which is expressed on a syntax tree as shown in Figure 3.28, can be applied to (sq 5), as in (double (sq 5)). String reduction leads to the following steps:

(S′ + I I (sq 5))
(+ (I sq 5) (I sq 5))
(+ (sq 5) (sq 5))

and so (sq 5) is evaluated twice.

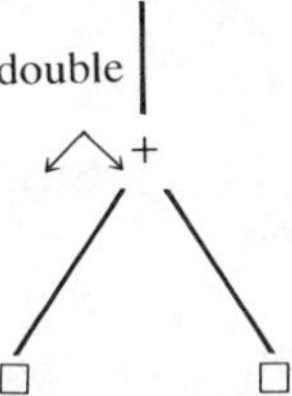

FIGURE 3.28 *Definition of 'double'*

Though this supports Curryed functions, and partial evaluation of infinite data structures, it is clearly inefficient. One method round this problem is to adopt a *graph reduction* mechanism. As the name suggests, this is most easily envisaged by way of graphs, Figure 3.29a, using the @ symbol to mean 'is applied to'.

The syntax tree is modified, and is no longer a tree in Figure 3.29b. Both branches of the '+' node point to the same expression. When this expression is evaluated, it will be replaced by a single node containing the value 25, and this value will be returned by both of the arcs of the + node. The final result, 50, will therefore be returned, but having evaluated (sq 5) only once. This mechanism is particularly useful for supporting *lazy evaluation*, in which parameters and their component parts are not evaluated until (if ever) they are needed, and then never again, since their value will be the same each time, owing to the property of *referential transparency*.

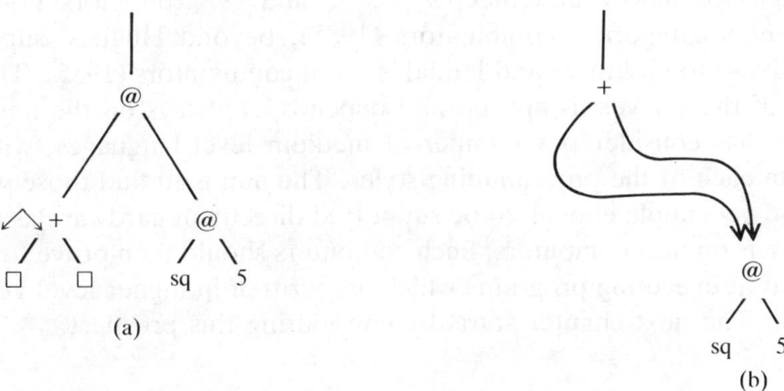

FIGURE 3.29 *Graph reduction of (double (S * I5))*

Figure 3.30 summarises the mechanisms which have been mentioned in this section, along with some properties. In particular, the correspondence between some styles, and their possible realisation, are noted.

3.3 CONCLUSIONS

Since the syntax tree carries the same information as the source text, and since it is used as the starting point in graph reduction, it is tempting to suggest that it could be used as a graphical programming language. Indeed, systems which use trees and

Imperative languages	*Functional languages*	*Implementation*	*No. times parameters are evaluated*
Call-by-value	Applicative order reduction	String reduction	1
Call-by-name	Normal order reduction	String reduction	As often as each is used (including 0)
Call-by-reference	Lazy evaluation	Graph reduction	0 or 1

FIGURE 3.30 *Evaluation mechanisms*

data-flow diagrams in this way have been investigated (deJong and Hankin 1982).

Combinators have been shown to be useful in the implementation of the reduction mechanisms. The ones which are described (Section 3.1.4) are fairly fine grain, merely specifying the movement of individual parameters within an expression. As with all questions of choosing an appropriate granularity, there is a trade-off to be made. At the fine grain extreme, too little work is performed at each stage to justify the high communications overhead of passing parameters each time. At the coarse grain extreme, vast monolithic functions are executed with little chance to share parts of the work with neighbouring processors. A spectrum of combinator levels has been identified, from the fine grain of Curry and Feys' S, K and I combinators (1958), through Kennaway and Sleep's ↙, ↘ and ↙↘ directors (1984), and Cousineau *et al.*'s categorical combinators (1985), beyond Hughes' supercombinators (1982, 1984) to Goldberg and Hudak's serial combinators (1985). The choice of which one of these levels is appropriate depends as always on the application.

This chapter has considered a number of medium level languages, with representatives from each of the programming styles. The aim is to find those which are expressive, and yet simple enough to be supported directly in hardware as the bases of instruction sets on new computers. Such computers should then prove to be particularly efficient at executing programs which are written in higher level versions of the same style. The next chapter starts by considering this prospect.

3.4 EXERCISES

3.1 Compile the following expression into Forth:

quadroot = [a,b,c] (0 − b + sqrt(b∗b − 4∗a∗c))/(2∗a)

3.2 Compile the expression from question 3.1 into S′, B′, C′, B and I–based combinators.

3.3 Redraw Figure 3.24 so that it traces the evaluation of the unoptimised code which is listed two lines below Figure 3.22.

4

FASTER EXECUTION AND PARALLEL COMPUTATION

When von Neumann and his contemporaries designed their computers (Burks *et al.* 1947) they had valves and relays to use as active components. Their design which, though seminal, still had much in common with the Analytical Engine (Babbage 1837), has been upgraded many times over the years to obtain better performance. Higher performance computers were made possible when the valves and relays could be replaced by transistors, the third generation resulted when small scale integration could be used, and the present generation has seen the emergence of the *computer on a chip*, made possible by VLSI. Thus performance enhancement has been achieved through improvements in hardware technology alone. Little has been changed over the four generations from von Neumann's, or even Babbage's, original designs. It has been suggested that this process cannot continue and that, for the next improvement in performance, the fifth generation, designers must look to different computation models. These will almost inevitably involve the extraction of parallelism, but this is far from a straightforward step to make. Even without the von Neumann bottleneck, the designer runs up against the dual problems: those of how to support so much parallel activity, and those of how to program so many autonomous processors.

The traditional model for program execution involves the use of a single processor fetching instructions and data from a single memory. The program counter and the data bus are both central in the design, and serve to ensure that only one instruction can be fetched at a time and that it can only operate on one item of data at any one time. This is the single instruction stream, single data stream model, SISD, as defined by Flynn (1972), and characteristically allows only one flow of control, or sequence of instructions, to thread its way through the program.

It is characteristic of the conventional computer that the individual operations are all very simple, they are all very repetitive, and there is an enormous amount of traffic travelling on the bus (Section 1.2.4). Many people, notably Backus (1978), consider that the bus is largely responsible for, and almost synonymous with, the von Neumann bottleneck. The remedy could be: (a) to accelerate traffic, (b) to reduce the volume of traffic, or (c) to remove the bottleneck altogether from the design.

In order to accelerate the traffic, the desinger could increase the clock speed. However, there is a limit to the extent to which this can be done, not least because of the bus and memory's ability to cope only with a certain maximum bandwidth. The second solution is considered next (in Section 4.1). The third is the more challenging option, and is the subject of the remainder of this chapter.

4.1 MEDIUM LEVEL INSTRUCTION SETS

The second option, that of reducing the number of accesses to the bus and memory, can be achieved by increasing the menu and the power of instructions in the processor's instruction set. The execution time of programs is reduced through needing fewer instruction fetches from memory per program.

The instruction sets for the first digital electronic computers consisted of operations which the electronic engineers found easy/cheap to implement. As languages were developed, so the electronics engineers started to receive feedback from the computer scientists as to how to extract greater performance from their hardware. They learned: which functions were most heavily used; which ones, if added, would become heavily used; and which presented the greatest inefficiencies.

Thus the trend in the 1960s was to provide bigger instruction sets, with many of the instructions performing quite complex operations. Instructions were provided for building and accessing stacks, for arithmetic expression evaluation and for efficient function calling. Large register banks were provided, exploiting locality during intermediate result evaluation. Complicated addressing modes were provided to use these registers, more specialised than those of Section 2.2.1, involving many parallel data transfers and subsidiary arithmetic operations. Instructions could then be provided to perform operations on the internal registers, and hence to execute without fetching further data from the memory.

Floating-point instructions were included. On some machines, tagged memory was provided – memory which held not only data, but information about the data. Integers, instructions, characters and floating-point numbers would each bear different tags, and so would be distinguishable, thus aiding the process of program development as well as that of program execution (Myers 1982). Burroughs are perhaps most famous in this area, designing computers in the 1960s whose instruction sets were tailored for executing Algol programs.

One disadvantage of the design of complex instruction set computers (CISC) is the need to provide the potentially massive amounts of hardware to decode each instruction. One execution-speed compromise is to use a *microcontroller* (μCPU)

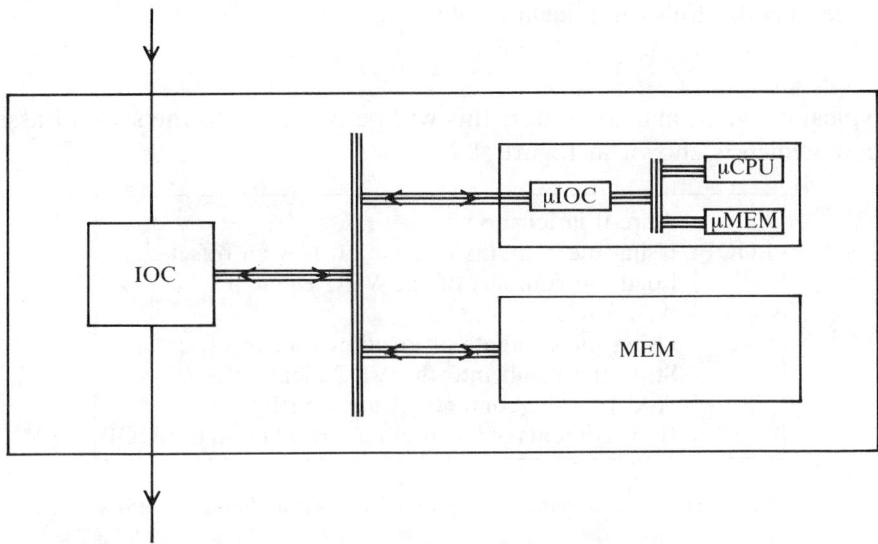

FIGURE 4.1 *A microcode-controlled CPU*

(Figure 4.1). This is a small, dedicated processor which has its own program, or *microcode*, stored in its own small, local (read only) memory. In effect, using the properties of von Neumann's stored-program idea, the microcontroller reads the CISCs instructions from main memory and manipulates them as data, like an interpreter handling pseudo-code. The reader is invited to consider what a picocontroller might do, and the nature of the granularity dependent design decisions which are entailed by its use.

Instead of making the computer very complicated, so that it might be powerful to a very broad, general class of application, the alternative is to design the computer so that it is extremely efficient at executing programs which are of a very restricted, specialised nature. This is seen, for example, in digital signal processors (DSP) (Yassaie 1986). By dedicating the design to one particular class of problem, the hardware can be optimised to extract as much performance from the special properties which the programs of its class possess. The penalty of this approach is that the design is then not generally applicable to a wide range of applications. There is therefore a trade-off between the value which is placed on high performance for a dedicated design, and that which is placed on its general usefulness. For a commercial computer designer, this trade-off is manifested as the balance between the price which customers are willing to pay for performance, and the size of the market.

For applications where vectors are manipulated routinely, it is worth considering a machine whose instruction set is specifically tuned to perform commonly occurring operations on entire vectors in one instruction. As an example, consider the following operation in Pascal:

```
FOR i := 0 TO 99 DO vec[i] := vec[i] + 3;
```

where 'vec' has the following declaration:

VAR vec = ARRAY [0..99] OF integer;

On a typical conventional computer, this will be compiled to the style of assembler operations which is shown in Figure 4.2.

```
       Store 0 in location I
LOOP:  Using the contents of location I as an offset ...
       Load the contents of the VEC element
       Add 3 to it
       Using the contents of location I as an offset ...
       Store the result into the VEC element
       Add 1 to the contents of location I
       If the contents of location I are ≤ 99 jump to LOOP
```

FIGURE 4.2 *Conventional assembler code to handle vectors*

The last seven instructions are executed 100 times, each one of them involving the six activities which are listed in Figure 1.13, four of which are transfers of data, or addressing information along the bus. Thus there are a total of 2804 bus transfers involved in Figure 4.2. However, the instructions might be instead realised by those of Figure 4.3, each of which is executed once, though the last one is more complicated that the others. As well as being fetched from memory (two bus transfers), the third instruction must perform 100 data read/write operations, each one involving three bus transfers: one to send the address; one to read the data; and one to write the new data back at the same address. Figure 4.3 therefore involves only 310 bus transfers to perform the same job as Figure 4.2, with a consequent improvement of the expected execution speed.

```
Store 0 in location FIRST
Store 99 in location LAST
Add 3 to vector VEC
```

FIGURE 4.3 *Possible assembler code on a vector-processing computer*

The alternative to tailoring the computer to its applications is to tailor it to a particular programming style. The Burroughs Algol computers have already been mentioned, and similar dedication can be made to the structured (Section 4.1.1) and declarative (Section 4.1.2) programming languages. The former is described next.

4.1.1 Structured imperative languages

In order to execute a structured language at the assembler level, an alternative to the branch and jump instructions must be provided in the instruction set. An experimental machine of this type was designed by Osmon (1978), in which data is held on an arithmetic stack, whilst instructions and program counters are interpreted on a control stack. Many practical machines, too, have been dedicated to the use of structured programming languages, but in fact operate in a conventional manner, using a conventional architecture, with the underlying microcode full of jumps and GOTOs. Provided, though, that this is hidden from the user's lowermost view of the machine, a better programming style can be encouraged.

Another concern, which is applicable to any dedicated language machine, is that the hardware might provide poor support for the facilities which are available in the language. For instance, Occam allows processes to communicate with any others, using any number of channels, but Transputers only physically support four nearest neighbours, each communicating along a single bidirectional channel. As with other languages like Fortran or Pascal run on standard computers, the mismatch is bridged by *semantic sugaring*, in which the language 'simulates' the desired behaviour using the resources which are available in the hardware. By clever mappings of the processes on to the processors, Transputer networks can simulate the effect of having more interconnections, in an analogous fashion to the way that virtual memory computers simulate the effect of having vast amounts of memory.

4.1.2 Declarative languages

For the design of multiprocessor declarative language machines, string reduction tends to be easier to implement than graph reduction, since it is the simpler of the two mechanisms in which to synchronise the passing and evaluation of parameters. However, the penalty involved in extensive copying of code on multiprocessor machines urges one in favour of adopting graph reduction as the execution model.

Lisp has been used as the basis of the assembler level for general purpose computers (Steele and Sussman 1980). Combinators too have been used both for real machines like Skim (Clarke *et al.* 1980) and for software simulations (Turner 1979), as have the higher level categorical combinators for the CAM (Cousineau *et al.* 1985).

Part of the motivation to find new designs for computer hardware rests with the observation that current computer designs are highly inefficient in their utilisation of hardware. For instance, most conventional computers can only use the arithmetic and logic unit *or* the memory; one is usually idle whilst the other is in use. Even when in demand the memory, containing 64 Kwords say, can only access one word at a time, and so at least 65 535/65 536 = 99.9985 per cent of the hardware is constantly idle. One might argue that this circuitry is employed in storing information, but the majority of it is only in temporary storage, and only remains there because of the bottleneck to its access. As technology improves and more transistors can be deployed in each circuit, the size of memory can be expected to increase and the utilisation will fall even further. There is a consequent need to make the memory do more useful work than mere storage and retrieval of single items of data. Since the use of declarative languages is to be encouraged, and these spend much time looking for function definitions and conducting extensive pattern-matching operations on the data, content addressing has been suggested as an extra function which memory could usefully perform.

With conventional memory (Figure 4.4) the memory-read operation requires an address to be supplied as input, and the data contents of that location are then returned as output. With content addressable memory (CAM) (Figure 4.5) the data are supplied as input and the address of the first location, which has those as its contents, is returned as output. The two memories therefore perform inverse memory-read operations. By combining the two functions in a single piece of hardware, with a control signal to select between the two options, the unit becomes an extremely powerful tool.

Further embellishments are possible, making the unit more expensive, and complicated, but increasing its performance. More control signals can be supplied, specifying that some of the data bits are to be ignored, that is to be treated as 'don't care' states, when the search is conducted. Thus, 'fuzzy' partial matching can be directly supported.

Instead of testing for equality, as has been so far described, the unit can test for locations whose contents are not equal to, less than, less than or equal to, greater than or equal to, or greater than a given value. Simple arithmetic functions also can

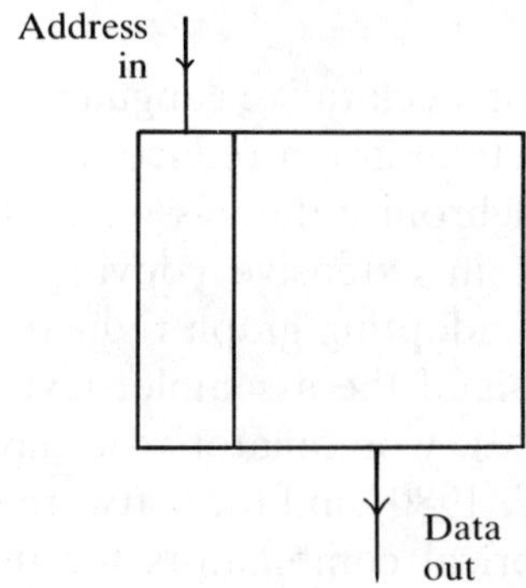

FIGURE 4.4 *Conventional memory*

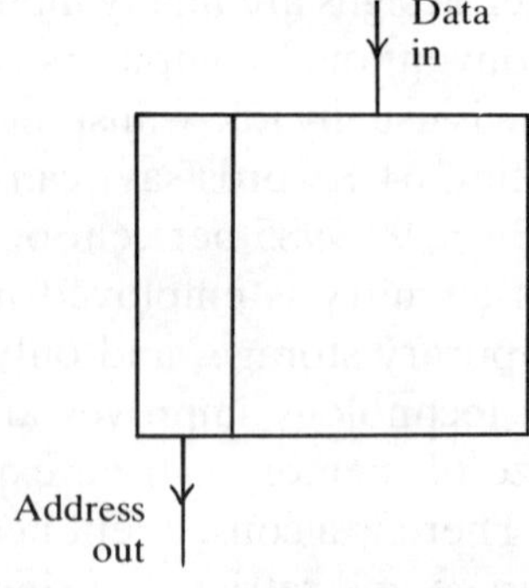

FIGURE 4.5 *Content addressable memory*

be added, for example to find locations whose contents when multiplied by one value become equal to a second value.

In Figure 4.5 it is assumed that if several locations pass the given test only one of their addresses, for example the earliest one, is presented to the address-out bus. By supplying even more control and data signals to the memory, specified conditional actions can be performed on *all* of the successfully matching locations. For instance, all locations whose present contents are equal to one given value can be made to take on a new value. Once again, simple processing capability can be added so that, instead of assignment, the selected locations can, for instance, undertake to increment the current contents by the given value, or to bitwise-And them with the given value.

The point of the above discussion is to highlight the scope of the work which the memory can be given to perform automonously of the central processor unit. It also shows that there is a midpoint at which a complicated content addressable memory becomes indistinguishable from a simple multiprocessor computer. Indeed, their purpose and aims are identical. A CAM, or associative memory, can be viewed either as a large memory with simple processing capability attached to the individual words (Foster 1976), or as a large processor array with memory distributed amongst the processors (Finnila and Love 1977, Lea and Streetharan 1979, Jones and Lea 1986b). However, the evolution of these ideas has arisen historically through the desire to construct multiprocessor computers, so this is the path which is traced next.

4.2 *MASSIVE-GRAIN PARALLELISM*

Programmers have long noticed that programs generally contain many sections which could be executed concurrently if only the resources were available. It is logical therefore to consider computers which can make use of more than one processor, the aim being to set many processors to work in parallel, each co-operating on executing a different part of the program (Chambers *et al*. 1984).

In general, there are two types of execution-time bottleneck: those which are held back by insufficient processing resources, and those which are restricted by inadequate input/output facilities (Kung 1982, Hwang and Briggs 1985). The former, the *compute-bound* problems, are limited by the numbers and speeds of the processors which are available, whilst the latter, the *input/output-bound* problems, are limited by the size and speed of the input/output channels (the *bandwidth*). Some problems exhibit both types of restriction, but this is frequently due to poor design of the system (for instance, a compute-bound problem which places a heavy burden on the communications channels by insisting that all intermediate results be stored non-locally).

Most of the present multiprocessor designs seem to be devoted to the more glamorous task of tackling the compute-bound problems. However, most of the major architecture-induced successes in computer design in the last forty years have been due to finding new ways of exploiting locality. Ironically, through devoting attention to easing the compute-bound bottleneck much of the burden has been taken from the input/output-bound bottleneck, but certain classes of problem, such as image sensing and graphics output, will always require provision for vast amounts of data to be received or transmitted externally to the system.

In the next section (Section 4.2.1) the degenerate case of independent parallelism is considered, and some loosely coupled networks are described afterwards (in Section 4.2.2). Section 4.3 considers network topologies in more general terms, as applicable to either loosely coupled or closely coupled systems. Section 4.4 describes some aspects of vertically parallel, closely coupled systems, and Section 4.5 considers the various arrangements for exploiting horizontal parallelism.

4.2.1 Independent parallelism

There are a number of arrangements for extracting parallelism from computer programs, as classified in Figure 4.6, and distinguished by the way in which the *processes*, that is the autonomous fragments of program, are mapped on to the *processors*. The simplest parallel system is one in which the components are not connected. An office might, for instance, wish to increase its word-processing, accountancy and technical throughput by buying many dozens of word processors and workstations. All of this work is executed concurrently, asynchronously and autonomously. There are no problems with intercomputer security and no complicated operating systems to run. It is also highly failure tolerant in a gracefully degradable fashion since, if one processor fails, the operation of none of the others is catastrophically impeded, and work can continue largely unaffected save for a reduction in the throughput of the department.

If one employee on one processor takes t time units to perform a given task, then he will take nt time units to perform n similar tasks. However, by using m employees on m processors, the n tasks will take nt/m time units, provided that $m \leqslant n$. The disadvantage is that no interaction is possible between systems. Two programmers, each working with their own computer, cannot co-operate on writing different parts of the same program. More importantly, as far as this book is concerned, two pro-

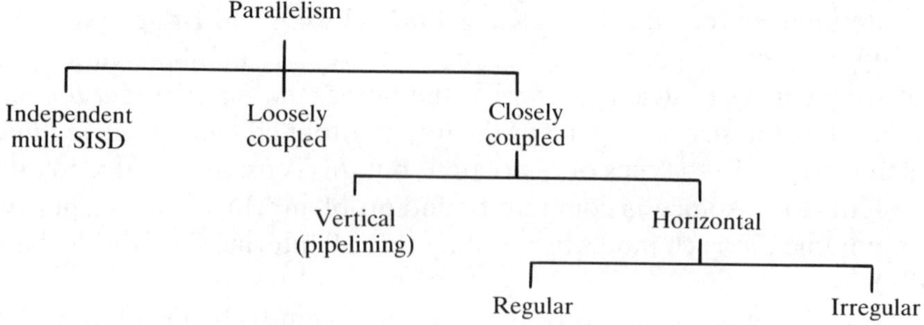

FIGURE 4.6 *Taxonomy of parallelism*

cessors cannot co-operate on executing different parts of the same program. The *granularity* is extremely coarse – indeed infinite to all intents and purposes, since nothing is ever communicated between the processors.

4.2.2 Loosely coupled networks

In order to economise on expensive hardware, many word processors and workstations are provided with facilities for networking, to enable each to access a few common hard-copy printers, disk units, etc. (Bennett 1984b). As a by-product, it then becomes feasible for people to co-operate in working on a single piece of data or program. Such systems still exhibit a very coarse granularity since only complete programs are communicated, and the idea of processors executing a single program remains largely unrealised.

An important concern is one of finding an economical interconnection strategy (Bennett 1984a). Many local area networks (LANs) use a shared bus topology, with word processors, workstations, hard-copy printers and disk units all accessible along the same bus. Ethernet is one such example. Before transmitting data on to the bus, the unit must first check that the bus is not already engaged by another transmitter. There is a protocol for resolving conflicts, and an addressing scheme to notify the addressee when data should be taken from the bus.

The Cambridge Ring uses another topology, this time taking the form of a large shift register. As the ring is clocked, data are shifted round the ring. Data are organised into discrete packets, each one bearing a destination address and several bytes of transmitted message. When only a few packets are being communicated, much of the ring will be empty; that is, instead of clocking data round, empty packets will be sent. When a unit needs to transmit a message it must first wait for one of these null passages to enter its part of the shift register. As with the Ethernet, all units must constantly look out for transmissions which are addressed to them.

These are two of the currently favoured LAN topologies. In common with closely coupled multiprocessor systems many other networking arrangements are possible, the most common of which are catalogued in the following section.

4.3 NETWORKING

There is often a need to allow any processor to communicate with any other. The most general, yet most highly tailored, solution would be to provide full point-to-point connections (Figure 4.7) and would be ideal were it not for its high implementation cost. In the past, this was a prohibitively expensive solution due to the cost of the extra logic which it entails. Even now that logic gates are cheap, it is the cost of the wiring which discourages its use. Moreover, it is not a solution which lends itself readily to *extensibility*, in which future enhancements of the system are anticipated.

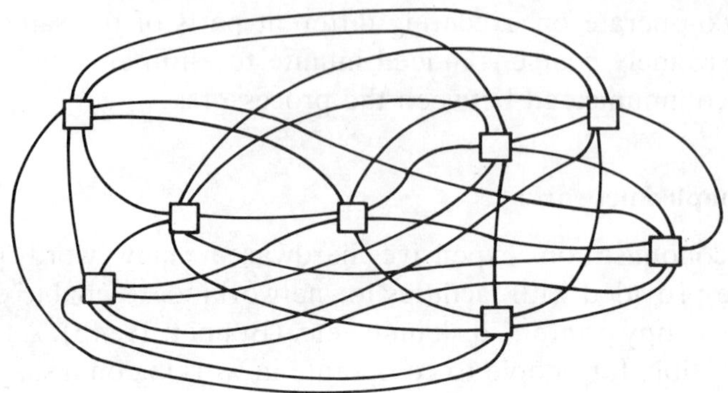

FIGURE 4.7 *Point-to-point connection*

A number of special case topologies have been developed therefore (Aspinall 1984), each making certain compromises by exploiting any regularity that is found within the target system. The choice of an appropriate one depends on the application, and the design philosophy of the remainder of the system. The most frequently encountered ones, each with very simple extensibility rules, can be classified as: (a) shared bus, (b) cross-bar exchange, (c) vector, (d) ring, (e) two-dimensional array, (f) star, (g) tree, (h) butterfly and (i) hypercube. This section briefly summarises these, dealing with them in an abstract fashion, treating each unit as an arbitrary black-box module.

4.3.1 Shared bus connection

All units are connected to the same bus (Figure 4.8). As well as data signals, the bus must carry control signals, one of which indicates when the bus is busy. When a unit needs to transmit a message to another, it first waits for the bus-busy signal to be removed. It then asserts the bus-busy signal itself, and inserts its data on to the bus, along with a destination address. Some embellishment is necessary to cater for clashes, where two or more units respond simultaneously to the removal of the bus-busy signal.

One major disadvantage of this system is that only one unit can send a single message at any instant. However, some systems make use of the fact that a single message can carry more than one address, so allowing messages to be broadcast to more than one unit.

4.3.2 Cross-bar exchange connection

Multiple transfers can be facilitated by providing more than one bus, as depicted by the horizontal lines in Figure 4.9. When a unit needs to transmit a message, the data are sent to the first array of switches, which engage the first bus that is found not to be busy. The destination part of the message is then used to establish which of the

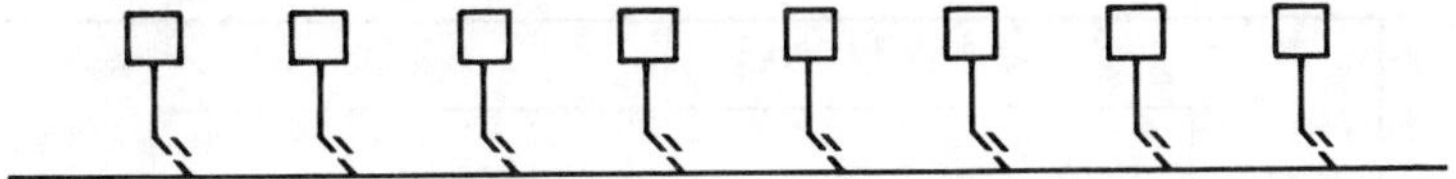

FIGURE 4.8 *Shared bus connection*

switches in the second array should be operated.

With the three-bus system of Figure 4.9, up to three transfers can be conducted simultaneously. When there are as many buses as there are units, and units still only transmit one message at a time, the cross-bar exchange is behaviourally identical to point-to-point wiring. It has the property, though, of enforcing regularity on the otherwise irregular structure which is depicted in Figure 4.7. It can be simplified by removing one of the banks of switches (Figure 4.10), leaving a single, square $N \times N$ matrix of switches, where N is the number of units in the system.

4.3.3 Vector connection

In Figure 4.11, the units are connected together like latches in a shift register. All of the links can be bidirectional, but units can communicate only with their two immediate neighbours, so to send a message over longer distances units must forward any received data which are not addressed to them. One disadvantage of this system is, therefore, its slow speed when non-local communication is common.

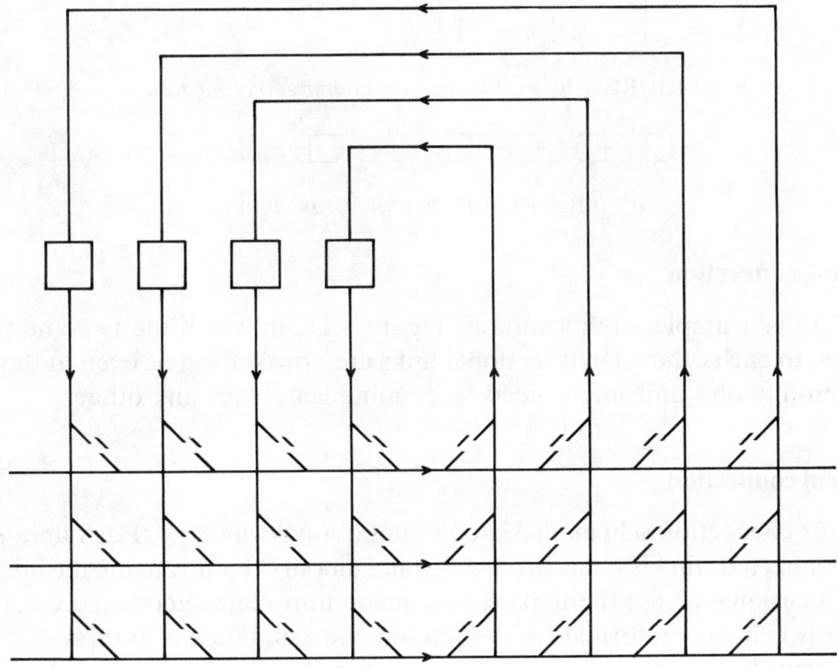

FIGURE 4.9 *Cross-bar exchange connection*

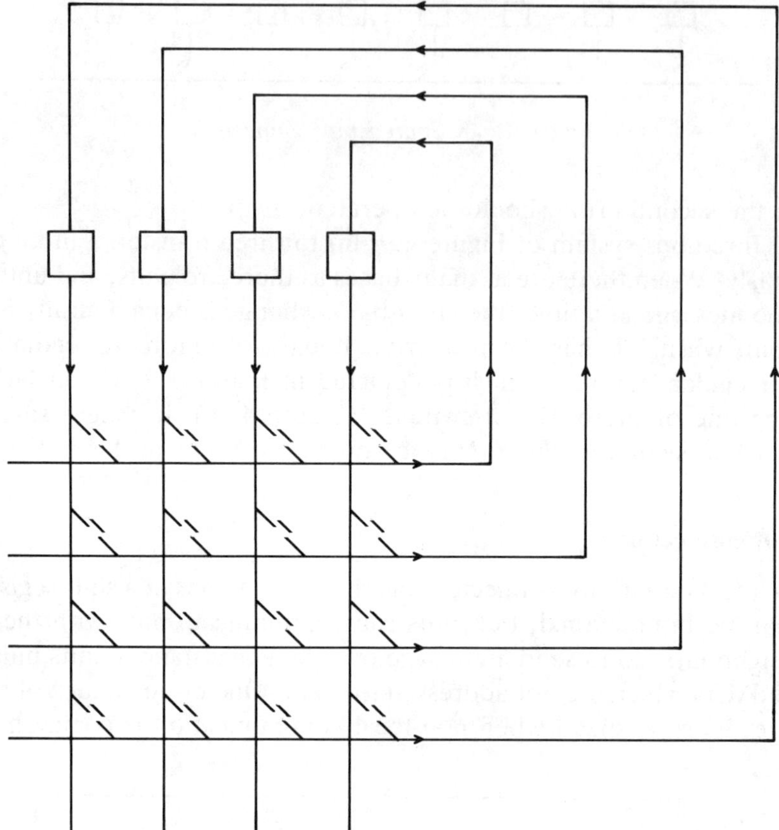

FIGURE 4.10 *Full cross-bar exchange connection*

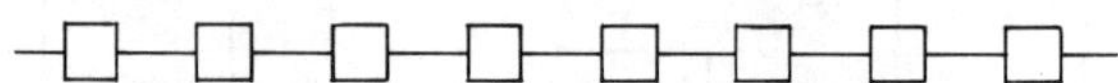

FIGURE 4.11 *Vector connection*

4.3.4 Ring connection

Figure 4.12 is a simple modification of Figure 4.11, in which the two end units are connected to each other. Unidirectional links are now sufficient, even in the general case when any one unit might need to communicate with any other.

4.3.5 Grid connection

The vector connection scheme has a one-dimensional topology. Each unit is said to be two-connected, that is it has two nearest neighbours. By arranging the elements in a two-dimensional array, the units can be made four-connected (Figure 4.13). One particularly convenient format for destination addresses then is to represent them as an (x,y) coordinate pair. This greatly simplifies the hardware for making routing decisions whether to transmit the message north, south, east or west.

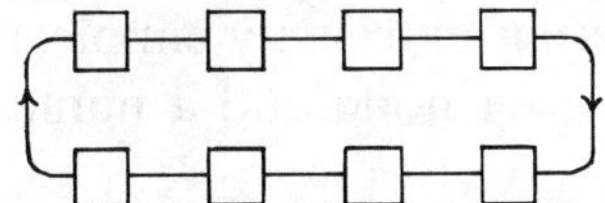

FIGURE 4.12 *Ring connection*

One common variant of Figure 4.13 is to make the grid eight-connected, thus allowing NW, NE, SW and SE connections in addition to the normal four. Another variant uses a six-connected grid, with each alternate row offset by half a column; conceptually at least the units are then hexagonal in shape. Finally, by extending the eight-connected grid idea to make a 16-connected grid, for instance, use can be made of non-nearest-neighbour connections, for example allowing direct communications with modules which are in the next row/column but one.

4.3.6 Star connection

With the star connection scheme, one module acts as the central 'master' unit, and the others are connected as its peripheral 'slaves' (Figure 4.14). In some contexts, the shared bus system can be considered to be a star configuration, in which the central module houses the bus and its associated logic. In other contexts, the star

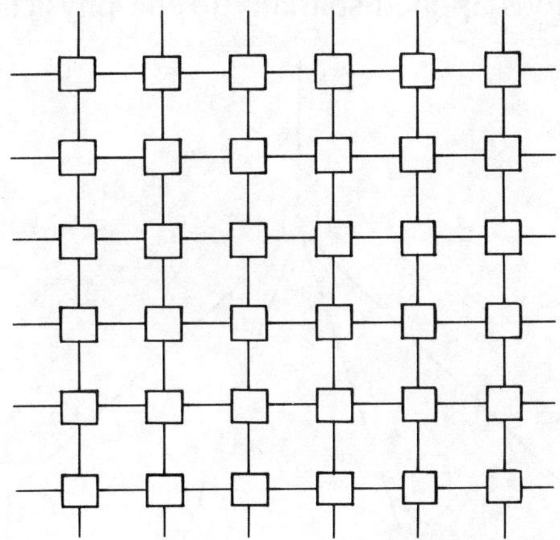

FIGURE 4.13 *Two-dimensional array connection*

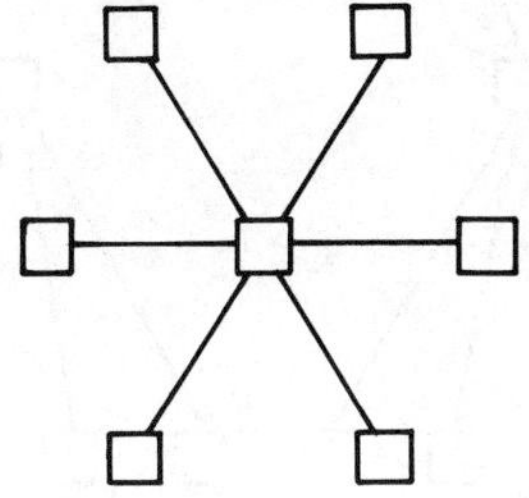

FIGURE 4.14 *Star connection*

arrangement can be viewed as an extremely simple tree, as described in the next section, with a single, central root node and a number of descendant modules.

4.3.7 Tree connection

Tree-shaped networks are especially convenient when the application is hierarchical in nature. Figure 4.15 shows a quaternary tree, that is a five-connected network. Although there is no global bus in this type of arrangement, carelessly designed architectures can still contain bottlenecks. If there is no constraint on where nodes can address their messages, only relatively few messages will be local, with the majority having to be forwarded by one or more nodes which are higher in the tree. In general, the nearer a node is to the root, the heavier will be the demand which it experiences merely forwarding messages from nodes in one of its subtrees to nodes in the others.

In the special case of a tree which has a maxium of two descendants, a binary tree, there is an arrangement known as the *H-tree* (Mead and Conway 1980) which maps readily on to a two-dimensional surface, such as a die of silicon (Figure 4.16).

Interestingly, Magó's use of the H-tree (1980) sometimes requires the system to be considered as a tree-shaped network, and sometimes as a linear array. Section 3.2.2 showed the three main ways of achieving this conversion in software. Figure 4.17 depicts these same methods applied spatially to the physical H-tree.

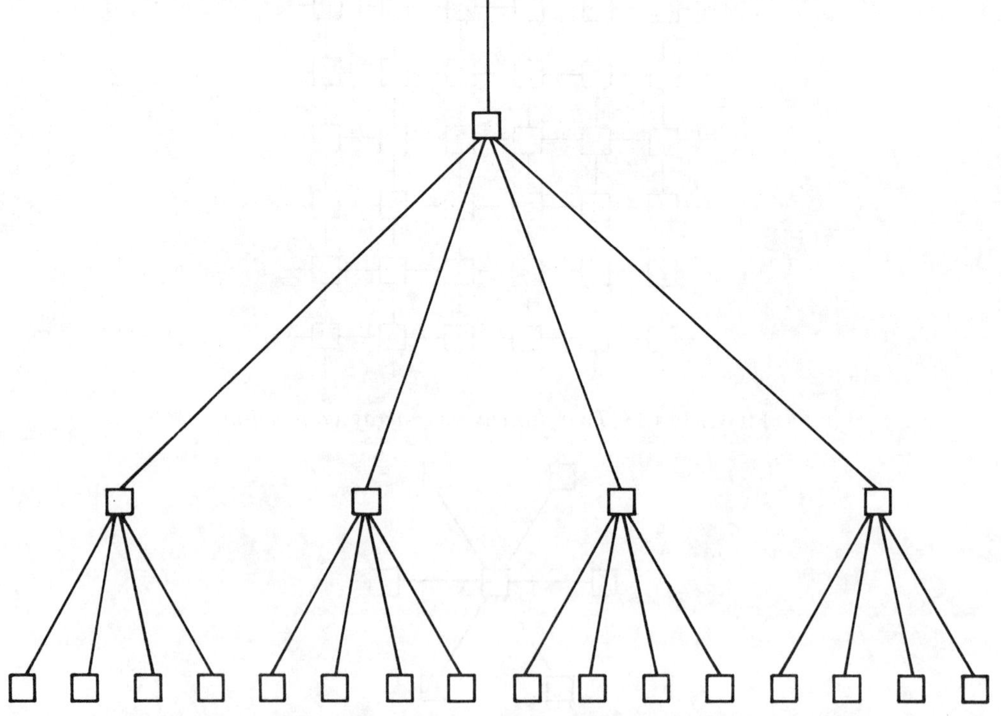

FIGURE 4.15 *Tree connection*

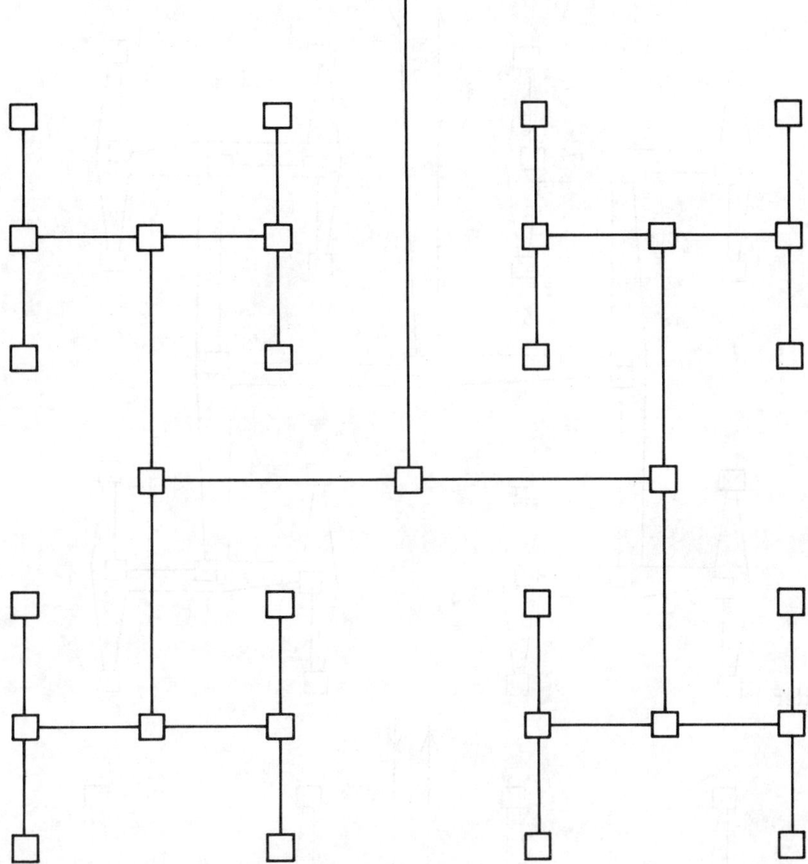

FIGURE 4.16 *H-tree connection*

4.3.8 Butterfly connection

Technically, the butterfly connection scheme is one particular member of a family of related systems (Hockney and Jesshope 1981). However, the popular literature tends to use the term as the generic name of the complete family, and this usage is continued here.

The system is normally depicted, as in Figure 4.18, with source modules arranged in a line at the top, destination modules arranged in a parallel line at the bottom, and a number of parallel layers of switching nodes arranged between them (Cripps *et al.* 1986, Brooks 1987). The characteristic which earns the technique its name is the regular pattern of crossover connections between the switch nodes.

One of the most quoted applications for this connection network is as dedicated fast-Fourier transform (FFT) hardware for the spectral analysis of a continuous stream of input data (Oppenheim and Schafer 1975). Another is the general purpose

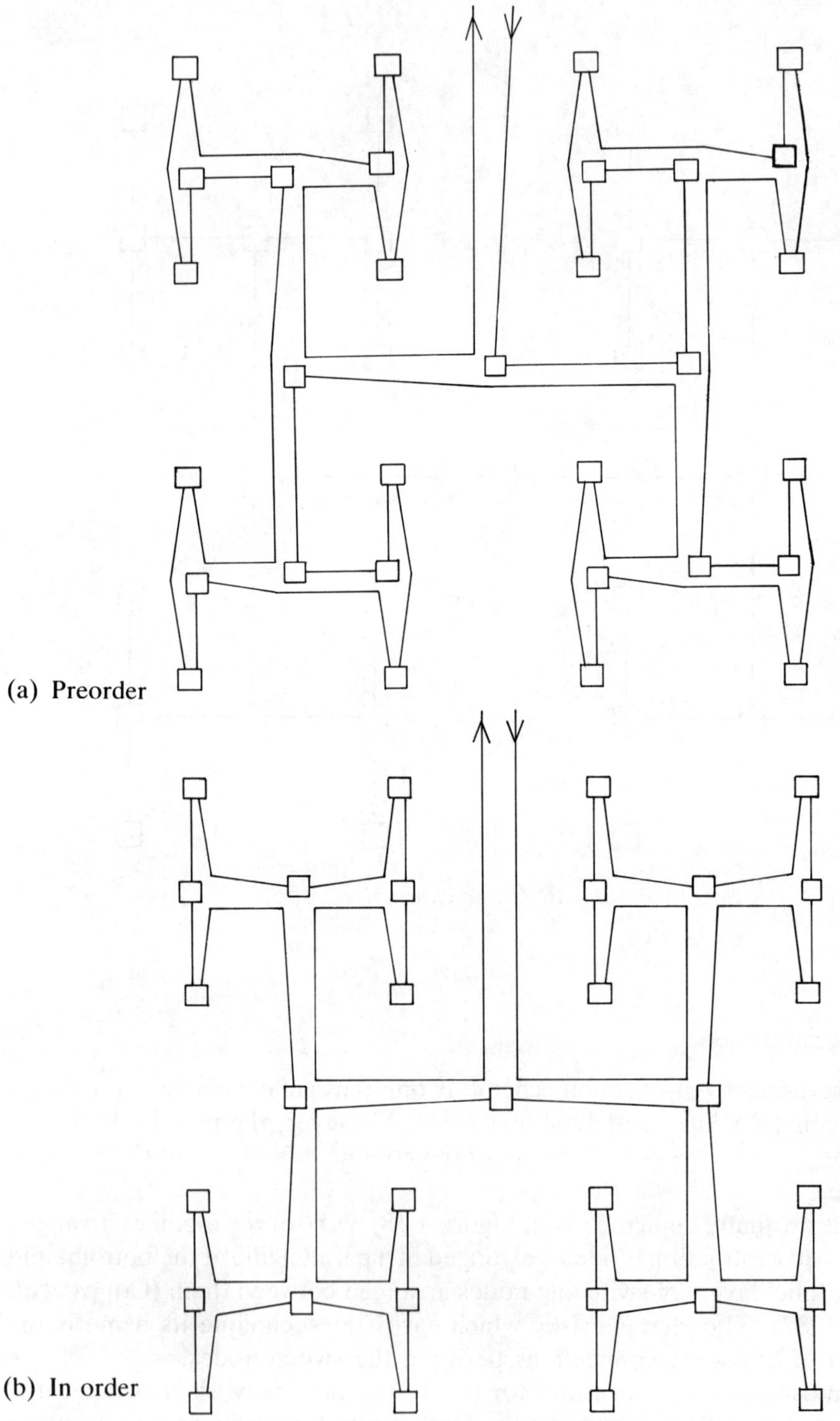

FIGURE 4.17 *Methods for connecting a tree as a linear array*

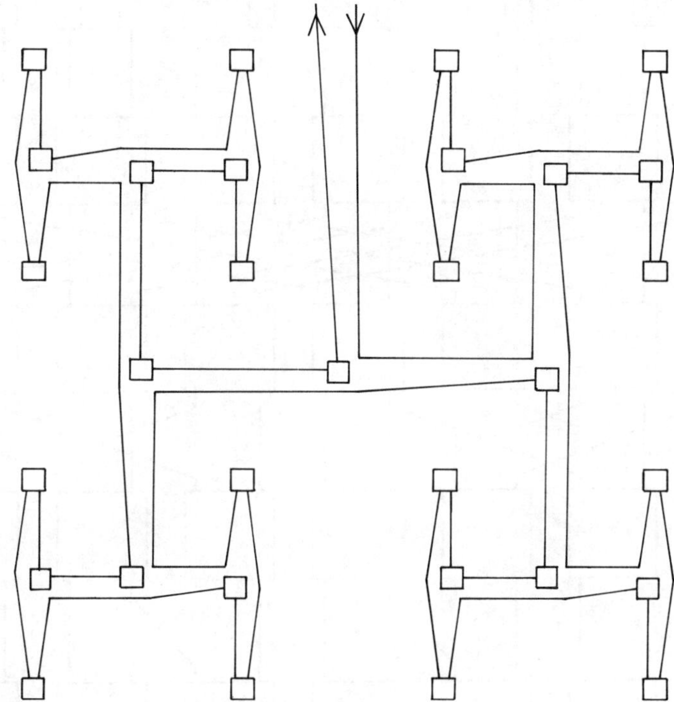

(c) Postorder

FIGURE 4.17 *continued*

Butterfly computer, which uses 16 processors connected to 16 memories via a network of four-way switching blocks.

If each destination module is given an address, represented as an integer to base 2, the two-way switches in the first layer (Figure 4.18) can be set according to the most significant bit of the address, and those in subsequent layers can be set according to successively less significant bits.

Systems have been proposed in which there is only one row of modules, that is so that Figure 4.18 is imagined topologically to be wrapped around the surface of a cylinder. Other systems embed the processors in the network, giving them the joint tasks of acting as source, destination and switching units (Figure 4.19).

Sleep and Burton (1981) observe that this arrangement can be used to map a 'virtual tree' on to the physical network of processors. Since every module can be said to have two successors below, and at least one predecessor above, a binary tree can be wrapped around the cylindrical network. Large trees will wrap around several times, burdening modules with several unrelated tasks to be conducted concurrently, but with the load fairly evenly spread between them. By using other connectivities, more highly branching trees can be supported directly.

4.3.9 Hypercube connection

Vectors are one-dimensional arrays, with a linear expansion law; adding new units to the system causes the longest message-forwarding time to grow in a linear fashion.

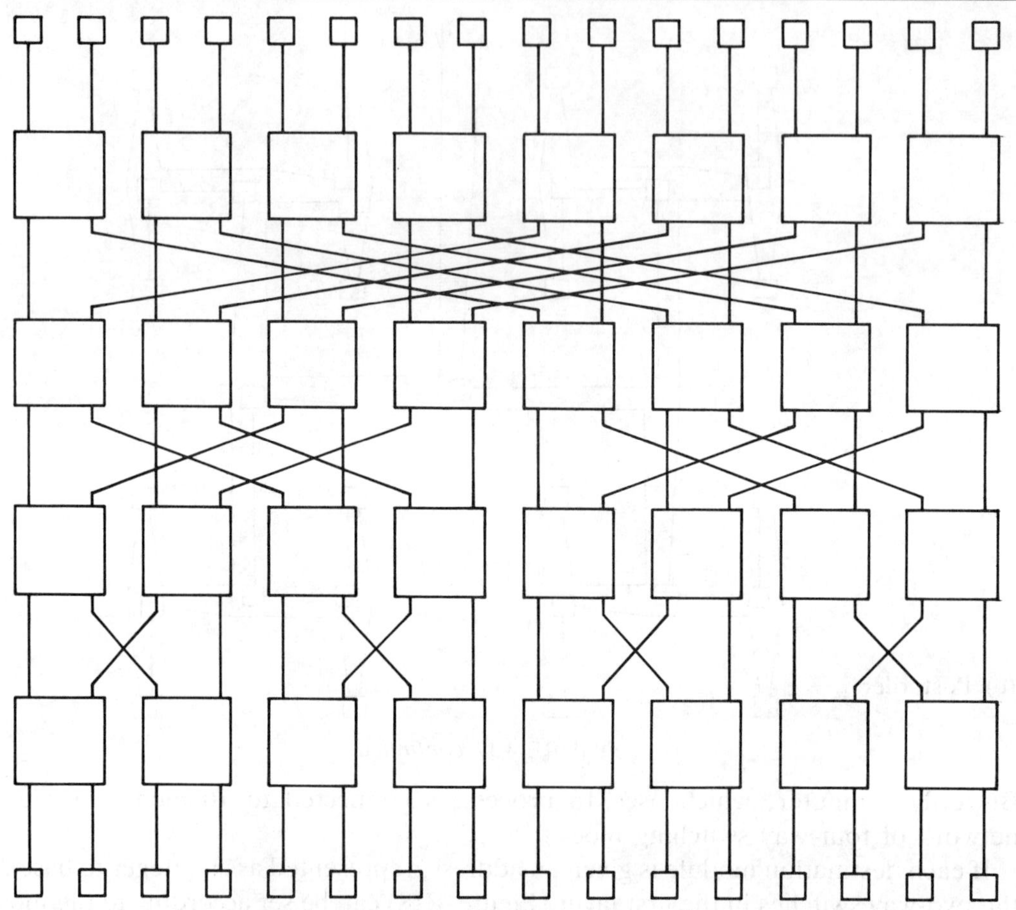

FIGURE 4.18 *Butterfly connection*

Two-dimensional arrays have a square-root expansion law, and cubic arrays have a cube-root expansion law. Hypercubes are just a generalisation, having an nth-root expansion law for an n-dimensional cube.

Just as a three-dimensional cube has 8 vertices, 12 edges and 6 square faces, so a four-dimensional cube, a *tessera*, has 16 vertices, 32 edges, 20 square faces and 8 cubes. In general, an n-dimensional hypercube* has 2^n vertices, $n2^{(n-1)}$ edges. It also has a maximum distance of n edges in order to travel from any one vertex to any other.

Multiprocessor architectures, for example the 12-dimensional one which is reported by Hillis (1985), have been constructed which make use of these properties. A module is placed at each vertex, and communications paths (wires) are laid between them along the edges. This forms a *binary hypercube*, so named because

* A new local definition of n is used here, as opposed to the 'globally reserved name' which was given at the front of the book, but consistent with the normal laws of 'scoping'.

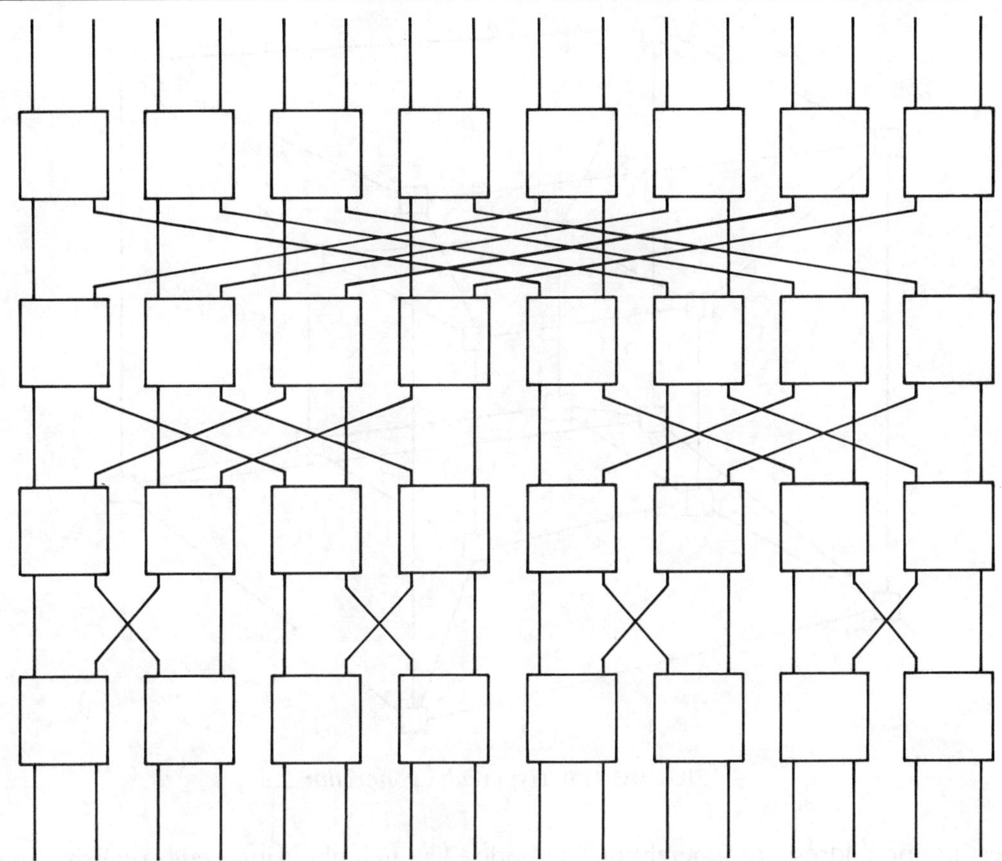

FIGURE 4.19 *Virtual tree connection*

every edge contains two modules (Figure 4.20). Other variants can be obtained by positioning modules along the edges, as well as at the two ends.

Implementing n-dimensional cubes on two-dimensional circuit boards and silicon slices is not a major conceptual problem. Most people are familiar with methods of representing three-dimensional cubes on two-dimensional paper, and similar methods exist for representing the higher dimensioned objects. The representation is only topological, using various lengths of wire to represent the equilength edges.

4.3.10 Packet-switched versus circuit-switched networks

There are two major types of network, each one applicable to any of the above topologies. However, to compare them, consider the hypercube topology as an example.

It was stated above that, for an n-dimensional hypercube, the worst-case communication path involves passing the message along n edges. If it acts as a *packet-switched network*, the source node sends its message, along with the

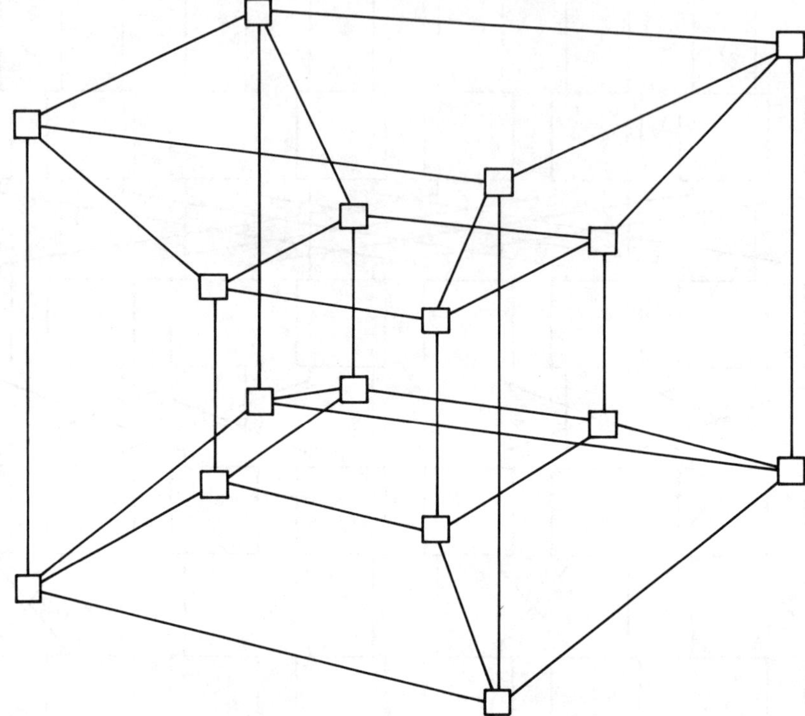

FIGURE 4.20 *Hypercube connection*

destination address, to a neighbouring node. The neighbouring node, realising that the message is not addressed to itself, sends it on to its neighbour in an appropriate direction. After *n* of these message-forwarding operations, the message arrives at the destination node. At each stage, the message is handled as a single unit (a packet). Once it has been passed to a neighbour, the node is free again to continue with the rest of its work, even though the message is still in transit. This is analogous to the process of sending messages through the postal system.

If it is a *circuit-switched network* instead, the analogy is with messages sent through the telephone system. The source node starts by setting up a route, first by contacting its neighbour and informing it of the address of the required destination node. Each of the nodes along the path to the destination are set into a receptive mode, in much the same way as each of the intervening exchanges in a telephone network being configured when a telephone number is dialled. Once the connection is made, the message can be transferred directly from the source node along the established path to the destination node. Just like the telephone exchange analogy, each of the nodes in the path must maintain the connection until the source node signals that it has reached the end of its message.

Loosely coupled and closely coupled systems can make use of either of these techniques. The next design decision which must be faced by the network designer, though, is the method by which the work of the nodes can be divided, shared and the returned results combined. The two major divisions, which are used to classify the available mechanisms, are described next, with vertical and horizontal parallelism described in Sections 4.4 and 4.5 respectively.

4.4 VERTICAL PARALLELISM: PIPELINING

Flynn (1972) identifies four classes of system, distinguished according to the method by which the data and instructions of the computation are shared between the processors. The data might be handled as a single stream or as many parallel streams, and similarly for the instructions (Figure 4.21).

Instruction handling	*Data handling*	
	Single stream	*Multiple streams*
Single stream	SISD	SIMD
Multiple streams	MISD	MIMD

FIGURE 4.21 *Flynn's classification*

The SISD class has already been discussed, being the basis of the conventional, von Neumann type of computer. So, taking the MISD (multiple instruction stream, single data stream) class of computers next, one method to organise many processors into co-operating on a single piece of work is to arrange them as a production line (pipeline). Each task is fed to the first processor, which performs one operation and passes the results to its neighbour. That processor performs a different single operation and passes the results on to its neighbour; meanwhile the first processor repeats its operation on the next task. On a multiprocessor system, the tasks are words from the main memory which are subjected to each of the processing stages, each one executing a different part of the microinstruction code.

MISD or pipelining is referred to also as vertical parallelism. In a flow chart (Figure 4.22) the operations in the pipeline are arranged in a vertical column, and data are envisaged entering in single file at the top, with results emerging from the bottom. It is apparent that pipelined systems are generally best suited by a vector interconnection scheme. If there are m stages to the pipeline, and the task is divided into m stages of equal duration, each one will take t/m time units (if the tasks are not of equal duration, the slowest stage sets the pace for the others). The first task therefore still takes t time units to execute, that is to emerge from the far end of the production line. However, the second task is only one stage behind, and will be completed t/m time units later, and the third task is immediately behind that. The time taken to process n tasks is therefore $t + (n - 1)t/m$. When n is sufficiently large, this tends to the value of nt/m that the independent parallelism system could achieve. The difference is that this system is more general: they need not be n distinct tasks, but n parts of a single job.

Figure 4.22 depicts a system which is capable of reading an arbitrarily large stream of numbers one at a time from an input source and subjecting each element to a number of scalar operations. The idea can be adapted so that, rather than being totally scalar, some of the operations can retain some limited memory of previous values. This has applications, such as in the design of non-recursive filters (Oppenheim and Schafer 1975).

If the processor whose assembler code is depicted in Figure 4.3 were completely limited by the speed of the bus, it would gain a substantial improvement in execution time over the system whose assembler code is represented in Figure 4.2. However, the third instruction is quite complicated; each one of its 100 internal cycles might take longer to execute than any of the other instructions. Behind the scenes, in the CPU, the same sort of operations are being performed as in the original program (Figure 4.23). However, the cycle time can be accelerated by arranging that the operations are each performed in a separate unit in a pipeline. As soon as the unit which is in charge of sending the address on to the bus has picked up a copy of the offset, and started to send the appropriate address, the unit which is in charge of adding one to it can start its process.

Apologies are extended to Flynn (1972) at this point since in his paper he does not

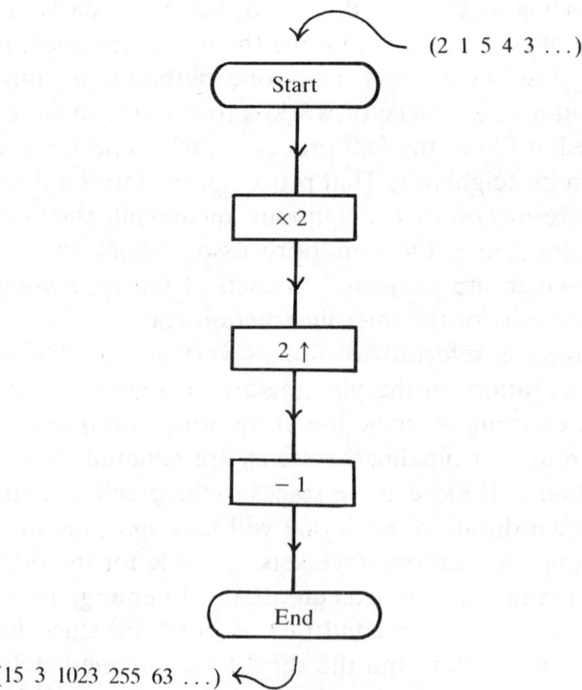

FIGURE 4.22 *Vertical parallelism*

consider this type of machine to be MISD. Most classification schemes, though, turn out to be highly dependent on the viewpoint of the observer. For a microcontroller implementation of a conventional computer, the latter's instructions are treated as data by the microcontroller, and so are part of the data stream. They are subjected to the multiple stages of the (micro)instruction streams, and so this text finds it convenient to classify this type of machine as MISD.

Form an offset from the start address
Load that element
Add 3 to it
Store that element back again
Add 1 to the offset
If it is still less than LAST loop again

FIGURE 4.23 *Microcode for the vector computer's ADD instruction*

Even within a conventional computer, there is scope for pipelining. Consider for example a variation of Figure 1.11, as depicted in Figure 4.24. This depicts the simple computer with its central processor unit broken into two independent, but communicating, processors. CPU1 can be responsible for the instruction fetch part of the instruction cycle:

1. Send contents of PC to address decoder.
2. Receive instruction from memory and pass it to CPU2.
3. Increment contents of PC.

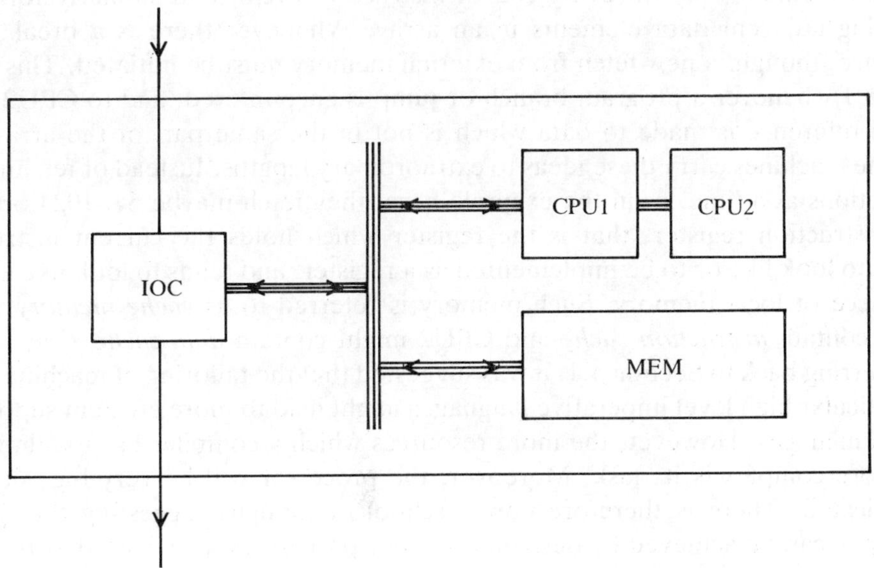

FIGURE 4.24 *Pipelined modification of a conventional computer*

CPU2 can be responsible for the execute part of the instruction cycle:

1. Send address of data to address decoder.
2. Receive data from memory.
3. Execute the instruction.

Once CPU1 has finished fetching the first instruction, and CPU2 has started to fetch data for it, CPU1 can start to fetch the next instruction.

Overall, therefore, instructions are processed at twice the original speed. This is only achieved, though, if there is sufficient spare bandwidth on the bus and memory since CPU1 and CPU2 cannot both have simultaneous access. One approach might be to provide two memory units connected on separate sets of buses. If instructions and data can be made to reside in separate memory units, then CPU1 and CPU2 can make simultaneous accesses without fear of clashes. However, this is not always possible or convenient, and so alternative means must be found for avoiding access clashes in the bus and memory.

In a processor that is more complicated than the one used here, there will be more internal work to be performed by each processor, for example manipulating internal registers without reference to external memory. Such periods of bus inactivity, if interleaved properly, can be used by the other processor. Adding registers to the processors, and complicating their instruction cycles, is therefore one technique for creating gaps in bus activity. Another method is to multiply the widths of the buses and memory. For instance, a 16-bit processor might be connected to 64-bit buses and memory. Whenever a fetch of one word is necessary, the processor actually fetches it with its three neighbouring words. The advantage of this technique lies in the fact that most programs access instructions in sequence. Thus CPU1 needs to access external memory only on every fourth instruction cycle, and similarly for CPU2 accessing adjacent data elements in an array. Whenever there is a break in the sequence, though, a new fetch from external memory must be initiated. This occurs to CPU1 whenever a program branch or jump is encountered, and to CPU2 whenever a reference is made to data which is not in the same part of the array.

Some machines carry these ideas to extraordinary lengths. Instead of fetching four instructions at a time, as in the example here, they fetch maybe 64, 1024 or more. The instruction register, that is the register which holds the current instruction, ceases to look like or to be implemented as a register, and tends to look like a small, fast piece of local memory. Such memory is referred to as *cache memory*. CPU1 might contain *instruction cache* and CPU2 might contain *data cache*.

Referring back to Section 4.1, it was suggested that the tailoring of machine design to particular high level imperative languages might lead to more efficient support for these languages. However, the more resources which a compiler has to administer, the more complex is its task. Moreover, the processor will be very big, slow and complicated. There is therefore now a school of thought suggesting that greater efficiency can be achieved by designing smaller processors, provided that the facilities which they offer are chosen very carefully. Instructions are included if they offer the best compromise between being heavily used, general purpose in their action and simple to support. Above all though, the instruction set is chosen for orthogonality: instructions are not included if their job can be performed by another which has already been included. In addition, the number of addressing modes is kept to a minimum by stripping out all of the general purpose registers, and all of the exotic addressing modes. All instructions are then designed to use the same addressing modes, so easing the tasks of both the hardware and the compiler. Such *reduced instruction set computers* (RISC) usually have very simple instructions. This means that complex high level tasks, as expressed in the high level language, involve the execution of large numbers of instructions, but as stated above this is inefficient in that it involves a large number of instruction-fetch cycles. To counter this, most RISCs are very heavily pipelined so that several instructions are at various stages of execution simultaneously. This is aided by the fact that all instructions take the same addressing modes, and so undergo the same operations in the pipeline.

Overall, vertical parallelism is relatively easy to use since the mechanism for synchronising the processes is simple. However, horizontal parallelism is more generally applicable, attracting much research attention, and is described next.

4.5 HORIZONTAL PARALLELISM

With horizontal parallelism, each of the activities can proceed without depending on others for input. Each of the subexpressions in Figure 4.25, for instance, can be evaluated in parallel and their values combined at the end.

There are two subclasses of horizontal parallelism: that in which the activity is identical in all processors (Section 4.5.1), and that in which it is not (Section 4.5.2). The former, a special case of the latter, is applicable where the data are highly regular and are subjected to identical operations. This is described next.

4.5.1 Regular structures

There is a large class of computer programs which involves the manipulating of enormous matrices. Examples are found in weather forecasting and other simulations. Each point in a multidimensional matrix might represent a point in the atmosphere, or a point in the bridge, aeroplane or motor car that is being designed. Even simulation of electrical circuits using languages like Spice-2 (Vladimirescu *et al.* 1980) involves the manipulation of matrices. Such manipulation is usually compute bound, and hence runs up against the execution-time bottleneck.

As an example of a typical operation, consider Figure 4.26, where two matrices are to be added element by element. No calculation interferes with, nor is influenced by, any other. In theory the elements of the result can be computed simultaneously.

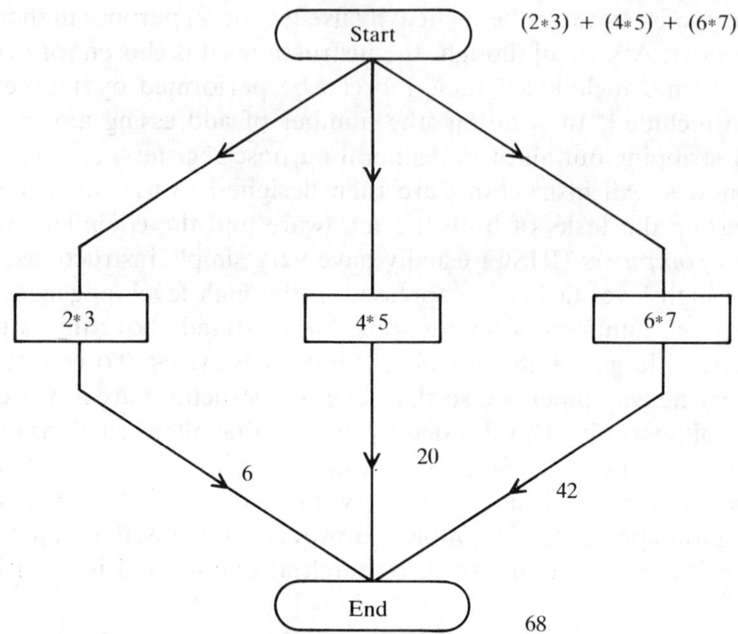

FIGURE 4.25 *Horizontal parallelism*

$$\begin{bmatrix} a_{1,1} & a_{1,2} & a_{1,3} \\ a_{2,1} & a_{2,2} & a_{2,3} \\ a_{3,1} & a_{3,2} & a_{3,3} \end{bmatrix} + \begin{bmatrix} b_{1,1} & b_{1,2} & b_{1,3} \\ b_{2,1} & b_{2,2} & b_{2,3} \\ b_{3,1} & b_{3,2} & b_{3,3} \end{bmatrix} = \begin{bmatrix} a_{1,1}+b_{1,1} & a_{1,2}+b_{1,2} & a_{1,3}+b_{1,3} \\ a_{2,1}+b_{2,1} & a_{2,2}+b_{2,2} & a_{2,3}+b_{2,3} \\ a_{3,1}+b_{3,1} & a_{3,2}+b_{3,2} & a_{3,3}+b_{3,3} \end{bmatrix}$$

FIGURE 4.26 *Matrix–matrix addition*

The above example entails no interelement communication. Even if it had been necessary to take a matrix and to compute a new value for each element from the mean of its neighbours, some interelement communication would be needed, but it would be entirely local, between physically adjacent neighbours.

This sort of potential for parallelism is fairly easy to locate; one knows when the problem is amenable to manipulation using matrices. It is also fairly easy to exploit, even using imperative languages. APL (Gilman and Rose 1984) and DAP-Fortran are examples of imperative languages which are excellent in this rôle.

Architectures which exploit this type of parallelism directly are often arranged as grids and arrays themselves, though a few are tree based, and organs such as CAM are vector shaped (Thurber 1976).

A sort of mixed SIMD and MISD architecture is produced when the data are divided into their component elements, each undergoing identical operation in identical processors, but with a steady pipelined flow of data elements from one processor to the next. For instance, systolic arrays (Moore *et al.* 1987), as described later, exhibit this.

4.5.2 Irregular structures

The final and most general category, MIMD (multiple instruction stream, multiple data stream), is the most difficult to harness, and is now considered. Earlier in this chapter (Section 4.1) it was suggested that by increasing the power of the instruction set the performance of the conventional SISD computer might be magnified. However, this still does not necessarily decrease the required bandwidth of traffic on the bus and memory. Although the number of accesses has been decreased, they tend to appear in bursts; the architecture still has to cater for the highest rate. Quiet periods simply represent wasted bandwidth. However, by putting more than one CPU on the bus whenever one processor is in a quiet, internal reference period, the bus and memory are available for one of the other processors. In order to make the processors co-operate on one program, interprocessor communication is needed. Many elaborate mechanisms could be chosen, but generally use is made of the fact that they all have access to the same global memory (Figure 4.27). One processor can leave a message for another simply by writing it at a mutually agreed address (Grimsdale 1984). This does not completely solve the problem of safe communication, however, and there are problems involved in programming these machines properly. Also, the technique is limited. Adding more processors achieves diminishing returns as more of the dead time on the bus is absorbed (Bux 1981).

One variant of this approach involves building a tree structure, with a bus at each level (Figure 4.28). The processors in each group can work with less risk of bus saturation. Communication from one processor to another in a distant group is made by routing the message out on to the external bus. A well-designed system ensures that usage of the external bus lies somewhere comfortably between the extremes of always idle and always saturated.

To justify the time penalty which is incurred whenever a message is transferred to a distant processor, it is usual to make the messages large. The system is therefore very coarse grain, sharing instructions at the function or complete program boundaries, and sharing data at the file level.

As an example of much finer granularity, for instance at the machine instruction level, consider the arithmetic expression:

$$\sin(x) + (1 + k) * \cos(y)$$

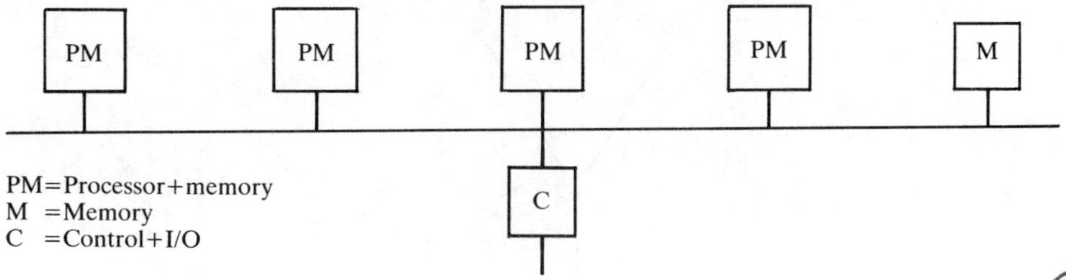

PM PM PM PM M

C

PM=Processor+memory
M =Memory
C =Control+I/O

FIGURE 4.27 *Shared bus architecture*

UNIVERSITY COLLEGE LIBRARY CARDIFF

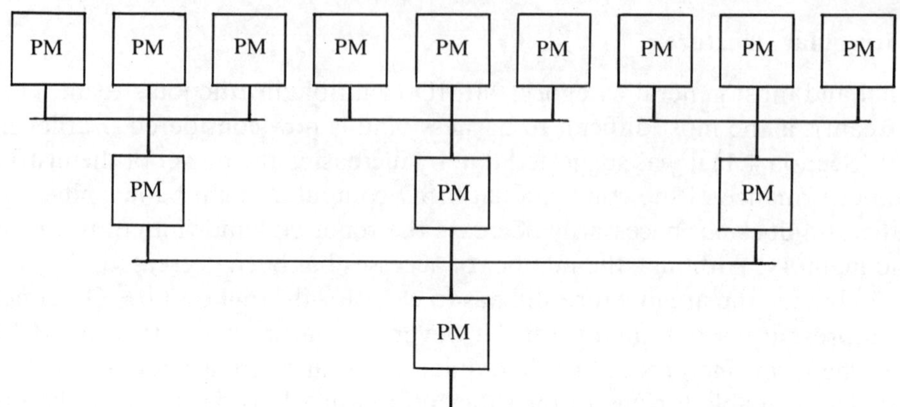

FIGURE 4.28 *Tree architecture*

Conventionally, the computer will evaluate this in a sequential manner. However, if, as in Figure 4.29, the expression is represented in the form of a syntax tree (a representation which is discussed in Section 3.2) the potential for parallel activity becomes apparent. Activity in each branch of the tree can be conducted in isolation from that in the other branches, that is it neither interferes with nor is influenced by any other. The potential for parallelism is measured by the width of the tree, and even this trivial example offers a potential parallelism of three at the cross-section which is labelled 'A____A'.

It is worth expending research effort to find ways of harnessing this type of parallelism because, as well as being useful to the vast majority of programs, it is also applicable to the extraction of regular parallelism too, which is just a special case. Thus a machine which exploits such a diffuse form of parallelism is completely general, and will also exploit regular parallelism when and where it is available. However, it should be noted that a general purpose machine will nearly always be outperformed by a specialist machine executing its specialist type of program. For

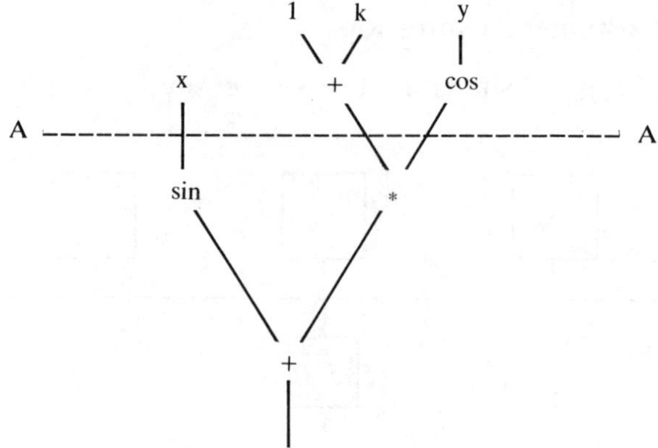

FIGURE 4.29 *Example of an arbitrary arithmetic operation*

example, an irregular parallelism machine executing a program which is predominantly matrix based is unlikely to perform as well on this program as a dedicated matrix-manipulating machine. This brings the discussion back to the trade-off between high performance specialist machines and the use of more generally applicable designs. The next section therefore discusses methods for measuring and quantifying performance, and methods by which it might be enhanced.

4.6 *PERFORMANCE*

One problem with MISD architectures is that normal programs do not consist entirely of vector operations, and so they rarely attain their maximum performance as quoted by their designers. The degrading factor is simply the overhead of setting up new addresses, and fetching new data into local (cache) memory. There is therefore a fairly smooth curve which can be plotted (Hwang and Briggs 1985) for the speed of the computation against the number of elements in the vectors which are being processed (Figure 4.30). For this, random, single element, scalar operations are treated as vectors of length one.

$$S_{k,*} = \frac{\text{execution time with scalars}}{\text{execution time with } k\text{-element vectors}}$$

and the maximum attainable relative speed is $s_{\infty,*}$, the relative speed when processing indefinitely long vectors.

As an example, the Cyber-205 attains only half of its maximum throughput,

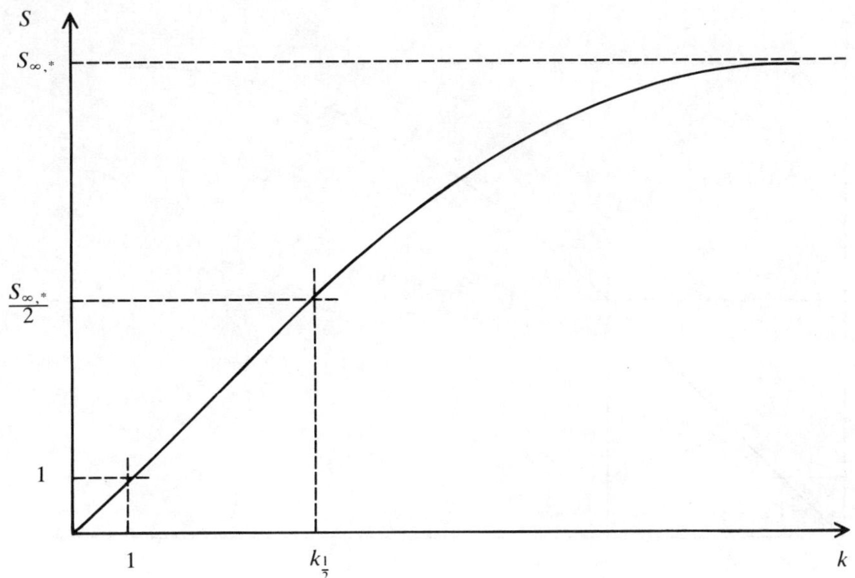

FIGURE 4.30 *Speed plotted against number of elements in the vector*

$S_{\infty,*}/2$, when processing vectors containing about 100 elements. Thus for the Cyber-205, $k_{\frac{1}{2}} \simeq 100$. However, with the Crayl, $k_{\frac{1}{2}} \simeq 4$, thus a Crayl is less severely affected by short vector lengths than is the Cyber-205.

Since scalar and short vector operations have such a serious effect on an MISD computer's performance, many compilers have been augmented with vectorisation preprocessors (Hwang and Briggs 1985). This therefore is yet another example of the considerable effort which designers are forced to expend, forcing regularity on problems which do not immediately exhibit it.

The curve of Figure 4.30 can be applied to SIMD architectures too (McBurney and Sleep 1986), where k represents the number of identical processes. In common with MIMD, SIMD architectures also have the characteristic curve of relative speed S plotted against number of processors, c (Figure 4.31) (Gurd *et al.* 1984). The relative speed is defined to be unity when only one processor is used, and:

$$S_{*,c} = \frac{\text{execution time on one processor}}{\text{execution time on } c \text{ processors}}$$

The maximum attainable relative speed is $S_{*,\infty}$, the relative speed when using an indefinitely large number of processors. The efficiency of the computer, as defined in some texts, is equal to $S_{*,\infty}/c$. The tailing-off of the curve, away from a linear growth with increasing c, is influenced by the fact that programs have a finite capacity for parallel activity, having only a finite number of primitive operations which can be executed in parallel. The speed of the computer whilst executing the program will not be bettered by adding more than this number of processors and will start to tail-off before this point. More importantly, the greater the number of processors in the machine, the bigger the machine is, and the more the com-

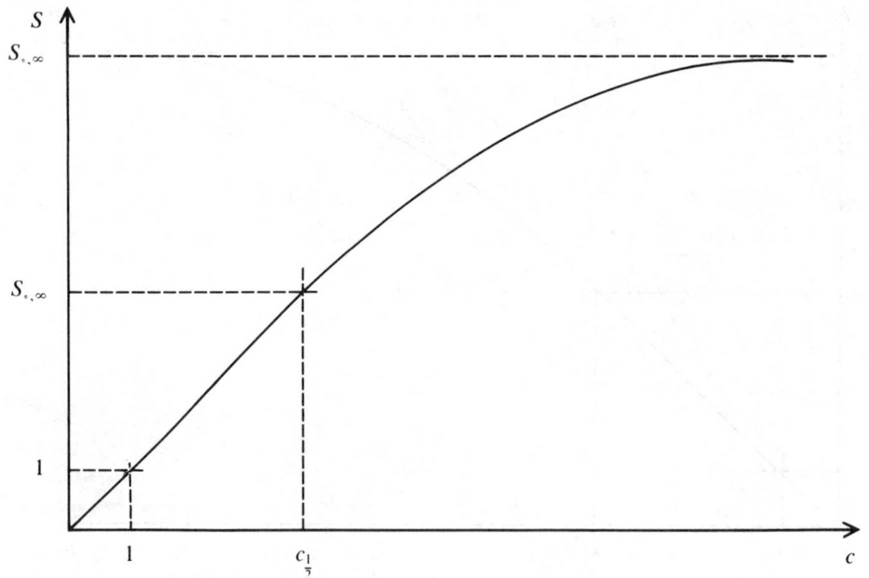

FIGURE 4.31 *Speed plotted against number of processors*

munications time between processors dominates the execution time within them. Unifying these two graphs, the relative speed, S, can be usefully plotted on a three-dimensional grid, $S_{k,c}$.

The next consideration is one of how to distribute processes amongst the processors. Static allocation is easiest, specified at compile-time. It would appear, though, that dynamic allocation involves a better use of resources, conducted at run-time, with busy processors sharing their processes with idle processors. However, this requires more housekeeping work to be performed, ascertaining which processors are busy or idle, remembering which processors are computing results for which others, etc. As a consequence, it is not always the case that dynamic allocation of processes to processors is more efficient than a static allocation. Judging which of the two is appropriate is not always clear either. For example, with weather forecasting, it is traditional to represent the atmosphere as an array of grid points at a certain spacing, and hence it would seem logical for the processing of the parameters of each point to be statically allocated to a separate processor. However, if the grid spacing is too fine then the problem becomes too large for the available resources, and if the grid spacing is too coarse the computation becomes inaccurate and worthless. The appropriate choice of grid spacing is therefore crucial, and might be set, for example, so that the program can just cope with the most intricate weather pattern which it is likely to encounter. But the fine grid pattern, although necessary when this case arises, is wasteful for the rest of the time, and in regions of calmer activity. Thus a dynamic allocation of more grid points and processors to regions of high activity and fewer processors to those of low activity represents a better use of resources.

As well as not always being optimal, 'obvious' mapping of the component processes of a program is not necessarily a highly parallel one. For instance, function application appears to present an ideal boundary at which to divide a program into processes, since each function is autonomous. Furthermore, the recursive functions cause large numbers of identical processes to be generated, which is seemingly ideal for use on parallel computers. However, the example of Figure 2.17 is still largely sequential in nature, with one recursion taking place after another, and little chance for work sharing. One promising line of study here concerns the use of a *divide-and-conquer* technique. In this, the problem is expressed in terms of at least two simpler, but roughly equal, subproblems. Instead of declaring that 'factorial(n) is the result of multiplying factorial($n-1$) by n', it is better to say that 'factorial(n) is the result of multiplying all of the numbers between 1 and n, and that this is the product of the multiplication of all the numbers between 1 and $n/2$ with the multiplication of all the numbers between $n/2+1$ and n'. Figure 4.32 shows a Pascal implementation of this definition.

Figure 4.33 represents an evaluation tree for the function in Figure 4.32, for example when it is applied to the number 7. Each of the nodes in the evaluation tree is a new process, and can be performed by a separate processor. Zapp is a multiprocessor architecture which uses this type of parallelism (Sleep and Kennaway 1984).

```
FUNCTION mult( m, n : integer ) : integer;
BEGIN
  IF m = n THEN mult := m
  ELSE mult := mult( m, (m+n)/2 ) * mult( ( m+n)/2+1, n );
END;

FUNCTION factorial( n : integer ) : integer;
BEGIN
  factorial := mult( 1, n );
END;
```

FIGURE 4.32 *Divide-and-conquer definition of 'factorial'*

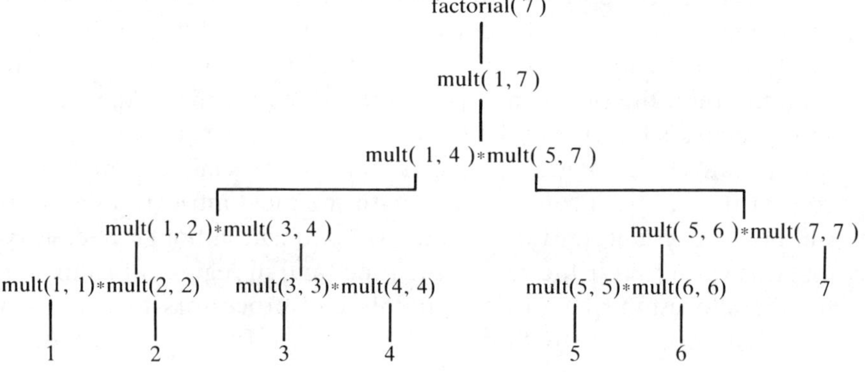

FIGURE 4.33 *Evaluation tree for 'factorial'*

Since large multiprocessor systems tend to be dominated by communciations time, careful thought must be applied, especially in dynamic allocation systems, to how the work is shared. In order to minimise the communication, it ought to be distributed locally whenever possible.

Whenever a busy processor is about to share some of its work with an idle processor, it must communicate the details of the new process, complete with relevant data. One option is to make a completely new copy of this data, so allowing the new processor to work autonomously with its own independent copy. However, in Section 3.2.5 it was shown that this 'string reduction' style of working is not always efficient. The other option, therefore, is not to send the data itself to the new processor, but to send references or pointers. However, the new processor then needs to send demands whenever one of the references is to be evaluated; this hence leads to an increased communications traffic. As ever, an appropriate balance must be found; some data are best copied, whilst others are best shared (Clack and Peyton Jones 1985, Burn *et al.* 1986, Abramsky and Hankin 1987).

It is also necessary to judge the correct level of granularity, in order to transmit neither long, complicated coarse grain messages infrequently, with relatively little scope for parallel work, nor deluges of trivial messages throughout the machine. The traditional levels of granularity include: task level, where complete programs are treated as the atomic elements of automonous process; the function level, as suggested in Figure 4.33; and the instruction level, where each machine instruction can be shipped to a separate processor for execution.

Since it is agreed that MIMD machines are most general purpose, much work has been devoted to their implementation. As usual, the many methods which have been investigated are best understood through classifying them and fitting them into a more general model, or view, of computation. This is the subject of the next section (Section 4.7). The section after that (4.8) describes some practical examples of machines which utilise some of these models.

4.7 MODELS OF COMPUTATION

Treleaven *et al.* (1982) present an excellent review of some of the alternatives to the conventional computation model. They identify three operations which occur during instruction handling on any computer: selection, examination and execution. They then identify three alternatives for each of these operations: control, data and demand. The three execution mechanisms, control-execution, data-execution and demand-execution, turn out to be identical, so only the differences in the selection (drive) and examination (flow) mechanisms are considered further.

In the *control-driven* selection model, instructions are selected by decree of some control pointer, in what is sometimes also called a *fetch cycle*. The control pointer, usually in the form of a program counter register, specifies the next instruction which is to be selected. Even in a multiprocessor version of this model, using a 'fork-join' type construct, such as Occam's 'PAR' (Jones 1985), instructions are selected by being referenced in one of the many program counters.

In the *control flow* examination model, instructions, once selected, are always accepted. They are not required to meet any further conditions and are passed straight over to be executed.

In the *data-driven* selection model, instructions are, conceptually at least, selected all of the time. For this to be realised literally, the system must have at least one processor for each instruction in the program; there are, however, several engineering compromises which reduce the need for quite so many processors.

In the *data flow* examination model, instructions are only accepted if all of their data are available. Thus in the expression (3+(4*5)), the addition operation cannot proceed because it does not yet have a simple number as its second argument, but the multiplication operation can proceed because both of its arguments are numeric. This model is also known as the *innermost expression* model, and is consistent with supporting the *applicative order reduction* mechanism (Section 3.2.5).

In the *demand-driven* selection model, instructions are selected only if their result is needed. For instance, a request for an answer to be printed on the user's terminal is a common source of demand signal.

In the *demand flow* examination model, which is alternatively known as the *reduction* model, all selected instructions are accepted but are only passed over for execution if all of their data are available. If any parameters are not yet available, a signal is sent to demand that the necessary instructions be evaluated. For instance, in the expression (3+(4*5)), the result of the addition operation might be needed by the user, but it cannot be evaluated until it has first sent a demand to the multiplication operation and has waited for the result to be received. This model is also known as the *outermost expression* model, and is consistent with supporting the *normal order reduction* and *lazy evaluation* mechanisms (Section 3.2.5).

In order to illustrate how these models can be made to work, the next section (4.7.1) compares the behaviours of three types of computer executing identical programs. Section 4.7.2 then generalises the classification scheme, and names some physical and experimental examples.

4.7.1 Examples of computer operation

It is convenient, but not necessary, to pair these models: control-driven selection with control flow examination; data-driven selection with data flow examination; and demand-driven selection with reduction. The behaviours of these three types of machine can be illustrated by considering how they would execute the example program shown in Figure 4.34.

```
a := 42;
b := 3 * 12;
c := a + 2 * b;
d := 2 * a − 6;
e := 17;
f := e + 33;
g := d + f;
print (c + d);
```

FIGURE 4.34 *An example program*

On control-driven, control flow computers, programs consist of a sequence of statements. Execution starts at the first statement, and when this has finished passes to the second. Execution passes on to subsequent statements in strict sequence, though in a more complicated program jumps to other parts of the sequence are permitted. The programmer must be aware of the sequence of control, and must write the program with it borne in mind. For instance, in Figure 4.34 the assignment to 'a' must be placed somewhere before the assignments to 'c' and 'd', otherwise erroneous results will occur.

On data-driven, data flow computers, the statements of the program can be presented in any order. If there are sufficient processors, conceptually one for each statement, the statements execute as soon as they can, that is as soon as all of the necessary data are available. Thus the assignments to 'a', 'b' and 'e' in Figure 4.34 can all proceed immediately. In the next cycle, the assignments to 'c', 'd' and 'f' can all proceed together. In the third cycle, the assignment to 'g' and the printing of the result of 'c+d' can occur together. All statements will then have been executed, so the machine stops.

On demand-driven, reduction computers, instructions start to execute as soon as a demand is made for them to do so. Again this means that the order of the statements is not important. In Figure 4.34 only the print statement starts to execute in the first cycle since this is a demand from the programmer for something to be printed. The values of 'c' and 'd' are not yet known, and so a demand is issued to the appropriate assignment statements. In the second cycle, therefore, the assignment statements to 'c' and 'd' start to execute, and demands are issued to the 'a' and 'b' assignment statements. In the third cycle, the assignment statements to 'a' and 'b' execute and return results since they do not need to demand any values themselves. These values are used by the assignment statements to 'c' and 'd' in the fourth cycle, and results are returned. In the fifth cycle, the print statement is able to make use of the 'c' and 'd' results, and to print the appropriate value on the terminal.

Four significant observations can be noted from this simple example. Firstly, the data-driven and demand-driven models each deduce which parts of the program can be executed in parallel without the programmer having to be aware of it himself. Secondly, the order of the statements in the program is not important to either of these two models. Thirdly, the data-driven computer executes the program in fewest cycles. Lastly, the demand-driven computer does not waste resources, for example on executing the assignments to 'e', 'f' and 'g' if their results are never needed.

The first of these observations is significant to systems which involve unspecified numbers of processors working in parallel. The ability to extract parallelism from programs without the user being aware of how much is available is very attractive. This is quite apart from the fact that it is definitely a bonus that the parallelism is extracted by the hardware, and is not left as another detail for the programmer to specify. In order to execute two subexpressions in parallel on either a data-driven or a demand-driven computer, there must be a guarantee that there is no interaction between the expressions. In this respect, the single assignment and declarative languages are ideal because of their avoidance of side effects.

Many major research issues remain to be solved though. One of these is the ironic problem of *throttling*. Because of the properties of divide and conquer, which many recursive algorithms exhibit, the amount of parallelism steadily builds up as the program executes. This is especially problematic with the data flow model, where the potential for parallel activity is harnessed so effectively and the limited resources of the practical machine are soon swamped.

Before naming some experimental machines which embody these properties, some further characteristics of instruction execution can be noted. This is undertaken in the next section.

4.7.2 Classification and examples

In addition to the models for instruction selection and instruction examination, machines vary as to how they hold the program in store. Some represent the program as large amorphous lumps, and others split the program into small fixed size packets. The former type are called *common-based* machines here, and the latter are called *packet-based* machines. Figure 4.35 depicts eight processors, each 'nibbling' away at a separate part of a program which is stored in common memory, and Figure 4.7 can be considered to represent eight processors passing packets to each other. In either case, each processor can work solely on the instructions and data which are held locally, and so gain the speed advantages inherent in local memory access.

When an instruction is executed, there are three variations of the mechanism for storing its result: some machines store results at any address anywhere in memory; others store the results in the data fields of the instructions which will consume them, effectively using a clean version of self-modifying code; and others store the results in place of the instruction which produced (supplied) them, so that subsequent calls on that function will find the result already evaluated.

According to this scheme, machines can be classified on a four-dimensional grid, using one dimension for each of: the selection model, the examination model, the type of structure which is used for holding the program, and the mechanism for storing the results. This grid is depicted in Figure 4.36 with a superset of the examples which are described by Treleaven *et al*. (1982) and Kennaway and Sleep (1984b). As usual with such classification schemes, the distinctions are not always easily made. Many architectures can be classified in one box when viewed at one level, and can be classified somewhere totally different when viewed at another. For instance, a course grained, pipelined system (MISD) of Figure 4.28-type computers (MIMD) might be implemented using conventional processor-memory units (SISD), which are constructed from bit-slice components (SIMD). Figure 4.36 must therefore be accepted only as a rough guide.

In order to reference the areas in Figure 4.36, each of the headings is abbreviated to an initial letter, and quoted in the order: selection model, examination model, program storage, result storage. Since the words data and demand begin with the same initial letter, they are referred to as data and need, D and N, respectively. Thus, for example, the Flagship machine can be found at location NRPS.

The majority of research, as witnessed by the population of the examples in Figure 4.36, seems to be concentrated on the leading diagonal. Thus, most work on control flow occurs in the CCxx region, for data flow in the DDxx region and for reduction

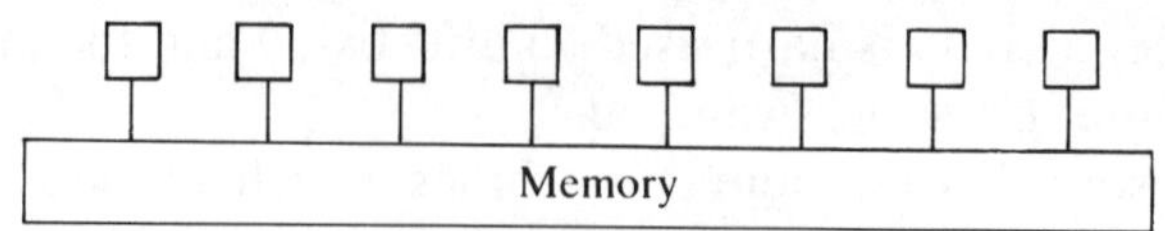

FIGURE 4.35 *Accessing parts of a program in common memory*

Examination \ Selection	Prog / Result	Control driven (C)		Data driven (D)		Demand driven (N)	
		Common (CxCx)	Packet (CxPx)	Common (DxCx)	Packet (DxPx)	Common (NxCx)	Packet (NxPx)
Control flow (C)	Global (xCxG)	**SISD** IBM4381 PDP11 8085	**MISD** Cray1 CDC205				
	Consumer (xCxC)						
	Supplier (xCxS)	**SIMD** DAP, Grid Illiac IV Wasp					
Data flow (D)	Global (xDxG)				Jumbo		
	Consumer (xDxC)	Tuki		DDMI GCF	MIT, Id MUDF, LAU,DDP		
	Supplier (xDxS)						
Reduction (R)	Global (xRxG)						
	Consumer (xRxC)			FFPM NRM		GMD Zapp	Cobweb1
	Supplier (xRxS)	SKRM Skim				Grip	Amps Flagship

FIGURE 4.36 *Table of computational models*

in the NRxx region (where x indicates a 'don't care' state). If these are considered to be the true examples of their type, then the machines below this diagonal can be considered to be simulations of their class. Thus CDxx might be considered to be a simulated data flow machine region, and CRxx and DRxx to be simulated reduction machine regions. It should be noted, though, that such simulations are still serious contenders as alternatives to the von Neumann model; indeed, it might be argued that they provide a healthy compromise which is not found in the machines of the leading diagonal.

Above the diagonal lie a series of unlikely machine types. A DCxx machine selects all of its instructions, and passes all of them unconditionally for execution. All programs execute in one machine cycle (with the print(c+d) statement of Figure 4.34 executing simultaneously with the other instructions), using whatever undefined values are held in the variables. An NCxx machine selects those instructions for which it needs results (just the print(c+d) instruction of Figure 4.34) and executes them unconditionally, again without waiting for any unresolved subexpressions to be evaluated. Finally, an NDxx machine selects those instructions for which results are needed (just the print(c+d) instruction again) and waits indefinitely for the subexpressions to return results, even though the subexpressions are never told that their results are needed.

Some other interesting areas are: CCCG – occupied by the conventional SISD computers; CCPG – occupied by MISD pipelined computers; CCCS – occupied by the SIMD array processors. All of the other major regions tend to be realised by MIMD machines. NRxC is a band which is occupied by the string reduction machines, whilst the band NRxS is used for graph reduction.

Section 4.7.1 described the different behaviours of the three major styles of instruction evaluation. Section 4.8 now repeats this, but with reference to computers which are based on real, existent hardware.

4.8 NOVEL ARCHITECTURE

Figure 4.36 tabulates some examples of real or experimental computers which illustrate some of the main points of the various classes. Figure 4.37 lists references for further reading for the machines which are not described by Treleaven *et al.* (1982).

Three of the machines are considered further here: data flow, reduction and cellular automata. The first two are general purpose classes of MIMD machine, and are represented by two practical examples. The third is more of a misfit, being a particular class of SIMD machine. All three examples, though, highlight certain properties which are relevant to later chapters.

4.8.1 Data flow machines

Jack Dennis' project at the Massachusetts Institute of Technology was started in 1974, and is the seminal work in this area. It was the first serious data flow architecture, upon which most of the others are based (Myers 1982, Treleaven *et al.* 1982). This section describes the operation of a hypothetical machine – one which is based on that of the Manchester University Data Flow machine, MUDF (Watson and Gurd 1982, Gurd *et al.* 1984) (Figure 4.38).

The program (for example the one from Figure 4.34) is compiled, and the object code is placed in the instruction store. Just as with a conventional computer, whose

Computer	*Reference*
IBM4381	IBM (1986)
PDP11	Hamacher *et al.* (1984)
8085	Intel (1979)
Crayl	Hwang and Briggs (1985)
Illiac IV	Thurber (1976)
Wasp	Lea (1986a)
Tuki	French and Glaser (1983)
Cobwebl	Shute and Osmon (1986)
SKRM	Turner (1979)
Grip	Peyton Jones *et al.* (1987)
Flagship	Dettmer (1986a)

FIGURE 4.37 *References for machines in Figure 4.36*

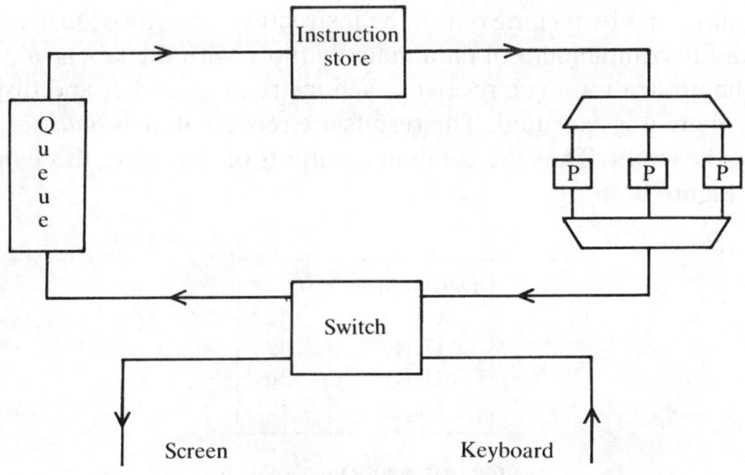

FIGURE 4.38 *A data flow machine*

object code is represented by a string of 16-bit words, so the object code of the MUDF-like machine is represented by a string of fixed length words. Here though, the length is likely to be substantially greater, 96 bits for instance. Each one of these is generally called a *packet*, or *token*, rather than a *word*, signifying that it conveys substantially more information.

Each packet is divided into six *fields:* a name, by which it can be referred; an op-code; a left argument field; a right argument field; and two destination fields, giving the names of two packets to which identical copies of the result can be sent. The argument fields can each contain a constant, or an indication that their value is presently unknown. The destination fields can each give: the name of the instruction packet to which the result should be sent and whether it should be sent to the left or right argument field, or else it can indicate that the copy of the result is not needed. Figure 4.39 illustrates this for the example program.

Name	*Operation*	*Left arg.*	*Right arg.*	*First dest.*	*Second dest.*
a:	NOP	42	0	c.L	t2.R
b:	MULT	3	12	t1.R	0
t1:	MULT	2	?	c.R	0
c:	ADD	?	?	t3.L	0
t2:	MULT	2	?	d.L	0
d:	SUB	?	6	g.L	t3.R
e:	NOP	17	0	f.L	0
f:	ADD	?	33	g.R	0
g:	ADD	?	?	0	0
t3:	ADD	?	?	t4.L	0
t4:	PRINT	?	0	USER	0

FIGURE 4.39 *Assembler representation of the instruction packets*

The program starts by picking out of the instruction store those instruction packets which have a full complement of data, namely those with the labels 'a', 'b' and 'e' in this case. The arbitration logic receives each instruction packet and dispatches it to a processor where it is executed. The results are represented as *data packets*, one for each copy of the result. Thus the combined outputs of the above three instructions is as listed in Figure 4.40.

Destination	*Data*
c.L	42
t2.R	42
t1.R	36
f.L	17

FIGURE 4.40 *Data packets*

These pass through the switch unit, through the queue, to the instruction store. Here, they are combined with the appropriate instructions, so leaving the program in the state as shown in Figure 4.41.

Name	*Operation*	*Left arg.*	*Right arg.*	*First dest.*	*Second dest.*
t1:	MULT	2	36	c.R	0
c:	ADD	42	?	t3.L	0
t2:	MULT	2	42	d.L	0
d:	SUB	?	6	g.L	t3.R
f:	ADD	17	33	g.R	0
g:	ADD	?	?	0	0
t3:	ADD	?	?	t4.L	0
t4:	PRINT	?	0	USER	0

FIGURE 4.41 *Assembler code for a MUDF-style machine*

The instructions which are named 't1', 't2' and 'f' now have full complements of arguments, and can be dispatched to the processors for execution. After a few more of these cycles, the final answer is packaged as the left argument of the PRINT instruction. This emerges from the processors as a data token bearing the address 'USER'. When this arrives at the switch unit, it is routed out to the user's screen, to be displayed.

The Manchester University Data Flow machine differs from the above description in a number of ways. Firstly, tokens are substantially longer, so that floating-point data can be represented as arguments. The time overhead which is involved in finding instructions in the instruction store, and routing them and the resultant data around the ring, necessitates performing fairly complicated operations at the processors for the operation to be worthwhile. Floating-point arithmetic is therefore supported at each of the 20 processor units. Secondly, the units are constructed from conventional SISD parts, and so each is sequential in operation. In particular, the instruction store can deal with only one token at a time. The queue unit is provided to help smooth the load, storing deluges of data packets until the instruction store is free to deal with them. The instruction store in fact represents the major bottleneck to the computation, and so on the Manchester machine its job is shared between two units: one for matching the incoming data packets in a content addressable fashion, and the other for dispatching the completed instruction packets to the processors.

4.8.2 Reduction machines

Another hypothetical design is described next, this time as an illustration of the operation of a reduction machine (Figure 4.42). Its operation is based on that of the Flagship computer (Dettmer 1986a).

As before, the program is compiled and represented on fixed length instruction packets, and these are stored in the memory elements (Figure 4.42). The choice of which memory element is used to store which packet is made by examining the binary bit pattern in the name field. For instance, if the pattern 0101 1000 1001 0111 is used as the representation of 'a', then it might be appropriate to store the instruction packet in the fifth memory (because 0101 is the binary for 5) where it can be found again quickly when its value is required.

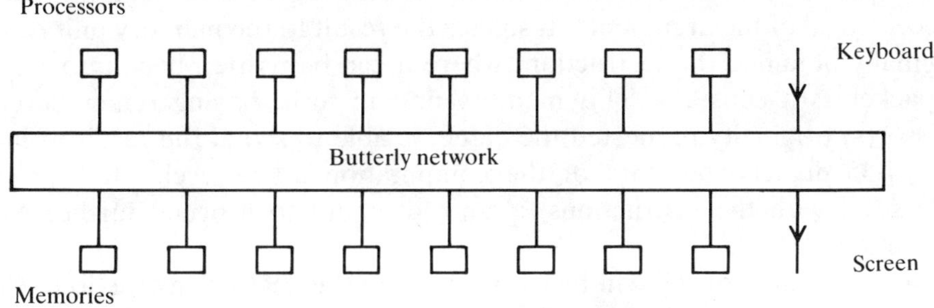

FIGURE 4.42 *A reduction machine*

For the example program which was illustrated before, the appropriate packets might be assembled as shown in Figure 4.43. The instruction packets are smaller because they do not need to carry any destination fields. However, the argument fields are slightly larger, needing to hold source addresses when the value of the argument is still unknown.

	Name	*Operation*	*Arguments*	
	a:		42	
	b:	MULT	3	12
	t1:	MULT	2	b
	c:	ADD	a	t1
	t2:	MULT	2	a
	d:	SUB	t2	6
	e:		17	
	f:	ADD	e	33
	g:	ADD	d	f
	t3:	ADD	c	d
!	t4:	PRINT	t3	

FIGURE 4.43 *Assembler code for a Flagship-style machine*

The computation starts by finding the application instructions. These are depicted in Figure 4.43 by the presence of an exclamation mark, and consist here of a single PRINT instruction. The processor prepares to print the argument, but finds that it is presently unknown. A command is sent to the memory which holds the 't3' packet. The memory prepares to send a value in reply, but finds that it is not yet evaluated, being an ADD operation, so it instead sends the instruction packet to another processor to be evaluated. This processor prepares to execute the instruction, but finds that neither argument is yet known. Commands are sent to the appropriate memories, demanding that the values of the 'c' and 'd' instructions be returned. These, in turn, are found to need further evaluation. The state of the program might then be as represented in Figure 4.44, with exclamation marks used to indicate that a copy of the instruction is awaiting execution in one of the processors.

Eventually the packets, like the one which bears the name 'a', are requested, not needing further execution. The memory unit sends the value back to the processor which requested it. This processor is able to proceed with its computation once it has received all of the arguments. It signals the result to the memory unit from which it originally obtained the instruction, where it can be written back into the instruction packet as a constant. This memory unit in turn, having remembered which processor(s) originally requested the value, is able to signal the result to it (them). Figure 4.45 depicts the state of the computation a few cycles further on from Figure 4.44, with the instructions 'c' and 'd' about to proceed further with their computations.

Finally, the value of 't3' will be overwritten in the PRINT instruction. The result can then be sent to the user's screen.

	Name	Operation	Arguments	
	a:		42	
	b:	MULT	3	12
	t1:	MULT	2	b
!	c:	ADD	a	t1
	t2:	MULT	2	a
!	d:	SUB	t2	6
	e:		17	
	f:	ADD	e	33
	g:	ADD	d	f
!	t3:	ADD	c	d
!	t4:	PRINT	t3	

FIGURE 4.44 *Assembler code for a Flagship-style machine*

	Name	Operation	Arguments	
	a:		42	
	b:		36	
	t1:		72	
!	c:	ADD	42	72
	t2:		84	
!	d:	SUB	84	6
	e:		17	
	f:	ADD	e	33
!	g:	ADD	d	f
!	t3:	ADD	c	d
	t4:	PRINT	t3	

FIGURE 4.45 *Assembler code for a Flagship-style machine*

The above example, and the one for the data flow machine (Section 4.8.1), are trivially simple and are intended only to give an idea of the operations which take place. The situation is complicated by the need to support repetition, in the form of either iterative loops or recursive function definitions. A description of these is beyond the scope of this chapter, and the interested reader is referred to Gurd *et al.* (1984) for MUDF, to Cripps *et al.* (1986) for Alice (a forerunner of Flagship) and to Higgs (1983) for a more detailed study of both.

4.8.3 Cellular automata

Cellular automata (Burks 1970) are a completely different type of machine, being a subclass of SIMD architecture. Their defining properties might be as listed in Figure 4.46.

One cellular automaton is well known by many home computer owners. Conway's 'Game of Life' automaton is generally viewed as a computer game, and illustrates

1. Composed of a (large) regular network of cells.
2. All cells are identical (or highly replicated).
3. Cells operate synchronously within the network.
4. Each cell has 'state'.
5. The state is updated at every clock cycle.
6. The next state is calculated from the cell's own previous state, and those of its neighbours.

FIGURE 4.46 *Properties of a cellular automaton*

the major properties of this class of processor. It is used as the first example, as the starting point on which the designs of more serious applications can be based.

An illustrative example

The cells in Conway's 'Game of Life' automaton are arranged in an eight-connected, two-dimensional array. The state of each one is either 'on' or 'off'. If it is on, and the states of less than two or more than three neighbours are also on, it turns itself off in the next cycle. If its state is off, and the cell is surrounded by exactly three neighbours whose states are on, the cell turns its state on in the next cycle. These decisions can be expressed as shown in Figure 4.47.

```
oldstate = state[self];
numneighb = state[N] + state [NE] + state[E] + state[SE] +
            state[S] + state[SW] + state [W] + state [NW];
IF (oldstate = on) AND (NOT (numneighb IN [2,3])) THEN state[self] := off
ELSE IF (oldstate = off) AND (numneighb = 3) THEN state[self] := on;
next;
```

FIGURE 4.47 *Rules for a single cell in Conway's Life*

Figure 4.47 shows that there is one rule for turning the cell's state off, and another for turning it on, and an implied default rule for keeping the state unchanged. Figure 4.48 shows three cycles of an array of cells obeying these rules. Each cell is represented either by a '•' or an '*', according to whether it is off or on respectively.

The rules (Figure 4.47) can be implemented using 70 transistors. One possible arrangement is depicted in Figure 4.49.

Although generally viewed as a game, this cellular automaton has serious theoretical implications (Codd 1968). However, a more practical subclass of cellular automaton is discussed next, namely that of the systolic array.

Systolic arrays

As well as the defining properties of cellular automata, systolic arrays are generally, but not universally, assumed to have the property that their data are communicated

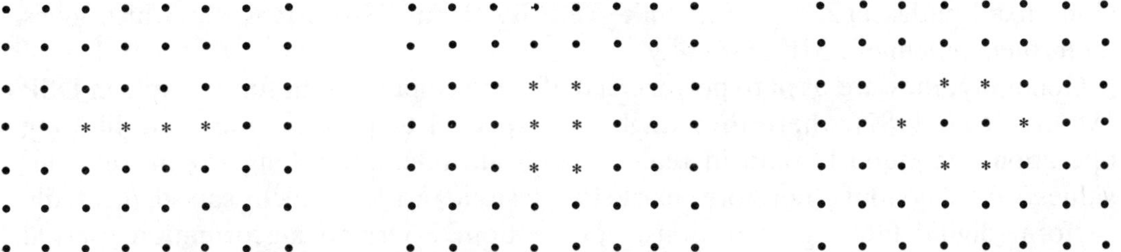

FIGURE 4.48 *Three cycles of Conway's Life*

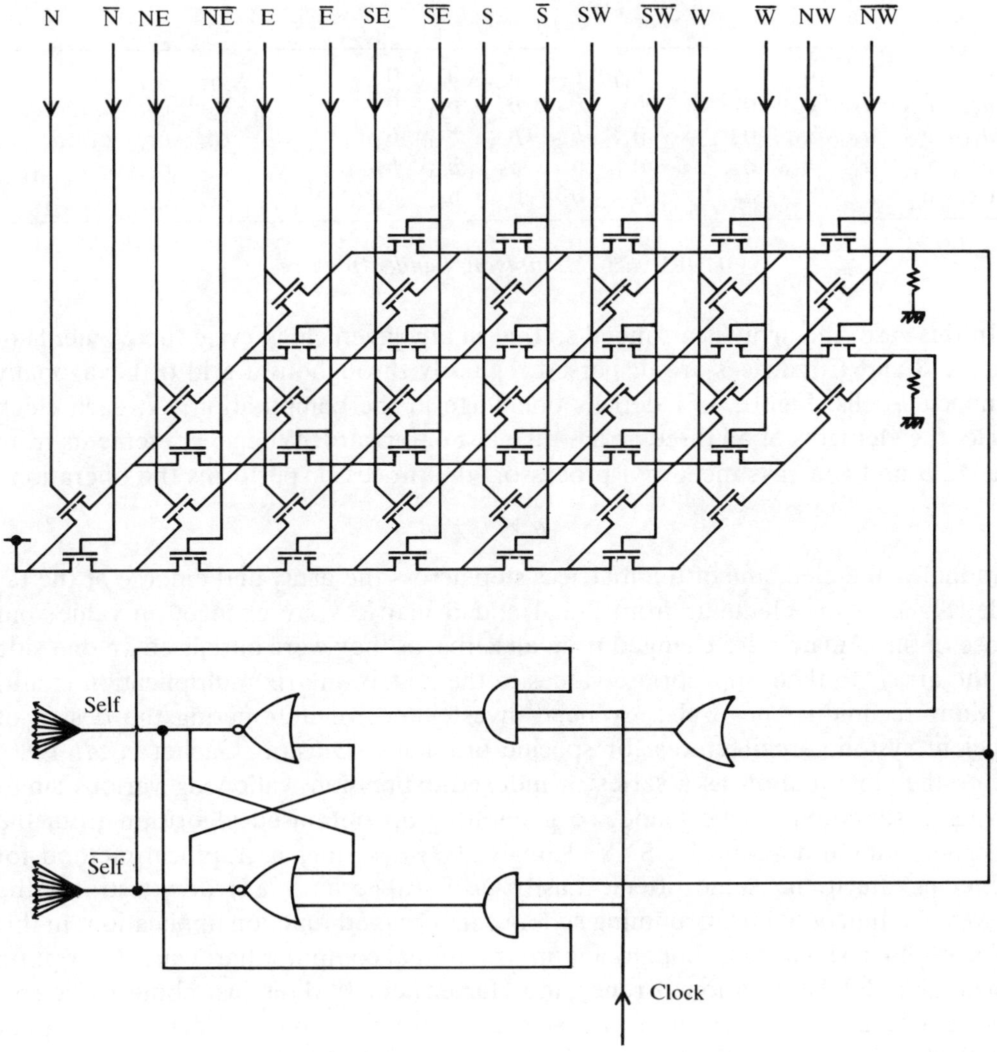

FIGURE 4.49 *Circuit diagram for a Conway Life cell*

along fixed paths, at a constant, finite velocity (Kung 1982). It is this which gives them their pipelined, MISD quality.

Generally, they are used to perform a dedicated computation, for example in DSP (Moore *et al.* 1987) where they might be expected to perform the same filtering operation continuously, and in real-time, on an indefinitely long stream of input values. Applications therefore exist for systolic arrays which can dedicatedly perform digital filtering operations, convolution, Fourier transformation, partial differential equation solving, pattern matching, relational database accessing, sorting, and other signal- and image-processing work. In much of this the banded matrix multiplication operation (Dettmer 1985) appears to be fairly central, and so is briefly illustrated here (Figure 4.50), using an example which is taken from Kung and Leiserson (1980).

$$\begin{matrix} a_{11} & a_{12} & 0 & 0 & 0 \\ a_{21} & a_{22} & a_{23} & 0 & 0 \\ a_{31} & a_{32} & a_{33} & a_{34} & 0 \\ 0 & a_{42} & a_{43} & a_{44} & a_{45} \\ 0 & 0 & a_{53} & a_{54} & a_{55} \end{matrix} \times \begin{matrix} b_{11} & b_{12} & b_{13} & 0 & 0 \\ b_{21} & b_{22} & b_{23} & b_{24} & 0 \\ 0 & b_{32} & b_{33} & b_{34} & b_{35} \\ 0 & 0 & b_{43} & b_{44} & b_{45} \\ 0 & 0 & 0 & b_{54} & b_{55} \end{matrix} = \begin{matrix} c_{11} & c_{12} & c_{13} & c_{14} & c_{15} \\ c_{21} & c_{22} & c_{23} & c_{24} & c_{25} \\ c_{31} & c_{32} & c_{33} & c_{34} & c_{35} \\ c_{41} & c_{42} & c_{43} & c_{44} & c_{45} \\ c_{51} & c_{52} & c_{53} & c_{54} & c_{55} \end{matrix}$$

FIGURE 4.50 *Multiplying banded matrices*

In this case, the array is arranged so that in any given clock cycle the elements of the A, B and C matrices are dispersed regularly throughout a grid of hexagonally connected cells. Figure 4.51 depicts one stage in the computation. At each clock cycle, the elements of all three arrays take a step forward. Whenever elements from the A, B and C arrays meet in a processor, the processor performs the operation:

$$c = a \times b + c$$

Gradually, the elements of the matrices step across the array and emerge at the far side. None of the elements from the A and B matrices are changed in value, but those of the C matrix are changed from all zeros, as they were initialised on one side of the array, to their appropriate values in the matrix–matrix multiplication result.

Many techniques have already been investigated for automating the design of efficient systolic architectures for specific problems. Diastol (Gachet *et al.* 1986) treats the computation as a series of indexed expressions, allowing various simplifying observations to be made, so generating an optimised algorithm from the designer's initial description. S. Y. Kung (1987) describes a graphical method for achieving much the same effect. Lastly, μFP (Sheeran 1985) demonstrates the power of a functional programming style, using Curryed function application, in this rôle. Within a single cell, though, a more traditional computer hardware description langauge (CHDL) notation (Breuer and Hartenstein 1981) is just about sufficient. Figure 4.52 gives a description of a single cell from the banded matrix multiplier array of Figure 4.51. The notation, such as data[self,SW] for instance, is used to

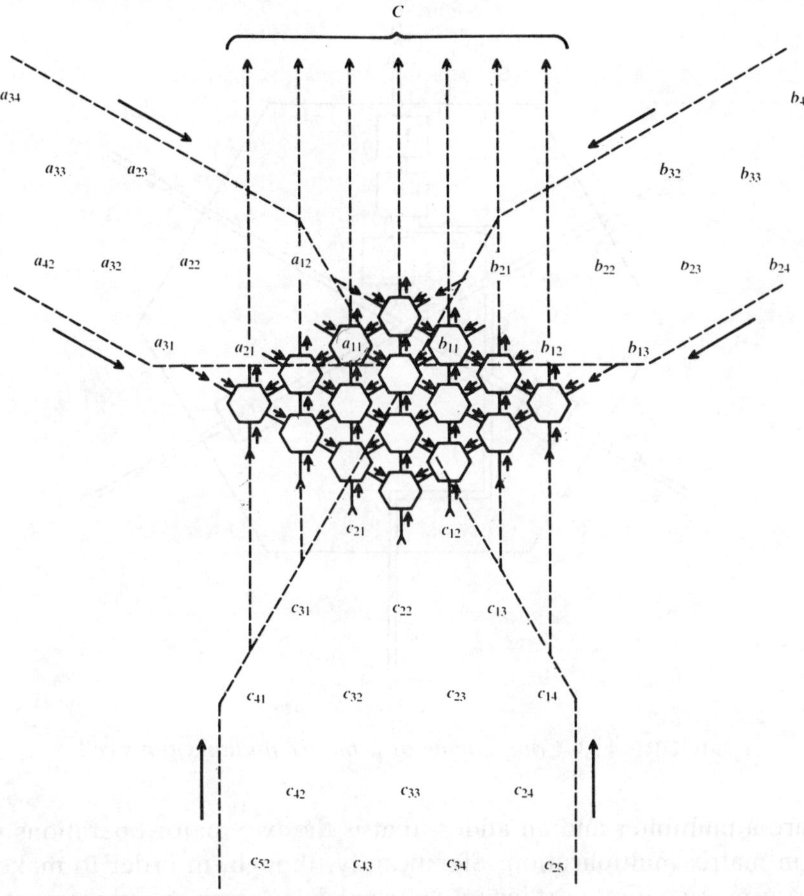

FIGURE 4.51 *Banded matrices multiplied in a dedicated filter (from Mead and Conway, Introduction to VLSI Systems, © 1980 Addison-Wesley Publishing Company, Inc. Reading, Massachusetts, p. 277, Fig. 8.12; reprinted with permission)*

```
data[self,E] := data[W,self] + ( data[NE,self] * data[SE, self] );
data[self,SW] := data[NE,self];
data[self,NW] := data[SE,self];
next;
```

FIGURE 4.52 *Rules for a single cell in the matrix–matrix multiplier*

indicate the state of a communications buffer which connects between the current cell, and its neighbour in the south-westerly direction. Using the notation of ISP' (Straubs 1980), all assignment operations are conducted concurrently whenever a **'next'** statement is executed.

Each element is extremely simple, as shown in Figure 4.53. The active com-

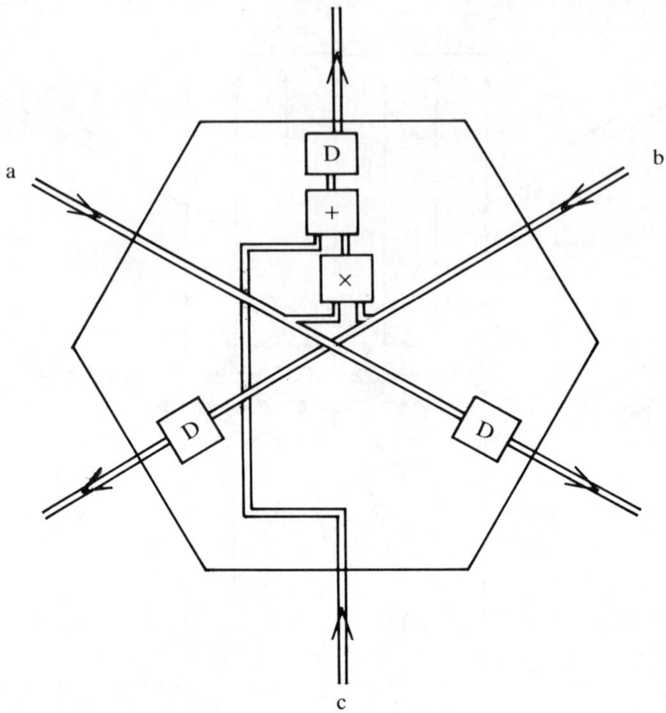

FIGURE 4.53 *Components of a matrix multiplication cell*

ponents are a multiplier and an adder, that is the two major operations which are involved in matrix multiplication. Significantly, though, in order to make it a true systolic array every output port incurs a latched delay, each one implemented using a single flip-flop.

In addition to the applications which were listed at the start of this section, systolic arrays can be used to implement low level arithmetic operations. For instance, a systolic array of full adders can be used to implement a parallel synchronous adder. A similar technique can be adopted to implement integer multiplication. In this, each of the data paths are one bit wide, and hence very fine grain. This is different to the example of Figure 4.51 where the data paths are several bits wide, and hence coarser grain. These bit-level systolic implementations of the parallel adder and multiplier can be used as the active components in Figure 4.53. Thus the example of Figure 4.51 becomes a hierarchical systolic array of systolic arrays.

One last point worth noting is the observation that, for certain types of off-line processing such as complicated image or graphics processing, it might be advantageous to have a less dedicated form of systolic array – one which can be configured to perform one transformation on the data and then reconfigured to perform the next transformation on the intermediate results. Fisher *et al.* (1985) are investigating such a programmable device to derive a more generally useful system.

4.9 CONCLUSIONS

Several ideas and computer classification schemes have been presented in this chapter. First the idea of adding complexity to the processor was considered. By making use of the general locality properties which are found in most programs, such as the storage of partial results and the provision for certain 'macro' scale operations, the traffic to and from memory via the data bus can be reduced. Through the need to share expensive computer equipment, the prospect of networking was considered. This led to the idea of designing multicomputer systems which could conduct work concurrently on a single program and so achieve a greater execution speed. This exploitation of coarse grain parallelism led, in turn, to the need for a fine grain version of these ideas for the design of multiprocessor computers. Flynn (1972) presented a very useful classification scheme for such systems, and each of these options was briefly considered. Of the four, MIMD is the one which is currently arousing most fifth generation research interest, and so a Treleaven *et al.* (1982) type of classification was introduced to break this class into finer divisions.

The previous four generations of computer have achieved greater execution speeds mainly by increasing the speed of operation of the components. As well as using faster transistors, this has required a reduction in the size of the modules, so mitigating against the use of complex processors with macroscopic instructions. The fifth generation cannot rely on further improvements in this area. Instead, the exploitation of locality and parallelism appears to be the most promising line of attack. This is particularly exciting because it concurs with the aims of computer scientists. These presently favour programming techniques which involve: little global communication and much local parameter-passing/result-returning, and the banishment of side effects so as to allow functions to behave as autonomous processes.

One final design decision, which has not been considered in this chapter, involves the choice between constructing the network from many identical processors or from a wide, but balanced, variety of different processors. For instance, the majority of the network might consist of integer arithmetic processors, with a few of them specialist in integer multiplication, and fewer still perhaps specialist in one floating-point instruction. Analogous to the dynamic-grid weather-forecasting example, this means that the majority of the network consists of small, fast, cheap processors for executing the majority of the work, and relatively few expensive ones for performing the specialist work. However, this idea, desirable as it sounds, is not ideal for implementation via WSI, for instance, as described in the next chapter. For this reason, this book favours the use of networks of identical processors, and proceeds now to show the massive advantages which this might make possible at the microelectronics level.

4.10 EXERCISES

4.1 Represent the program of Figure 4.54 in the reduction computer style of Figure 4.43, and trace the cycles of its execution.

```
x := 3;
y := 4;
z := 5;
p := x*y + y*z + z*x;
q := 3*x*x + 4;
print( p );
```

FIGURE 4.54 *Example program*

4.2 Represent the program of Figure 4.54 in the data flow computer style of Figure 4.39, and trace the cycles of its execution. (You will need to make use of the NOP instruction's ability to send copies of its left argument to two destinations.)

5

CONFIGURATION

STRATEGIES

Fault and failure tolerance can be achieved most easily in systems which are highly regular. The presence of a fault or failure will render a whole cell inoperative, but the presence of an inoperative cell will not render the whole device unusable. This chapter classifies some of the topological techniques which can be used to achieve this (Figure 5.1) though, understandably, it cannot hope to be a complete list. It uses two examples, a random access memory and a processor array, as vehicles with which to illustrate the characteristics of each technique.

As always, the appropriate choice of technique depends on the application. The more elaborate the reconfiguration scheme is, the more hardware is required to interface the circuits. This extra overhead is itself prone to faults and failure, and must be minimised if the technique is not to be self defeating. The cost of the reconfiguration logic, in terms of additional device and circuit yield hazards, can be justified only if it is minimal in comparison to that of the payload logic. This generally means that the complexity of the reconfiguration machinery must be significantly less than that of the circuits which are to be reconfigured.

In order to compare the various available techniques for fault/failure tolerance, some elementary statistics will be necessary. However, the treatment which is given next (Section 5.1) is not intended to be a precise one, but rather one that gives a feel for the relationships of the various parameters. A catalogue of configuration strategies follows after it, starting in Section 5.2.

5.1 TERMINOLOGY AND STATISTICS

Studies in WSI are relatively new, and the terminology has not yet stabilised. In many cases, arbitrary decisions must be made, choosing between one term or another, given that either choice will result in conflict with someone else's terminology. This section defines the terms as they as used in this book, but with due acknowledgement that this is not a universally agreed terminology. On the whole, though, it is that of Dickson (1984), and is mostly self explanatory. When in doubt, the reader

DIRECT REPLACEMENT
- Patching
- Integer replication

LINEAR FINAL DEVICE
- Bypass
- Meander cutting
- Meander growth
- Spiral growth

RECTANGULAR FINAL DEVICE
- Standby-spare replacement
- Standby-spare cell replacement
- Standby-spare hybrids
- Rotary switch connection

TREE-SHAPED FINAL DEVICE
- Tree cutting
- Tree growth

PATH REDUNDANCY
- Perfect harvest
- Convex wrapping
- Multidimension topologies

TIME REDUNDANCY

NON-NEAREST-NEIGHBOUR INTERCONNECTION
- Partitioned bypass
- Corridor routing
- Diogenes
- Tree of matrices
- Divide-and-conquer matrix–matrix mapping

MASKING REDUNDANCY
- Modular redundancy
- Block parity
- Hamming correction

FIGURE 5.1 *Summary of techniques for fault/failure tolerance*

should refer to the list of Globally reserved names at the front of the book, and to the Glossary and Index at the end, each of which refer to defining descriptions, as they apply here.

A *device* is a packagable object, such as a semiconductor memory chip. The word *circuit* is used here to mean ‘a region of the device whose failure is caused by just one fault within the region’. Thus, for a circuit to work, it must be fault free. In the traditional approach, there is only one circuit per device but in WSI, where the aim is for the device to occupy an entire wafer, it might contain many circuits. A *cell* is the result of a logical partition of a circuit, such as a single flip-flop from a memory array, or a single processor from a processor array. There are often many cells in each circuit.

Defects are unavoidably introduced during the fabrication of semiconductor circuits. They are caused by *dislocations*, and other *flaws* in the crystal structure, and through *blemishes* on the reticles and masking layers. They are also caused on a larger scale by accidents, and human error, such as mask misalignment and incorrect chemical mixtures and temperatures, during fabrication. The most serious of these are called *faults*, and are the catastrophic defects which prevent circuits from working and which are present from the time of fabrication. A *failure*, on the other hand, is the cessation of function of a previously working circuit whilst it is in service.

Yield is measured as the ratio of the number of working items to the number of fabricated items. For instance, the *circuit yield*, **y**, runs from zero (no circuits work) to unity (every circuit works). Other meaningful measures are the *device yield*, *Y*, and the *cell yield*, *y*. *Reliability* is measured as the probability of an item failing within a given time. It, too, is applicable as a measurement for devices, circuits and cells.

Defect tolerance is the ability to cope with defects, and is used to keep the cell yield, *y*, as high as possible. It is often achieved by relaxing the design rules. For instance, 1 μm blemishes can be tolerated by using 5 μm design rules. The larger defects, which are not so tolerated, manifest themselves as faults.

Fault tolerance is the ability to cope with any faults that are accidentally built into the device. It is used to keep the device yield, *Y*, as high as possible. They are detected at the end-of-manufacture test stage. Any that escape this test eventually manifest themselves as failures when the circuit is in service. It should be noted, though, that Saucier and Trilhe (1986a, b) use a different name to mean this (as noted in the Glossary).

Failure tolerance is the ability to cope with any failures which develop whilst the device is in service. It is used to keep the device reliability, *B*, as high as possible. Again, Saucier and Trilhe (1986a, b), and Anderson and Lee (1981) differ in their choice of terminology here (as noted in the Glossary).

Independently of the amount and quality of the fault/failure tolerance in the device, there will always be a *hardcore* which is not fault/failure tolerant. The hardcore of the system is defined in Anderson and Lee (1981) as consisting of the critical components which must operate reliably if system failures are to be prevented.

Some applications can be described as *fixed aim*; for instance, they require a final device with *m* rows and *n* columns, and must ignore any which are surplus to their requirements. There are other applications where the final size of the array is not important, and they are said to exhibit *graceful degradation*. This is the ability to work with an uncertain number of resources. When applied to fault tolerant systems, the device harnesses as many resources as it can from those which are functioning correctly. When applied to failure tolerant systems, parts of the device are taken out of service, but the overall device continues to function, albeit using its diminished resources and with a reduced performance.

The first common example which comes to mind of a fixed aim device is the random access memory (RAM). The intention, for instance, might be to build a high speed memory to perform the function which is currently implemented by backing store (Bentley and Jesshope 1986; Dettmer 1986b). Although it is an application upon which redundancy has already been used for many years, it is not necessarily very applicable to some of the techniques which are described here, but it is extraordinarily good as an illustration. Therefore a memory of m words, each n bits wide, is used as a common example throughout this chapter. In the diagrams, m is taken to be eight, and n is taken to be four, though of course in practice m is likely to be much larger than this. All of the methods which are described in this chapter, when applied to the memory example, fail if a flaw occurs in the address decoder, or in any of the data-bus, row-select, write/not-read or power supply lines, each of which, therefore, must be considered to be part of the hardcore. However, the aim is merely to improve the yield of working devices, and not necessarily to achieve the ultimate aim of 100 per cent device yield.

For the graceful degradation illustrations, a 16×16 nearest-neighbour interconnection (NNI) processor array is used. However, neither this nor the RAM is intended to be a restrictive example. Many arrangements for multiprocessor arrays can be fixed aim devices, especially the SIMD architectures. Similarly, gracefully degradable memories are feasible, and commonly found in mass storage.

5.1.1 Fault-free processing

The traditional method could be called *fault-free* processing, or *100 per cent yield* (Aubusson and Catt 1978). Wafers are processed with a number of circuits on them: those which are fault free can be packaged; those which contain one fault or more will not work properly and so are discarded. As circuit complexity is increased, so the circuit area increases, and the proportion which are fault free tends to zero.

Wafer sizes are normally quoted in terms of the wafer diameter, d. These are traditionally measured in inches. For consistency of units, though, this text will assume that a four-inch wafer has a diameter of 100 mm. For a number of reasons, it is normal to leave a margin round the edge of the wafer, of width δd. Typically, this could be about 10 mm (Ferris-Prabhu *et al.* 1987). The effective diameter is thus $d'=d-2\,\delta d$, and the usable area is $W=\pi d'^2/4$.

The number of devices which are fabricated on each wafer is called '*num*' here. If each device has an area of A, then simplistically there will be about W/A such devices on a wafer, that is $num=W/A$. For VLSI, A is about 100 mm^2.

Faults on the wafer of semiconductor are assumed, for the present, to be random in their distribution. Their density is D, measured in units of 'faults per unit area', and typically might have a value about five per square centimetre, that is 0.05 mm^{-2}.

Using conventional fabrication techniques, the presence of a single fault within a device causes a circuit element such as a transistor not to function properly, and as a result the whole device is unusable. Here, the number of usable devices on the wafer is called the '*crop*'. The ratio of *crop*/*num* is called the *device yield*, Y. It is a number between zero and unity, indicating the proportion of fabricated devices which are working properly. Because it is a number between zero and unity, it can also be used to indicate a probability; given any device chosen at random it is the probability that it is one of the working ones. It is dependent on the fault density and the area of the device, thus $Y=\nu(D,A)$, the definition of which is discussed in Section 5.1.2. The effect of increasing A is to reduce *num*, and usually also to reduce Y, therefore causing a two pronged attack on the crop. As A is increased, not only is there an increase in the area that is wasted each time, but also in the probability that the area will be wasted.

Most of the devices which are considered in this text are composed of large numbers, c, of identical cells each of area a, and hence $A=ca$. The position of the cell on the wafer's surface can be specified using polar coordinates. The distance of the centre of the cell from the centre of the wafer is r. Its angular position, θ, is determined by measuring anticlockwise from a line which passes through the wafer's centre, and which runs parallel to the wafer's primary flat (Figure 5.2).

Lastly, the minimum transistor size is an important parameter. In keeping with Mead and Conway (1980), this text uses λ as the unit of length, and refers to it as the *grid size*. The minimum size of a transistor is then $2\lambda \times 2\lambda$. The value of λ has a direct effect on the cell area, a, the maximum switching speed, τ, and the fault density, D. Two of these have implications on the yield function, $v(D,a)$, as is described next.

5.1.2 The yield function

Present day commercial circuits are about 10 mm square, containing lines and transistors which are only 2 μm wide (i.e. $\lambda \simeq 1$ μm). The circuit is *written* into the semiconductor crystal by a series of photographic exposures, each one bearing a different pattern. There could well be 12 of these exposures, each one aligned with its predecessors to a greater accuracy than ± 1 μm throughout the 10 mm × 10 mm area. To make matters worse, the final layers are written over a surface which is far from flat, having had previous layers of materials etched and deposited, and having been warped from repeated temperature cycling, over a 1000°C range, placed in hostile

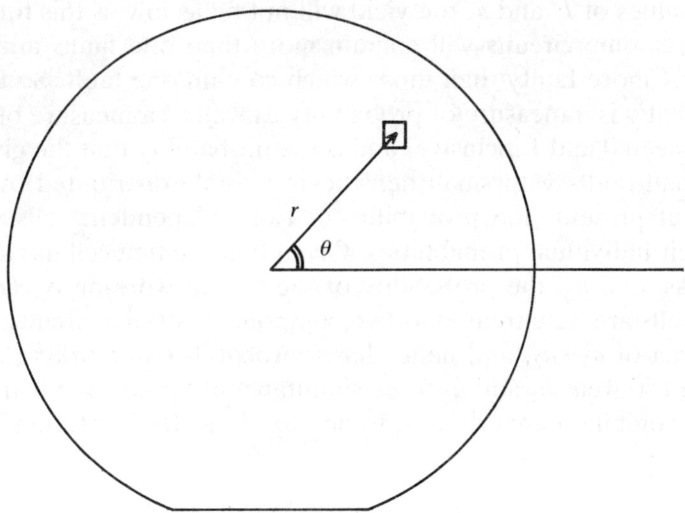

FIGURE 5.2 *Polar coordinate references on a wafer*

atmospheres and highly corrosive chemical baths. It is little wonder that not every circuit works.

Given any cell at random, the probability of finding that it is a working one is y, which is also the *cell yield*. Because they are independent events, assuming that faults can be approximated by point defects occurring at random, the probability of finding a device with c cells all working is the product of the individual probabilities. Thus $Y=y^c$.

Yield is dependent on two major parameters: the expected number of faults per unit area, and the circuit's area, $y=v(D,a)$. The first is process dependent, for example, depending on the grid size, λ, the type of transistor used, the maximum temperature encountered during fabrication and the number of fabrication steps, whilst the second is partly process dependent (grid size, λ) and partly design dependent (number of transistors used). Since this function is so important to WSI, its nature will be discussed further. Rather than copying the theoretical derivations which can be found in countless other texts (for example Bertram 1983), the derivation here will be purely intuitive. Readers for whom this is an insufficient treatment are referred to Bertram's chapter for the more formal treatment.

To start the derivation, assume that: the number of faults per unit area is extremely small, the faults themselves are miniscule, the area of the circuit is very small, and the faults are dispersed randomly. Then the proportion of circuits with at least one fault in them will be approximated by: Da. For example, if $D=0.001\ \text{mm}^{-2}$, and $a=0.01\ \text{mm}^2$, the number of faults per cell is about 0.000 01, that is about 1 cell in 100 000 contains a fault. Since the presence of a single fault in a circuit is enough to prevent the whole circuit from functioning, the proportion of faulty circuits is also given by Da, and the yield of good circuits is therefore given by:

$$y = 1 - Da$$

For larger values of D and a, the yield will not be as low as this formula predicts, largely because some circuits will contain more than one fault, and this does not make them any more faulty than those which contain one fault. So the next step is to recognise that y is a measure of probability as well as a measure of yield. It takes on values between 0 and 1 inclusive, and is the probability that the given cell works. Since only small faults with small densities randomly distributed over small areas are assumed at present, the probability of two independent cells working is the product of their individual probabilities. Given that the first cell has area a_1, and the second cell has area a_2, the probability of them both working is $v(D,a_1).v(D,a_2)$.

If the two cells are now treated as two components of one circuit, the overall circuit has an area of a_1+a_2, and hence has a probability of working of $v(D,a_1+a_2)$. The condition for areas a_1 and a_2 to be simultaneously fault free is the same as that of finding the combined area, a_1+a_2, to be fault free. By inspection it can be noted that since:

$$v(D,a_1)\,v(D,a_2) = v(D,a_1+a_2)$$

and it is known that v decreases with increasing a, then:

$$\begin{aligned} v(D,a) &= F(D)^{-a} \\ &= e^{-af(D)} \end{aligned}$$

where $f(D)=\ln(F(D))$. The nature of $f(D)$ is such that it lies in the range 0 to ∞ for v to lie in the range 1 to 0, respectively. Also, since the series expansion of v is:

$$1 - af(D) + \frac{a^2f(D)^2}{2} - \frac{a^3f(D)^3}{6} + \ldots$$

then the original intuitive estimate for very small D and very small a, $y=1-Da$, will be satisfied when $f(D)=D$. Thus the new estimate for v is:

$$y = v(D,a) = e^{-Da}$$

This is the Poisson model for estimating circuit yield. It should be emphasised again though that this only holds when the initial assumptions are valid, namely: the areas of the cells are small, the fault density is low, the faults are small, and the faults are not clustered but are distributed randomly. As soon as any one of these assumptions fails, the relationship $v(D,a_1+a_2)=v(D,a_1)v(D,a_2)$ ceases to hold too.

5.1.3 Fault tolerance

In order to tolerate faults and failures, it is proposed that C cells should be fabricated within each device. C is chosen sufficiently larger than c for there to be a high chance that c working cells might be found amongst those fabricated. In general, these cells are grouped so that there are $\mathbf{c}$ cells per circuit, and hence $C/\mathbf{c}$ circuits in the device.

Each circuit occupies an area of $\mathbf{a}=\mathbf{c}a+\delta a$, made up from the payload logic area, $\mathbf{c}a$, plus the fault/failure tolerance logic area, δa. Any fault/failure in the latter can be treated in the same way as a fault/failure in the former, but it would seem prudent to ensure that $\delta a \ll \mathbf{c}a$ in order that faults/failures in the extra circuitry will cause an insignificant decrease in the circuit yield, $\mathbf{y}=v(D,\mathbf{a})=y^{\mathbf{c}}v(D,\delta a)$.

Figure 5.3 shows that the area of the device is $A'=(C/\mathbf{c})\mathbf{a}+\delta A$, where δA represents the area of the extra hardcore which is contributed by the control and glue logic for the fault/failure tolerance circuitry. The yield of the reconfigured circuits, V, depends on the particular fault/failure tolerance strategy which is being used, as will the values of δa and δA. It is imperative that $\delta A \ll ca$ if any improvement is to be experienced in the device yield, $Y'=Vv(D,\delta A)$.

As well as imposing additional area and yield hazard overheads, the fault/failure tolerance hardware introduces an extra time delay into signal paths. If this threatens to jeopardise the performance of the system, it might be acceptable to treat the critical timing paths as hardcore, and hence not to degrade their performance further with fault/failure tolerance logic.

In order to compare the relative merits of each of the fault/failure tolerant techniques, several measures have been suggested. The first is the *replication factor*, R. This is a measure of the scale of redundancy which is employed, $R=C/c$. When rectangular arrangements of cells are used, the device is fabricated with M rows and N

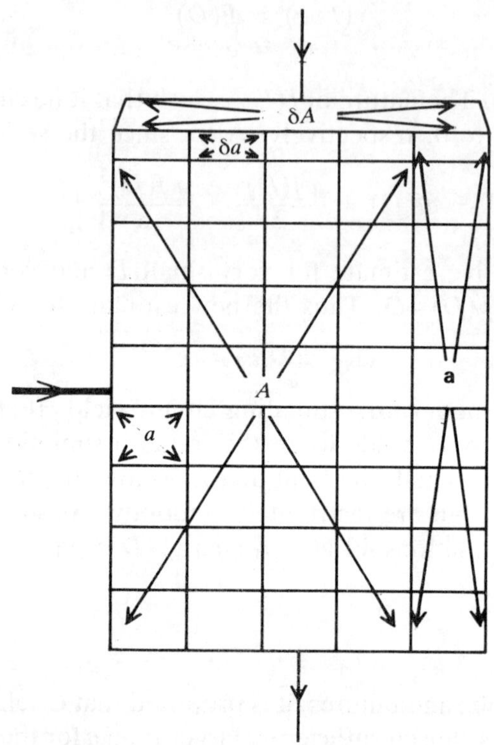

FIGURE 5.3 *Areas of an 8 × 4 array implemented as an 8 × 5 array*

columns, that is $C=MN$. Of these, the device is to utilise m rows and n columns, that is $c=mn$, and so $R=MN/mn$. The *replication overhead*, or *redundancy* as it is called in some texts, is one less than this, $R-1$. Another commonly used measure is the *harvest* (Rosenberg 1986), which is the ratio of utilised items to usable items. Thus the *cell harvest*, which has also been variously known as *cell utilisation* or *cell usage*, is the ratio of utilised cells to working cells, $h=c/(Cy)=1/(Ry)$. Like yield, its value runs from zero when nothing is utilised, to unity when everything is utilised. It is possible, indeed desirable, for the harvest to exceed the yield. For instance, if 1000 cells are fabricated, and only 10 of them work, then the cell yield is 1 per cent, but if the device is able to make use of 9 of the working cells, then the cell harvest is 90 per cent. Generally, this is not the case though, and the cell harvest falls sharply when the cell yield is reduced below some threshold value.

Within the device, the number of working cells is Cy. This means that the number of faulty cells is $C(1-y)$. For all of the fixed aim techniques, for any given cell yield, y, the cell harvest, h, bears a constant relationship to the replication factor, R, *viz.* $h=1/(Ry)$.

There is another measure of silicon utilisation called the *relative device area*. This is defined as the ratio of the final area of the device to the area of the payload logic, thus $rda=A'/A$. Other texts prefer to use the *relative device overhead*, which is one less than this, $rdo=rda-1$. It should be noted that VLSI has a less than perfect value for *rda*, too. Space is required for scribe lines, safety margins, bond pads and signal drivers between the circuits. Indeed, Aubusson showed (1979), that, for one strategy at least, the *rda* for the wafer scale device could be less than that for the VLSI equivalent.

With ULSI in particular, the *crop* is an important figure of merit. It has the value $crop' = WY'/A'$. In order to experience improvement, that is for $crop' > crop$, Y'/Y must be larger than A'/A. In other words, the device yield must increase by a larger factor than the area does.

Lastly, two other figures of merit might be considered for certain applications. The minimum number of faulty cells that can kill the device, the *best-case failure*, is K_{min}, and the maximum number of faulty cells that can be tolerated, the *worst-case success*, is F_{max}.

5.1.4 Failure tolerance

Most machines are prone to failure, with the failure rate distributed according to the characteristic curve of Figure 5.4. Three major periods are highlighted. During the first (infant mortality) any machines which, though they appear to be correctly manufactured, are so poorly constructed that they fail very early in their life. Those machines which survive this period tend to be those which are constructed as near perfectly as could be expected, and failures are rare. After the expected lifetime of the machine, components start to wear out and the failure rate rises again.

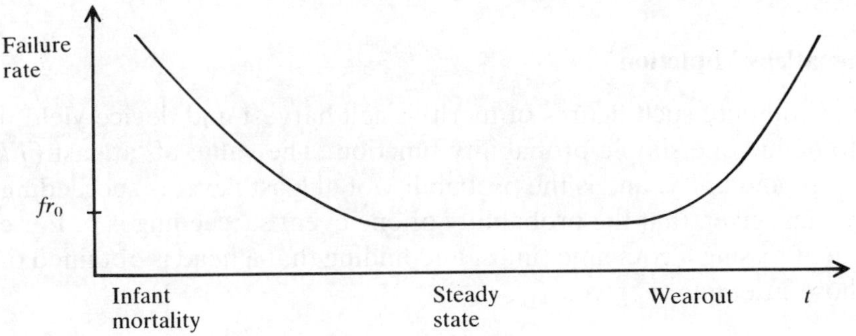

FIGURE 5.4 *Periods of failure*

When the machines are conventional integrated circuits, the customer can expect circuits to fail only rarely, always within the steady state period of the devices' lives. The manufacturer protects the customer from the infant mortality phase by subjecting each circuit to a running-in process, and discarding those which fail during this time. The customer is protected from the wearout phase simply by virtue of the fact that the lifetime of electronics systems tends to be much shorter than that of the integrated circuits (which is perhaps of the order of a hundred years, or much more).

During the steady state phase, integrated circuit failures are attributable to metal migration (the gradual thinning of metal conductors), ion migration (the gradual absorption of metal ions into the semiconductor substrate) and corrosion. External bond connections are therefore highly vulnerable, and the pin count represents the best measure for predicting the reliability for VLSI circuits. For WSI, the steady state period might be shorter lived, and the failure rate might be much higher, perhaps dominated by metal migration in the heavily used signal leads.

During the steady state phase, the failure rate is constant, fr_0. The *mean time to failure* (MTTF) is the inverse of this (Bertram 1983), and is used here as the metric of reliability. The cell reliability, b, the circuit reliability, $\mathbf{b}$, and the device reliability, B, are the respective mean times to failure of these items.

The probability that any given working cell will be still working after t units of time is $p=e^{-t/b}$. The probability of several independent cells all working after t units of time is given by the product of their individual probabilities, thus $P=p^c$, and hence $B=b/c$.

The reliability of each failure tolerant circuit $\mathbf{b}=(b\ \delta b)/(b+\mathbf{c}\ \delta b)$, where δb is the reliability of the failure tolerance logic area, δa. The aim is for this to increase the device reliability from $B=b/c$ to $B'=\mathbf{cb}\ \delta B/(\mathbf{cb}+C\ \delta B)$, where δB is the reliability of the extra hardcore area, δA.

Two important concerns with failure tolerant systems are those of determining whether it can cope with intermittent failures, and whether it can fail cleanly, that is without loss of data, and without pulling the rest of the system down. Neither of these issues is addressed here, but the interested reader is referred to Anderson and Lee (1981).

5.1.5 The 'atleast' function

In order to compute such figures of merit as cell harvest and device yield, it is convenient to define one simple probability function. The value of 'atleast (j,k,p)' lies between zero and unity, and is the probability of at least j events succeeding out of a total of k tries, given that the probability of one event succeeding is p. For example, the chance of tossing a coin nine times, and finding that a head is obtained on at least five of those attempts, is given by:

$$\text{atleast}(5, 9, 0.5)$$

The definition of 'atleast' is given below, and is the standard one for the binomial expansion. (A Pascal implementation of this definition can also be found in Appendix 2.)

$$\text{atleast}(j, k, p) = \sum_{i=j}^{k} \frac{k!}{(k-i)!\ i!}\ p^i(1-p)^{k-i}$$

Some special cases exist, as depicted below. The last one arises because the probability of there being at least one success is the same as that of there not being zero successes.

$$\text{atleast}(k, k, p) = p^k$$
$$\text{atleast}(k-1, k, p) = kp^{k-1} - (k-1)p^k$$
$$\text{atleast}(0, k, p) = 1$$
$$\text{atleast}(1, k, p) = 1 - (1-p)^k$$

There is now a case-by-case description of the logical techniques which are available for fault/failure tolerance. The physical methods by which these can be realised are discussed in Chapter 6, as is the performance of the reconfiguration algorithms and how it might be maximised. Throughout this, it is assumed that both δa and δA are negligible. This is a very naïve assumption, and likely to be invalid for many applications. It is justified here though for the clarity and simplicity of the illustrations which would otherwise be lost. It is left to the reader, having gained some idea of the relative merits of the alternative techniques, to repeat the analysis in more detail for the specific application on which it is to be used.

5.2 DIRECT REPLACEMENT

The most obvious approaches involve the wholesale replication of circuits, with no dependence on any regularity which the device might possess. Consequently, they are as equally applicable to non-regular structures as they are to regular ones.

5.2.1 Patching

Just as flaws in cloth can be repaired by being covered with a patch, so too can flaws in a wafer of semiconductor (Figure 5.5). The device is fabricated in the normal way, and each of the cells is tested in turn. Whenever a faulty one is found, it is disconnected from the device and an external copy is physically bonded in its place.

In practice, a coarser granularity is used. It would be practical only to use circuits which are at least as coarse grain as LSI devices, such as blocks of memory, or simple processors.

5.2.2 Integer replication

The above technique is exceptional. Most fault/failure tolerant techniques, as found in the remainder of this chapter, rely on making use of the resources which are provided together on a single piece of semiconductor. For example, the next, intuitively simple, technique involves replicating every circuit, possibly several times, but only using one of the working copies. The higher the replication factor, the higher is the tolerance to low cell yields, but the lower is the cell harvest.

Performance-wise, there is little effective difference between device replication and the conventional technique of testing devices, and discarding them until a

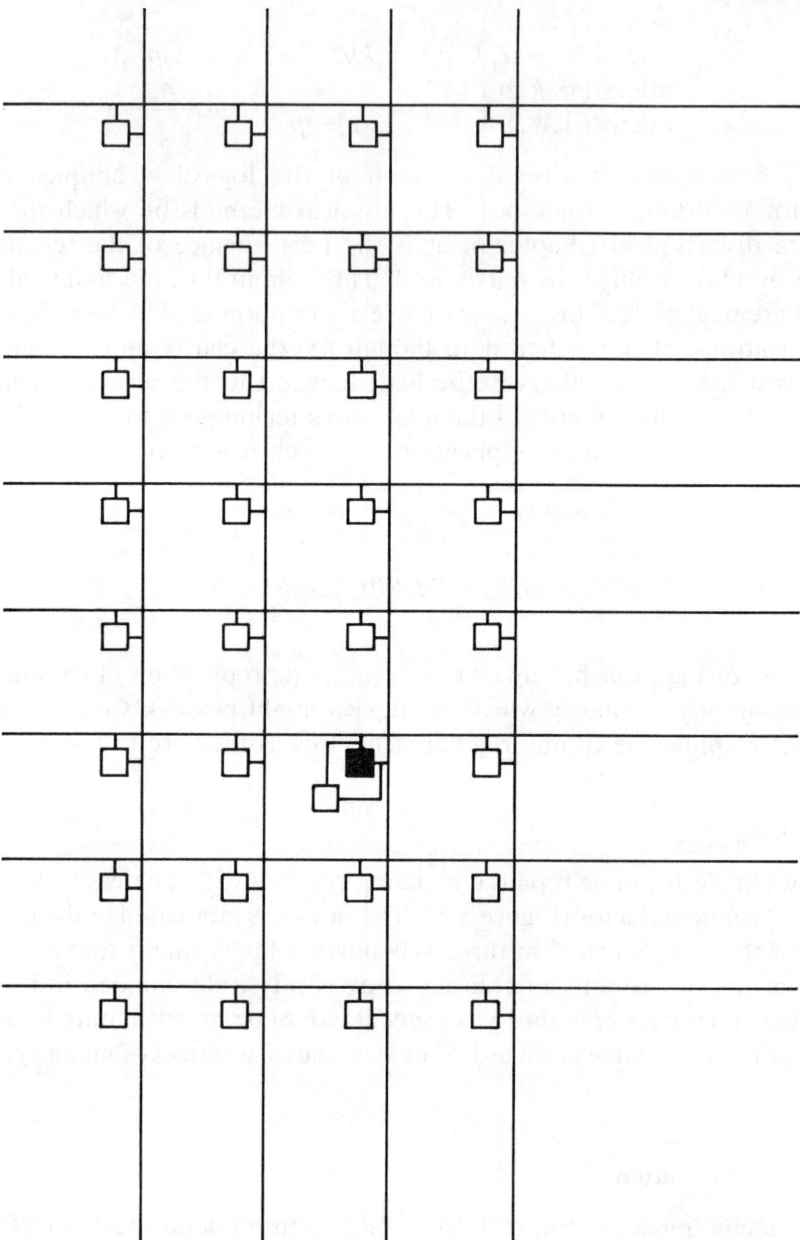

FIGURE 5.5 *Patching*

working one is discovered. Indeed, device replication, in common with all of the fixed aim techniques, suffers the additional disadvantage that the packaged device size is much larger, by a factor R. This approach, therefore, is rarely beneficial.

Instead of replicating the devices, column replication can be used. Figure 5.6 illustrates the technique, using a replication factor of two. The reader is invited to

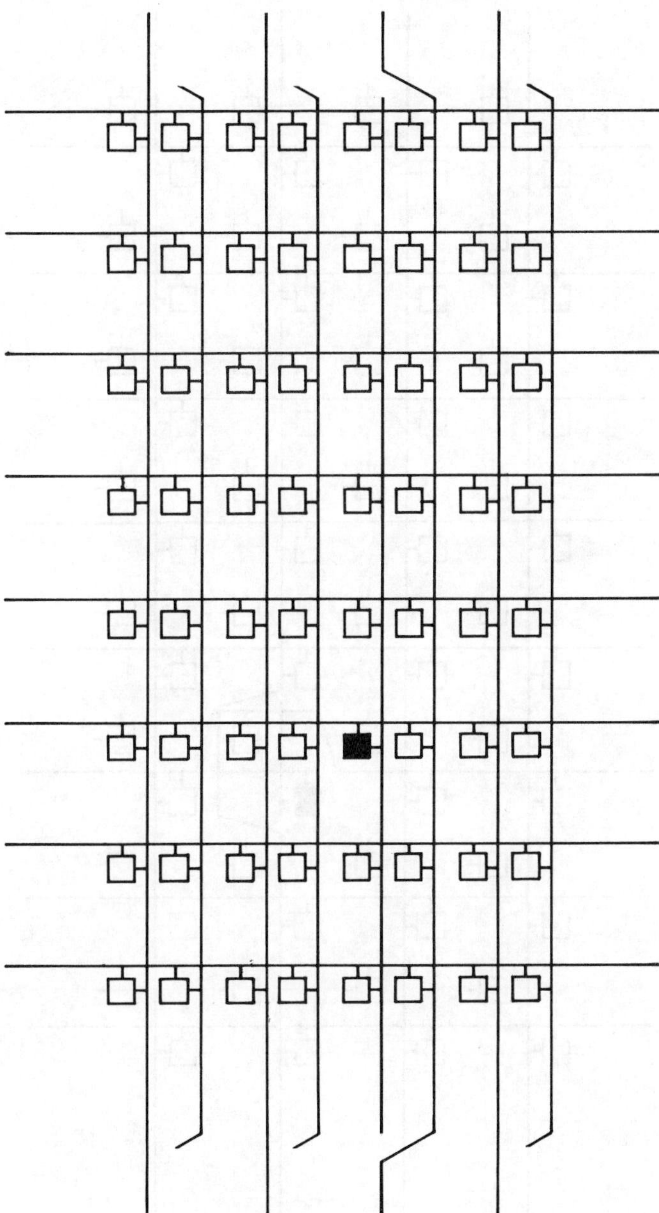

FIGURE 5.6 *Fixed aim column-orientated replication*

confirm that this technique can be applied equally well for row replications. For rectangular devices, with fewer columns than rows, row replication involves finer grain circuits, that is with fewer cells in each, **c**.

The finest grain variant of this series of approaches is *cell replication* (Figure 5.7), in which any cell can be switched in or out independently of the others. In Figure 5.8, the performances of the four techniques are calculated.

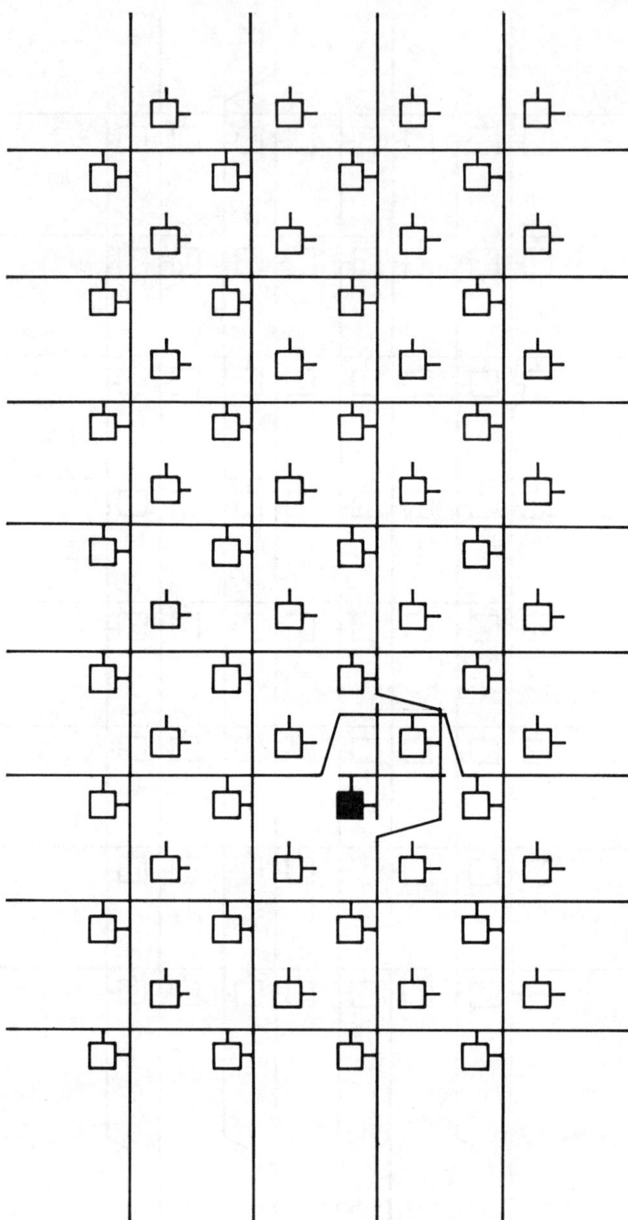

FIGURE 5.7 *Fixed aim cell-orientated replication*

In general, the device yield, Y', increases as the grain size is reduced from device replication to cell replication. For rectangular devices, this means that orientating the replication around the shortest dimension (the rows in the eight by four example which is used above) produces a better device yield. In practice, the cost of adopting a finer grain size is the increase in the areas, δA and δa, which has not been included in the calculations of Figure 5.8.

Device replication		*Column replication*	*Row replication*	*Cell replication*
Min. working cells in circuit:	mn from mn	m from m	n from n	1 from 1
Circuit yield:	y^{mn}	y^m	y^n	y
Min. working circuits in group:	1 from R	1 from R	1 from R	1 from R
Group yield:	$1-(1-y^{mn})^R$	$1-(1-y^m)^R$	$1-(1-y^n)^R$	$1-(1-y)^R$
Min. working groups in device:	1 from 1	n from n	m from m	mn from mn
Device yield (Y'):	$1-(1-y^{mn})^R$	$(1-(1-y^m)^R)^n$	$(1-(1-y^n)^R)^m$	$(1-(1-y)^R)^{mn}$

FIGURE 5.8 *Performance of fixed aim integer replication*

There are no gracefully degradable versions of these techniques because of their inability to use more than one circuit from each group. This is the 'cost' which is incurred for the advantage of independence from any regularity (or lack of) in the device.

In the worst case, the technique could fail if there are R faulty cells, if they all occur in the same group, with one fault in each of the circuits of the group. At the opposite extreme, the technique can cater for $(R-1)mn$ faulty cells, so long as there is exactly one working circuit in every group. Figure 5.9 illustrates these two cases for column replication.

5.3 LINEAR FINAL DEVICE

Rather than representing RAM, the following examples assume the use of sequential access memory, in the form perhaps of a massive shift register. This type of memory might still have an address decoder: a counter which is incremented each time the shift register is clocked, and which represents the address of the presently exposed bit. In a first-in/first-out (FIFO) queue, data are inserted at one end and are read out again sometime later at the other, to be optionally fed back in again. This is not a new idea; many of the computers from the 1950s used mercury delay lines in this way (Randell 1982). Even modern computers make extensive use of magnetic tape storage, where data are stored sequentially on the magnetic tape and at a later date they can be read sequentially back again in the same order. A large wafer scale shift register might be envisaged, therefore, for use as a solid state replacement for a magnetic tape or disk drive. This is particularly attractive to the home computer market, where the cost of mass storage is prohibitive (Dettmer 1986b).

Another application of serial access memory, the last-in/first-out (LIFO) queue, or stack, requires the use of bidirectional shift registers. The reader is invited to consider the implications that this has on the implemention of Forth-based computers (Section 3.1.2).

Outside of the applications for memory, many of the multiprocessor computer architectures make use of a vector-connected arrangement of processing elements. Lea and Streetharan (1979), and Shute and Osmon (1986) suggest two architectures

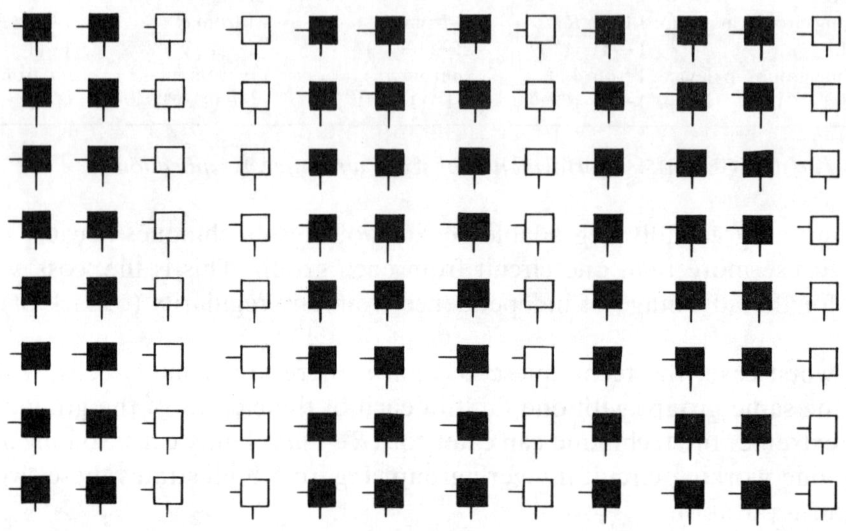

Successful

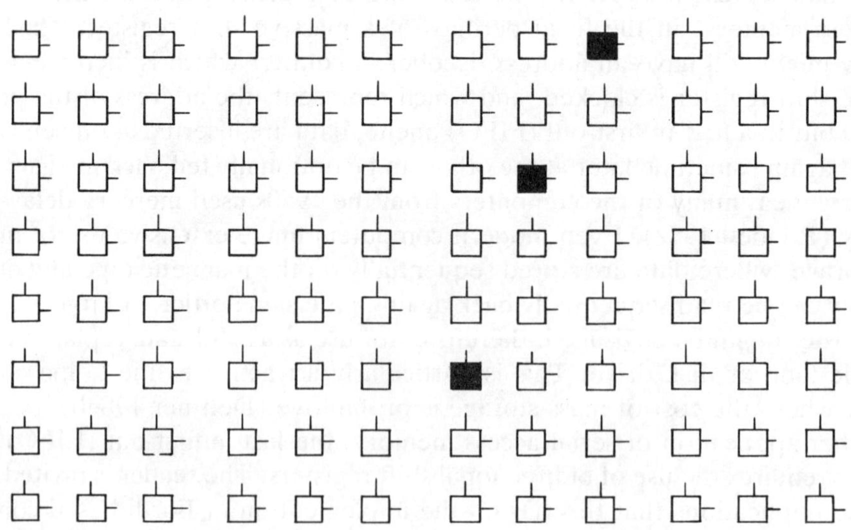

Failed

FIGURE 5.9 *Examples of best-case failure and worst-case success*

which are able to make use of some of the techniques which are described in this section.

Most of the techniques are gracefully degradable in nature, harvesting as many working cells as they can. Fixed aim applications can still be implemented, simply by truncating the growth of the chain when it has reached the desired length. The calculation of the device yield then becomes one of determining the probability that the chain can be made to grow to a certain minimum length, for example as investigated by Aubusson and Gledhill (1978).

5.3.1 Bypass

Perhaps the most obvious, most commonly used technique to achieve gracefully degradable networks involves the placement of suitable bypass connections (Figure 5.10). These can be optionally switched into operation whenever a faulty cell is encountered, so configuring the faulty physical chain into a fault-free logical chain.

The bypass operation can be considered, in abstract terms, to be simply a matter of using conventional two-way switches (Figure 5.11). More practical methods are considered in Chapter 6.

Leighton and Leiserson (1986) derive statistics on the maximum expected hop length. Since the longest hop length determines the maximum communications speed, if the system is used synchronously, this study is of primary importance.

Often, when the cells are simple, the complexity of the bypass switches is comparable with that of the cells. In such cases, it is advantageous to increase the granularity of the fault/failure tolerance. Hedge and Lea (1986), for instance, employ bypass connection which skips four cells at a time whenever any one of them is found to be faulty.

5.3.2 Meander cutting

The less expensive approach is to run a line along one side, bypassing any loops which are not fault free. This is depicted in Figure 5.12.

Figure 5.12 shows that, even for a cell yield of about 90 per cent, the cell harvest is particularly low (about 28 per cent). Figure 5.13 derives the performance figures for the general case.

5.3.3 Meander growth

When the system is initiated, a test signal is supplied to a circuit at the edge of the wafer. If this circuit proves to be faulty, others have to be tested until a working one is found. The aim of the approach is then to wind a snake of connections through the working cells, avoiding the faulty ones (Figure 5.14).

The irregular physical structure of the final configuration makes the performance statistics very messy. The reader is probably best advised to resort to empirical techniques, such as simulation runs.

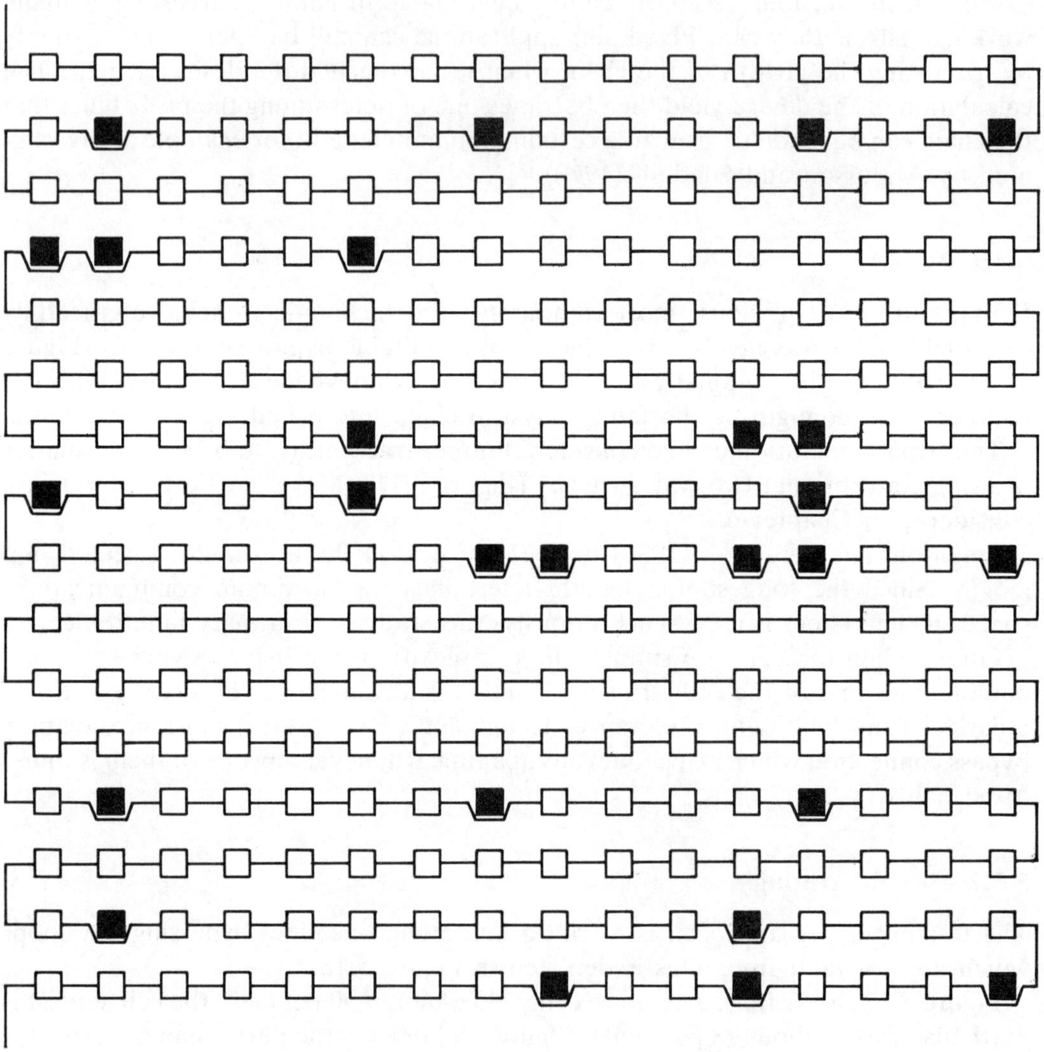

FIGURE 5.10 *Gracefully degradable bypass*

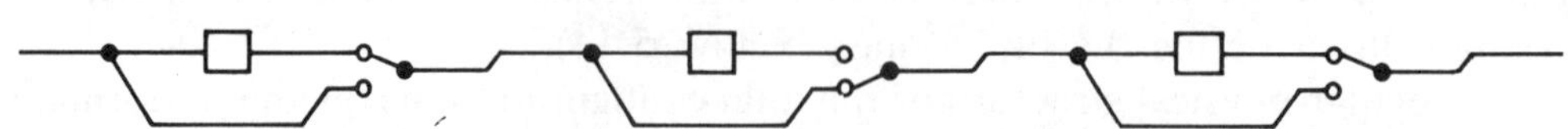

FIGURE 5.11 *Bypass switches*

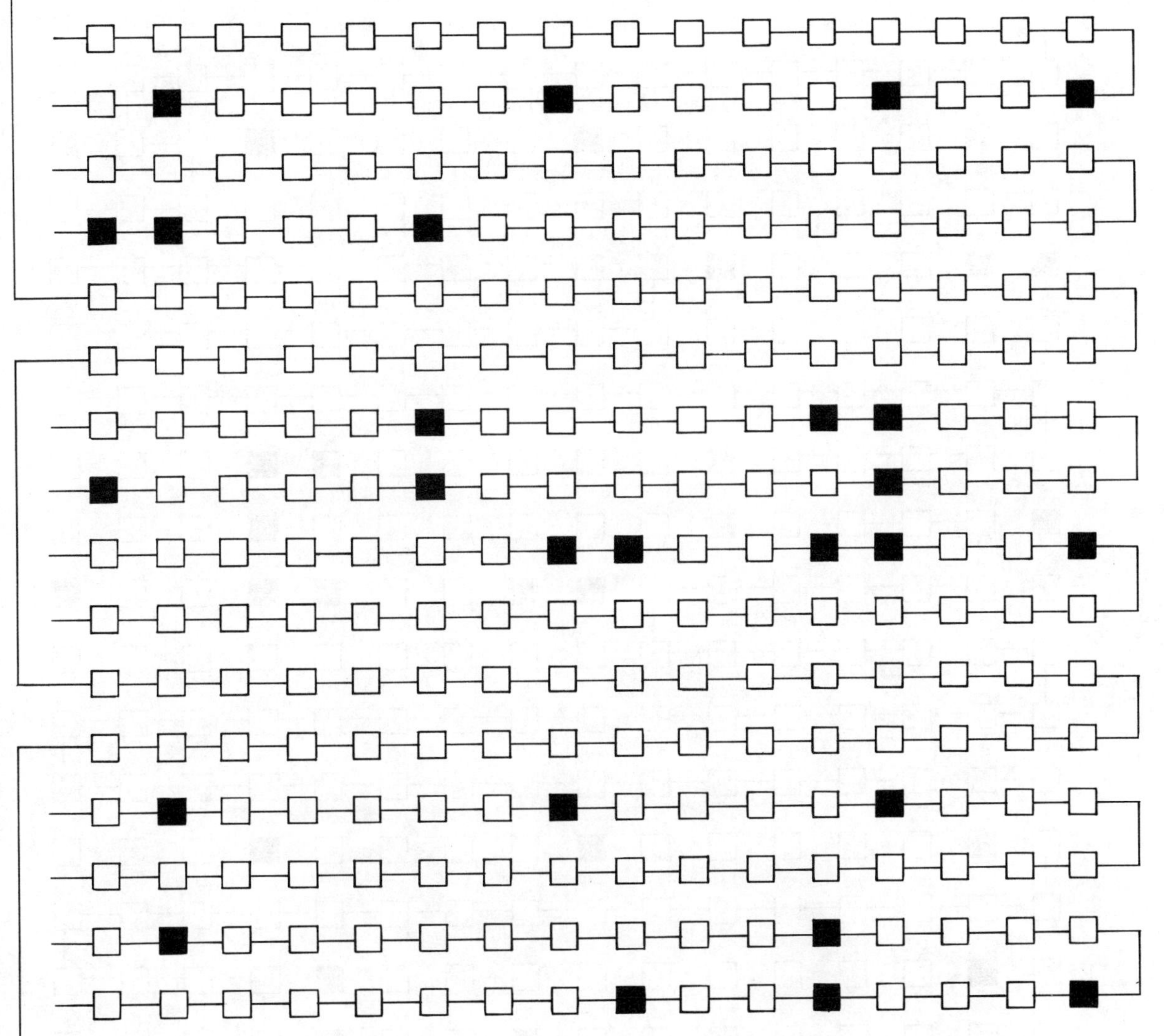

FIGURE 5.12 *Gracefully degradable meander cutting*

Meander yield:	y^{2N}
Device yield (Y'):	$1-(1-y^{2N})^{M/2}$
Number of working meanders:	$\frac{M}{2}y^{2N}$
Number of utilised cells:	MNy^{2N}
Number of working cells:	MNy
Cell harvest (h):	y^{2N-1}

FIGURE 5.13 *Performance of gracefully degradable meander cutting*

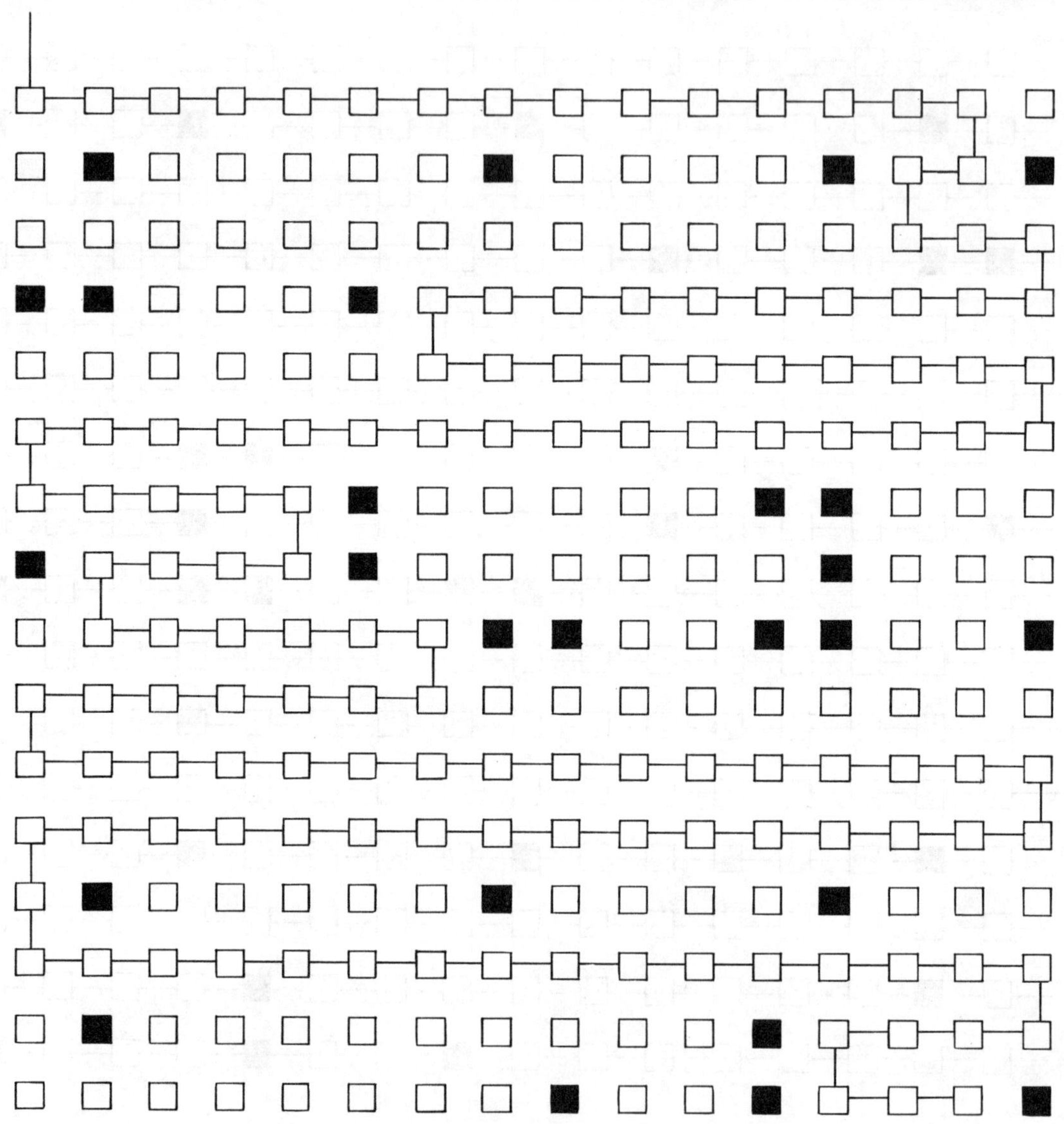

FIGURE 5.14 *Gracefully degradable meander growth*

5.3.4 Spiral growth

Using an algorithm which is attributed to Catt (1974), a working cell is first found, as before. Having established that it is fully working, this cell tries one of its neighbours, and tests to see if it too is fully functioning. If it is, the process is repeated with the new cell. In Figure 5.15, each new cell first tests the next neighbour in a clockwise direction from the side on which the spiral entered it. If it finds that this is the edge of the wafer, it tries the next cell round. If the new cell is fully functioning, and has not been connected already, it can be added to the spiral.

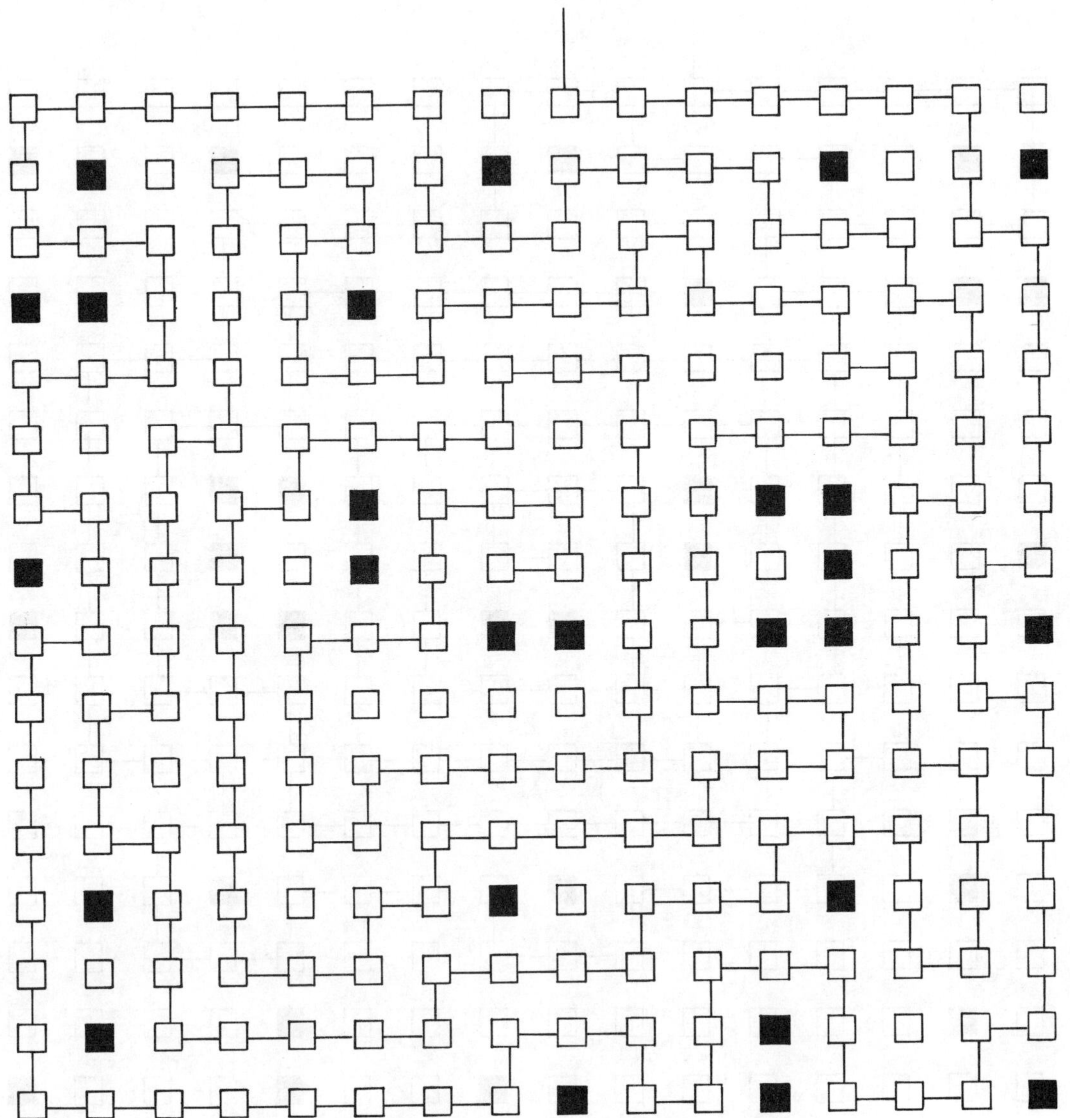

FIGURE 5.15 *Gracefully degradable inward-grown Catt spiral*

Gradually, because of the clockwise test sequence, a clockwise spiral is built. This technique is used in Anamartic's 20 Mbyte memory project. The intention is to use the silicon wafer memory in place of a Winchester disk unit on home computers (Dettmer 1986b). On occasions, it is necessary to back out of cells if, though they are working, they have found that each of their neighbours is unavailable. Figure 5.15 shows that the spiral not only avoids faulty circuits, but also some which are fully working. These are excluded because they are in *blind alleys*.

Figure 5.16 depicts a system in which the spiral is grown from the centre outwards. This is in fact less efficient than the inward-grown spiral of Figure 5.15, because the

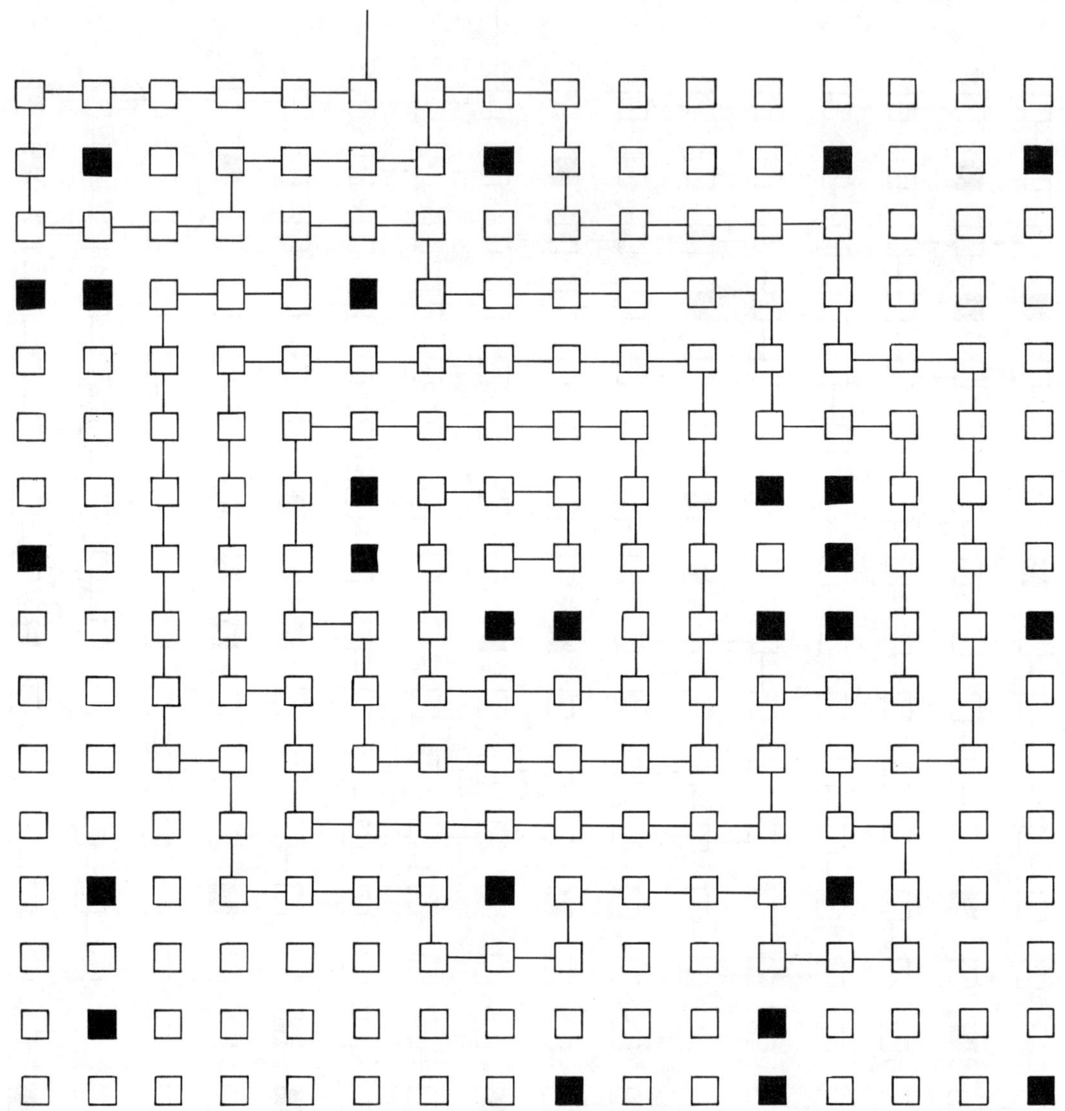

FIGURE 5.16 *Gracefully degradable outward-grown Catt spiral*

spiral divides the wafer when it first reaches the edge, leaving several unharvestable regions. However, the advantage of outward-grown spirals is that they start from the higher yield region at the centre, where the chance of finding a working bondable cell is greater.

The device yield is $1-(1-y)^z$ where z is the number of cells from which the spiral can be started (Catt called these *chip-z* sites). Again, the cell harvest might best be obtained by relying on empirical results, such as those reported by Aubusson and Gledhill (1978).

The technique might fail in the presence of z faulty cells. The maximum number of faulty cells tolerated is $C-1$, so long as a chip-z cell is the one working cell.

5.4 RECTANGULAR FINAL DEVICE

Much research has concentrated on applications which require a two-dimensional array of cells. There are many compute-bound problems which have a strong two-dimensional content which map easily on to arrays of co-operating parallel processors. Since wafers and printed circuit boards are two-dimensional writing surfaces, design of such processor arrays seems potentially very profitable, and it is not surprising that a large amount of work is presently concentrated on this area.

Because of the highly regular nature of processor and memory arrays, a few spares can be shared between a large number of circuits. This is analogous to a motor car carrying just one, not four, spare wheels, to replace whichever of the road wheels fails first. In this way, fractional replication factors between one and two are possible, even for the fixed aim applications.

5.4.1 Standby-spare replacement

Using a standby-spare column technique, faulty columns can be replaced by one of the spares which is provided. For instance, the memory can be fabricated as eight five-bit words, and so the replication factor is 1.25. If a fault is found in one of the columns the column is ignored, and the spare column is used instead.

Figure 5.17 shows a slight variation of the method in which, rather than using the extra column directly as a replacement, the neighbouring one is used. Subsequent columns are then each required as replacements for their predecessors. The main advantage of this technique is that the extra connections, though more numerous, are all local, involving fewer crossover connections, each one being nearest neighbour instead. It is this variant which is reported for Inmos' static memory (Edwards 1985).

If it is necessary to cater for more than one faulty cell per device, the array can be fabricated with more than one spare column. But then the interconnection is no longer quite nearest neighbour since provision must be made to connect to the next but one or more distant neighbours.

Figure 5.18 depicts the memory fabricated as nine four-bit words, so using a replication factor of only 1.125. This is lower than that for the equivalent version of standby-spare column because of the rectangular nature of the device, there being fewer cells in a row than there are in a column.

The performance for standby-spare column is calculated in Figure 5.19. The corresponding calculation for the standby-spare row approach appears to produce a better device yield for a given cell yield. This again stems from the fact that the rows are finer grain than the columns in the rectangular arrangement of Figure 5.17. Once again, this conclusion might be reversed once the areas of δa and δA are taken into account.

The best-case failure and worst-case success can be calculated, for example for standby-spare column: the technique might fail if there are $N-n+1$ faulty cells, assuming the worst case where all the faults occur in different columns (Figure 5.20).

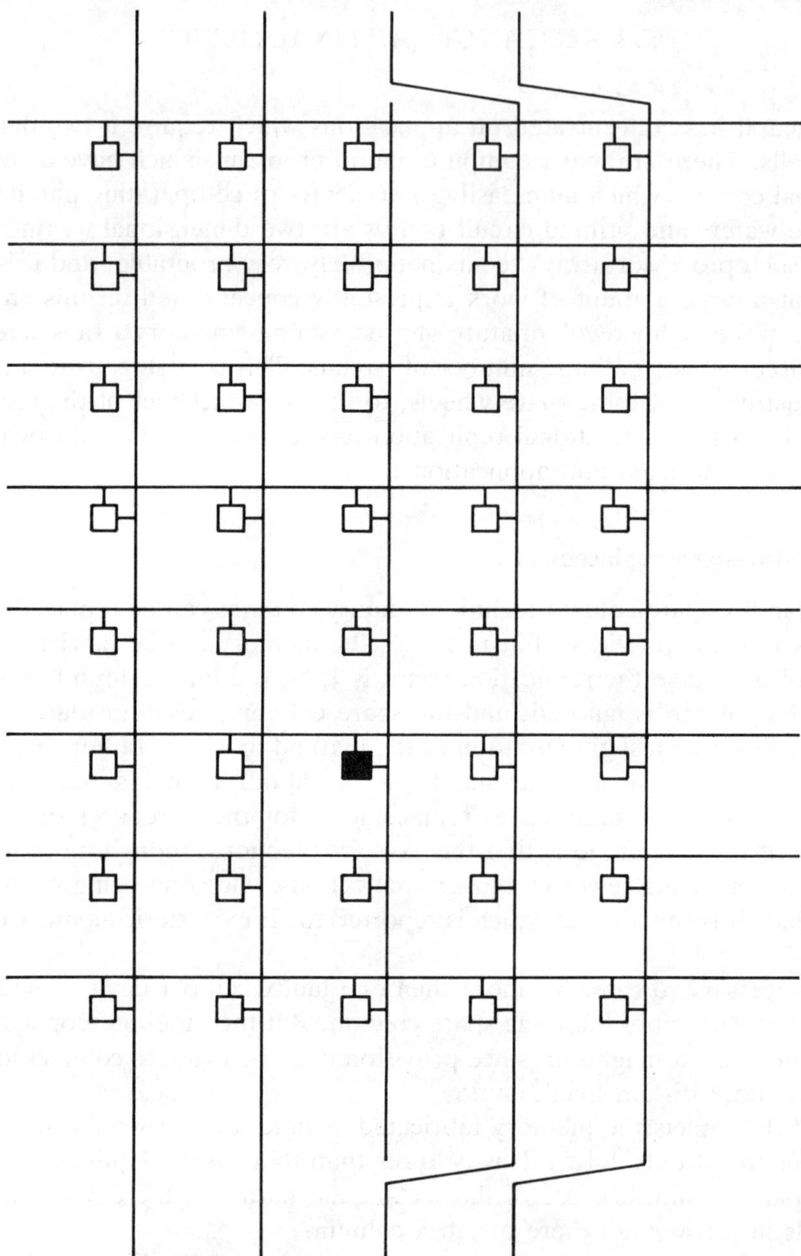

FIGURE 5.17 *Fixed aim standby-spare column*

The maximum number of faulty cells tolerated is $mN-mn$, when they all lie in the same $N-n$ columns.

When used for graceful degradation applications, some method is usually needed to connect cells along the other dimension. For example, gracefully degradable standby-spare column connection can be combined with a bypass technique along

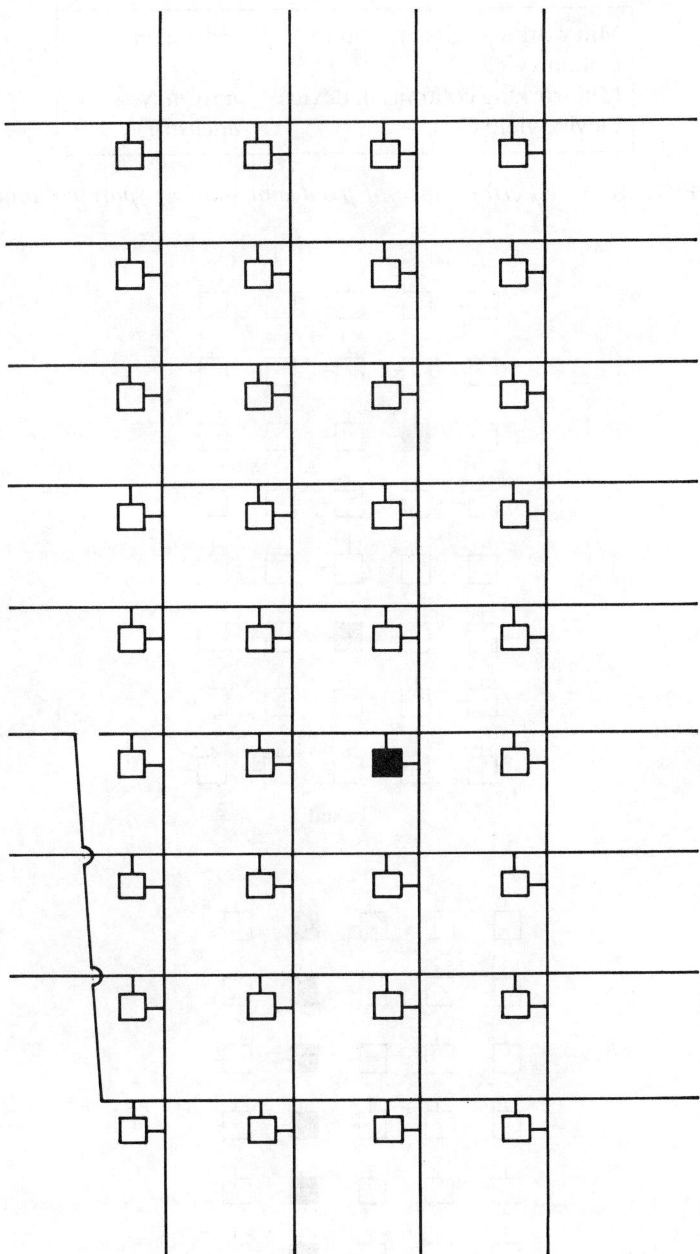

FIGURE 5.18 *Fixed aim standby-spare row*

the rows (Figure 5.21). There are fixed aim applications, too, for which this is appropriate. For instance, Moore *et al.* (1986) use it to implement a systolic array.

The performance of a gracefully degradable array is calculated in Figure 5.22. In this, it is assumed that the degenerate case of one working column is acceptable as the worst case of a working device.

Min working cells in column:	m from m
Column yield:	y^m
Min working columns in device:	n from N
Device yield (Y'):	$atleast(n,N,y^m)$

FIGURE 5.19 *Performance of fixed aim standby-spare column*

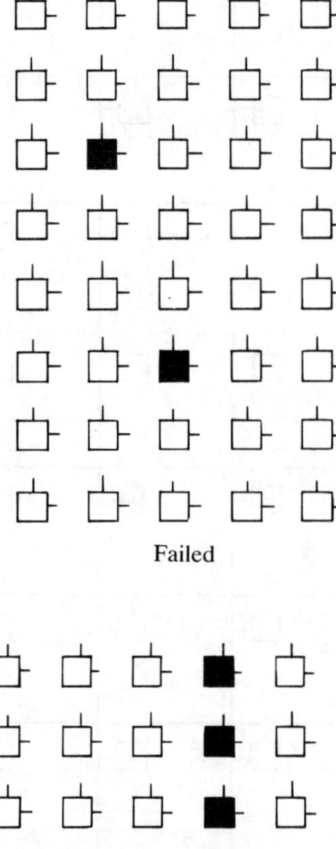

FIGURE 5.20 *Examples of best-case failure and worst-case success*

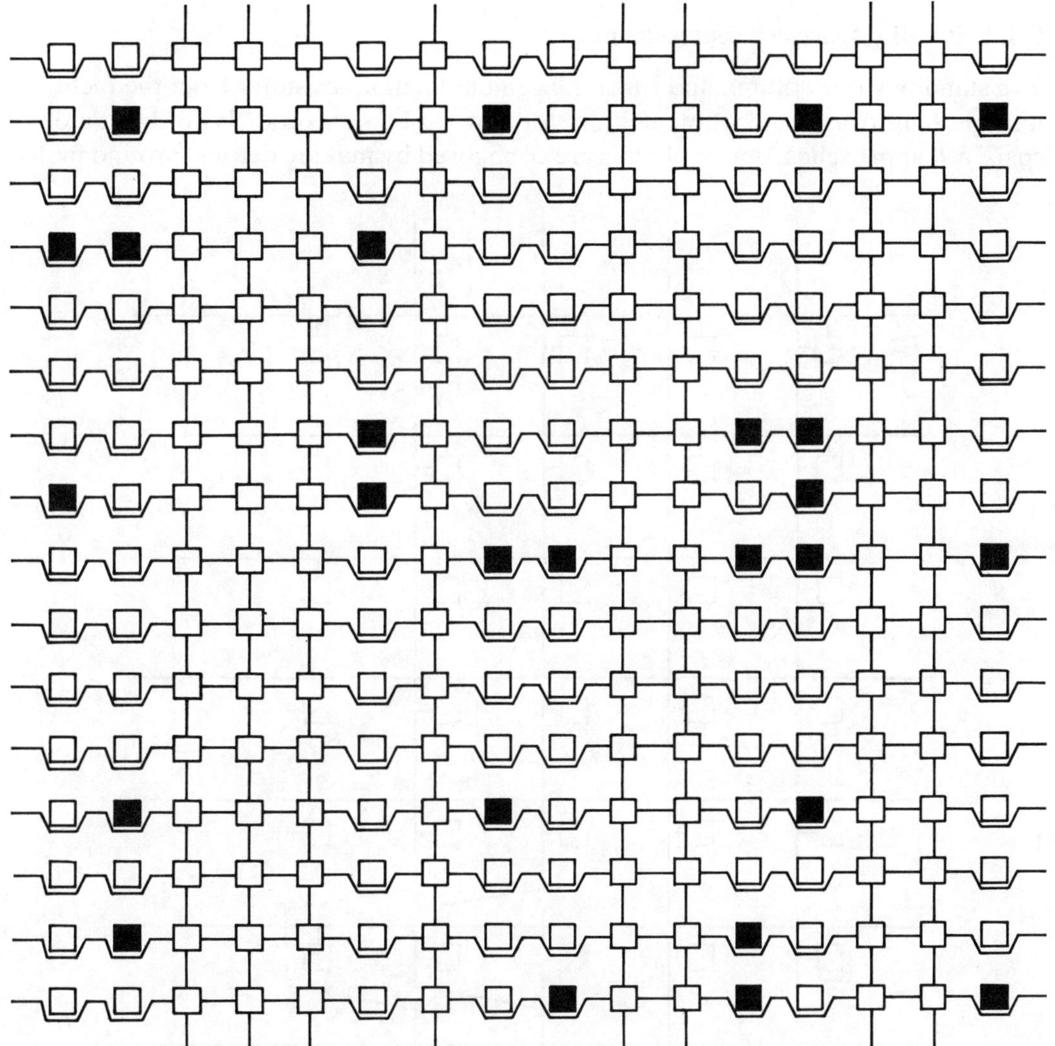

FIGURE 5.21 *Gracefully degradable standby-spare column*

Column yield:	y^M
Device yield (Y'):	$1-(1-y^M)^N$
Number of working columns:	My^M
Number of utilised cells:	MNy^M
Number of working cells:	MNy
Cell harvest (h):	y^{M-1}

FIGURE 5.22 *Performance of gracefully degradable standby-spare column*

5.4.2 Standby-spare cell replacement

The standby-spare column and row replacement techniques suffer from the fact that a single fault causes the whole column, or row, to be sacrificed. With the standby-spare cell approaches, good columns are configured by making detours around faulty

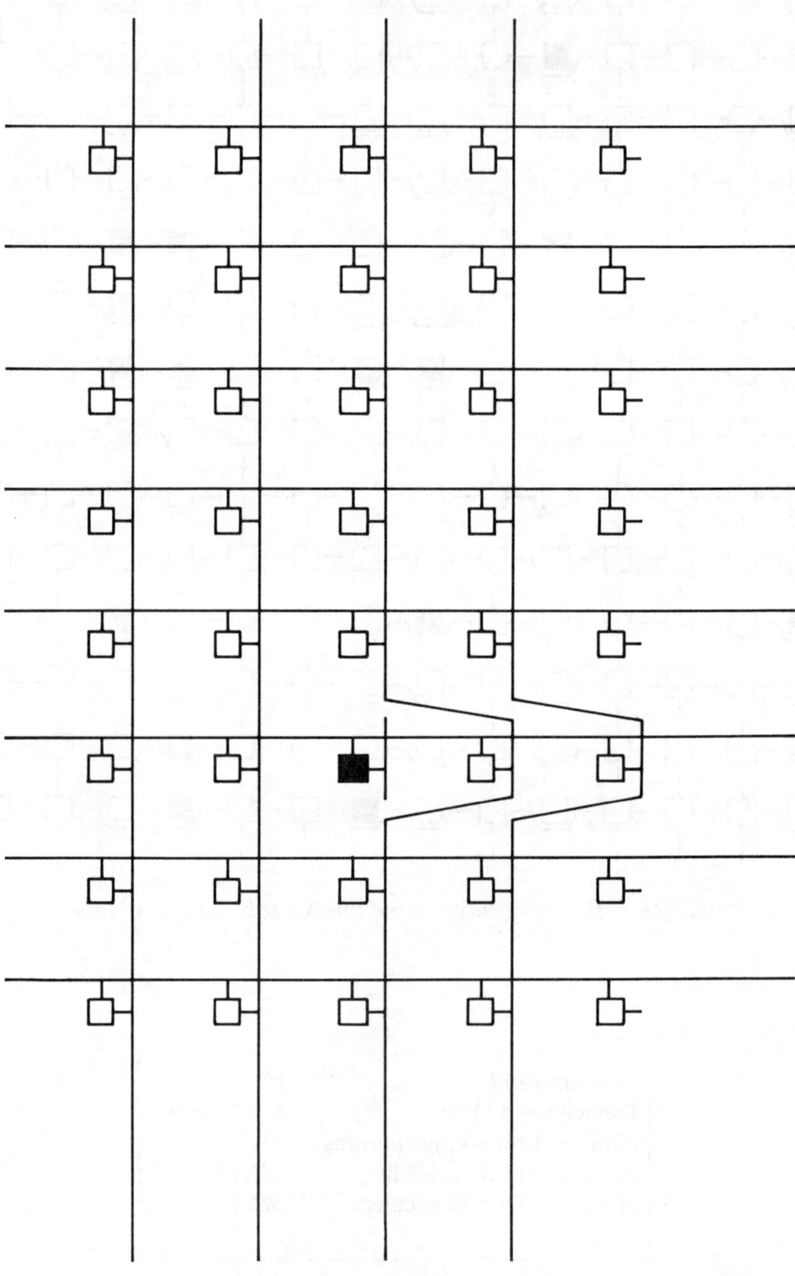

FIGURE 5.23 *Fixed aim column-orientated standby-spare cell*

cells. It is possible to imagine a system which upon discovering a faulty cell makes links to a cell in the spare column. It is more usual, though, for the system to use a similar nearest-neighbour shuffling approach to the one which was adopted for the standby-spare column approach. When a faulty cell is found, it is replaced by the neighbouring cell in the next column. Subsequent columns then need to supply cells as replacements for the ones which have been commandeered by previous columns. This is depicted in Figure 5.23.

The advantage of this method lies in the fact that one spare column is enough to tolerate many faulty cells, so long as there are never more than one of them in the same row. Therefore, this approach is more tolerant of decreasing cell yields than is standby-spare column. This again follows from the fine granularity of the cell-orientated approaches, with the consequent disadvantage that the effects on δa and δA might modify its eventual attractiveness. The row-orientated version of this is used, though, by Evans *et al.* (1986).

Again, it is possible to add more than one spare column to improve the performance. However, this solution is not quite as straightforward as it might at first appear. If only nearest neighbour detours are allowed there are problems which are caused by *ramping in* and *ramping out* in the routing algorithm. In Figure 5.24, the detour begins one row earlier than would otherwise have been expected, and finishes one row later.

Alternatively, nearest-neighbour interconnection can be abandoned, and methods can be used such as the one which Leighton and Leiserson (1986) attribute to Greene. In this, each row is interspersed with routing channels (Figure 5.25).

A problem analogous to that of ramping in and out occurs when the number of channels is less than the width of the worst-case, contiguous group of faulty cells which is expected. Leighton and Leiserson describe how the algorithm must be capable of discarding columns which cannot be connected through a lack of space on the interrow channels.

The performance for column-orientated standby-spare cell is calculated in Figure 5.26, assuming that ramp-in and ramp-out is not a problem. The technique might fail if there are $N-n+1$ faulty cells (Figure 5.27); this assumes the worst case, where all the faults occur in the same rows. The maximum number of faulty cells tolerated is $mN-mn$, so long as there are only $N-n$ faulty cells in each row.

For graceful degradation, bypass connections are needed in the other dimension. Figure 5.28 displays a gracefully degradable system using column-orientated standby-spare cell with row-orientated bypassing.

The performance of the gracefully degradable column-orientated standby-spare cell approach is derived in Figure 5.29. The number of working columns is dictated by the number of faults in the worst-affected row. Consequently, it is not sufficient to compute the mean number of working cells per row, but needs also the minimum number per row. For this analysis, the minimum number is taken to be three standard deviations below the mean value. The standard deviation of circuit yield could have been taken into account when calculating the performance of the standby-spare column approach too, but since the circuits are much larger there, consisting of

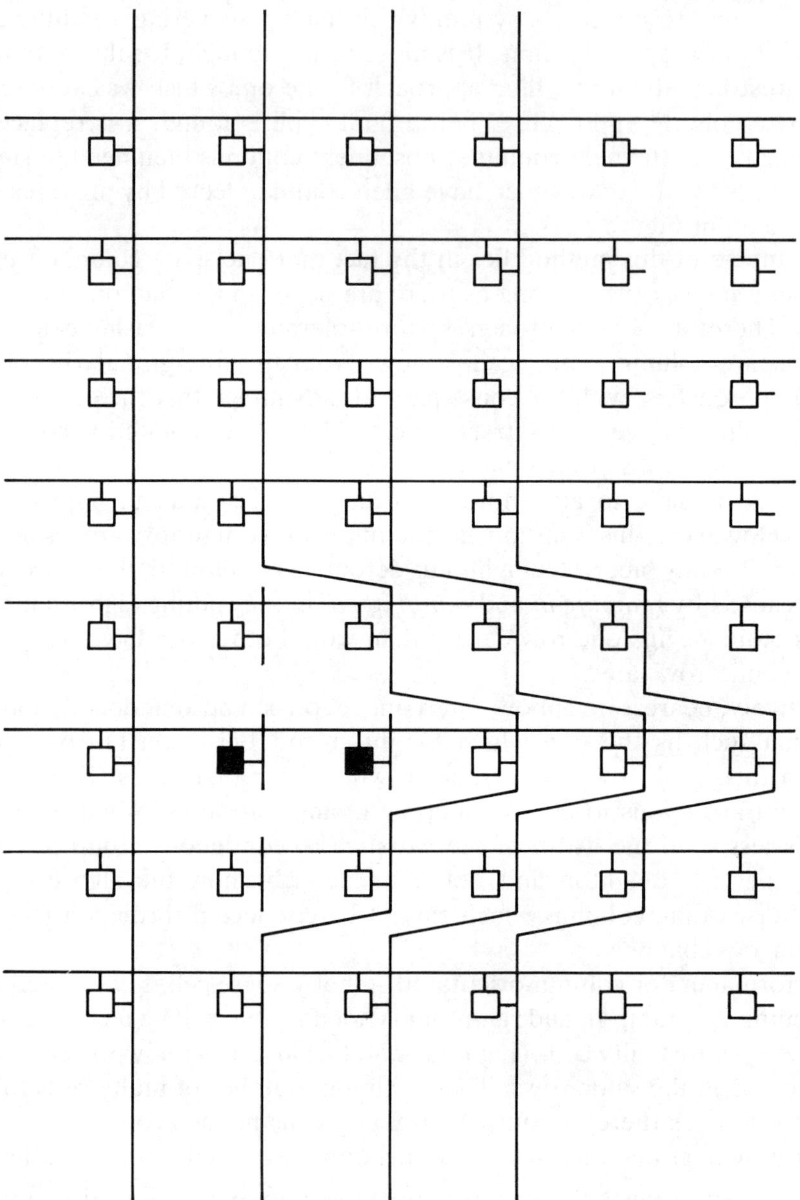

FIGURE 5.24 *Fixed aim standby-spare cell, with two columns of spare cells*

whole columns of M cells, the expected standard deviation will be substantially smaller.

5.4.3 Standby-spare hybrids

One of the shortcomings of the standby-spare approaches is that a fault/failure in one of the major buses will cause the whole device to fail. Straight, via-less metal

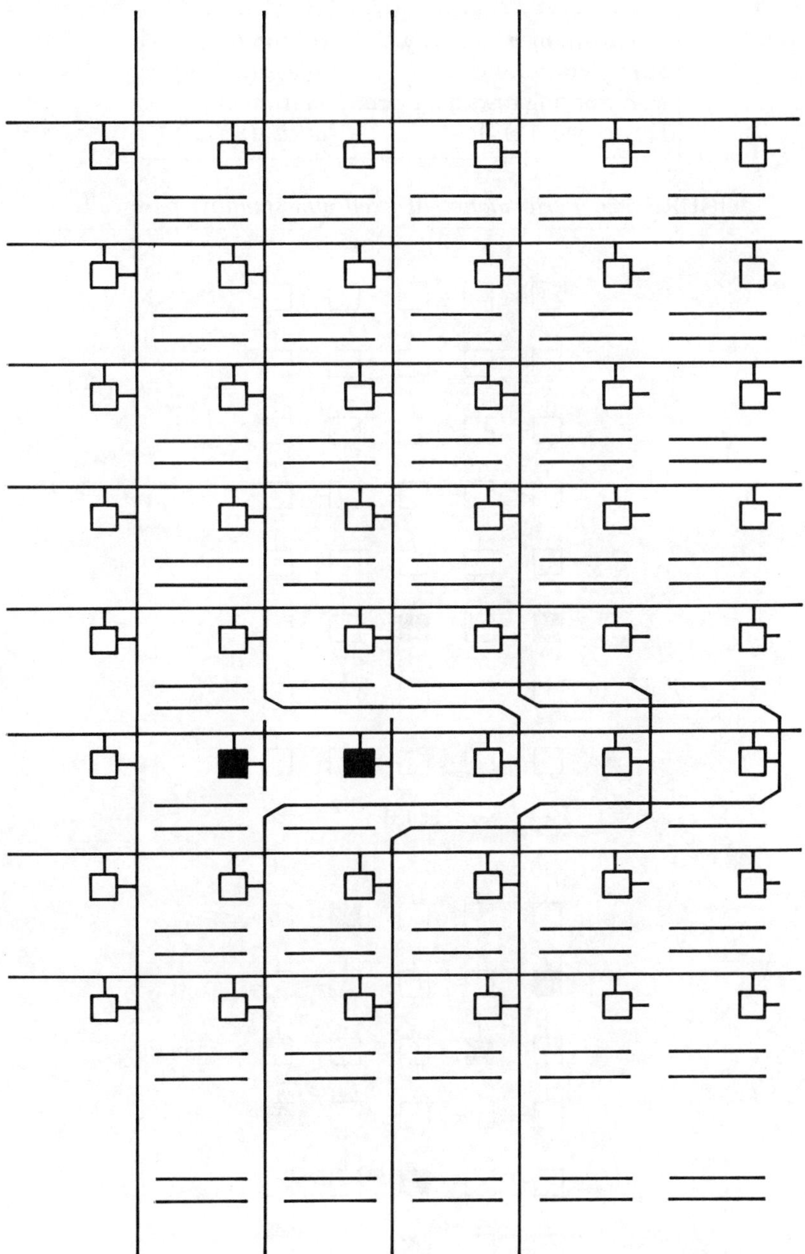

FIGURE 5.25 *Fixed aim standby-spare cell, with two columns of spare cells*

tracks yield extremely well. Therefore, the standby-spare and bypass approaches are generally quite reasonable options. However, if there are likely to be problems in passing buses over potentially faulty cells, combinations of column- and row-orientated approaches can be used to ensure that cells are used only if they are

Min working cells in row:	n from N
Row yield:	$atleast(n,N,y)$
Min working rows in device:	m from m
Device yield (Y'):	$atleast(n,N,y)^m$

FIGURE 5.26 *Performance of fixed aim standby-spare cell*

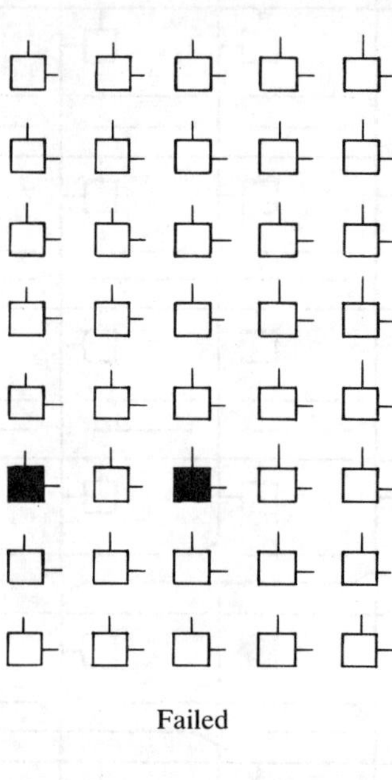

Failed

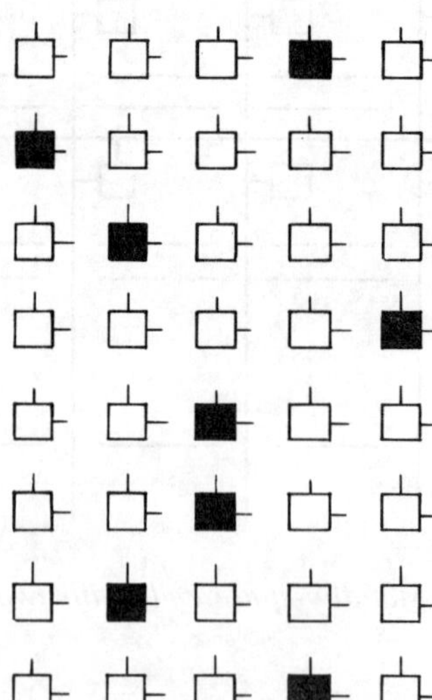

Successful

FIGURE 5.27 *Examples of best-case failure and worst-case success*

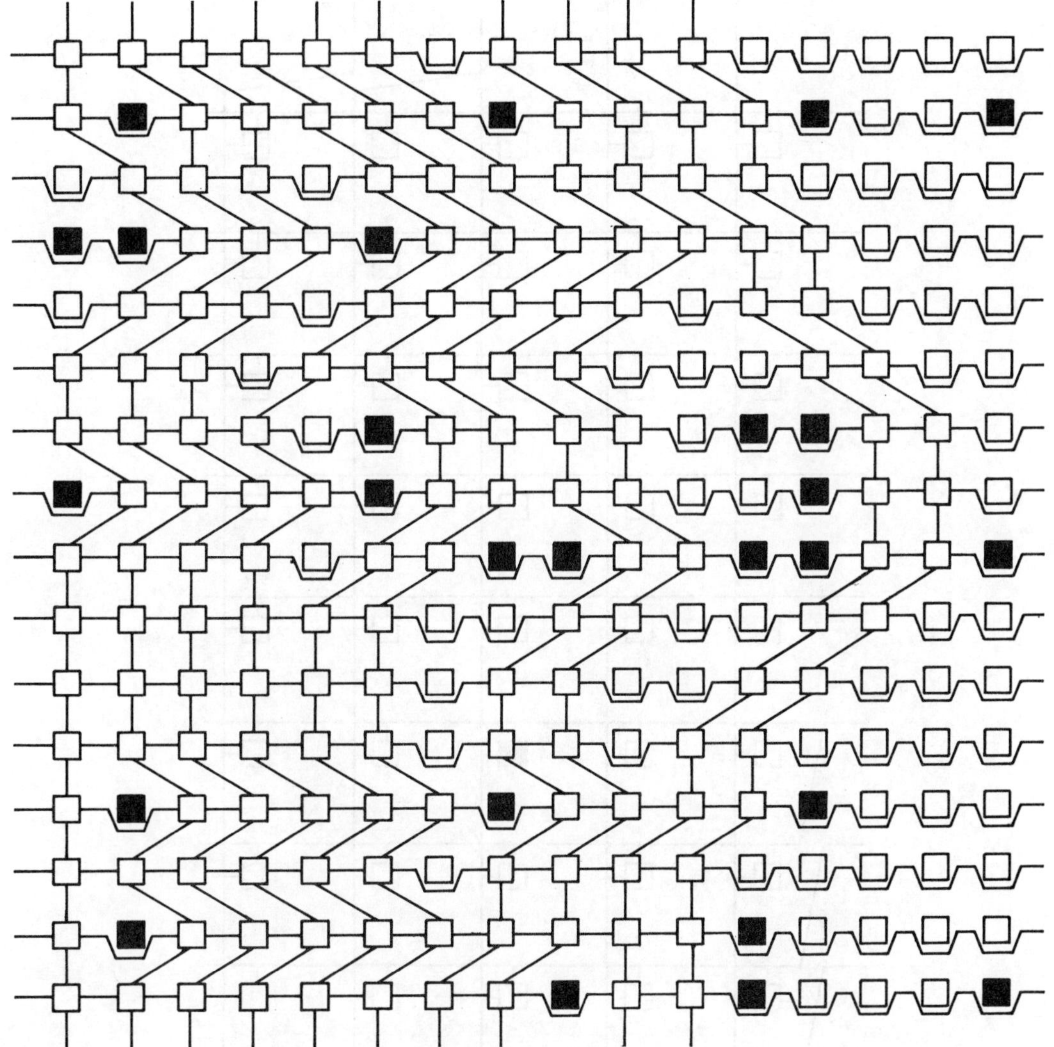

FIGURE 5.28 *Gracefully degradable column-orientated standby-spare cell*

Device yield (Y'):	$(1-(1-y)^N)^M$
Number of working columns:	$Ny - 3\sigma$
Number of utilised cells:	$M(Ny - 3\sigma)$
Number of working cells:	MNy
Cell harvest (h):	$1 - \dfrac{3\sigma}{Ny}$

FIGURE 5.29 *Performance of gracefully degradable standby-spare cell*

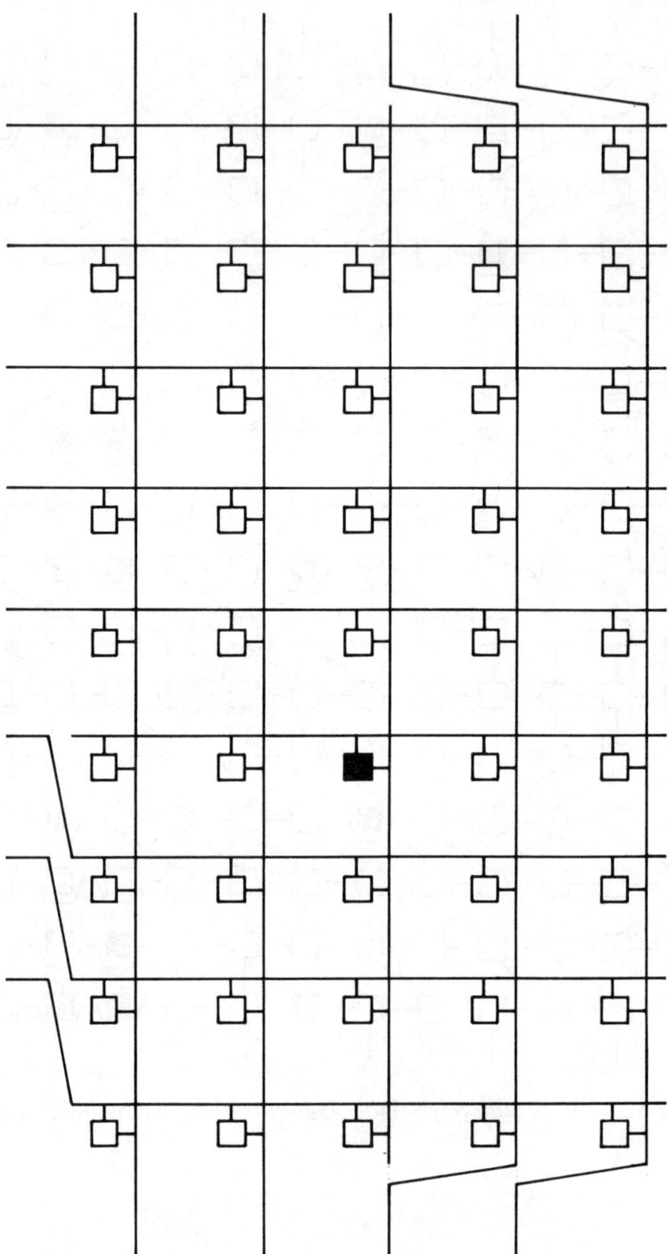

FIGURE 5.30 *Fixed aim standby-spare column and row*

in good columns *and* good rows. For example, Figure 5.30 depicts the use of the standby-spare column and row approach.

The other hybrid combinations, which have the same advantages of avoiding faulty regions completely, are 'column-orientated standby-spare cell and standby-spare row', 'standby-spare column and row-orientated standby-spare cell' and

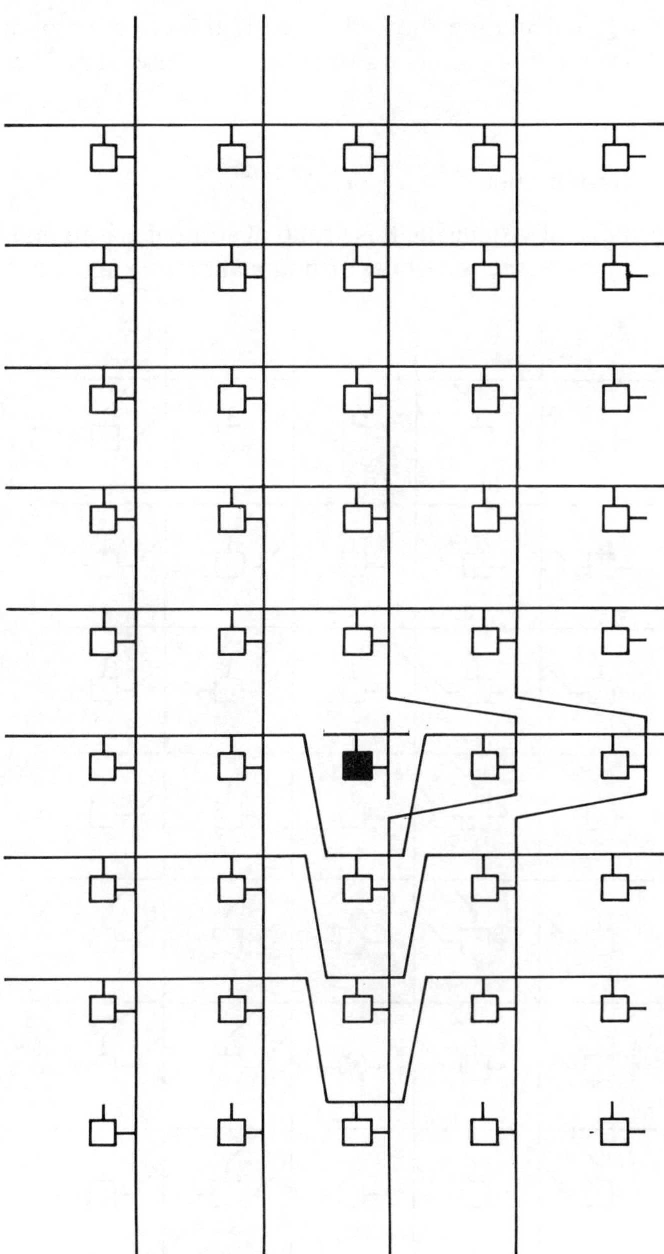

FIGURE 5.31 *Fixed aim column- and row-orientated standby-spare cell*

'column- and row-orientated standby-spare cell'. With the last of these, problems exist when two cells are neighbours in the same logical row *and* are neighbours in the same logical column (Evans *et al*. 1986). In Figure 5.31, which requires 32 cells to act as an 8 × 4 array, 33 cells are actually employed. The reason is that two of the cells act in tandem, storing the same data at all times, and therefore act as if they were one cell. When calculating the cell harvest, the effective number of utilised cells remains 32 since it is completely transparent to the user that 33 cells are actually employed.

5.4.4 Rotary switch connection

The best way, perhaps, of visualising this group of strategies is to imagine a two-pole switch placed at every intersection of the orthogonal buses. Figure 5.32, for instance,

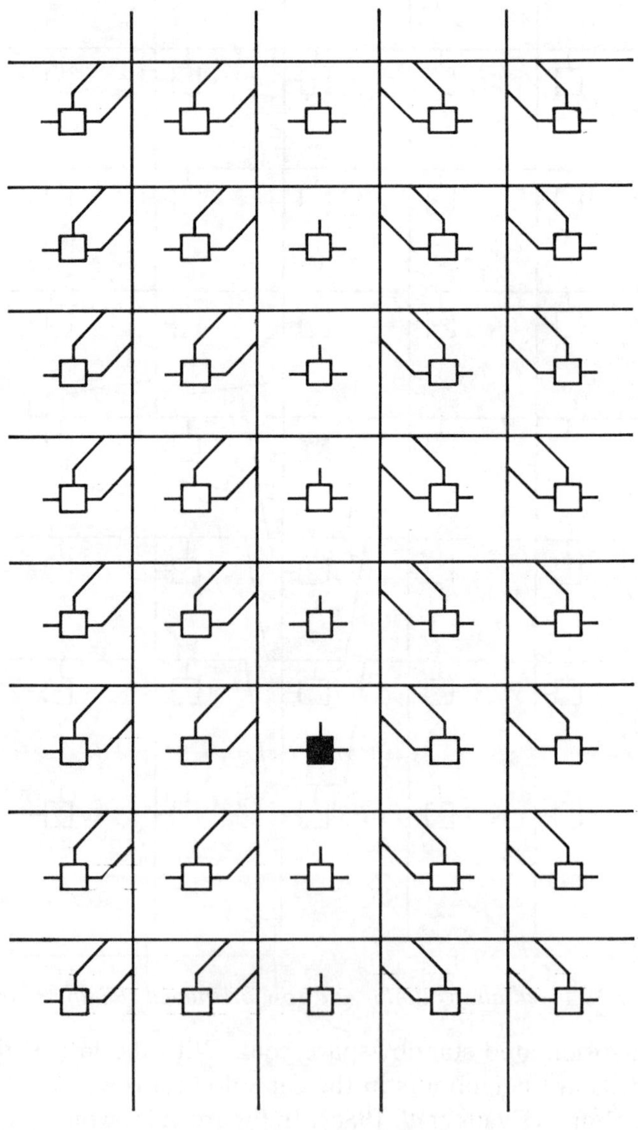

FIGURE 5.32 *Fixed aim column-orientated ganged rotary switch connection*

depicts 32 two-pole, two-way switches, each of which can be set in its SW or SE position. For the first strategy, the switches are ganged in their columns.

In practice, the switches can be realised using pairs of complementary transistors, each driven by common control lines. The technique has the same performance as standby-spare column, and the former is therefore one means of implementing the latter. This only holds for one spare column though, that is when $N=n+1$. Similarly, the row-orientated ganged rotary switch connection and standby-spare row connection strategies are only comparable when $M=m+1$.

For the unganged version, the rotors have the same swing (Figure 5.33) as they

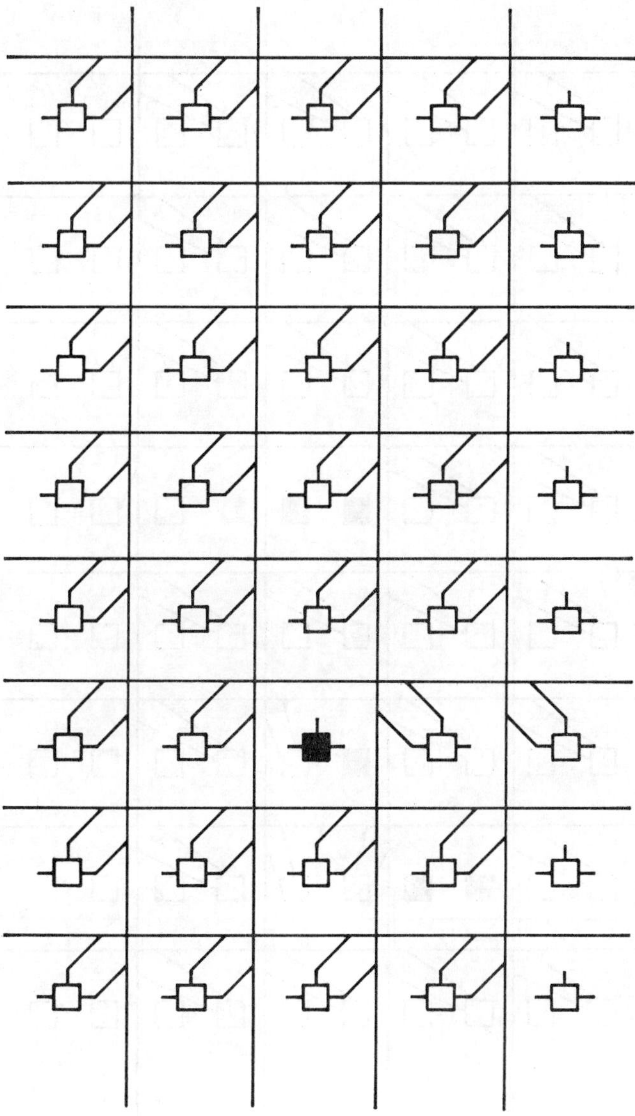

FIGURE 5.33 *Fixed aim unganged column-orientated rotary switch connection*

did in Figure 5.32, but they are free to move independently of each other. When $N=n+1$, this is a possible implementation of the column-orientated standby-spare cell strategy. Similarly, the row-orientated equivalents can be compared when $M=m+1$.

Figure 5.34 shows another variant. By providing an extra column, as in Figure 5.33, and then replicating each one, the device yield can be improved at the expense of the cell harvest. The switches are two-pole, four-way and hence more complicated. Again, this will be reflected in the values of δa and δA and so does not appear in the analysis here.

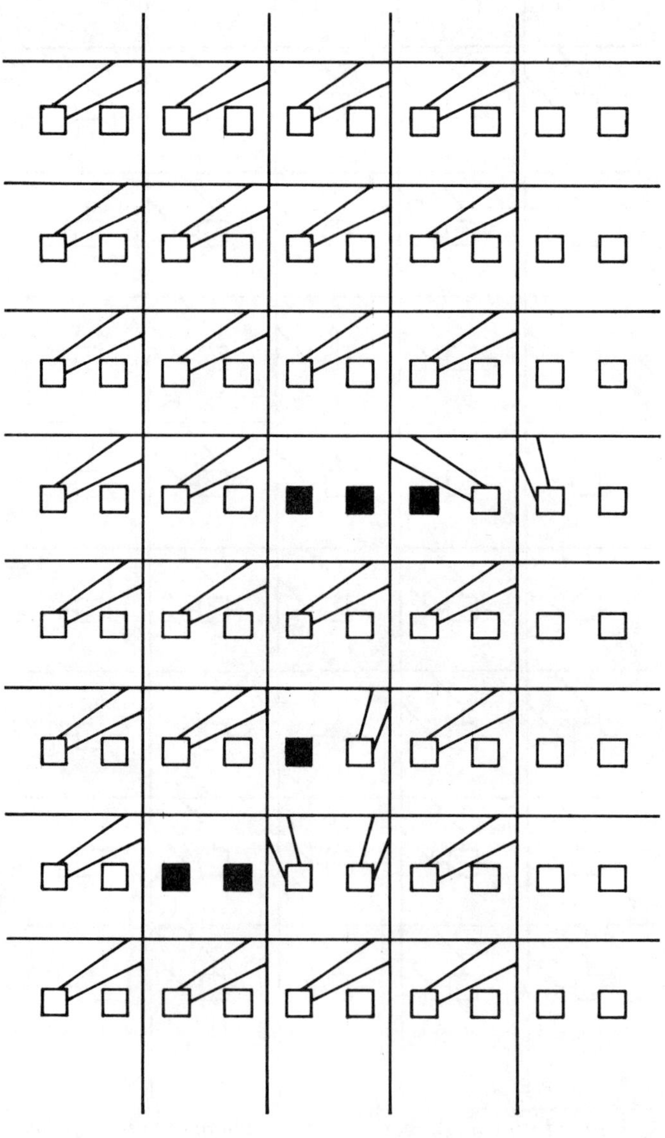

FIGURE 5.34 *Four-way column-orientated unganged rotary switch connection*

The four-way switches are also used in Figure 5.35, but are given a full circle of swing (Jesshope and Bentley 1986b), for example scanning in the clockwise direction of NW, NE, SE, SW. When faulty cells are encountered the spare cell from the same row is tried first, but when the cell yield is lower, then cells can be taken from the adjacent row instead. The technique has a remarkable ability to recover from the effects of relatively heavy clusters of faults. Despite the heavy clusters which are depicted in Figure 5.35, the routing is back to normal by the time it reaches the bottom.

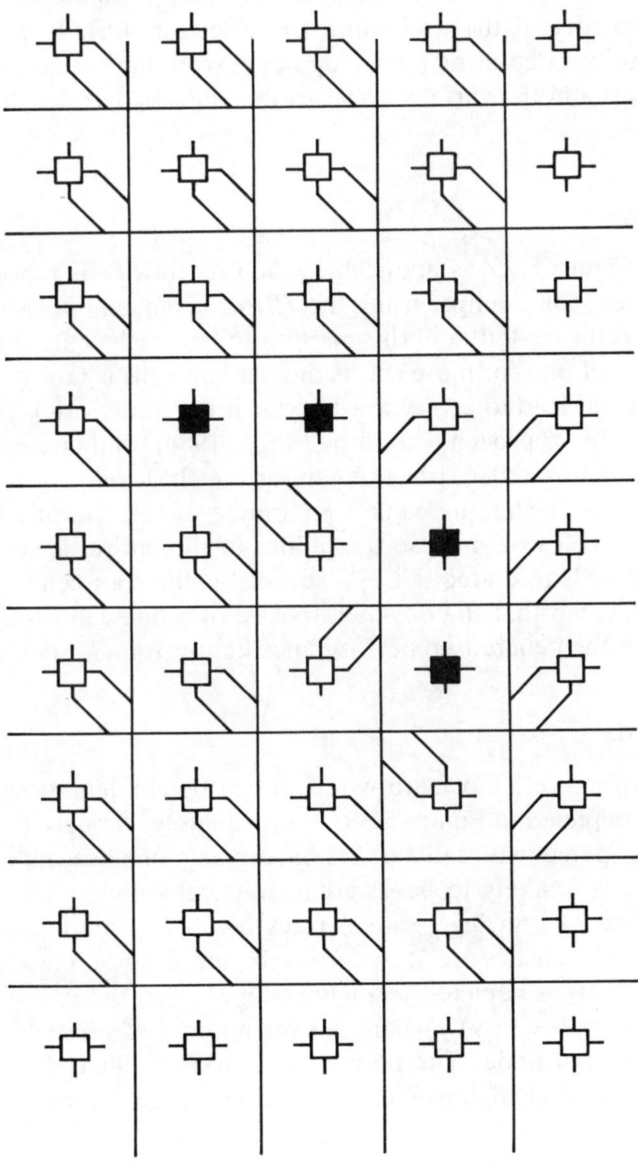

FIGURE 5.35 *Fixed aim row- and column-orientated rotary (unganged)*

In each of the techniques which have been described so far, it is often important to specify the order in which the circuits are tested. It has been assumed, in Figure 5.35, that rows are tested in a top-to-bottom order, in a left-to-right raster scan.

5.5 TREE-SHAPED FINAL DEVICE

Many multiprocessor architectures adopt a tree-shaped topology, so attempting to harness the properties of the evaluation tree (Section 4.6). In principle, memory too could be implemented using a tree topology, with the storage elements, the flip-flops, at the leaves and the various stages of the address decoder dispersed amongst the branch nodes.

5.5.1 Tree cutting

This approach (Figure 5.36) is applicable when the device is fabricated as a hard-wired physical tree, for example using the *H-tree* arrangement (Mead and Conway 1980). The root cell is tested, and this goes on to test each of its child cells. When a parent cell finds that one (or more) of its descendant cells is faulty, it simply ignores it (them). This could lead to a very low harvest if the faulty cell is found near to the root of the tree. This approach is used by Magó (1980), and an n-ary tree version is used by Jones and Lea (1986a) at their 'interbranch' level.

Pessimistically, the technique cannot guarantee to tolerate any faulty cells since a fault in the root cell would cause the failure of the entire device. The maximum number of faulty cells tolerated is $C-1$, so long as the root cell is the one which is working, and provided that the degenerate case of a one-cell system is acceptable. Figure 5.37 shows the generalised performance figures for a k-ary tree with L levels.

5.5.2 Tree growth

When the tree structure is not hard-wired, it can be configured from the available working cells as depicted in Figure 5.38. Unfortunately, though, the tree which this generates is very sparse, with most nodes having only one descendant. Consequently, the technique is unlikely to be of great practical value.

Another method of growing (sparse) trees involves a modification to the Catt-spiral idea in which branches are grown from the spiral, once it has formed, from the blind-alley cells. This is depicted in Figure 5.39.

The device yield is $1-(1-y)^z$, where z is the number of sites which are capable of being used as the root node. The number of working cells is Cy, and the number of utilised cells can be as high as Cy, except when there is a complete ring of duds fencing off areas of working cells, as depicted in Figure 5.41. The circuit harvest under this strategy can be very high, and is likely to be unity even for quite moderate cell yields, almost completely independent of y.

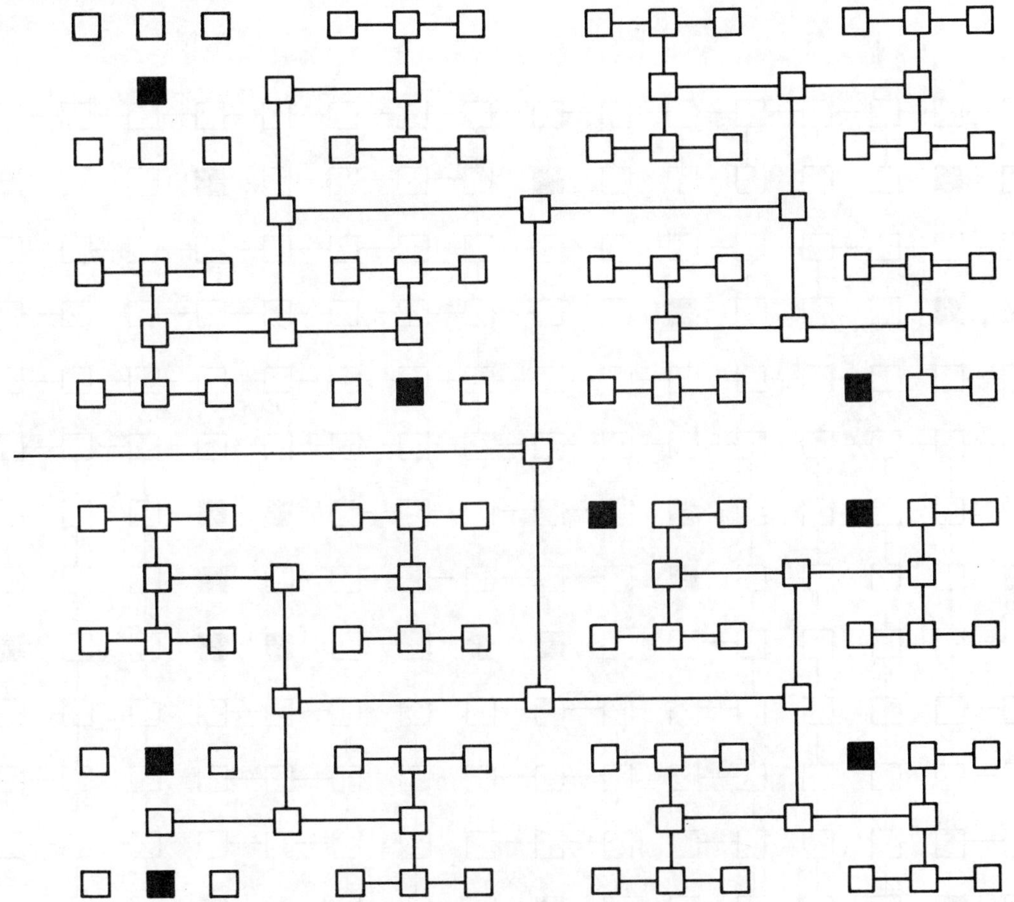

FIGURE 5.36 *Gracefully degradable tree cutting*

Device yield (Y'):	y
Levels within the tree:	L
Number of fabricated cells:	$C = \dfrac{k^L - 1}{k - 1}$
Number of utilised cells:	$y \cdot \dfrac{(ky)^L - 1}{(ky) - 1}$
Number of working cells:	Cy
Cell harvest (h):	$\dfrac{1}{C} \cdot \dfrac{(ky)^L - 1}{(ky) - 1}$

FIGURE 5.37 *Performance of gracefully degradable k-ary tree cutting*

Pessimistically, the techniques might fail in the presence of z faulty cells. The maximum number of faulty cells tolerated is $C-1$, so long as one of the root cells is the one working cell.

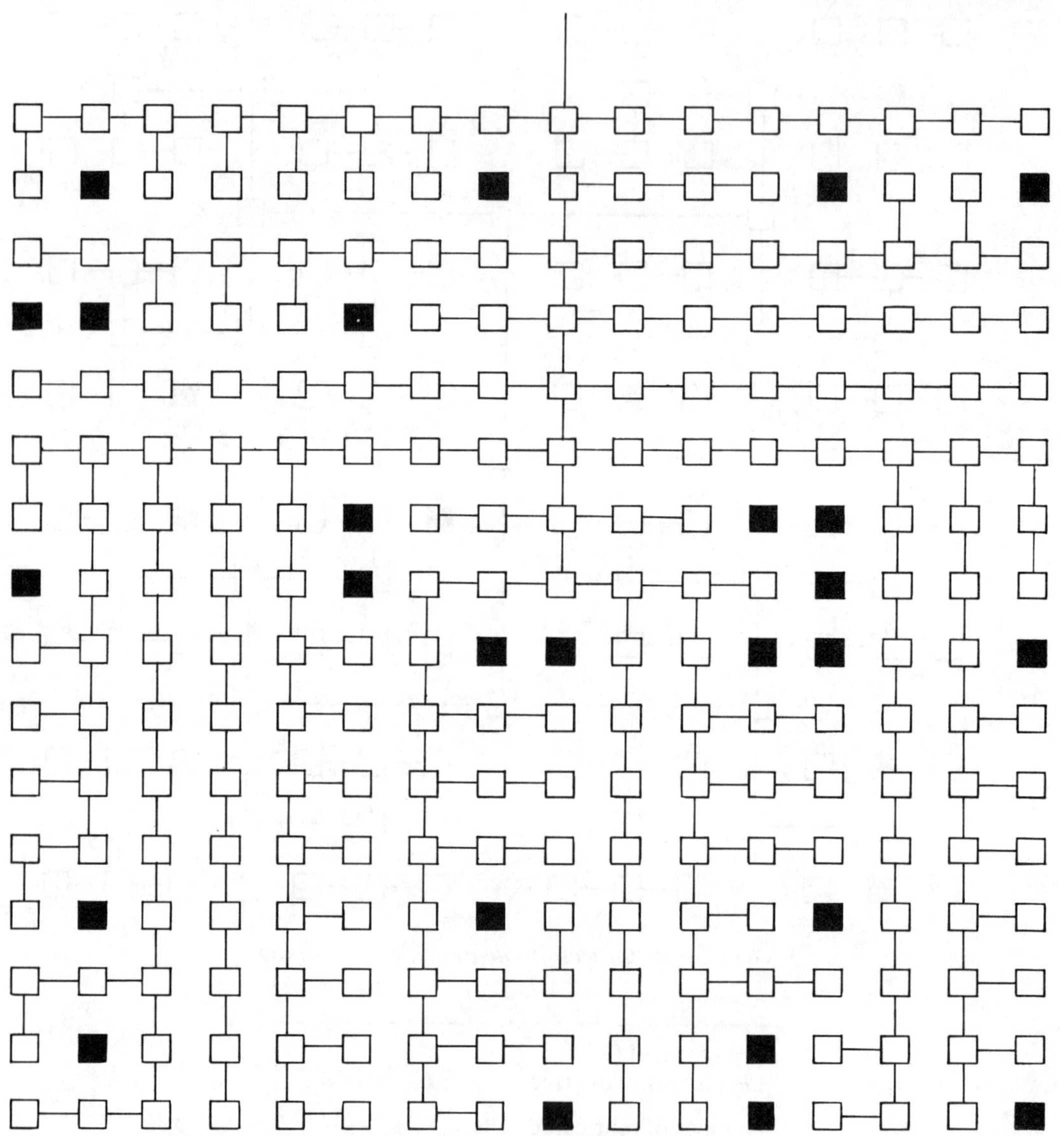

FIGURE 5.38 *Gracefully degradable tree growth*

5.6 PATH REDUNDANCY

When very highly connected topologies are used, data which are communicated from one processor to another have a large number of paths from which to choose. If one path is blocked by faulty processors, or is congested or is unavailable for some other reason, the next best route can be used instead. As the number of faulty paths is increased so the performance of the communications network falls, but in a graceful fashion.

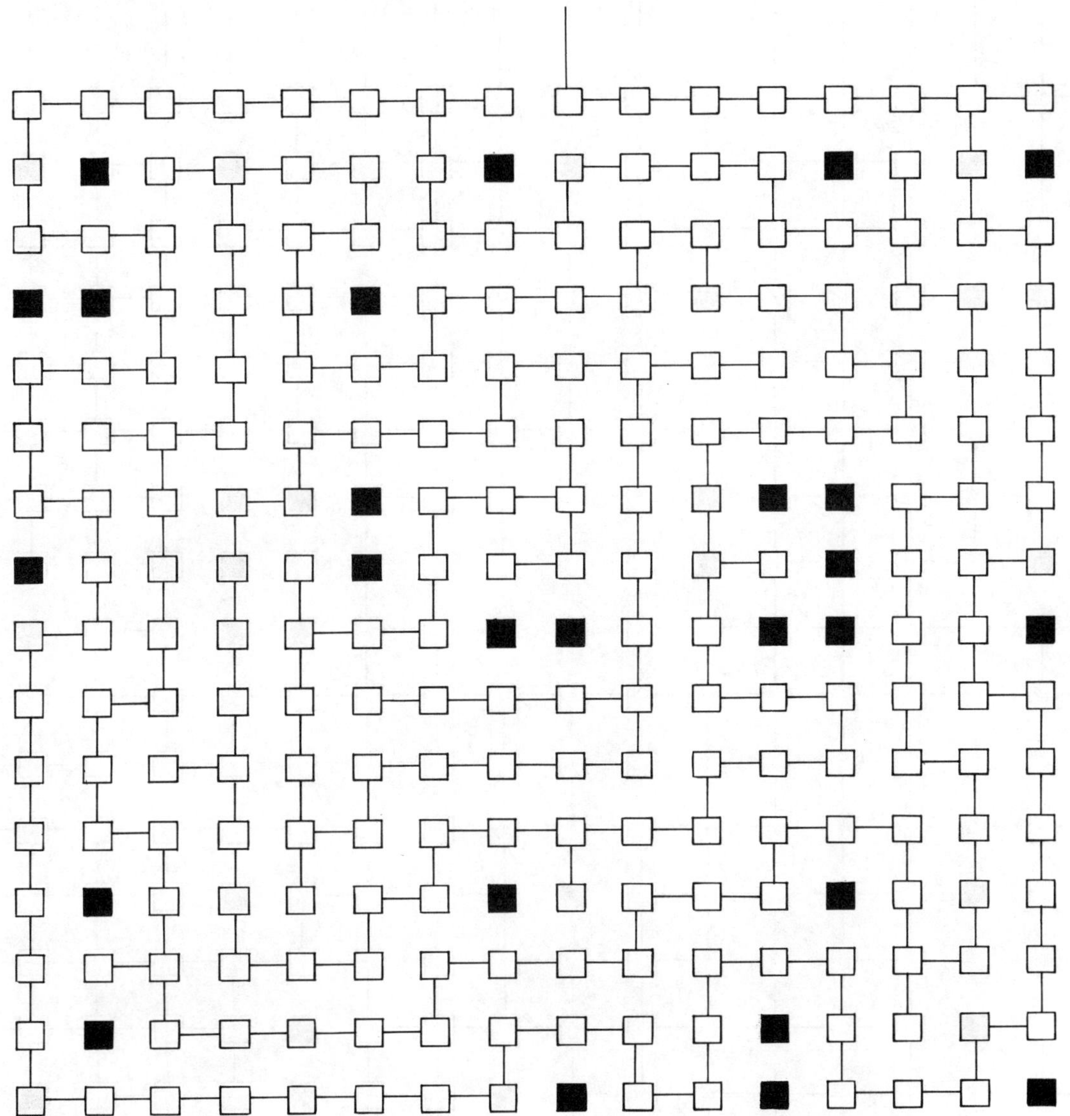

FIGURE 5.39 *Gracefully degradable inward-grown Catt spiral with spurs*

5.6.1 Perfect harvest

For consistency with the next section, the description of the (near) perfect harvest technique is reserved for Figure 5.42, using an eight-connected grid. However, for consistency with preceding sections, Figure 5.40 displays the technique as applied to a four-connected grid.

Simplistically, the device needs at least one of the cells round the circumference to be working, and to be connectable to the outside world. The device yield is therefore

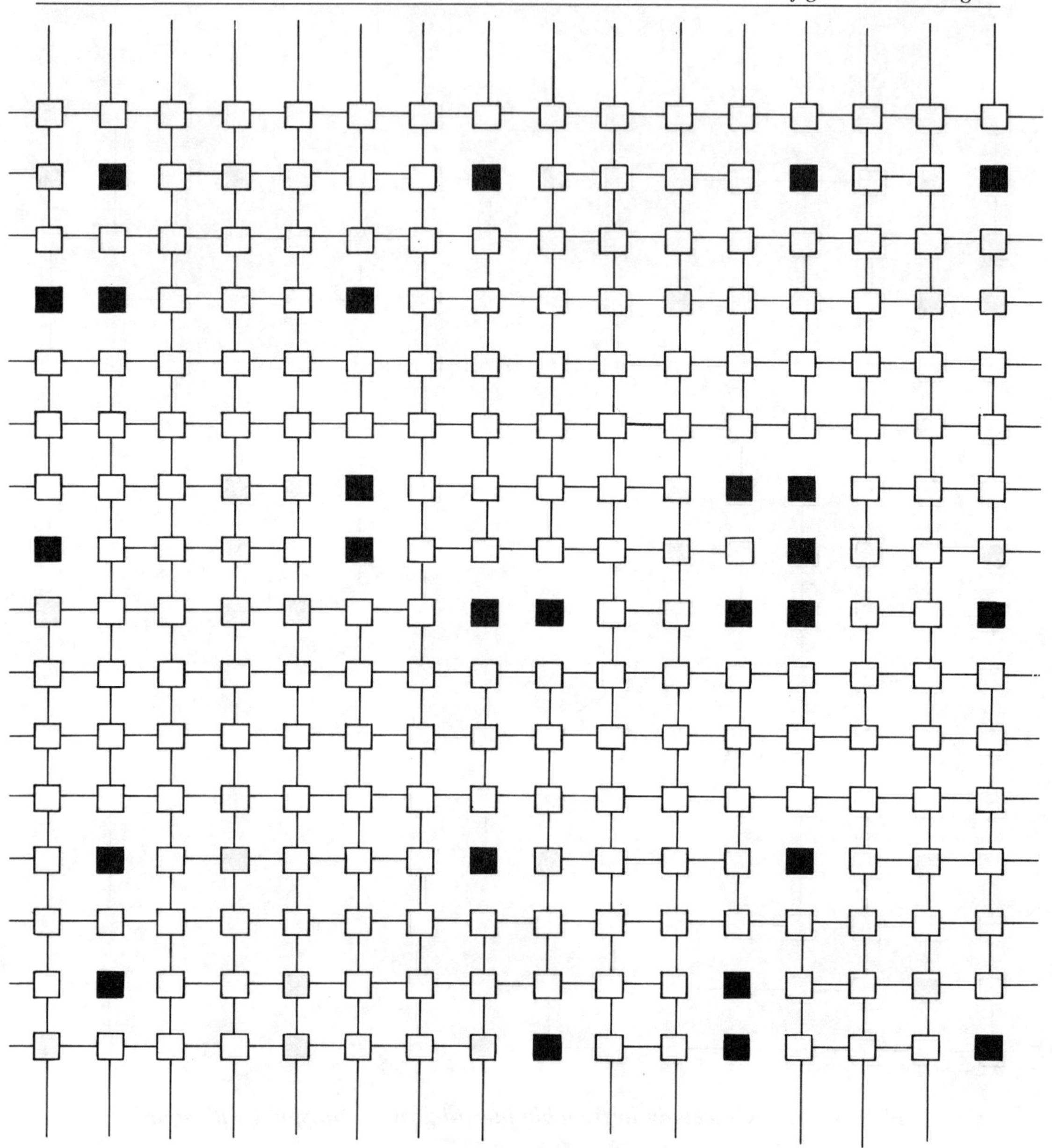

FIGURE 5.40 *Gracefully degradable perfect harvest*

$1-(1-y)^{(2(M+N)-4)}$. For nearest-neighbour interconnection, assuming that there are no boxed-off regions like the one depicted in Figure 5.41, the cell harvest tends to unity, and is almost completely independent of y.

The technique might fail in the presence of $2(M+N)-4$ faulty cells, assuming that

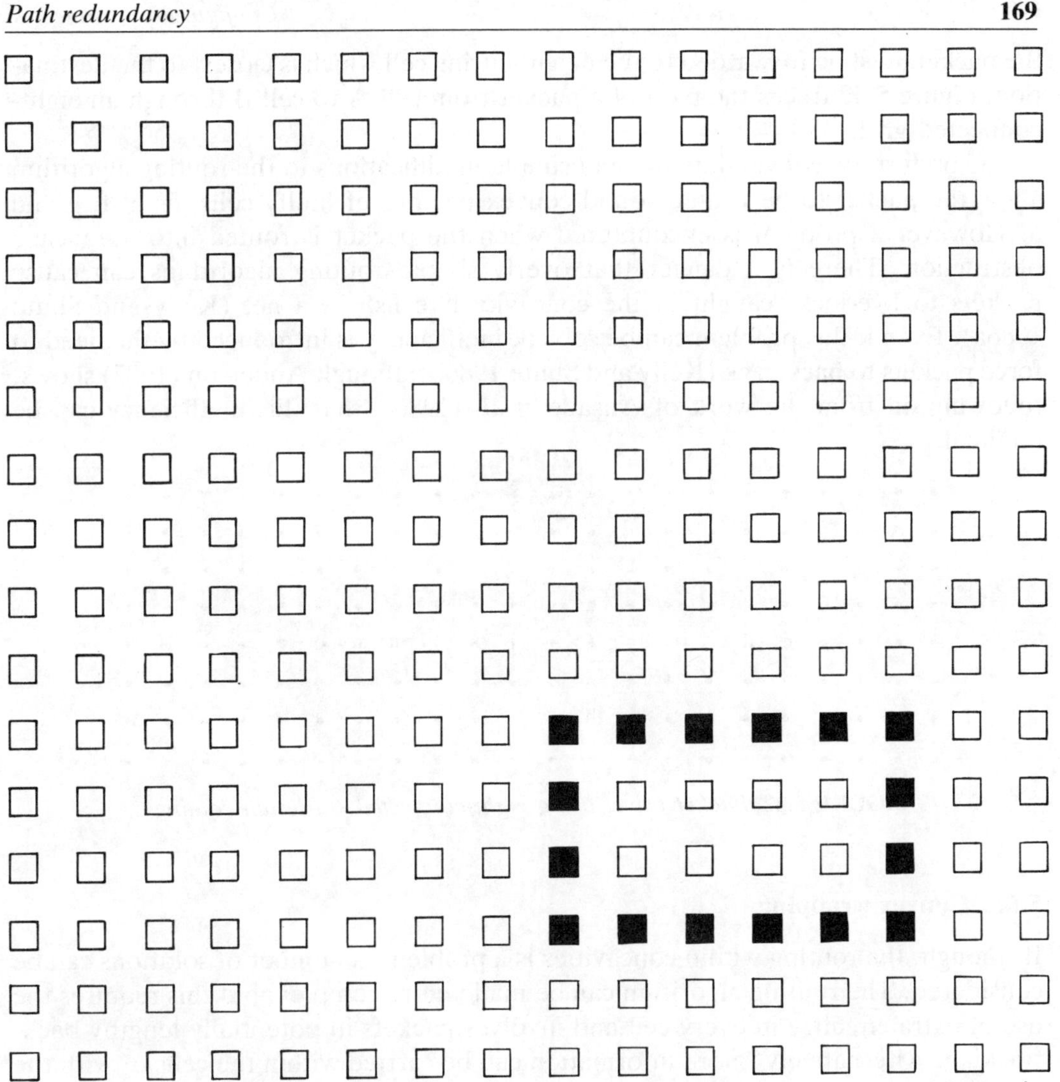

FIGURE 5.41 *Unharvestable cells surrounded by a hedge*

all of the faults occur at the edge of the device. The maximum number of faulty cells tolerated is $C-1$, so long as an edge cell is the one which is working.

A few words are perhaps necessary to describe, briefly, the sort of architecture which might be able to make use of this potentially attractive strategy. Consider the construction of a packet-based multiprocessor computer such as the one described by Anderson *et al.* (1987). There is a requirement to communicate packets between processors. The packets must carry a destination address to indicate the name of the cell to which they should be dispatched. Whenever a packet arrives in a cell, the cell first checks for its own address in the destination field. If the address does not match, the packet must be forwarded to the neighbouring cell which is closest to the destination. Figure 5.42 traces the path of a packet from cell A to cell B through an eight-connected grid.

The path starts conventionally, and simple modifications to the routing algorithm allow the packet to be routed round convex patches of faulty cells, as at f, g and h. However a problem is encountered when the packet is routed into a concave obstruction. There is a danger that overly simple routing algorithms can cause packets to live-lock, caught in the concavity like fish in a net (Kelly and Shute 1986a). Even if this problem can be solved, inefficiency is introduced by the need to force packets to backtrack (Kelly and Shute 1986b); though Anderson (1987) shows, following on from the work of Ansade *et al.* (1986), that this inefficiency can be minimal.

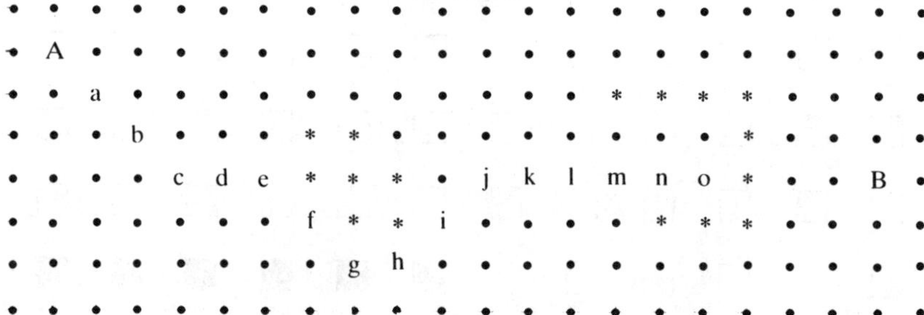

FIGURE 5.42 *Packet travel using eight-connected Cartesian routing*

5.6.2 Convex wrapping

If, though, the routing within concavities is a problem, a number of solutions can be considered. The routing algorithm can be made more complex, but this requires the use of extra circuitry in every cell and involves packets in potentially lengthy backtracking. Alternatively, more information can be carried within the cells or with the packets to log the history of any given packet (in order to avoid sending it more than once along the same path), or in the form of global maps of the working parts of the whole wafer, or local maps of sections of it. In each case, large amounts of extra circuitry are required and, in the case of information carried on the packets, extra time is required to transmit the massively long packets. All of these suggestions, though, have attempted to use all of the cells: they have tried to achieve a 100 per cent cell harvest, even though there is a less than 100 per cent cell yield. Experience with fault tolerant algorithms indicates, perhaps, that this is unreasonably greedy and that the sacrifice of working cells must be expected. This sacrifice, manifested as a reduced harvest, is used to buy a better layout: one which allows a simpler and faster routing algorithm to operate. Instead of travelling through the layout which is depicted in Figure 5.42, the packets actually find the one which is shown in Figure 5.43. The cells which are marked '+' are working ones which have turned themselves off.

The technique 'wraps' concave patterns of faulty cells inside a convex envelope

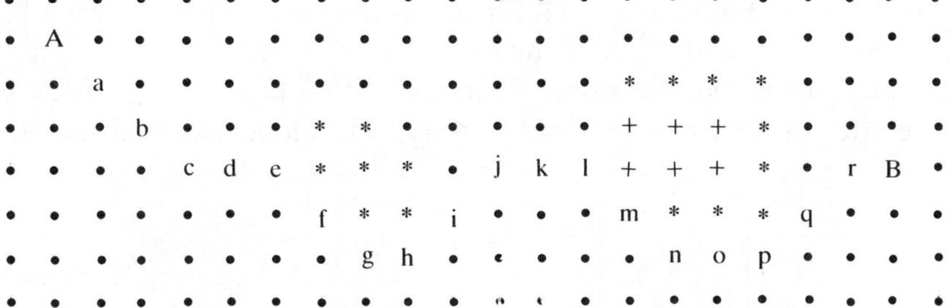

FIGURE 5.43 *Packet travel after convex wrapping*

by sacrificing the working ones which lie in the concavities. Thus nothing more complicated than a simple wall following routing algorithm is required since only convex regions of unusable cells are encountered.

5.6.3 Multidimension topologies

The hypercube, as described in Section 4.3.9, is a very highly connected network, there being $k2^{(k-1)}$ connections between the 2^k cells on a k-dimensional cube, that is an average of $k/2$ connections per cell. These connections are used primarily to minimise the worst-case communication time. However, the large number of interconnections can be useful if some of the routes are broken, or are congested. If the best route is not available for communication, there are plenty of alternative routes.

The Connection Machine (Hillis 1985) is an example of an application which uses the hypercube. Zapp (Sleep and Burton 1981) is an example which uses a butterfly network. The physical realisation of either topology, using WSI, is beset with problems, though, since the act of mapping multidimensional networks on to two-dimensional wafer surfaces involves conductor tracks crossing over each other on a grand scale.

5.7 *TIME REDUNDANCY*

To obtain an $m \times n$ arrangement of cells a completely different style of approach can be used, involving the fabrication precisely of an $m \times n$ rectangle of cells; then wherever there is a faulty cell a neighbouring cell oscillates between performing its own function and that of its faulty neighbour (Negrini and Stefanelli 1986). Understandably, there is a reduction in the throughput from the system. In effect, this is an adaption of the techniques of *time sharing*, or *time division multiplexing*.

The physical cell harvest is 100 per cent, but in Figure 5.44 $(mn)-2$ of the cells are working at only half capacity. This leads to a notion perhaps of temporal cell harvest: the ratio of the utilised capacity to that available. In general, this is $(mn)/(kmny)$, that is $1/(ky)$, where k is the number of tasks which are allocated to the most heavily burdened cell, and is 2 in Figure 5.44. Since k is the temporal replication factor, this technique is consistent with each of the other fixed aim strategies, in that $h=1/(ky)$. However, to its advantage, the value of the replication factor, the slow-down factor, is selectable after the device manufacture stage. Thus a perfect grid can work at full

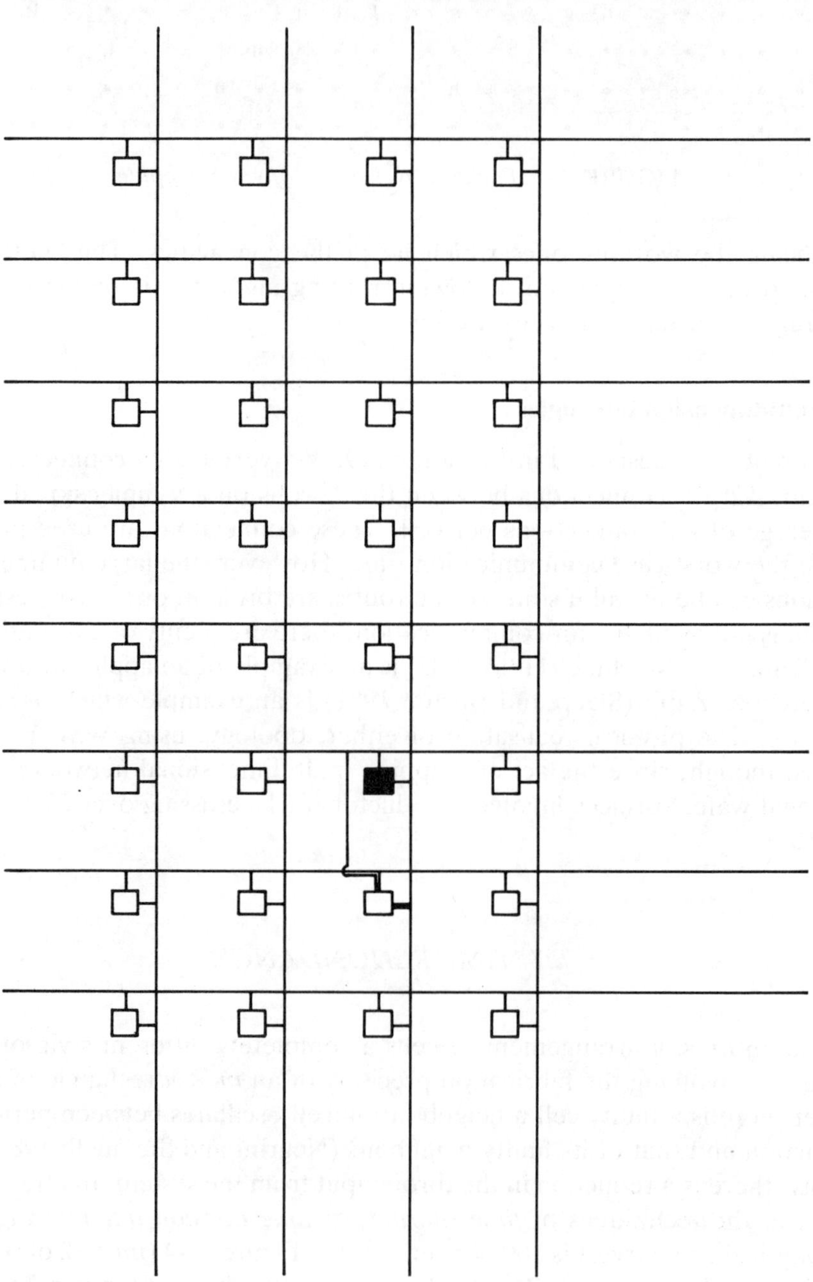

FIGURE 5.44 *Fixed aim column-orientated time redundancy*

speed, $k=1$, and only those with faults need be made to work at slower speeds.

Row- or column-orientated versions are both possible, with the work of faulty cells being taken over by a working neighbour in the same row or column respectively. One variation, for instance in the column-orientated version, involves restricting cells so that they can take over the work of the cell only in a given direction, for instance the cell to the north. Figure 5.45 depicts the best-case failure and worst-case success of such a system, assuming that the northernmost cells in each column are able to monitor for faults for their cylindrically mapped 'neighbours' at the southernmost end. Another variation is to allow cells to monitor for faults in any direction, but then some protocol must be established to resolve conflicts when several cells offer to take over the work of a single faulty cell.

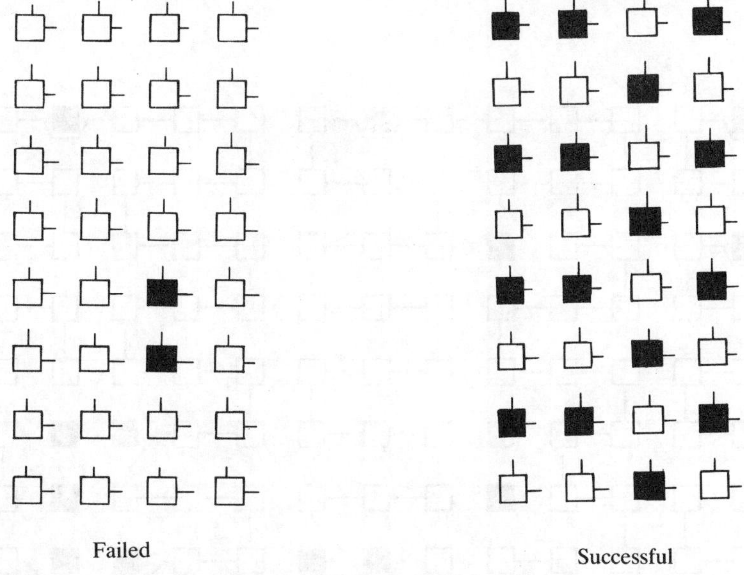

FIGURE 5.45 *Examples of best-case failure and worst-case success*

5.8 NON-NEAREST-NEIGHBOUR INTERCONNECTION

This chapter, with a few notable exceptions, has been preoccupied with NNI. The reasons for this preoccupation are the applicability to the local communications ideas which are involved in supporting declarative languages, and the undesirability of complicated long distance interconnections in microelectronics (Sutherland and Mead 1977). For other applications, where this consideration is no longer appropriate, connections other than to nearest neighbours can be considered. The possibilities are, of course, greater even than the incomplete list which is given above for NNI. However, some notable examples can be briefly mentioned here.

5.8.1 Partitioned bypass

Leighton and Leiserson (1986) suggest that when the cell yield is fairly low the expected hop lengths using the strategy of Figure 5.10 are non-optimal. By dividing the two-dimensional array into a number of subarrays, growing a bypassing chain of good cells in each and then interconnecting the chains, they calculate an expected hop length which is substantially better for relatively low cell yields, and perhaps only marginally worse when the cell yield is high. Thus the expected path-lengths are more uniform from one device to another, and hence easier to design, with timing in mind. They also indicate an optimum size for dividing the grid for one particular cell yield, $y=0.5$. For the purposes of the illustration in Figure 5.46, though, an arbitrary subgrid size is used.

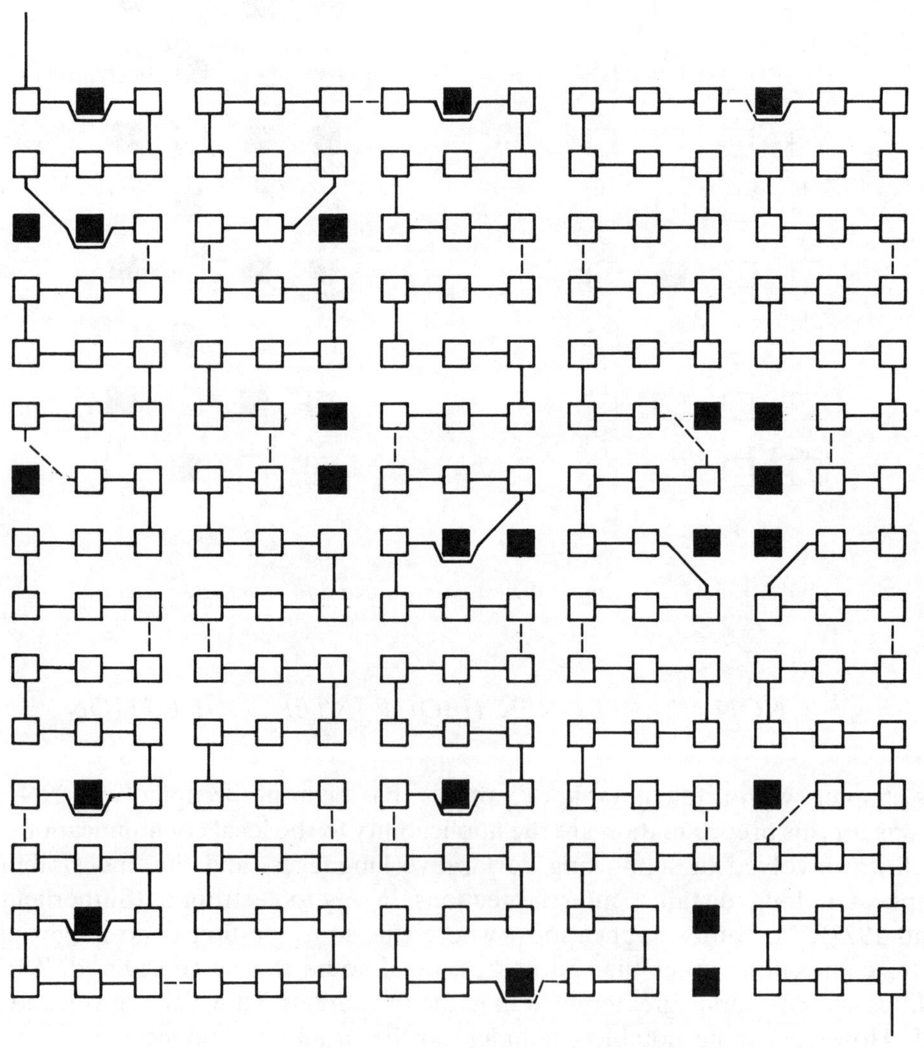

FIGURE 5.46 *Gracefully degradable partitioned bypass*

5.8.2 Corridor routing

Hedlund (1986) suggests a technique (one which has also been investigated by Chevalier and Saucier 1986), which allows for the configuration of arbitrary topologies on a regular mesh of cells and switching units. Figure 5.47 depicts an 8 × 8 array of cells embedded in a 17 × 17 four-connected switching matrix.

By sending initialising information to the switching nodes, paths can be configured in the mesh of Figure 5.47, for instance, to make the device behave as a linear network. Figure 5.48 depicts each of the connected routes shown by a solid line, and each of the disconnected routes omitted.

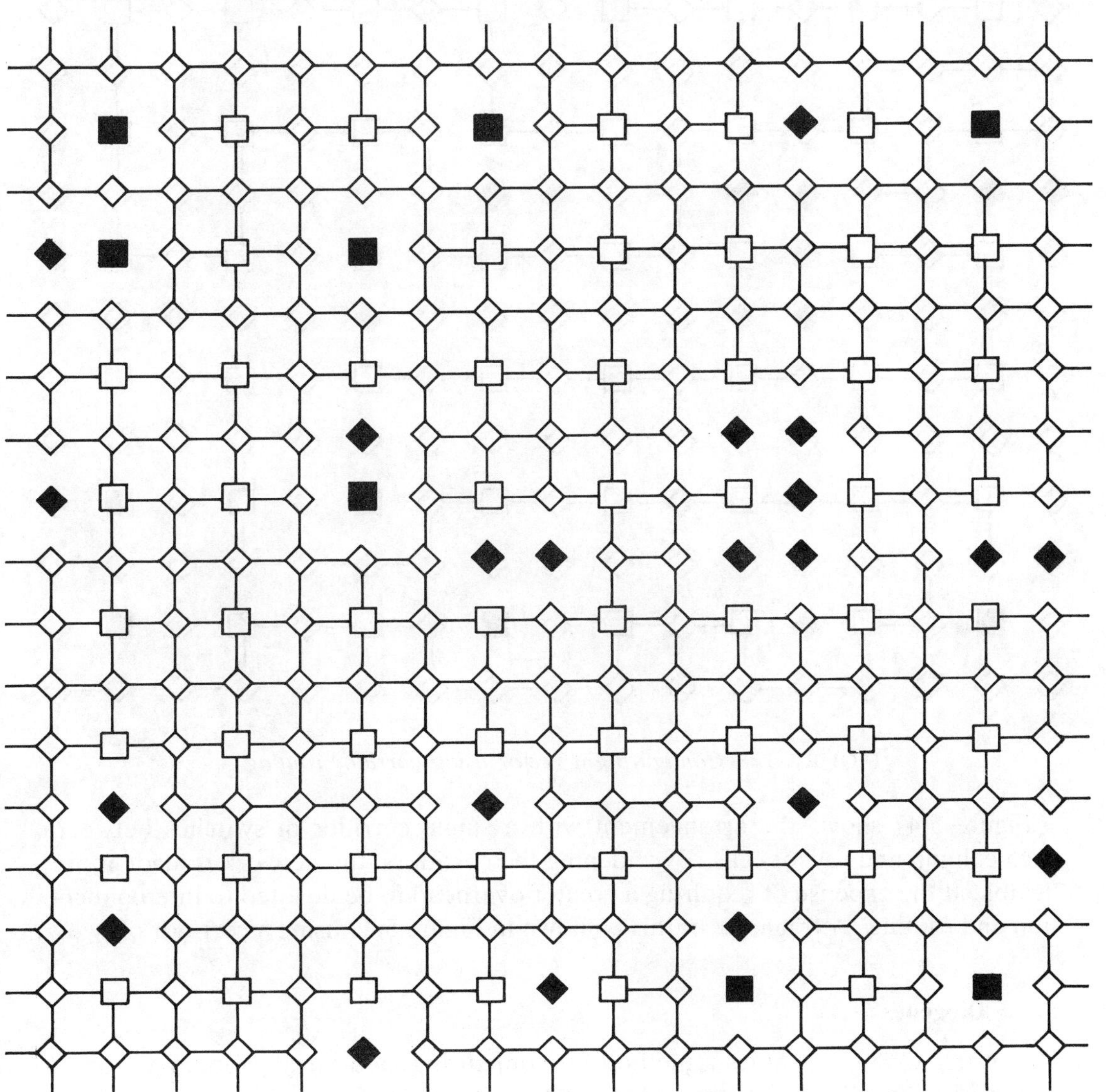

FIGURE 5.47 *Corridor routing*

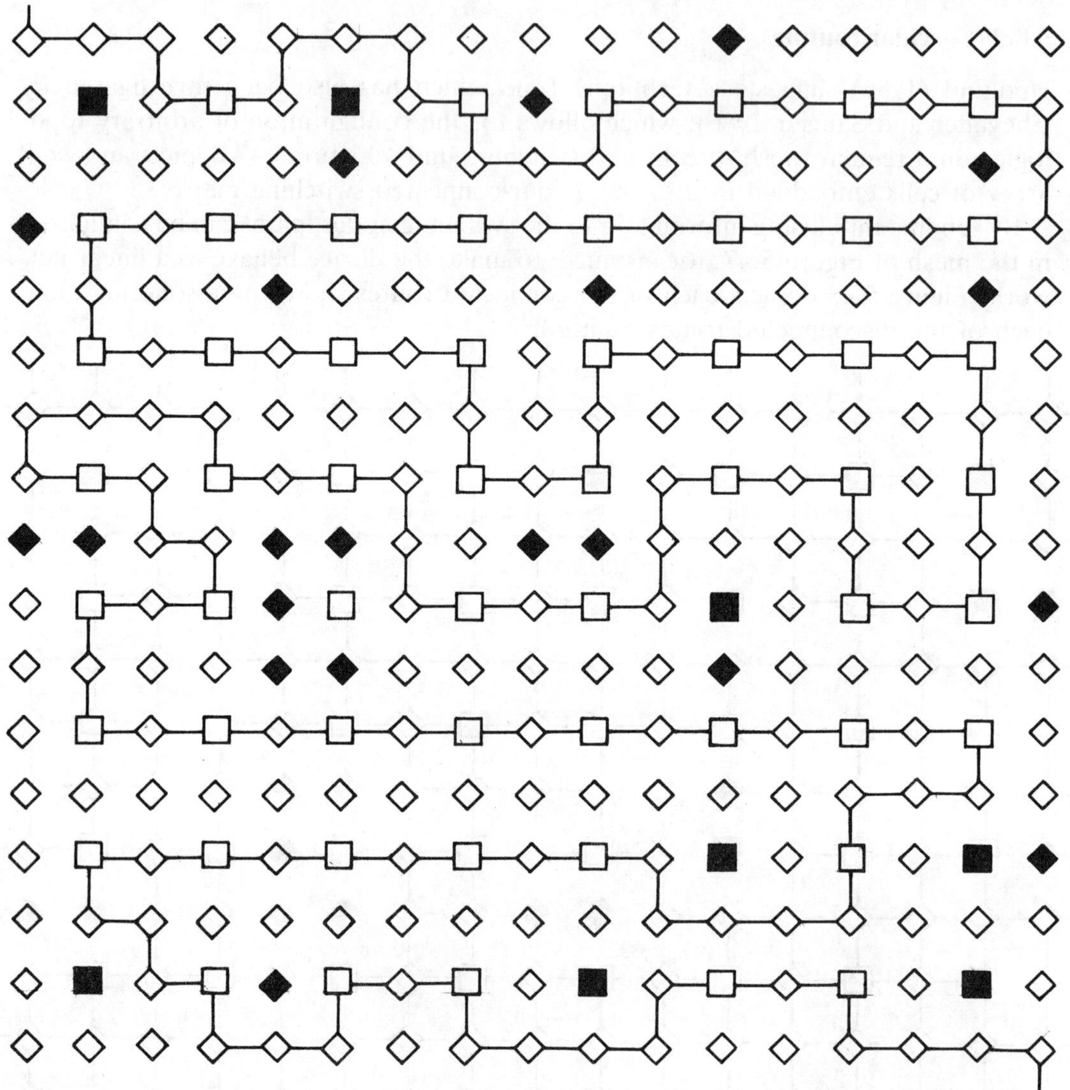

FIGURE 5.48 *Configuring a vector using corridor routing*

Figure 5.47 shows the arrangement with a single corridor of switches between each column and row of cells. By widening the corridors, the network is made more flexible at the expense of requiring a greater overhead to be devoted to interconnection and routing. A fragment of this is shown in Figure 5.49 using a corridor of two.

5.8.3 Diogenes

Rosenberg (1986) describes a method for configuring an arbitrary topology from a linear array of cells. Above the cells there lies a number of pathways, with switching between each (Figure 5.50).

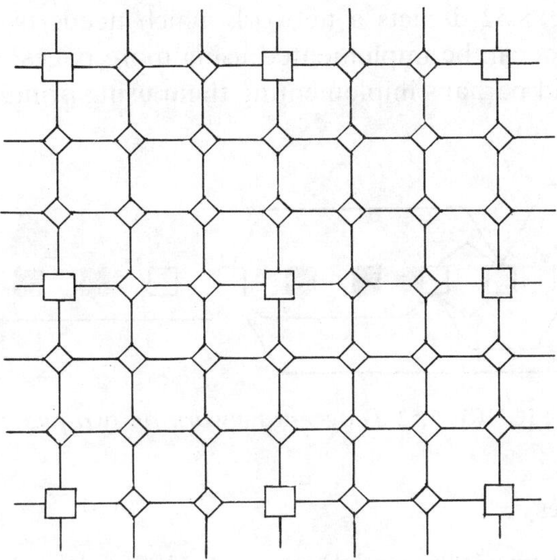

FIGURE 5.49 *Corridor of two routing*

FIGURE 5.50 *Diogenes*

By making and breaking connections, the desired network can be configured. For instance, Figure 5.51 depicts the first seven working cells configured as a binary tree.

The only restrictions on the configuration are that: there must be sufficient pathways for the complexity of the most complicated network which is to be built, and no logical paths can cross. For the binary tree, the first restriction means that at least $\lg(c)$* pathways must be provided, whilst the second is not a problem, as demonstrated in Figure 5.51.

For more complicated networks, Rosenberg suggests that the routing should be provided on many pages, with the linear array of cells arranged along the spine.

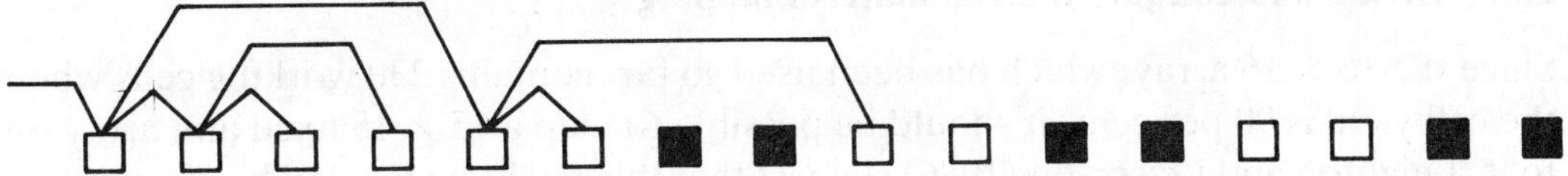

FIGURE 5.51 *Diogenes tree growth*

* $\lg(c) = \log_2(c)$.

For instance, Figure 5.52 depicts a network which needs two pages. Even more complicated networks can be implemented using more pages, visualising them as a loose-leaf binder, and perhaps implementing them using printed circuit boards on a common backplane.

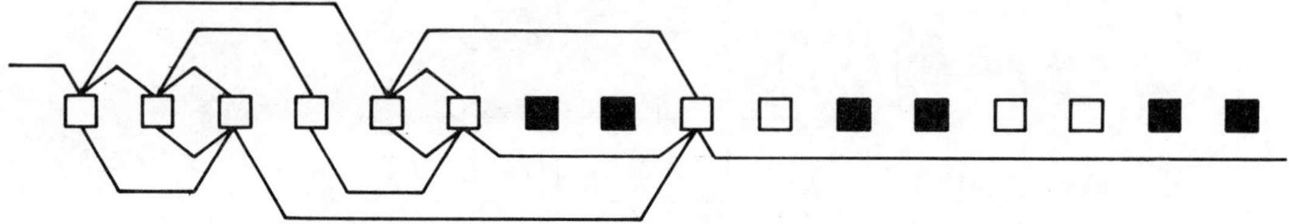

FIGURE 5.52 *Diogenes network on two pages*

5.8.4 Tree of matrices

Leighton and Leiserson (1986) and Rosenberg (1986) describe an arrangement in which arbitrary networks can be implemented on a binary tree of matrix connections, feeding into a linear array of cells (Figure 5.53). Again, the intention is to set the switches in the network so as to make the arrangement behave as some other logical structure.

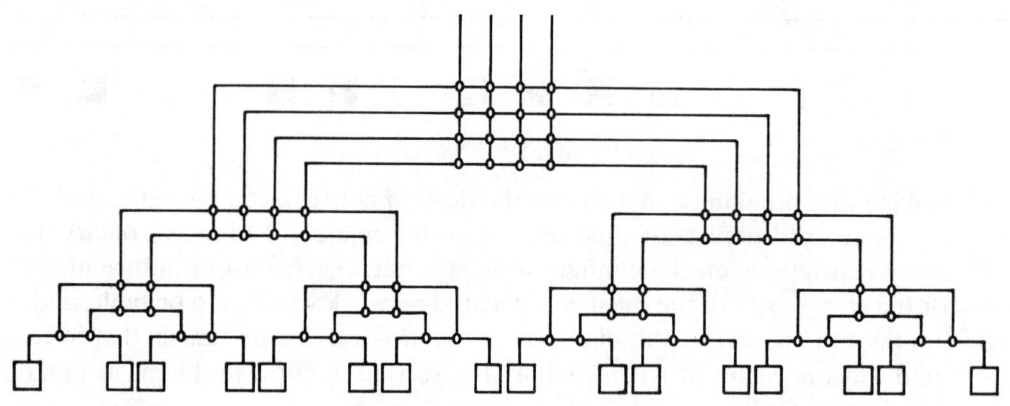

FIGURE 5.53 *Tree of matrices*

5.8.5 Divide-and-conquer matrix–matrix mapping

Since the 16 × 16 array, which has been used so far, contains 230 working cells when the cell yield is 90 per cent, it should be possible to map a 15 × 15 fixed aim array on to it. Leighton and Leiserson (1986) suggest that this might be tackled by distributing the elements from the target array evenly over the cells of the physical array. This in turn suggests the use of a divide-and-conquer algorithm.

Figure 5.54a depicts a 15 × 15 array, which might represent a systolic array. The first step involves dividing the physical array into two equal subarrays, for instance

$a_{1,1}$	$a_{1,2}$	$a_{1,3}$	$a_{1,4}$	$a_{1,5}$	$a_{1,6}$	$a_{1,7}$	$a_{1,8}$	$a_{1,9}$	$a_{1,10}$	$a_{1,11}$	$a_{1,12}$	$a_{1,13}$	$a_{1,14}$	$a_{1,15}$
$a_{2,1}$	$a_{2,2}$	$a_{2,3}$	$a_{2,4}$	$a_{2,5}$	$a_{2,6}$	$a_{2,7}$	$a_{2,8}$	$a_{2,9}$	$a_{2,10}$	$a_{2,11}$	$a_{2,12}$	$a_{2,13}$	$a_{2,14}$	$a_{2,15}$
$a_{3,1}$	$a_{3,2}$	$a_{3,3}$	$a_{3,4}$	$a_{3,5}$	$a_{3,6}$	$a_{3,7}$	$a_{3,8}$	$a_{3,9}$	$a_{3,10}$	$a_{3,11}$	$a_{3,12}$	$a_{3,13}$	$a_{3,14}$	$a_{3,15}$
$a_{4,1}$	$a_{4,2}$	$a_{4,3}$	$a_{4,4}$	$a_{4,5}$	$a_{4,6}$	$a_{4,7}$	$a_{4,8}$	$a_{4,9}$	$a_{4,10}$	$a_{4,11}$	$a_{4,12}$	$a_{4,13}$	$a_{4,14}$	$a_{4,15}$
$a_{5,1}$	$a_{5,2}$	$a_{5,3}$	$a_{5,4}$	$a_{5,5}$	$a_{5,6}$	$a_{5,7}$	$a_{5,8}$	$a_{5,9}$	$a_{5,10}$	$a_{5,11}$	$a_{5,12}$	$a_{5,13}$	$a_{5,14}$	$a_{5,15}$
$a_{6,1}$	$a_{6,2}$	$a_{6,3}$	$a_{6,4}$	$a_{6,5}$	$a_{6,6}$	$a_{6,7}$	$a_{6,8}$	$a_{6,9}$	$a_{6,10}$	$a_{6,11}$	$a_{6,12}$	$a_{6,13}$	$a_{6,14}$	$a_{6,15}$
$a_{7,1}$	$a_{7,2}$	$a_{7,3}$	$a_{7,4}$	$a_{7,5}$	$a_{7,6}$	$a_{7,7}$	$a_{7,8}$	$a_{7,9}$	$a_{7,10}$	$a_{7,11}$	$a_{7,12}$	$a_{7,13}$	$a_{7,14}$	$a_{7,15}$
$a_{8,1}$	$a_{8,2}$	$a_{8,3}$	$a_{8,4}$	$a_{8,5}$	$a_{8,6}$	$a_{8,7}$	$a_{8,8}$	$a_{8,9}$	$a_{8,10}$	$a_{8,11}$	$a_{8,12}$	$a_{8,13}$	$a_{8,14}$	$a_{8,15}$
$a_{9,1}$	$a_{9,2}$	$a_{9,3}$	$a_{9,4}$	$a_{9,5}$	$a_{9,6}$	$a_{9,7}$	$a_{9,8}$	$a_{9,9}$	$a_{9,10}$	$a_{9,11}$	$a_{9,12}$	$a_{9,13}$	$a_{9,14}$	$a_{9,15}$
$a_{10,1}$	$a_{10,2}$	$a_{10,3}$	$a_{10,4}$	$a_{10,5}$	$a_{10,6}$	$a_{10,7}$	$a_{10,8}$	$a_{10,9}$	$a_{10,10}$	$a_{10,11}$	$a_{10,12}$	$a_{10,13}$	$a_{10,14}$	$a_{10,15}$
$a_{11,1}$	$a_{11,2}$	$a_{11,3}$	$a_{11,4}$	$a_{11,5}$	$a_{11,6}$	$a_{11,7}$	$a_{11,8}$	$a_{11,9}$	$a_{11,10}$	$a_{11,11}$	$a_{11,12}$	$a_{11,13}$	$a_{11,14}$	$a_{11,15}$
$a_{12,1}$	$a_{12,2}$	$a_{12,3}$	$a_{12,4}$	$a_{12,5}$	$a_{12,6}$	$a_{12,7}$	$a_{12,8}$	$a_{12,9}$	$a_{12,10}$	$a_{12,11}$	$a_{12,12}$	$a_{12,13}$	$a_{12,14}$	$a_{12,15}$
$a_{13,1}$	$a_{13,2}$	$a_{13,3}$	$a_{13,4}$	$a_{13,5}$	$a_{13,6}$	$a_{13,7}$	$a_{13,8}$	$a_{13,9}$	$a_{13,10}$	$a_{13,11}$	$a_{13,12}$	$a_{13,13}$	$a_{13,14}$	$a_{13,15}$
$a_{14,1}$	$a_{14,2}$	$a_{14,3}$	$a_{14,4}$	$a_{14,5}$	$a_{14,6}$	$a_{14,7}$	$a_{14,8}$	$a_{14,9}$	$a_{14,10}$	$a_{14,11}$	$a_{14,12}$	$a_{14,13}$	$a_{14,14}$	$a_{14,15}$
$a_{15,1}$	$a_{15,2}$	$a_{15,3}$	$a_{15,4}$	$a_{15,5}$	$a_{15,6}$	$a_{15,7}$	$a_{15,8}$	$a_{15,9}$	$a_{15,10}$	$a_{15,11}$	$a_{15,12}$	$a_{15,13}$	$a_{15,14}$	$a_{15,15}$

(a)

$a_{1,1}$	$a_{1,2}$	$a_{1,3}$	$a_{1,4}$	$a_{1,5}$	$a_{1,6}$	$a_{1,7}$	$a_{1,8}$	$a_{1,9}$	$a_{1,10}$	$a_{1,11}$	$a_{1,12}$	$a_{1,13}$	$a_{1,14}$	$a_{1,15}$
$a_{2,1}$	$a_{2,2}$	$a_{2,3}$	$a_{2,4}$	$a_{2,5}$	$a_{2,6}$	$a_{2,7}$	$a_{2,8}$	$a_{2,9}$	$a_{2,10}$	$a_{2,11}$	$a_{2,12}$	$a_{2,13}$	$a_{2,14}$	$a_{2,15}$
$a_{3,1}$	$a_{3,2}$	$a_{3,3}$	$a_{3,4}$	$a_{3,5}$	$a_{3,6}$	$a_{3,7}$	$a_{3,8}$	$a_{3,9}$	$a_{3,10}$	$a_{3,11}$	$a_{3,12}$	$a_{3,13}$	$a_{3,14}$	$a_{3,15}$
$a_{4,1}$	$a_{4,2}$	$a_{4,3}$	$a_{4,4}$	$a_{4,5}$	$a_{4,6}$	$a_{4,7}$	$a_{4,8}$	$a_{4,9}$	$a_{4,10}$	$a_{4,11}$	$a_{4,12}$	$a_{4,13}$	$a_{4,14}$	$a_{4,15}$
$a_{5,1}$	$a_{5,2}$	$a_{5,3}$	$a_{5,4}$	$a_{5,5}$	$a_{5,6}$	$a_{5,7}$	$a_{5,8}$	$a_{5,9}$	$a_{5,10}$	$a_{5,11}$	$a_{5,12}$	$a_{5,13}$	$a_{5,14}$	$a_{5,15}$
$a_{6,1}$	$a_{6,2}$	$a_{6,3}$	$a_{6,4}$	$a_{6,5}$	$a_{6,6}$	$a_{6,7}$	$a_{6,8}$	$a_{6,9}$	$a_{6,10}$	$a_{6,11}$	$a_{6,12}$	$a_{6,13}$	$a_{6,14}$	$a_{6,15}$
$a_{7,1}$	$a_{7,2}$	$a_{7,3}$	$a_{7,4}$	$a_{7,5}$	$a_{7,6}$	$a_{7,7}$	$a_{7,8}$	$a_{7,9}$	$a_{7,10}$	$a_{7,11}$	$a_{7,12}$	$a_{7,13}$	$a_{7,14}$	$a_{7,15}$
$a_{8,1}$	$a_{8,2}$	$a_{8,3}$	$a_{8,4}$	$a_{8,5}$	$a_{8,6}$	$a_{8,7}$	$a_{8,8}$	$a_{8,9}$	$a_{8,10}$	$a_{8,11}$	$a_{8,12}$	$a_{8,13}$	$a_{8,14}$	$a_{8,15}$
$a_{9,1}$	$a_{9,2}$	$a_{9,3}$	$a_{9,4}$	$a_{9,5}$	$a_{9,6}$	$a_{9,7}$	$a_{9,8}$	$a_{9,9}$	$a_{9,10}$	$a_{9,11}$	$a_{9,12}$	$a_{9,13}$	$a_{9,14}$	$a_{9,15}$
$a_{10,1}$	$a_{10,2}$	$a_{10,3}$	$a_{10,4}$	$a_{10,5}$	$a_{10,6}$	$a_{10,7}$	$a_{10,8}$	$a_{10,9}$	$a_{10,10}$	$a_{10,11}$	$a_{10,12}$	$a_{10,13}$	$a_{10,14}$	$a_{10,15}$
$a_{11,1}$	$a_{11,2}$	$a_{11,3}$	$a_{11,4}$	$a_{11,5}$	$a_{11,6}$	$a_{11,7}$	$a_{11,8}$	$a_{11,9}$	$a_{11,10}$	$a_{11,11}$	$a_{11,12}$	$a_{11,13}$	$a_{11,14}$	$a_{11,15}$
$a_{12,1}$	$a_{12,2}$	$a_{12,3}$	$a_{12,4}$	$a_{12,5}$	$a_{12,6}$	$a_{12,7}$	$a_{12,8}$	$a_{12,9}$	$a_{12,10}$	$a_{12,11}$	$a_{12,12}$	$a_{12,13}$	$a_{12,14}$	$a_{12,15}$
$a_{13,1}$	$a_{13,2}$	$a_{13,3}$	$a_{13,4}$	$a_{13,5}$	$a_{13,6}$	$a_{13,7}$	$a_{13,8}$	$a_{13,9}$	$a_{13,10}$	$a_{13,11}$	$a_{13,12}$	$a_{13,13}$	$a_{13,14}$	$a_{13,15}$
$a_{14,1}$	$a_{14,2}$	$a_{14,3}$	$a_{14,4}$	$a_{14,5}$	$a_{14,6}$	$a_{14,7}$	$a_{14,8}$	$a_{14,9}$	$a_{14,10}$	$a_{14,11}$	$a_{14,12}$	$a_{14,13}$	$a_{14,14}$	$a_{14,15}$
$a_{15,1}$	$a_{15,2}$	$a_{15,3}$	$a_{15,4}$	$a_{15,5}$	$a_{15,6}$	$a_{15,7}$	$a_{15,8}$	$a_{15,9}$	$a_{15,10}$	$a_{15,11}$	$a_{15,12}$	$a_{15,13}$	$a_{15,14}$	$a_{15,15}$

(b)

FIGURE 5.54 *Dividing the target array into two subarrays*

by splitting it vertically through the middle. The aim is to map the elements of the target array evenly over the working cells of the physical subarrays. The target array is divided so that the number of elements in each half is proportional to the number of working cells in each half of the physical array. Thus, the two halves of the physical array contain respectively 116 and 114 working cells, so the target array is divided in the ratio of 116:114, that is to the nearest integers 113:112 (Figure 5.54b).

As is traditional with divide-and-conquer algorithms, the process is repeated recursively. Each of the physical subarrays is divided into two equal halves, using a horizontal split this time, and the numbers of working cells are counted in each half. The elements of the two target subarrays are then divided in the same ratio. For the physical array, the counts of working cells for the NW, SW, NE and SE quadrants are respectively 56, 60, 59 and 55. For the target array, the ratio of 56:60 is about 55:58, and the ratio of 59:55 is about 58:54. Figure 5.55a depicts a suitable division. Figure 5.55b shows the next level of recursion, having divided each of the quadrants further.

The exact position for the dividing line is often quite flexible. Some heuristics, which seem to work, suggest that: undue zig-zagging of the line should be avoided early in the algorithm's application (for instance in Figure 5.54b), dividing partitions should be aligned with those in neighbouring subarrays whenever possible, and the ratio of maximum height to minimum width of the newly partitioned subarrays should be kept as square (or 2:1 rectangular) as possible.

Since the physical grid contains 230 working cells, and the target array needs only 225, there will be five unharvested cells. These act in the algorithm a little like the 'don't care' states in a Karnaugh map (Lewin 1985). The mapping of the target array on to the physical grid is somewhat like stretching a uniform rubber sheet to fit over an irregular surface. In some regions, the lattice lines on the rubber sheet undergo quite drastic stretching and contortion. The availability of unharvested cells, if placed carefully, can be used to 'release the tension' in some of the more contorted regions.

Figure 5.56 shows the final partitioning of the target array down to a level which corresponds to the division of the physical array into two by two subarrays. Figure 5.57 shows the final mapping of this on to the physical grid.

5.9 *MASKING REDUNDANCY*

All of the techniques described so far contrive to connect spare cells in place of faulty ones. The techniques which are described in this section also require redundant hardware, but this time all of it is in constant use. When data are stored in a memory, for example, redundant data are stored with it. When the data are retrieved, a check is made on the extra data, and this information is used to make any necessary corrections *on line*. Thus masking redundancy provides a route to the implementation of on-line failure tolerance.

$a_{1,1}$ $a_{1,2}$ $a_{1,3}$ $a_{1,4}$ $a_{1,5}$ $a_{1,6}$ $a_{1,7}$ $a_{1,8}$ $a_{1,9}$ $a_{1,10}$ $a_{1,11}$ $a_{1,12}$ $a_{1,13}$ $a_{1,14}$ $a_{1,15}$

$a_{2,1}$ $a_{2,2}$ $a_{2,3}$ $a_{2,4}$ $a_{2,5}$ $a_{2,6}$ $a_{2,7}$ $a_{2,8}$ $a_{2,9}$ $a_{2,10}$ $a_{2,11}$ $a_{2,12}$ $a_{2,13}$ $a_{2,14}$ $a_{2,15}$

$a_{3,1}$ $a_{3,2}$ $a_{3,3}$ $a_{3,4}$ $a_{3,5}$ $a_{3,6}$ $a_{3,7}$ $a_{3,8}$ $a_{3,9}$ $a_{3,10}$ $a_{3,11}$ $a_{3,12}$ $a_{3,13}$ $a_{3,14}$ $a_{3,15}$

$a_{4,1}$ $a_{4,2}$ $a_{4,3}$ $a_{4,4}$ $a_{4,5}$ $a_{4,6}$ $a_{4,7}$ $a_{4,8}$ $a_{4,9}$ $a_{4,10}$ $a_{4,11}$ $a_{4,12}$ $a_{4,13}$ $a_{4,14}$ $a_{4,15}$

$a_{5,1}$ $a_{5,2}$ $a_{5,3}$ $a_{5,4}$ $a_{5,5}$ $a_{5,6}$ $a_{5,7}$ $a_{5,8}$ $a_{5,9}$ $a_{5,10}$ $a_{5,11}$ $a_{5,12}$ $a_{5,13}$ $a_{5,14}$ $a_{5,15}$

$a_{6,1}$ $a_{6,2}$ $a_{6,3}$ $a_{6,4}$ $a_{6,5}$ $a_{6,6}$ $a_{6,7}$ $a_{6,8}$ $a_{6,9}$ $a_{6,10}$ $a_{6,11}$ $a_{6,12}$ $a_{6,13}$ $a_{6,14}$ $a_{6,15}$

$a_{7,1}$ $a_{7,2}$ $a_{7,3}$ $a_{7,4}$ $a_{7,5}$ $a_{7,6}$ $a_{7,7}$ $a_{7,8}$ $a_{7,9}$ $a_{7,10}$ $a_{7,11}$ $a_{7,12}$ $a_{7,13}$ $a_{7,14}$ $a_{7,15}$

$a_{8,1}$ $a_{8,2}$ $a_{8,3}$ $a_{8,4}$ $a_{8,5}$ $a_{8,6}$ $a_{8,7}$ $a_{8,8}$ $a_{8,9}$ $a_{8,10}$ $a_{8,11}$ $a_{8,12}$ $a_{8,13}$ $a_{8,14}$ $a_{8,15}$

$a_{9,1}$ $a_{9,2}$ $a_{9,3}$ $a_{9,4}$ $a_{9,5}$ $a_{9,6}$ $a_{9,7}$ $a_{9,8}$ $a_{9,9}$ $a_{9,10}$ $a_{9,11}$ $a_{9,12}$ $a_{9,13}$ $a_{9,14}$ $a_{9,15}$

$a_{10,1}$ $a_{10,2}$ $a_{10,3}$ $a_{10,4}$ $a_{10,5}$ $a_{10,6}$ $a_{10,7}$ $a_{10,8}$ $a_{10,9}$ $a_{10,10}$ $a_{10,11}$ $a_{10,12}$ $a_{10,13}$ $a_{10,14}$ $a_{10,15}$

$a_{11,1}$ $a_{11,2}$ $a_{11,3}$ $a_{11,4}$ $a_{11,5}$ $a_{11,6}$ $a_{11,7}$ $a_{11,8}$ $a_{11,9}$ $a_{11,10}$ $a_{11,11}$ $a_{11,12}$ $a_{11,13}$ $a_{11,14}$ $a_{11,15}$

$a_{12,1}$ $a_{12,2}$ $a_{12,3}$ $a_{12,4}$ $a_{12,5}$ $a_{12,6}$ $a_{12,7}$ $a_{12,8}$ $a_{12,9}$ $a_{12,10}$ $a_{12,11}$ $a_{12,12}$ $a_{12,13}$ $a_{12,14}$ $a_{12,15}$

$a_{13,1}$ $a_{13,2}$ $a_{13,3}$ $a_{13,4}$ $a_{13,5}$ $a_{13,6}$ $a_{13,7}$ $a_{13,8}$ $a_{13,9}$ $a_{13,10}$ $a_{13,11}$ $a_{13,12}$ $a_{13,13}$ $a_{13,14}$ $a_{13,15}$

$a_{14,1}$ $a_{14,2}$ $a_{14,3}$ $a_{14,4}$ $a_{14,5}$ $a_{14,6}$ $a_{14,7}$ $a_{14,8}$ $a_{14,9}$ $a_{14,10}$ $a_{14,11}$ $a_{14,12}$ $a_{14,13}$ $a_{14,14}$ $a_{14,15}$

$a_{15,1}$ $a_{15,2}$ $a_{15,3}$ $a_{15,4}$ $a_{15,5}$ $a_{15,6}$ $a_{15,7}$ $a_{15,8}$ $a_{15,9}$ $a_{15,10}$ $a_{15,11}$ $a_{15,12}$ $a_{15,13}$ $a_{15,14}$ $a_{15,15}$

(a)

$a_{1,1}$ $a_{1,2}$ $a_{1,3}$ $a_{1,4}$ $a_{1,5}$ $a_{1,6}$ $a_{1,7}$ $a_{1,8}$ $a_{1,9}$ $a_{1,10}$ $a_{1,11}$ $a_{1,12}$ $a_{1,13}$ $a_{1,14}$ $a_{1,15}$

$a_{2,1}$ $a_{2,2}$ $a_{2,3}$ $a_{2,4}$ $a_{2,5}$ $a_{2,6}$ $a_{2,7}$ $a_{2,8}$ $a_{2,9}$ $a_{2,10}$ $a_{2,11}$ $a_{2,12}$ $a_{2,13}$ $a_{2,14}$ $a_{2,15}$

$a_{3,1}$ $a_{3,2}$ $a_{3,3}$ $a_{3,4}$ $a_{3,5}$ $a_{3,6}$ $a_{3,7}$ $a_{3,8}$ $a_{3,9}$ $a_{3,10}$ $a_{3,11}$ $a_{3,12}$ $a_{3,13}$ $a_{3,14}$ $a_{3,15}$

$a_{4,1}$ $a_{4,2}$ $a_{4,3}$ $a_{4,4}$ $a_{4,5}$ $a_{4,6}$ $a_{4,7}$ $a_{4,8}$ $a_{4,9}$ $a_{4,10}$ $a_{4,11}$ $a_{4,12}$ $a_{4,13}$ $a_{4,14}$ $a_{4,15}$

$a_{5,1}$ $a_{5,2}$ $a_{5,3}$ $a_{5,4}$ $a_{5,5}$ $a_{5,6}$ $a_{5,7}$ $a_{5,8}$ $a_{5,9}$ $a_{5,10}$ $a_{5,11}$ $a_{5,12}$ $a_{5,13}$ $a_{5,14}$ $a_{5,15}$

$a_{6,1}$ $a_{6,2}$ $a_{6,3}$ $a_{6,4}$ $a_{6,5}$ $a_{6,6}$ $a_{6,7}$ $a_{6,8}$ $a_{6,9}$ $a_{6,10}$ $a_{6,11}$ $a_{6,12}$ $a_{6,13}$ $a_{6,14}$ $a_{6,15}$

$a_{7,1}$ $a_{7,2}$ $a_{7,3}$ $a_{7,4}$ $a_{7,5}$ $a_{7,6}$ $a_{7,7}$ $a_{7,8}$ $a_{7,9}$ $a_{7,10}$ $a_{7,11}$ $a_{7,12}$ $a_{7,13}$ $a_{7,14}$ $a_{7,15}$

$a_{8,1}$ $a_{8,2}$ $a_{8,3}$ $a_{8,4}$ $a_{8,5}$ $a_{8,6}$ $a_{8,7}$ $a_{8,8}$ $a_{8,9}$ $a_{8,10}$ $a_{8,11}$ $a_{8,12}$ $a_{8,13}$ $a_{8,14}$ $a_{8,15}$

$a_{9,1}$ $a_{9,2}$ $a_{9,3}$ $a_{9,4}$ $a_{9,5}$ $a_{9,6}$ $a_{9,7}$ $a_{9,8}$ $a_{9,9}$ $a_{9,10}$ $a_{9,11}$ $a_{9,12}$ $a_{9,13}$ $a_{9,14}$ $a_{9,15}$

$a_{10,1}$ $a_{10,2}$ $a_{10,3}$ $a_{10,4}$ $a_{10,5}$ $a_{10,6}$ $a_{10,7}$ $a_{10,8}$ $a_{10,9}$ $a_{10,10}$ $a_{10,11}$ $a_{10,12}$ $a_{10,13}$ $a_{10,14}$ $a_{10,15}$

$a_{11,1}$ $a_{11,2}$ $a_{11,3}$ $a_{11,4}$ $a_{11,5}$ $a_{11,6}$ $a_{11,7}$ $a_{11,8}$ $a_{11,9}$ $a_{11,10}$ $a_{11,11}$ $a_{11,12}$ $a_{11,13}$ $a_{11,14}$ $a_{11,15}$

$a_{12,1}$ $a_{12,2}$ $a_{12,3}$ $a_{12,4}$ $a_{12,5}$ $a_{12,6}$ $a_{12,7}$ $a_{12,8}$ $a_{12,9}$ $a_{12,10}$ $a_{12,11}$ $a_{12,12}$ $a_{12,13}$ $a_{12,14}$ $a_{12,15}$

$a_{13,1}$ $a_{13,2}$ $a_{13,3}$ $a_{13,4}$ $a_{13,5}$ $a_{13,6}$ $a_{13,7}$ $a_{13,8}$ $a_{13,9}$ $a_{13,10}$ $a_{13,11}$ $a_{13,12}$ $a_{13,13}$ $a_{13,14}$ $a_{13,15}$

$a_{14,1}$ $a_{14,2}$ $a_{14,3}$ $a_{14,4}$ $a_{14,5}$ $a_{14,6}$ $a_{14,7}$ $a_{14,8}$ $a_{14,9}$ $a_{14,10}$ $a_{14,11}$ $a_{14,12}$ $a_{14,13}$ $a_{14,14}$ $a_{14,15}$

$a_{15,1}$ $a_{15,2}$ $a_{15,3}$ $a_{15,4}$ $a_{15,5}$ $a_{15,6}$ $a_{15,7}$ $a_{15,8}$ $a_{15,9}$ $a_{15,10}$ $a_{15,11}$ $a_{15,12}$ $a_{15,13}$ $a_{15,14}$ $a_{15,15}$

(b)

FIGURE 5.55 *Dividing the target array into four and eight subarrays*

$a_{1,1}$	$a_{1,2}$	$a_{1,3}$	$a_{1,4}$	$a_{1,5}$	$a_{1,6}$	$a_{1,7}$	$a_{1,8}$	$a_{1,9}$	$a_{1,10}$	$a_{1,11}$	$a_{1,12}$	$a_{1,13}$	$a_{1,14}$	$a_{1,15}$
$a_{2,1}$	$a_{2,2}$	$a_{2,3}$	$a_{2,4}$	$a_{2,5}$	$a_{2,6}$	$a_{2,7}$	$a_{2,8}$	$a_{2,9}$	$a_{2,10}$	$a_{2,11}$	$a_{2,12}$	$a_{2,13}$	$a_{2,14}$	$a_{2,15}$
$a_{3,1}$	$a_{3,2}$	$a_{3,3}$	$a_{3,4}$	$a_{3,5}$	$a_{3,6}$	$a_{3,7}$	$a_{3,8}$	$a_{3,9}$	$a_{3,10}$	$a_{3,11}$	$a_{3,12}$	$a_{3,13}$	$a_{3,14}$	$a_{3,15}$
$a_{4,1}$	$a_{4,2}$	$a_{4,3}$	$a_{4,4}$	$a_{4,5}$	$a_{4,6}$	$a_{4,7}$	$a_{4,8}$	$a_{4,9}$	$a_{4,10}$	$a_{4,11}$	$a_{4,12}$	$a_{4,13}$	$a_{4,14}$	$a_{4,15}$
$a_{5,1}$	$a_{5,2}$	$a_{5,3}$	$a_{5,4}$	$a_{5,5}$	$a_{5,6}$	$a_{5,7}$	$a_{5,8}$	$a_{5,9}$	$a_{5,10}$	$a_{5,11}$	$a_{5,12}$	$a_{5,13}$	$a_{5,14}$	$a_{5,15}$
$a_{6,1}$	$a_{6,2}$	$a_{6,3}$	$a_{6,4}$	$a_{6,5}$	$a_{6,6}$	$a_{6,7}$	$a_{6,8}$	$a_{6,9}$	$a_{6,10}$	$a_{6,11}$	$a_{6,12}$	$a_{6,13}$	$a_{6,14}$	$a_{6,15}$
$a_{7,1}$	$a_{7,2}$	$a_{7,3}$	$a_{7,4}$	$a_{7,5}$	$a_{7,6}$	$a_{7,7}$	$a_{7,8}$	$a_{7,9}$	$a_{7,10}$	$a_{7,11}$	$a_{7,12}$	$a_{7,13}$	$a_{7,14}$	$a_{7,15}$
$a_{8,1}$	$a_{8,2}$	$a_{8,3}$	$a_{8,4}$	$a_{8,5}$	$a_{8,6}$	$a_{8,7}$	$a_{8,8}$	$a_{8,9}$	$a_{8,10}$	$a_{8,11}$	$a_{8,12}$	$a_{8,13}$	$a_{8,14}$	$a_{8,15}$
$a_{9,1}$	$a_{9,2}$	$a_{9,3}$	$a_{9,4}$	$a_{9,5}$	$a_{9,6}$	$a_{9,7}$	$a_{9,8}$	$a_{9,9}$	$a_{9,10}$	$a_{9,11}$	$a_{9,12}$	$a_{9,13}$	$a_{9,14}$	$a_{9,15}$
$a_{10,1}$	$a_{10,2}$	$a_{10,3}$	$a_{10,4}$	$a_{10,5}$	$a_{10,6}$	$a_{10,7}$	$a_{10,8}$	$a_{10,9}$	$a_{10,10}$	$a_{10,11}$	$a_{10,12}$	$a_{10,13}$	$a_{10,14}$	$a_{10,15}$
$a_{11,1}$	$a_{11,2}$	$a_{11,3}$	$a_{11,4}$	$a_{11,5}$	$a_{11,6}$	$a_{11,7}$	$a_{11,8}$	$a_{11,9}$	$a_{11,10}$	$a_{11,11}$	$a_{11,12}$	$a_{11,13}$	$a_{11,14}$	$a_{11,15}$
$a_{12,1}$	$a_{12,2}$	$a_{12,3}$	$a_{12,4}$	$a_{12,5}$	$a_{12,6}$	$a_{12,7}$	$a_{12,8}$	$a_{12,9}$	$a_{12,10}$	$a_{12,11}$	$a_{12,12}$	$a_{12,13}$	$a_{12,14}$	$a_{12,15}$
$a_{13,1}$	$a_{13,2}$	$a_{13,3}$	$a_{13,4}$	$a_{13,5}$	$a_{13,6}$	$a_{13,7}$	$a_{13,8}$	$a_{13,9}$	$a_{13,10}$	$a_{13,11}$	$a_{13,12}$	$a_{13,13}$	$a_{13,14}$	$a_{13,15}$
$a_{14,1}$	$a_{14,2}$	$a_{14,3}$	$a_{14,4}$	$a_{14,5}$	$a_{14,6}$	$a_{14,7}$	$a_{14,8}$	$a_{14,9}$	$a_{14,10}$	$a_{14,11}$	$a_{14,12}$	$a_{14,13}$	$a_{14,14}$	$a_{14,15}$
$a_{15,1}$	$a_{15,2}$	$a_{15,3}$	$a_{15,4}$	$a_{15,5}$	$a_{15,6}$	$a_{15,7}$	$a_{15,8}$	$a_{15,9}$	$a_{15,10}$	$a_{15,11}$	$a_{15,12}$	$a_{15,13}$	$a_{15,14}$	$a_{15,15}$

FIGURE 5.56 *Final partitioning of the target array*

Two subclasses are identified by Anderson and Lee (1981): *failure correction* (Section 5.9.1) and *error correction* (Section 5.9.3). The first involves the overriding of faulty hardware, whilst the second involves the remedying of erroneous data. One example of the first is described next.

5.9.1 Modular redundancy

Modular redundancy is very closely related to the integer replication redundancy techniques, but instead of disconnecting faulty circuits all circuits are left permanently connected. A *voting circuit* is then employed to arbitrate between the values which are returned. When less than half of the circuits have failed, the voting circuit relies on the majority decision. When more than half of the circuits have failed, the outcome depends on the nature of the cells. If the results from the cells are only one bit wide, as they might be in the memory example, the failure of more than half of the circuits is catastrophic, and the device fails. If the cells are more complicated, there might still be sufficient good circuits to out-vote the faulty ones, each of which is likely to be producing a different wrong answer. For instance in pentuple modular redundancy, where $R=5$, if three faulty circuits respectively supply the answers 2, 7 and 4 and the other two supply the correct answer 6 then this value overrules the others.

Figure 5.58 depicts the more common *triple modular redundancy* (TMR) where

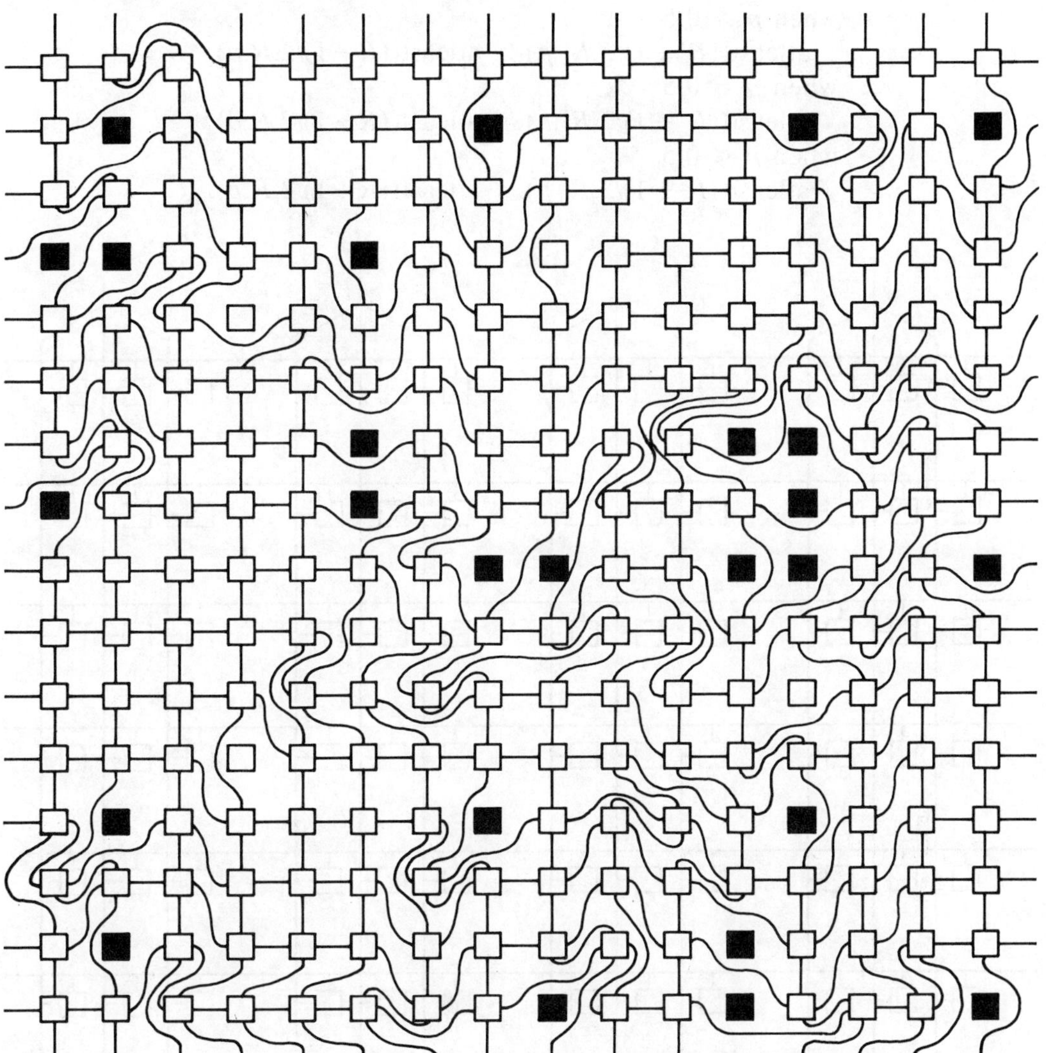

FIGURE 5.57 *Schematic representation of the 15 × 15 array*

$R=3$, showing how this is an adaptation of the column replication technique. The reader is invited to confirm that the idea is also applicable to the device replication and the cell replication techniques.

The bit-level TMR system of Figure 5.58 is failure tolerant and able to cope not only with circuits which are faulty from the manufacturing stage, but also with circuits which develop faults whilst they are in service. This is bought at the expense of tolerating only one fault/failure in three, as opposed to two faults in three which could be tolerated by the equivalent column replication architecture.

Figure 5.59 derives the performance figures for column-orientated modular redundancy. In this, it is important to note the following property, which works for any odd value of R and its successor $R'=R+2$:

when $p > 0.5$
  $\text{atleast}((R'+1)/2, R', p) > \text{atleast}((R+1)/2, R, p)$
when $p = 0.5$
  $\text{atleast}((R'+1)/2, R', p) = \text{atleast}((R+1)/2, R, p)$
when $p < 0.5$
  $\text{atleast}((R'+1)/2, R', p) < \text{atleast}((R+1)/2, R, p)$

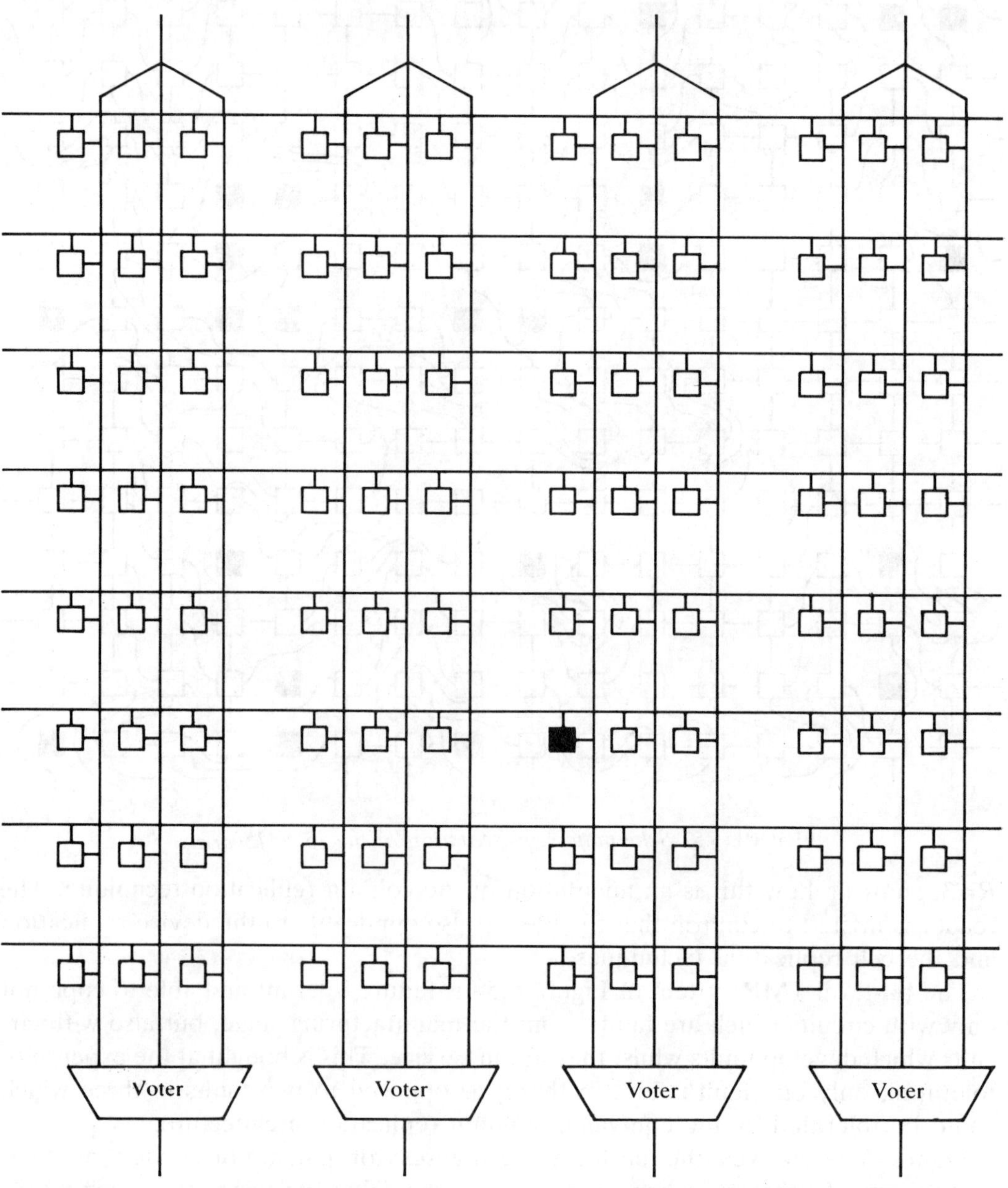

FIGURE 5.58 *Fixed aim triple modular column redundancy*

Min. working cells in column:	m from m
Column yield:	y^m
Min. working columns in group:	$\frac{R+1}{2}$ from R
Group yield:	atleast $\left(\frac{R+1}{2}, R, y^m\right)$
Min. working groups in device:	n from n
Device yield (Y'):	atleast $\left(\frac{R+1}{2}, R, y^m\right)^n$

FIGURE 5.59 *Performance of fixed aim R-plex column modular redundancy*

It follows that R-plex modular redundancy is only beneficial if the circuit yield is greater than 50 per cent. For R-plex column redundancy, the device yield is atleast$((R+1)/2, R, y^m)^n$, and the technique works only when $y^m > 0.5$. For R-plex device redundancy, the device yield is atleast$((R+1)/2, R, y^{mn})$, and the technique works only when $y^{mn} > 0.5$. For R-plex cell redundancy, the device yield is atleast$((R+1)/2, R, y)^{mn}$, and the technique works when $y > 0.5$. Thus modular redundancy is not always applicable. R-plex cell redundancy, where the grain size is small and $p=y$, is more likely to be beneficial than R-plex device redundancy, where the grain size is larger and $p=y^{mn}$.

5.9.2 Block parity

With parity-bit detection, each n-bit word is stored as an $(n+1)$-bit value. The value of the extra bit is computed by performing modulo 2 addition on the other n bits. When the word is retrieved again it is necessary only to recompute the parity of the data bits and to compare them against the one which was stored. If the two values differ an error is known to have occurred in one of the bits.

However, it is not sufficient for failure tolerance purposes to know that an error has occurred. It must be possible to locate the point of error exactly and to correct it. One way of achieving this is through the use of block parity. For this, the memory example is implemented with an extra row and column. The cells in the spare column are used to store the parity bit which is computed as each word is stored. The cells in the spare row are used to store a similar *parity bit* for each column (Figure 5.60). If any cell is faulty and unable to store binary digits correctly, a check of the parity bits will pinpoint which column and which row contains the offending cell, and hence which bit needs to be inverted when the memory is read.

5.9.3 Hamming correction

When the Hamming correction techniques are applied to the memory example, parity information is only calculated on a row basis. However, several parity bits are calculated for each row, each one being derived from a different set of bits. Using the example of four-bit words:

1 1 1 0 1
1 1 0 1 1
0 0 0 1 1
1 1 0 0 0
0 0 1 1 0
1 1 1 1 0
1 1 0 0 0
1 1 0 1 1
0 0 1 1 0

FIGURE 5.60 *Fixed aim block parity*

d4	d3	d2	d1

the idea requires that a seven-bit encoding of the information be used:

d4	d3	d2	p3	d1	p2	p1

Four of the bits are simply copied from the original data, and the remaining three bits are parity bits. It is convenient to give these bits new names:

h7	h6	h5	h4	h3	h2	h1

The parity bits are determined using modulo 2 addition as follows:

$$
\begin{aligned}
p1 &= d1 \oplus d2 \oplus d4 \\
\text{i.e } h1 &= h3 \oplus h5 \oplus h7 \\
p2 &= d1 \oplus d3 \oplus d4 \\
\text{i.e } h2 &= h3 \oplus h6 \oplus h7 \\
p3 &= d2 \oplus d3 \oplus d4 \\
\text{i.e } h4 &= h5 \oplus h6 \oplus h7
\end{aligned}
$$

Some (long) time later, when the data are retrieved, modulo 2 addition is used again to determine the following signals:

$$
\begin{aligned}
s1 &= h1 \oplus h3 \oplus h5 \oplus h7 \\
s2 &= h2 \oplus h3 \oplus h6 \oplus h7 \\
s3 &= h4 \oplus h5 \oplus h6 \oplus h7
\end{aligned}
$$

Because of the way in which h1, h2 and h4 were derived, the values of s1, s2 and s3 should each be zero. If this is the case, h1, h2 and h4 can be discarded, and the remaining four data bits retrieved and sent to the output. If one of the cells is faulty, though, it will not correctly remember its stored bit and some or all of s1, s2 and s3 will contain a logical '1'. Again, because of the way in which h1, h2 and h4 were generated, it is now possible to read s3, s2 and s1 as a three-bit integer, the value of which is the name of the bit which is faulty. For example if s3, s2 and s1 take on the

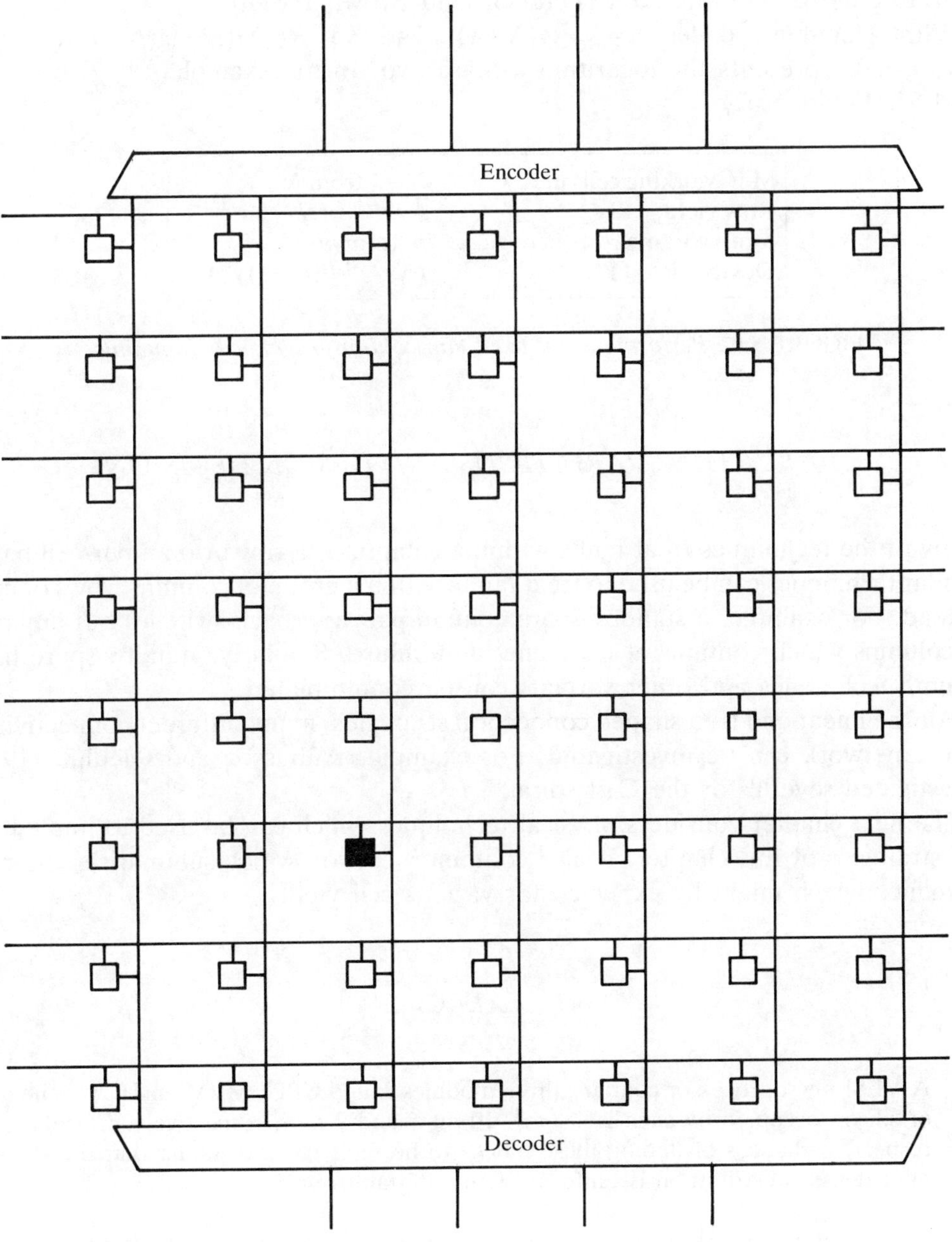

FIGURE 5.61 *Fixed aim column-orientated Hamming redundancy*

values '1', '1' and '0' respectively, it means that h6 has the erroneous value. The value of h6 can, therefore, be inverted. Having made this correction, the values of h1, h2 and h4 can be discarded, and the remaining four data bits sent to the data bus.

Figure 5.61 depicts a system which uses Hamming codes can tolerate any number of faulty cells so long as there are no more than one per row. Other codes exist for tolerating more than one fault (Peterson and Brown 1961).

With Hamming codes $n=N-\lg(N+1)$, and so $R=N/(N-\lg(N+1))$, where lg as usual represents the logarithm to base two. In the example, $N=7$, $n=4$ and $R=1.75$ (Figure 5.62).

Min. working cells in row:	$N-1$ from N
Row yield:	$Ny^{N-1}+(N-1)y^N$
Min. working rows in device:	m from m
Device yield (Y'):	$(Ny^{N-1}+(N-1)y^N)^m$

FIGURE 5.62 *Performance of fixed aim column-orientated Hamming*

5.10 FURTHER VARIATIONS AND DESIGN DECISIONS

Many of the techniques treat faults within a column or a row or on a per-cell basis. Similar techniques can be used to treat faults within a group of columns, rows or cells instead. For example, a standby-spare column-pair approach switches out any pair of columns which contains at least one fault/failure. Similarly, standby-spare half-column techniques and other variants can be contemplated.

For the linear and tree-shaped connection strategies, many different connectivities of the network can be investigated. For example, Aubusson and Gledhill (1978) investigated several for the Catt spiral.

The next chapter considers physical techniques which can be used to implement the strategies of this chapter. It also contains a section which summarises the performance which might be expected for various cell yields.

5.11 EXERCISES

5.1 A VLSI microprocessor contains three modules called CPU, MEM and IOC. The area of silicon occupied by each is 4 mm^2, 10 mm^2 and 2 mm^2 respectively. Calculate the respective chances of finding these blocks to be fault free, assuming that the Poisson fault density distribution is uniform, with 0.05 faults/mm^2.

5.2 If 1000 of the microprocessors from question 5.1 are tested, how many might be expected to work?

5.3 Assuming that the processors in question 5.1 are square and that a large number of them are needed, arranged in a square grid on the wafer, calculate the proportion of wafers on which every processor works. (Assume that the wafer diameter is 150 mm, and that a 9 mm safety border is to be left around the circumference.)

5.4 Calculate the cell yields, the predicted cell harvests and the actual cell harvests for each of the fixed aim and graceful degradation diagrams depicted in this chapter.

5.5 How must Figure 5.40 be modified to depict the arrangement for a four-connected array configured using convex wrapping?

5.6 Draw the interconnection scheme for a graceful degradation standby-spare column and row configuration. (A blank grid is available, if required, on page 215.) What are the values of the cell yield and cell harvest?

6
CONFIGURATION
IMPLEMENTATION AND PERFORMANCE

Chapter 5 describes logical strategies for the configuration of non-perfect devices; this chapter describes the physical techniques by which they might be implemented. Regardless of whether fault or failure tolerance is adopted, reconfiguration is achieved by deploying switches between the circuits. For fault tolerance, these can be realised by *fuses* to break unwanted circuits, *antifuses* to make wanted circuits (Chapman 1986) or methods for physically writing conductor track across the wafer surface. For failure tolerance, the switches are realised using transistors, with appropriate control logic to determine whether the transistor should be conducting or non-conducting.

These techniques can be divided into a number of classes as depicted in Figure 6.1. The alternative names, as indicated by parentheses, are mostly those which are used by Anderson and Lee (1981). *Fault tolerance* (Section 6.2) involves reconfiguration at the manufacture stage, and is a fairly manual technique, involving the static connection of good circuits and the disconnection of faulty ones. *Off-line failure tolerance* configuration (Section 6.3) can undergo reconfiguration whilst the device is in service, but all work must be aborted whilst it does so. Lastly, *on-line failure tolerance* configuration (Section 6.4) can undergo reconfiguration while a computation is in progress and is a spontaneous process which need not even be brought to the user's attention. First, though, the impracticality of wafer scale defect tolerance is discussed.

6.1 DEFECT TOLERANCE (FAULT-FREE WAFERS)

In principle, the circuit could be fabricated in the conventional manner, and only those which are fault free over the entire wafer used. If the device yield is kept sufficiently high, for example 90 per cent, then only one wafer in ten is discarded. Since the device area, A, is a large, fixed value, namely the area of the entire wafer, the device yield, Y, can be increased to such a high value only by reducing the fault

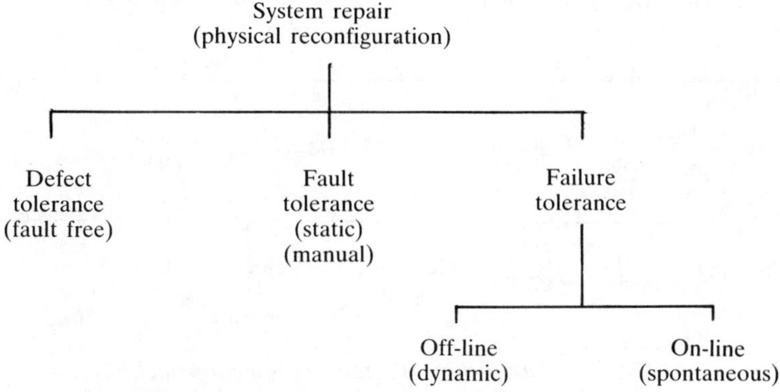

FIGURE 6.1 *Techniques for physical reconfiguration*

density, D. This can be achieved by increasing the grid size, λ, but the packing density falls as a result. Therefore, the penalty is that the increased area occupied by each feature allows fewer transistors to be placed on the wafer, and the main aim of WSI is missed. Figure 6.2 lists some example values to demonstrate the impracticality of this method. The top line is assumed empirically from observation of current VLSI, using the Poisson fault distribution model. Subsequent lines are extrapolated from these figures, assuming that the fault distribution, D, is inversely proportionally to the square of the grid size, λ.

Required device area $A = W$ *(mm²)*	*Required device yield* Y	*Required fault density* D	*Required feature size* λ *(mm)*	*Required transistor count* $\varkappa$	*Obtained device yield* Y
13 273		5.0×10^{-2}	1	60 000 000	6.0×10^{-289}
13 273	0.90	7.9×10^{-6}	79	10 500	
13 273	0.50	5.2×10^{-5}	31	69 000	
13 273	0.10	1.7×10^{-4}	17	230 000	

FIGURE 6.2 *Defect tolerance for 150 mm diameter wafer with 10 mm margin*

Although it is impractical as a technique for fabricating the bulk of the device, defect tolerance can still be used to great effect in restricted areas. In particular, it can be used in the regions which are occupied by each circuit's hardcore logic.

6.2 *FAULT TOLERANCE (STATIC CONFIGURATION)*

The implementations for fault tolerance are also known as *programmed interconnection* techniques (Aubusson and Catt 1978) owing to their similarities to the methods

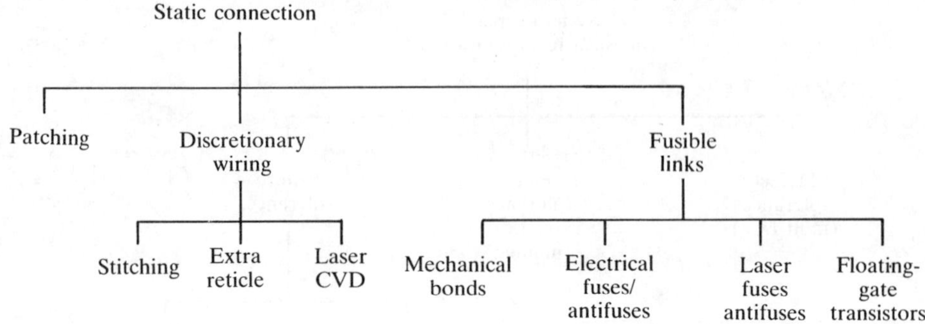

FIGURE 6.3 *Taxonomy of static connection techniques*

which are used for programmable read-only memory (PROM), and programmable logic array (PLA). Suitable subdivisions are listed in Figure 6.3.

The next three sections deal respectively with patching, discretionary wiring and fusible links. Of these, the last is the best researched, and so greater emphasis is placed on Section 6.2.3.

6.2.1 Patching

It is possible to disconnect faulty circuits, and to connect good ones over them. Usually, the 'patch' is the mirror image of the circuit which it replaces so as to enable it to be placed face down on the faulty circuit. In this way the external connection pads, in the form of solder bumps, on the *flip-chip* will align with those of the faulty circuit. R.W. Johnson *et al.* (1986) describe a similar idea in which the chips are inserted into holes which are cut into the wafer. Conventional bonding is then used to stitch the electrical connections between the chips and the wafer.

The idea of the *silicon mother-board* or *superhybrid* is related to the patching technique. In this, the wafer is used only to carry conductor tracks, and conventional silicon chips are fixed to it in the same way that they might be fixed to a thick-film substrate or a printed circuit board (PCB). The idea is, therefore, intermediate to those of thick-film and WSI (Johnson 1986). Its main advantage over PCB is the higher packing density which it makes possible. Its main advantage over thick-film is the close matching of thermal coefficients of expansion, which is especially important when the intention is to work, say, at liquid nitrogen temperatures in order to realise an enhanced reliability and performance (Johnson 1984). The advantages over pure WSI are that the technology is available now, able to use memory and processor parts which have been tested and produced in high volume, and hence which are cheap and readily available.

6.2.2 Discretionary wiring

Under the discretionary wiring approaches, the circuits are fabricated as normal, but are left isolated from one another. The last stage of the fabrication process involves testing each one and making a map of where the working circuits are located. The map is used to drive bonding equipment to *stitch* the good circuits together, bonding between the bond pads on neighbouring circuits.

In another approach, a reticle is constructed according to the map and used to etch a final layer of interconnecting metal. However, the need for a customised reticle for each wafer makes this an expensive option.

In yet another series of approaches, the map is used to direct an electron beam or a laser to write the interconnection pattern directly into the wafer. In the former, the beam is used to pattern a photoresist layer, prior to etching of an underlying layer of metal. In the latter, the conducting paths are synthesised directly by the laser, using a laser-induced chemical vapour deposition (CVD) technique. For this, the wafer is enveloped in a suitable chemical atmosphere, and a laser beam tracks across the surface, reflected by computer-controlled mirrors. The local heating of the wafer's surface breaks down the gases to synthesise the necessary solid conductor deposit (Burns 1986).

All of these approaches fail when faults are introduced by the last stage in the fabrication process. The bonding operation, the committing of the last layer of metal and the writing of the wiring pattern can each be considered to be risky operations.

6.2.3 Fusible links

Since the use of fusible links is the most investigated route to fault tolerance, this group of techniques is studied in greater detail here. Once again, the device is presented to the text station and each circuit is tested. Depending on which configuration strategy is to be adopted, connections are made and others are broken so as to avoid any faulty circuits. Conceptually, this could be implemented using a series of two-way switches, as in Figure 6.4 which depicts a possible arrangement to realise the standby-spare column configuration strategy.

In practice, the effect can be achieved by blowing strategically placed fuses and making strategically placed antifuses. This is depicted in Figure 6.5. A *fuse*, of course, is a piece of conductor which normally makes an electrical connection, but when melted the conductor flows away, so breaking the connection. By analogy, an *antifuse* is a gap in conductor, that is electrical isolation, but when melted conductor flows in to fill the gap, and so makes electrical contact.

More simply, the same effect can be achieved with fuses only. This is shown in Figure 6.6. In a similar way, the effect could be achieved using antifuses only.

The memory example of Chapter 5 is capable of a much simpler logical connection for the standby-spare row approach (Moore 1986c) since the rows are only ever selected one at a time. Instead of making physical connections to the spare row, the address decoder can be used to perform the work. In Figure 6.7, then sixth row is disconnected, by blowing the fuse in the select line, and the 'AND' gate in the decoder for the spare row has the appropriate fuses blown so that it responds instead to this address. It must be emphasised, though, that this works for this memory example purely because the cells do not communicate with each other, so the physical

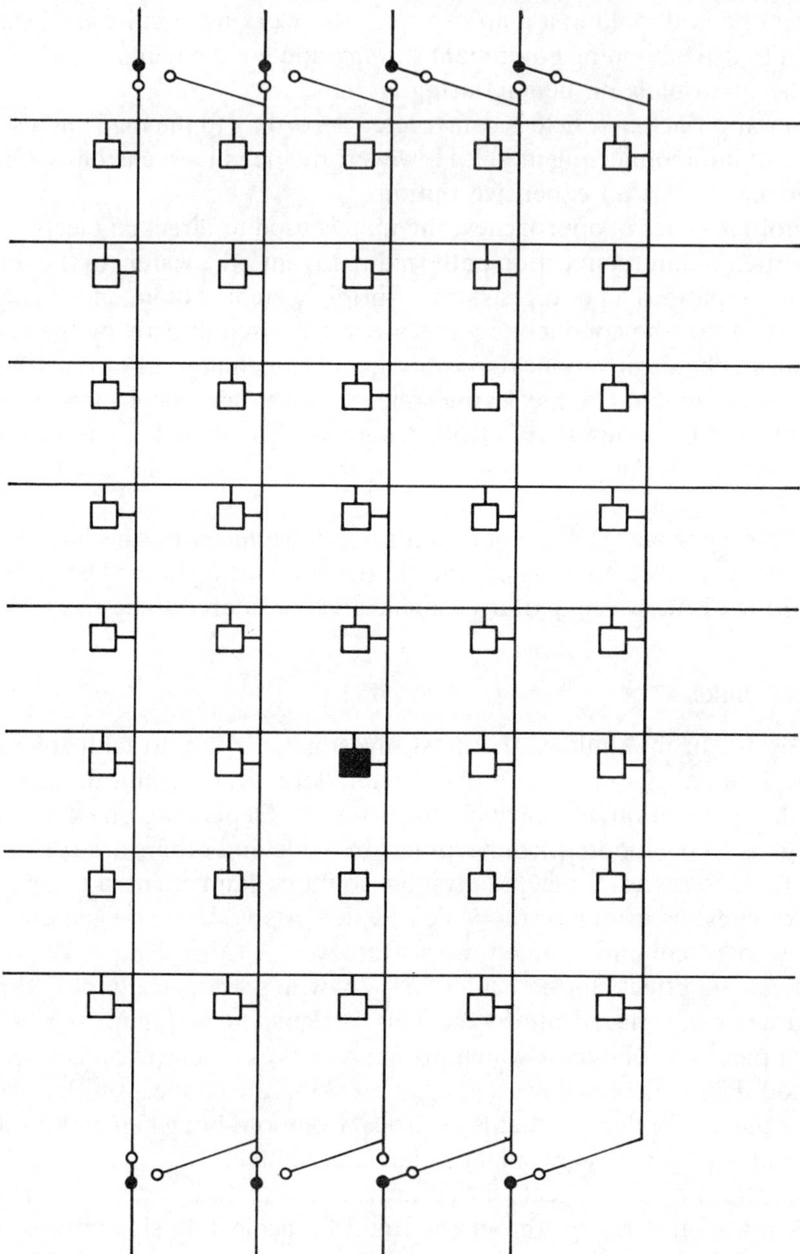

FIGURE 6.4 *Switches used to implement standby-spare column*

location is of little consequence and only one of the rows is activated at any one time. The technique cannot be applied to the columns because they are all used simultaneously, nor to processor array applications because they have an interconnect topology which must be preserved.

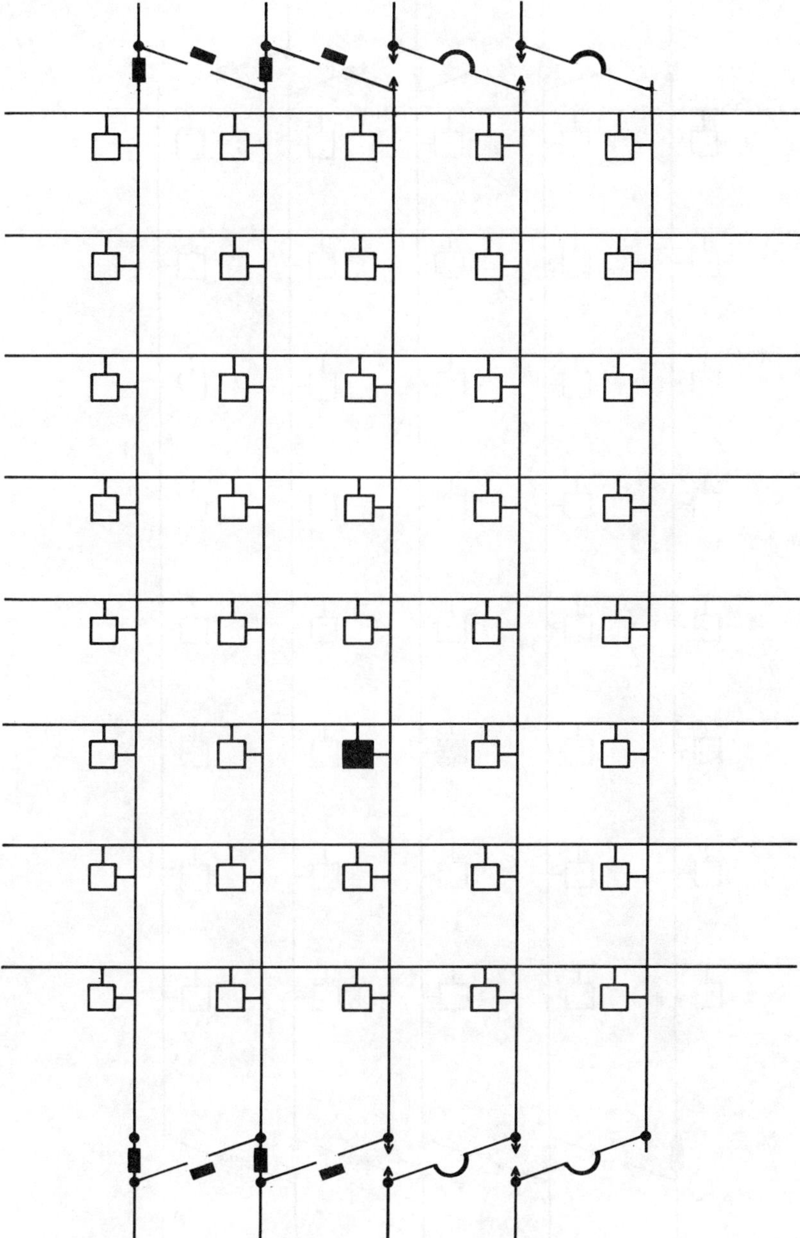

FIGURE 6.5 *Fuses and antifuses used to implement standby-spare column*

The physical methods for implementing fuses and antifuses were listed in Figure 6.3. Each one is now studied separately in the order: mechanical, electrical, laser control and electron beam control.

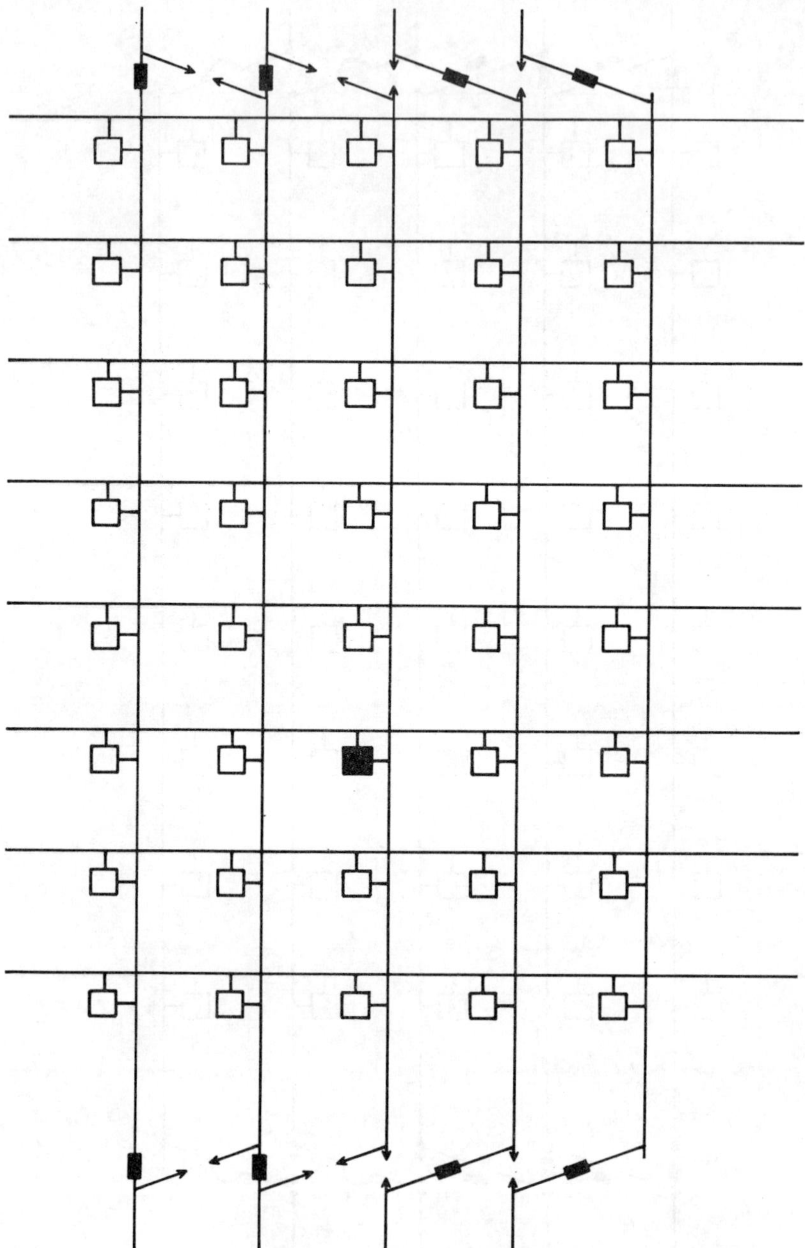

FIGURE 6.6 *Fuses used to implement standby-spare column*

Mechanical breaking and bonding

The simplest idea, conceptually, is to cut the metallised tracks which connect to faulty cells. Chisels in the form of ultrasonic probe tips have been used in laboratory prototyping/experimental environments, but the idea is unlikely to become feasible

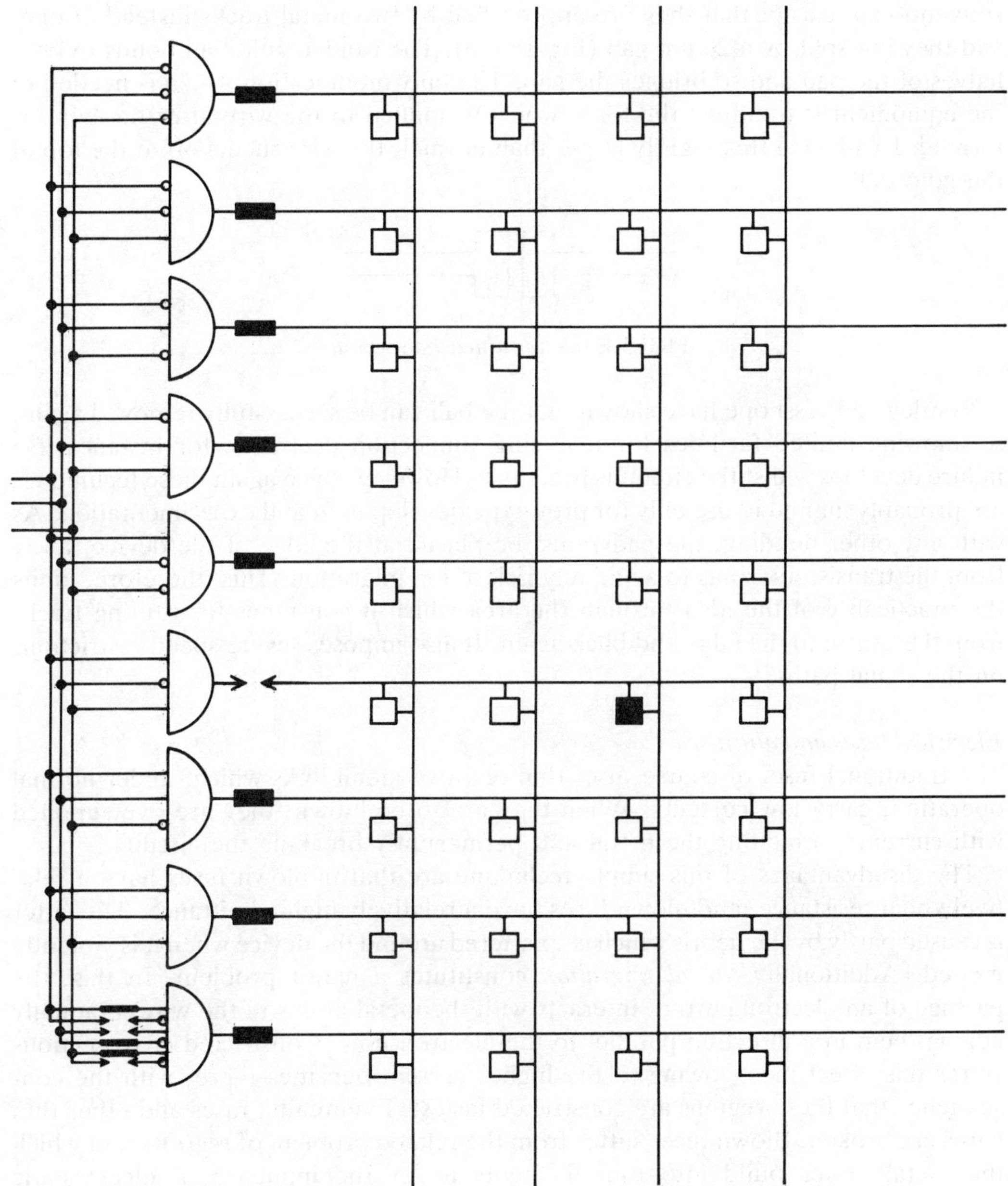

FIGURE 6.7 *Fixed aim standby-spare rows implemented in the address decoder*

for production purposes, owing to its slow operation and its tendency to cause more damage than it repairs.

Jesshope and Bentley (1986a) have investigated the opposite idea, that of making mechanical connections. They describe a method, using modified gold-wire bonding equipment, to weld gold balls on to circuit-breaking bonding pads. These pads are conventional, except that they are approached by two metal tracks instead of one, and they are split by a 20 μm gap (Figure 6.8). The welded gold ball bonds to both halves of the pad and so bridges the gap. The only modification which is needed to the equipment is to adjust the force which is applied to the wire after the bond is formed. By making this slightly larger than normal, the wire sheers off at the top of the gold ball.

FIGURE 6.8 *Modified bond pad*

Bentley and Jesshope have shown that the ball can be successfully removed again, so allowing limited facilities for reversing connection decisions, for instance if a failure develops whilst the circuit is in service. However, once again these techniques are probably limited to use only for prototype development and experimentation. As with any other bonding, the pads must be placed at the edge of the device, away from the transistors, so as to avoid any risk of ion migration. This, therefore, limits the practicality of the idea through the area which it consumes for routing tracks from the centre to the edge and back again. It also imposes severe speed restrictions on the signal paths.

Electrical fuses and antifuses

The traditional fuse, of course, uses thin resistive metal links which, under normal operation, carry low currents. When they are to be blown, they are oversupplied with current, so melting the metal and permanently breaking the circuit.

The disadvantages of this simple technique are that unblown fuses have a relatively high resistance, and blown fuses have a relatively high admittance. The latter is caused partly by the debris which is splattered around the device when it is violently melted. Additionally, *metal migration* constitutes a major problem. In this, the passage of an electron current interacts with the metal atoms in the wire, gradually edging them in a direction parallel to the electron flow. Constricted cross-sections suffer this effect most, owing to the higher current densities there, with the consequence that these regions are constricted fastest. Eventually, fuses and other thin wires are broken. Blown fuses suffer from the related problem of *regrowth*, in which the metal atoms build into thin filaments under the influence of electrostatic attraction.

Laser fuses and antifuses

By aiming a laser at strategically placed fuses (Chapman 1986), the energy of the laser is absorbed, so causing the connection to melt. The opposite effect, that of making circuits by laser heating, is achieved by Chapman using the laser antifuse which is depicted in Figure 6.9. A fairly low power, long duration, laser pulse is used so as to minimise the splatter damage which would otherwise occur. When laser power is applied the second layer metal melts, as does the intervening insulation,

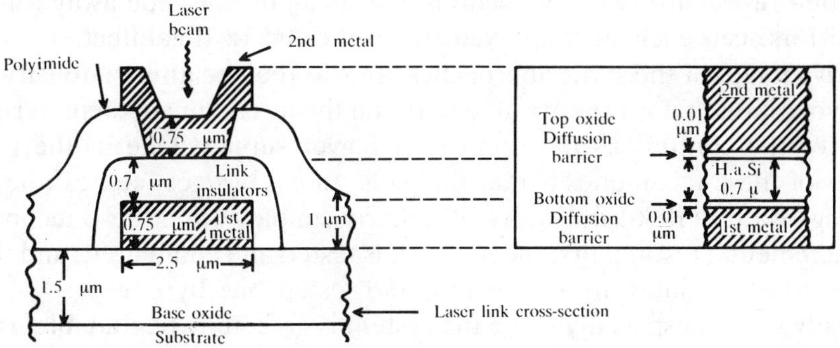

FIGURE 6.9 *Cross-section of a laser antifuse (from Jesshope and Moore, Wafer Scale Integration, p. 205, © 1986 Adam Hilger, IOP Publishing Ltd, Redcliffe Way, Bristol; reprinted with permission of Lincoln Laboratory, Massachusetts Institute of Technology, Lexington, Massachusetts)*

forming an aluminium–silicon alloy in roughly equal proportions with a resistance of less than one ohm.

The above *pyrolytic* method uses the power of the laser directly to bring about the state change in the antifuse. By using chemicals which actively react to the laser light, lower power densities can be used. This *photolytic* method promises, therefore, to reduce the risk of laser damage to the rest of the circuit. Nicolas (1986) investigates this, together with a number of speed, power, spot size and wavelength trade-offs.

Floating-gate transistors

The floating-gate transistor is a metal oxide semiconductor field effect transistor (MOSFET) which, as well as having insulation beneath the gate to isolate it from the channel, has insulation completely surrounding it. The transistor is normally non-conducting, but by injecting a strong enough signal through the oxide to the gate, for example by using a focused electron beam (Girard *et al.* 1986), sufficient charged particles can be placed in the embedded gate to ensure that the transistor remains conducting even when the beam is subsequently removed.

A floating-gate transistor can be made, therefore, to behave like a normally conducting device (a fuse) or a normally non-conducting device (an antifuse). Moreover, because it can behave as either, the decision can be reversed at a later date, for instance if a failure develops in the device during normal service.

6.2.4 Summary of static configuration techniques

With the fault tolerant techniques, it is generally assumed that configuration is performed as a fabrication step, with the manufacturer testing and configuring the device before releasing it to the customer. Any failures which develop later, while the device is in service, will mean that the device must be discarded. For particularly valuable devices though, which might include *all* wafer scale systems, there might be some scope for reworking through the reversing of earlier configuration decisions.

Uncommitted fuses/antifuses, connections which can be chiselled away for floating-gate transistors, can each be employed, theoretically, to this effect.

Some advantages of the static approaches are: (a) their relative simplicity, and (b) their non-volatility, that is they are able to retain the interconnection pattern without the need for the continuous provision of a power supply. One of the secondary advantages of these techniques is that the pads, fuses, bridges, etc. can be used for test probing. Raffel (1986) notes that it is fairly simple, using these techniques, to conduct incremental testing; first the network is tested and configured, and then each of the functional modules are connected, and tested one by one.

One disadvantage, especially when the system is gracefully degradable, is that the capacitive and conductive loading on lines, particularly the global ones, is unpredictable at design time, as noted by Chapman (1986). Furthermore, the interconnection lengths and capacitances are typically high, and in the worst case very high. The circuitry which drives these lines must cater for the worst-case electrical drive and time delay. Thus the cost of low-yielding wafers, measured in terms of area occupied, operating speed and the power consumed, is born even by high-yielding wafers (Leighton and Leiserson 1986).

Some other disadvantages are: (a) circuit testing and configuration is conducted at fabrication time and contributes, therefore, to the cost of the device; (b) the act of making and breaking the programmed connections can itself cause faults; (c) the diversity of the technologies used, such as fuses with metal oxide semiconductor (MOS), which might not necessarily be compatible; (d) a poor ability to deal with infant mortality; and (e) although they exhibit fault tolerance, they do not exhibit failure tolerance. The next group of techniques address this last problem.

6.3 OFF-LINE FAILURE TOLERANCE (DYNAMIC CONFIGURATION)

With this series of techniques, if a failure occurs during the device's lifetime the testing procedure can be repeated and a new configuration pattern can be applied. For this to take place, the present (corrupted) computation must be abandoned and restarted from a convenient point once the device has been reconfigured.

Instead of using fuses and connectors to break and make links, the approaches which are described in this section use transistors. Figure 6.10 shows the possible correspondence between these styles, and the reader is invited to confirm that

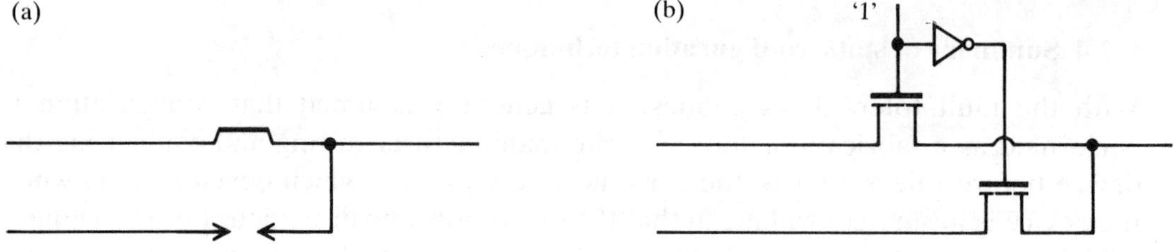

FIGURE 6.10 *Transistors used instead of fuses and antifuses*

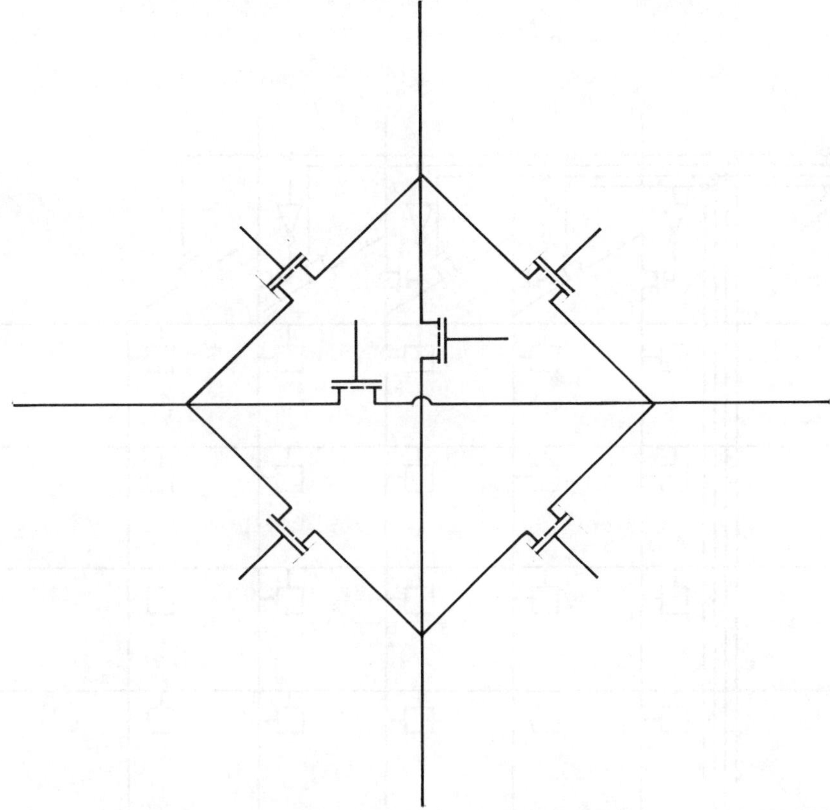

FIGURE 6.11 *Transistors used to implement a crossing-point switch*

either is applicable for use in Figure 6.5 and the bypass switches of Figure 5.11. Similarly, transistors can be used to implement the switches of Figure 5.47 (Katevenis and Blatt 1986), as depicted in Figure 6.11.

The control data to the transistors are volatile, and therefore require: (a) a power supply to be connected continuously to the configuration logic, (b) backing to be used or (c) reconfiguration to be repeated at every power-up. The methods of deriving this data, either from external connections (Section 6.3.1), internal latches (Section 6.3.2) or internally generated (Section 6.3.3) are each described next.

6.3.1 External pattern storage

Cell testing is first conducted externally and a map of the fault/failure pattern is generated. This is used to derive an appropriate pattern of signals for application to the external pins and thence to the routing transistors. The principal limitation of this system is the small number of spare pins which can be devoted to this use. Only configuration strategies which need very little information, for example standby-spare column, are generally applicable (Figure 6.12).

The next problem is one of how to generate the map of fault distribution and

UNIVERSITY COLLEGE LIBRARY CARDIFF

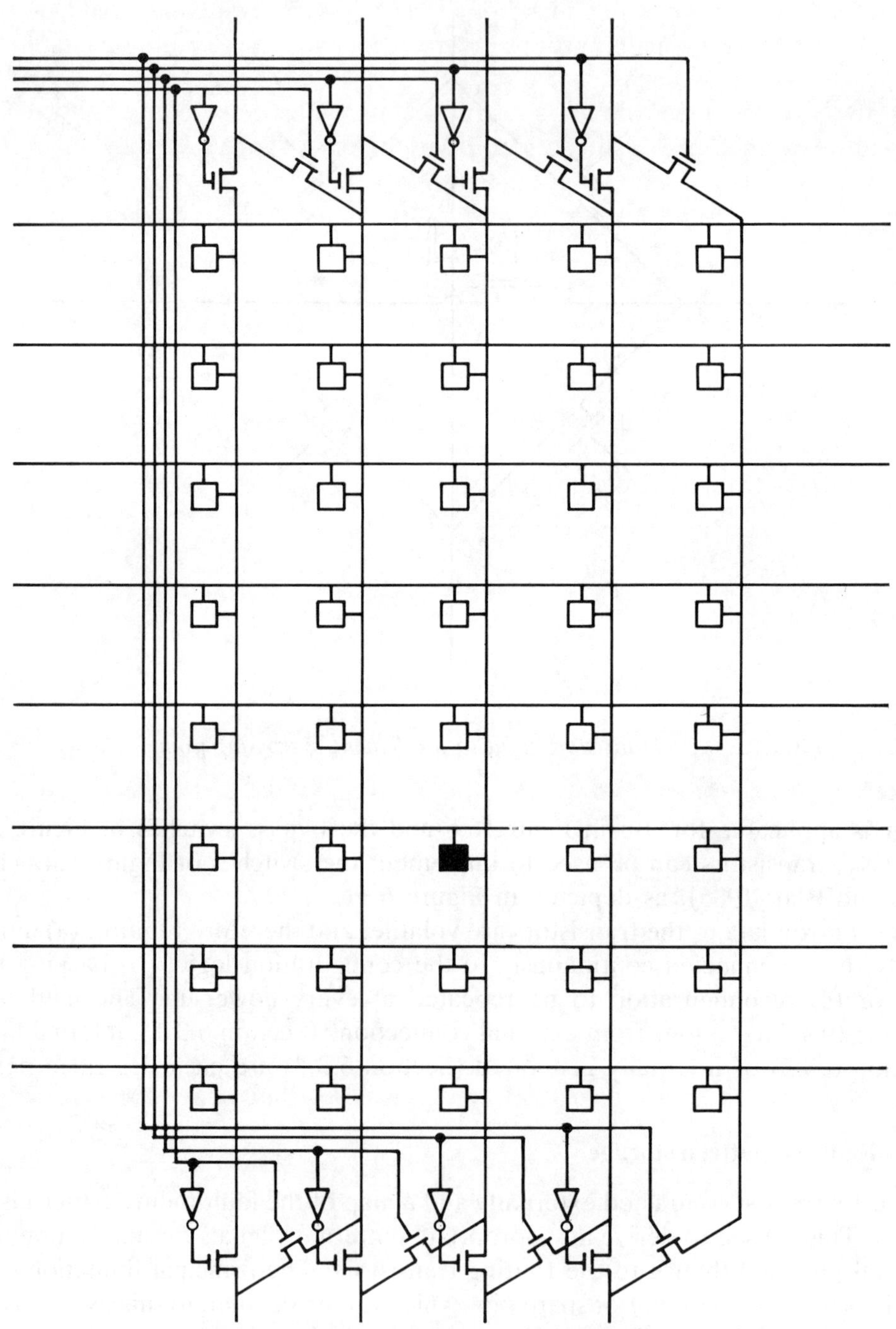

FIGURE 6.12 *Patterns stored locally*

hence the required pattern of control signals. Trial and error testing is possible for small systems, employing only a few circuits. With this, the external system applies various control patterns until it finds one which yields a properly working system. By careful design, it is possible to adopt a binary search, divide-and-conquer style of testing, which isolates smaller groups of circuits in each test, locating the faulty ones with greater accuracy each time.

Another possible idea is to use a testing scheme which can identify faulty columns of circuits and another which can identify faulty rows. Together, they can pinpoint the faulty circuits and identify them for isolation.

6.3.2 Internal pattern storage

In an alternative approach (Figure 6.13) the signals for the routing transistors are stored in a large register rather than on the pins of the device. If this register is arranged as a shift register, then only one pin is needed from which to load the initial pattern. However, in all operational respects this approach is the same as those of Section 6.3.1, with testing still conducted off-line and externally (Catt 1974).

Since the control pattern is introduced serially, Chevalier and Saucier (1986) and Genestier *et al.* (1986) suggest that incremental testing could be conducted, with little extra cost. Thus off-line failure tolerance is able to use this technique just as readily as Johnson (1986) and Raffel (1986) show for fault tolerance (in Section 6.2.1 and 6.2.3 respectively).

One potential problem with this approach is the size of the shift register. There is certainly no point in making it bigger than the payload logic, especially if it is not fault tolerant itself. Normally, though, large shift registers will be dispersed throughout the device (i.e. each circuit will contain a few elements from the overall register). This has the advantage that the pattern is dispersed amongst the routing transistors, and also that the elements of the shift register are as fault/failure tolerant as the payload circuits, that is contributing to the area δa rather than to δA.

6.3.3 Internal control

Catt's idea was that the testing could be performed by the processors on the wafer, rather than in an expensive external computer. However, his original idea still assumed that the co-ordination of the test sequence is performed by a special processor on the wafer, which he called 'chip-z'. It is possible to modify the idea so that more of the test function is performed by each processor. This has the immediate advantage of speeding up the process, since there is no longer a need for the test results to be returned all the way across the device to chip-z each time.

In general, the principle adopted in these approaches is to initiate the test externally, applying it to just one cell, and then to use the tested, working cells as they are discovered to test their neighbours. The process is recursive, with some of the approaches making use of divide-and-conquer, highly parallel test sequences, thus reducing the cost of the test and configuration time. The parallelism in the test

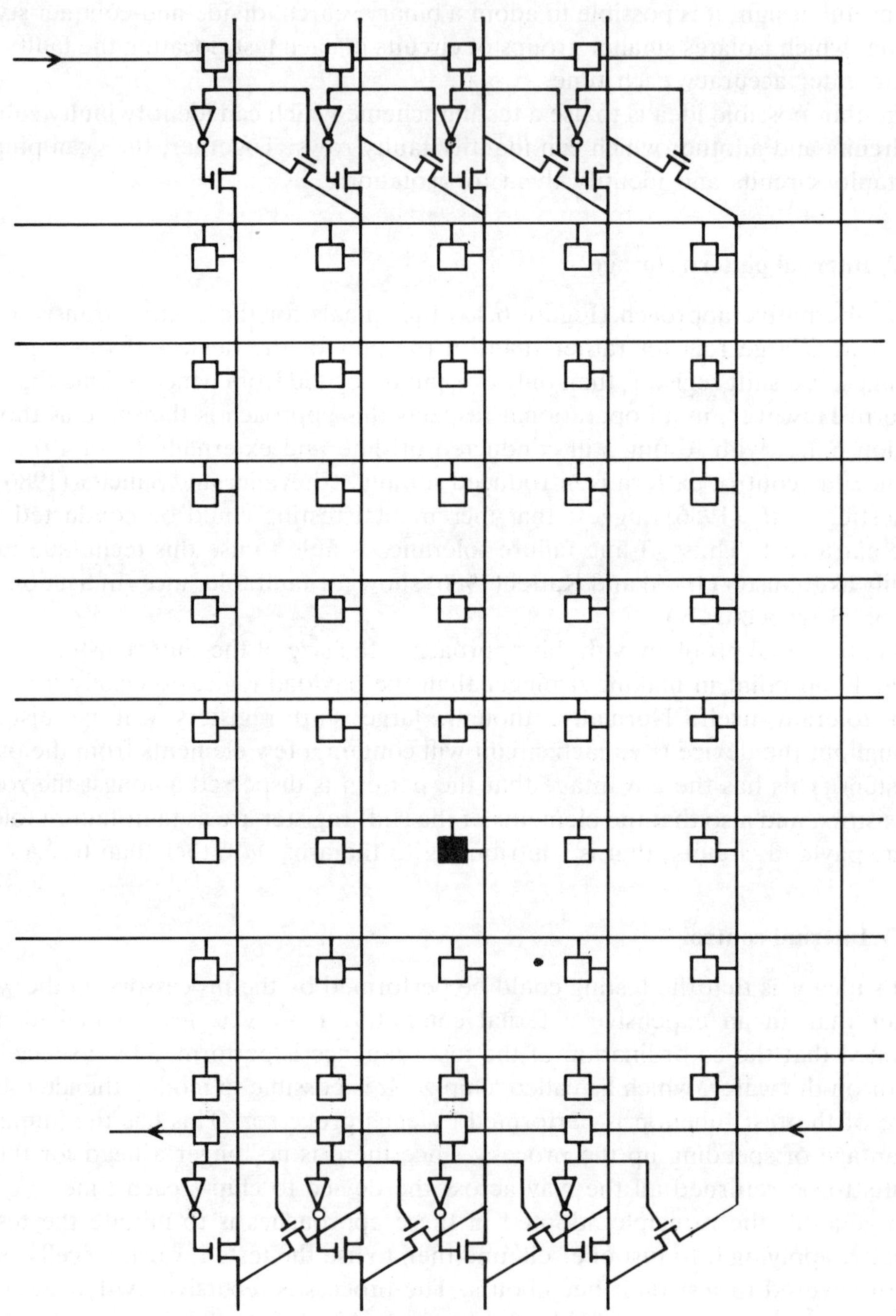

FIGURE 6.13 *Patterns stored on internal latches*

sequence depends on how many cells are commanded to take over at each recursion. For the internal control variant of the Catt spiral algorithm this value is unity, that is the test is sequential and takes about the same time as when the test had been conducted externally and, although this is not contributory to the purchase cost, it becomes part of the recurring ownership cost.

The design of better control logic might be usefully approached through the study of cellular automata (Section 4.8.3). Here, the cellular automation is not used to perform the computation, but rather to arrange the interconnection network. Thus the payload processors ride 'pick-a-back' on the simple automaton's processors, and make use of the interconnection network which it establishes. The remainder of this section explores the cellular automation rules which could be used to implement several of the fault/failure tolerance strategies of Chapter 5. When used for establishing an interconnection network, monotonic cellular automata are generally used; either there is no rule for putting the cell into the 'on' state, or there is no rule for putting it into the 'off' state. Johnstone *et al.* (1987) consider the circuitry which these rules could involve, and show that even the most complex of these algorithms can be realised using about seventy transistors.

A language is required in which to express the hardware requirements. The one which is chosen here is based on ISP' (Straubs 1980), which is a derivative of ISP, as described by Bell and Newell (1971). Certain simplifying notations have been adopted, in particular that 'on=true=1' and 'off=false=0'. Thus the expression 'on+off+on' usefully evaluates to 2.

Rectangular final device

Figure 6.14 shows the trivial rules for a cellular automation realisation of the standby-spare column scheme. Initially, the states of the cells are reset and externally generated signals are injected at the southern end. *M* cycles later some signals emerge from the northern end, indicating which columns can be used in the system.

```
IF state[S] = on THEN state[self] := on;
next;
```

FIGURE 6.14 *Cellular automaton rules for standby-spare column*

A suitable algorithm for implementing the row-orientated standby-spare cell approach is described by Evans *et al.* (1986) in the form of a truth table for an asynchronous combinatorial circuit employing 20 gates per cell. This can be expressed for a synchronous cellular automaton as listed in Figure 6.15 for the column-orientated version. Use is made of directional signals, thus 'requested[NW,self]' is the request signal which is sent by the neighbour in the north-west to the current cell, and 'available[self,NW]' is the availability signal which the current cell can send in reply. These are all initialised to their 'off' state. Cells which pass the test for correct working then assert each of their 'available' signals. Configuration is initiated by injecting 'request' signals at the northern end. Some $2N$ cycles later (Evans *et al.*

1986), 'request' signals emerge at the southern end and 'available' signals at the northern end, indicating which columns can be used by the system.

```
available[self,NW] := on;
available[self,N]  := NOT requested[NW,self];
available[self,NE] := NOT (requested[NW,self] AND requested[N,self]);
requested[self,SW] := available[SW,self];
requested[self,S]  := available[S,self] AND (NOT available[SW,self]);
requested[self,SE] := available[SE,self] AND
                      (NOT (available[S,self] OR available[SW,self]));
next;
```

FIGURE 6.15 *Cellular automaton rules for standby-spare cell*

Linear final device

In order to construct a clockwise, inward-grown Catt spiral, or an anticlockwise, outward-grown one, the first processor is set into action by being supplied with an externally generated 'request' signal. Then as each new processor is added to the spiral it runs the configuration algorithm of Figure 6.16.

```
diri := succ(diri);
IF requested[diri,self] = on THEN BEGIN
  available[self] := off;
  doro := dori;
  FOR i := 1 TO (numofsides - 1) DO BEGIN
    diro := succ(diro);
    IF available[diro] = on THEN BEGIN
      WHILE rejected[diro] = off DO requested[self,diro] := on;
        requested[self,diro] := off;
    END;
  END;
  rejected[self] := on;
END;
next;
```

FIGURE 6.16 *Cellular automaton rules for Catt spiral*

The algorithm in Figure 6.16 assumes that each cell has two flags: the first is called 'available', and is initially on in each of the working cells, and off in each of the others; the other is called 'rejected' and is normally off. It also has two cyclic counters 'diri' and 'diro'; the former is the direction from which the spiral entered the cell, and the latter is the direction in which it will finally leave. (The function 'succ(dir)' computes the clockwise successor of 'dir'.) This algorithm deals with blind alleys, backtracking out of them by use of the 'rejected' flag.

Tree-shaped final device
The tree of Figure 5.38 was grown by using the cellular automaton algorithm which is given in Figure 6.17. This assumes that an external signal, called 'prevail', is applied globally to every cell. It represents an imaginary 'wind' blowing over the array, first from the north, backing around each point of the compass. Initially all states are reset, and a state signal is injected into a cell at the edge of the wafer. The wind prevails in a constant direction until no new cells are turned on as a result of a faulty cell or the edge of the wafer being encountered. The process is complete when no new cells are turned on with the wind blowing from any direction. In Figure 5.38, the wind backs a total of 11 positions, that is 990°, or 2.75 complete cycles, the last 270° of which are engaged in checking that no growth is possible in any direction.

```
IF state[prevail] = on THEN state[self] := on;
next;
```

FIGURE 6.17 *Cellular automaton rules for tree growth*

Since the 'prevail' signal is supplied globally across the wafer, it is fortunate for timing reasons (Section 7.1) that it varies only relatively slowly. Since it must be represented using two or three bits in the respective cases of four- and eight-connected grids, it would seem that Gray codes would be an appropriate choice of representation.

Convex wrapping
Convex wrapping is different to most of the other approaches; whereas the others are positive harvesters, collecting what good cells they can, convex wrapping is a negative harvester, collecting everything that works and then discarding those which cannot be utilised.

The aim is to make sure that every harvested cell can forward data packets which are 'in transit'. For this, there must either be at least one through path, that is for an eight-connected grid there must be at least one pair of opposite working neighbours from the following: N–S, W–E, NW–SE or NE–SW. Alternatively, for highly connected networks, even when there are no direct paths, forwarded packets might need only be subjected to a small diversion; for instance a packet which is travelling north is still making progress towards its goal even if it is diverted to the north-west or north-east. These conditions are summarised by stating that a cell, in an eight-connected network, sacrifices itself only if both of the following conditions are met simultaneously:

1. There exist no pairs of working opposite neighbours.
2. It has three or more adjacent dud or sacrificed neighbours.

For example, the cell at location C2 in Figure 6.18a meets both conditions and so must be sacrificed, but the cell at D2 in Figure 6.18b does not meet the first condition, there being a NW–SE passage. The cell at location C3 in Figure 6.18c is analogous to the one at C2 in Figure 6.18a and so must be sacrificed, but the cell at location C3 in Figure 6.18d has a rich choice of simple diversion paths, so does not meet the second condition and need not be sacrificed.

```
   123456        123456        123456        123456
 A ......      A ......      A ......      A ......
 B .****.      B .****.      B ..**..      B ..**..
 C ..***.      C .****.      C ...*..      C .*....
 D ..***.      D ..***.      D ...*..      D ...*..
 E ......      E ......      E ......      E ......

    (a)           (b)           (c)           (d)
```

FIGURE 6.18 *Examples of pattern which are to be convex wrapped*

In fact, the single condition: 'A cell sacrifices itself if it has four or more adjacent dud or sacrificed neighbours', is sufficient since if this is met then the conditions (1) and (2) above must be met also. This is embodied in the rules in Figure 6.19. It is assumed that, initially, the state is 'on' in each cell which passes the test for correct working, and 'off' in all others.

```
oldstate = state[self];
IF (oldstate=on) AND (longestchainoff(N,NE,E,SE,S,SW,W,NW,N) >= 4)
  THEN state[self] := off;
next;
```

FIGURE 6.19 *Cellular automaton rules for convex wrapping*

6.4 ON-LINE FAILURE TOLERANCE (SPONTANEOUS CONFIGURATION)

Previous sections have investigated the use of defect, fault and off-line failure tolerance. This section discusses the realisation of the most powerful, but also the most expensive class of techniques, which is able to tolerate failures even whilst the device is in operation. Of the techniques which are discussed in Section 5.9, the implementation of modular redundancy (Section 6.4.1) is described as an example of a *failure correction* technique, and Hamming (Section 6.4.2) is described as an example of an *error correction* technique.

6.4.1 Modular redundancy

Usually odd numbers are chosen for the repetition factor, three being a fairly common choice, giving rise to TMR. Each of the repetitions is given the task of performing the same operation, and hence should all generate the same results. The results are collated by a *voting circuit* and the majority decision is taken. Even if one of the repeated circuits issues erroneous results, it will be out-voted by the other circuits. Figure 6.20 depicts a suitable voting circuit for bit-level TMR.

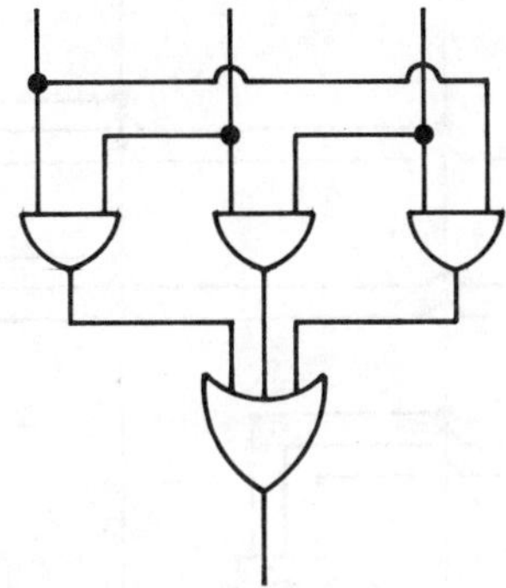

FIGURE 6.20 *A voter cell for bit-level triple modular redundancy*

6.4.2 Hamming correction

The Hamming encoder of Section 5.9.3 can be realised by the circuit shown in Figure 6.21. In this, the parity states are calculated by the modulo 2 addition units, each of which consists of a binary tree of two-input exclusive-or gates.

Similarly, the decoder can be realised as shown in Figure 6.22. Again, extensive use is made of modulo 2 addition units, the internal construction of which can be found in Appendix 1.

6.5 *PERFORMANCE*

Now that a wide variety of logical techniques have been described in Chapter 5, along with some possible physical implementation in this chapter, various performance measures and comparisons can be noted. The most important characteristic for a VLSI or ULSI manufacturer is the crop, because this is the number of devices which will share the overall wafer-processing costs. However, for the manufacturer of wafer-sized arrays, the most important characteristics are: the device yield, Y, which is the probability that a given wafer will work and the proportion of fabricated wafers which do work; the reciprocal of the relative device area, $1/rda$, which measures the physical efficiency of the fault/failure tolerance algorithm, being the ratio of payload area to total semiconductor area; and the cell harvest, h, which measures the logical efficiency of the fault/failure tolerance algorithm, being the ratio of the number of payload cells to total available cells. All three measures tend to decrease sharply when the cell yield falls below some critical value, as depicted in Figure 6.23. This shape is typical of most fault tolerance algorithms, the main

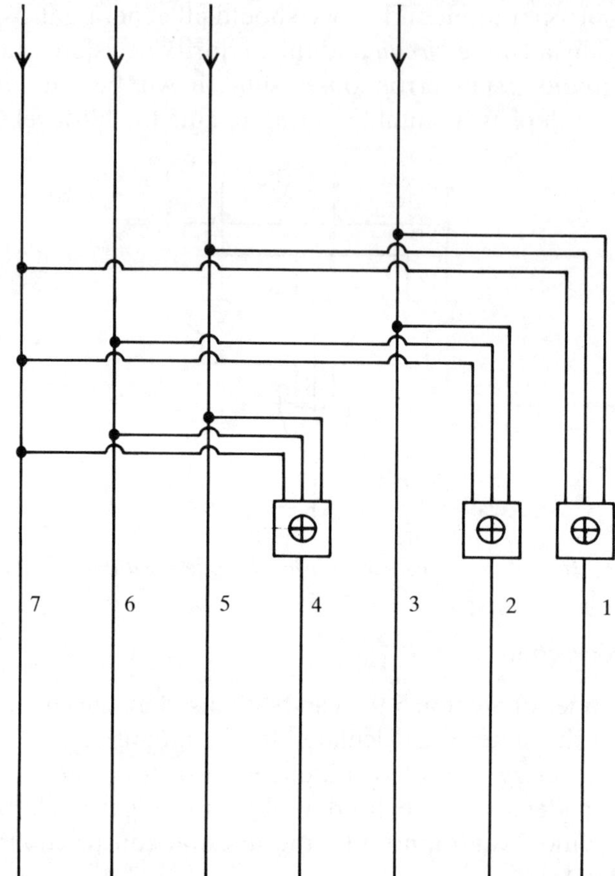

FIGURE 6.21 *Circuit diagram for Hamming encoder*

distinction being the position and gradient of the point of inflection. The rise of the step tends to become steeper, and to be displaced to the left, as the connectivity of the grid is increased. The latter effect is desirable, but the effect of the steeper cut-off is more problematic, and could have serious implications to an inconsistently yielding fabrication line.

Figure 6.24 lists the algebraic expressions for the device yield and cell harvest for some of the gracefully degradable techniques which are considered in Chapter 5. Not only do different sized devices result from using different techniques, but the size also varies with the number and distribution of the faults. The variable nature of the final device need not be a major problem if for instance a select-on-test technique is adopted, similar to the ones which were used in the 1960s to grade transistors according to their gain. Even in the 1980s, magnetic disks are sold with various numbers of working segments, thus confirming that the approach is applicable to memory too.

For fixed aim applications, the reciprocal measures tend to be more useful: thus *rda* instead of 1/*rda*, and the replication factor, *R*, instead of cell harvest, *h*,

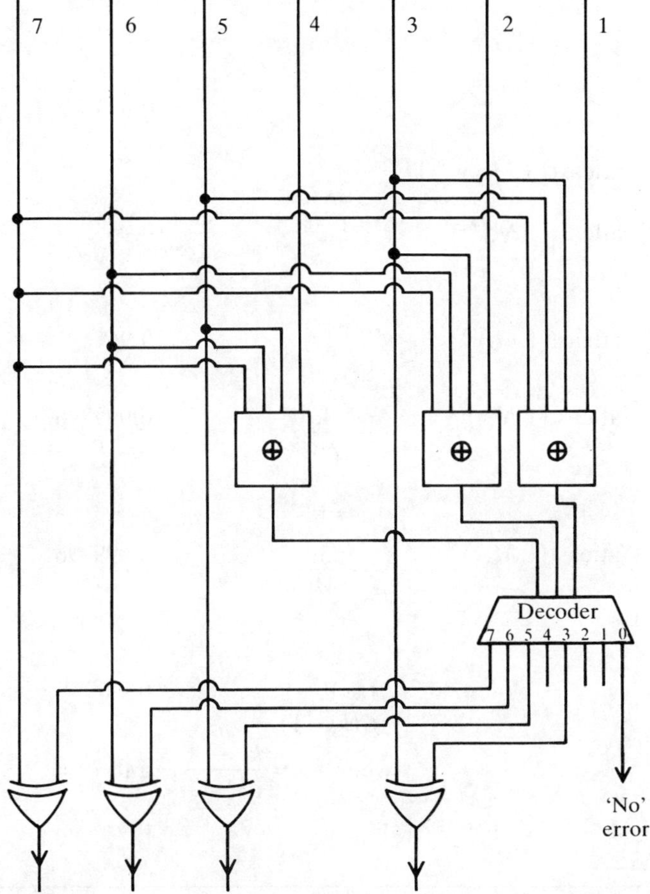

FIGURE 6.22 *Circuit diagram for Hamming decoder*

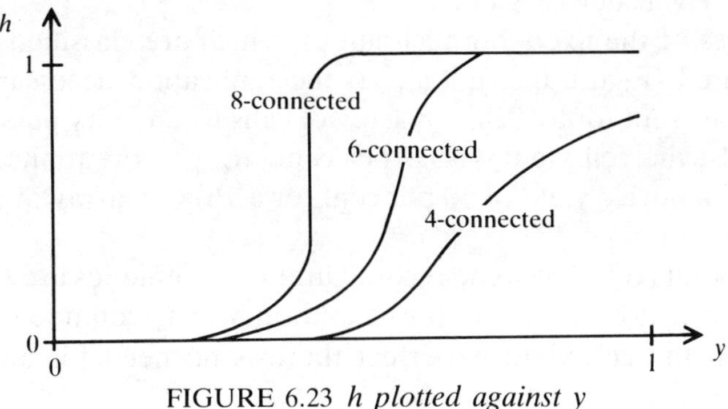

FIGURE 6.23 *h plotted against y*

	Y'	h	Y'_{proc}	h_{proc}
Fault free	y^c	1	1.9×10^{-12}	1
Bypass	y	1	0.9	1
Meander cutting	$\text{atleast}\left(1, \frac{M}{2}, y^{2N}\right)$	y^{2N-1}	0.24	0.038
Standby-spare column	atleast$(1,N,y^M)$	y^{M-1}	0.96	0.21
Standby-spare row	atleast$(1,M,y^N)$	y^{N-1}	0.96	0.21
Standby-spare cell column orientated	atleast$(1,N,y)^M$	$1 - \frac{3\sigma}{Ny}$	0.999996	0.58 where $\sigma = 2$
Standby-spare cell row-orientated	atleast$(1,M,y)^N$	$1 - \frac{3\sigma}{My}$	0.999996	0.58 where $\sigma = 2$
Tree cutting	y	$\frac{(ky)^L - 1}{C(ky-1)}$ where $C = \frac{k^L - 1}{k-1}$	0.9 and $k = 2$	0.53
Tree growth	y	~ 1	0.9	1

FIGURE 6.24 *Summary chart for graceful degradation techniques*

remembering that $h = 1/(Ry)$. A good reconfiguration algorithm is one which gives low values for these. They give an indication of what size of device needs to be fabricated to achieve a given device yield.

The performances of the fixed-aim techniques, which are classified in Chapter 5, can now be tabulated (Figure 6.25). R_{mem} is the replication necessary to obtain a device yield of 50 per cent for a 1024 × 8 array of cells when, very pessimistically for single memory cells, the cell yield is 99.9 per cent. R_{proc} is the replication which is necessary to obtain a device yield of 50 per cent for a 16 × 16 array of cells when the cell yield is 90 per cent.

Moore (1986b) points out that some reconfiguration techniques are so complicated that they are, at best, not worth the effort and, at worst, counter-productive. He observes that when the cell yield is perfect there is no need for any fault/failure

	Y'	R_{mem}	R_{proc}
Fault free	y^c	2500	3.6×10^{11}
Device replication	atleast$(1,R,y^c)$	2500	3.6×10^{11}
Column replication	atleast$(1,R,y^m)^n$	6	16
Row replication	atleast$(1,R,y^n)^m$	2	16
Cell replication	atleast$(1,R,y)^c$	2	3
Standby-spare column	atleast(n,Rn,y^m)	2.75	5.3125
Standby-spare row	atleast(m,Rm,y^n)	1.008	5.3125
Standby-spare cell column orientated	atleast$(n,Rn,y)^m$	1.125	1.3125
Standby-spare cell row-orientated	atleast$(m,Rm,y)^n$	1.003	1.3125
N-modular device redundancy	atleast$\left(\frac{R+1}{2},R,y^c\right)$	non-converging	
N-modular column redundancy	atleast$\left(\frac{R+1}{2},R,y^m\right)^n$	non-converging	
N-modular cell redundancy	atleast$\left(\frac{R+1}{2},R,y\right)^c$	3	9

FIGURE 6.25 *Summary chart for fault and failure tolerance techniques*

tolerance. When it is between 90 and 100 per cent (Figure 6.26) all of the techniques produce similarly high cell harvests, so it is sensible to choose the simplest one. When it is somewhere between 70 and 90 per cent the performances of the different techniques are beginning to diverge, but only to the extent that the simplest ones are seen to be unsuitable and the moderately complicated ones are only marginally worse than the over complicated ones. This trend is perhaps extended a little further in the cell yield range of 30 to 70 per cent. With cell yields below this perhaps fault/failure tolerance is fighting a losing battle, and not worth applying.

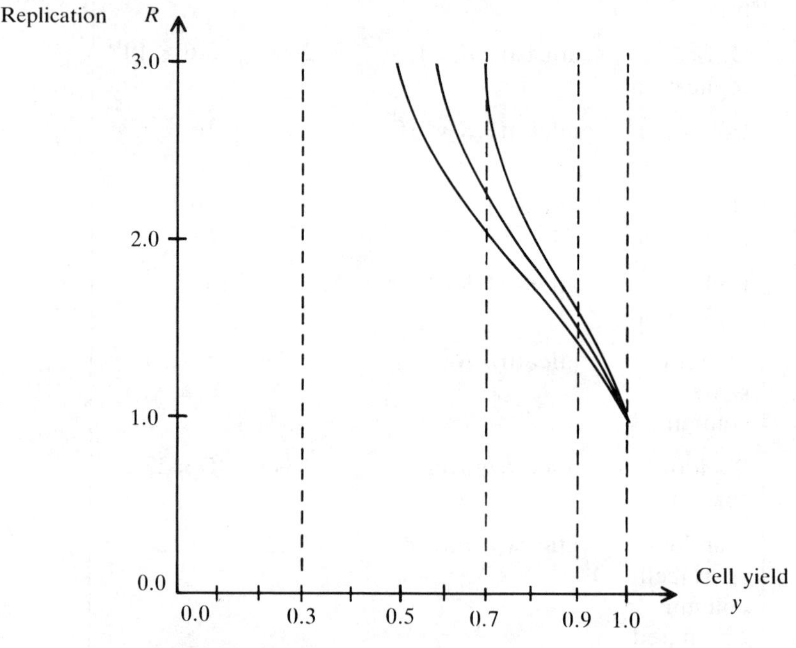

FIGURE 6.26 *The zones of fault tolerance*

Lastly, it should be noted that too much emphasis should not be placed on maximising the device yield, cell harvest and inverse relative device area to the exclusion of other important considerations. The next chapter describes how there are major problems involved in distributing signals and power over the wafer scale device, and then dissipating the power afterwards. Many of these problems occur even when the cell yield is 100 per cent, but they are heightened by the unpredictable nature of the location of faults. Reconfiguration strategies might need to be concerned not only with harvesting as many cells as possible, but also with making sure that signal path-lengths, current densities in power leads and power dissipation are balanced throughout the device. Strategies might need to be prepared to sacrifice working cells if they otherwise would place an undue burden on the power supply, etc. The next chapter should, therefore, be read with this in mind, even though it is primarily concerned with only the massive problems which occur even with perfect cell harvests.

6.6 EXERCISES

6.1 Using a copy of the blank grid of Figure 6.27, redraw Figure 5.38 for a tree which is grown on an eight-connected grid. Through how many degrees does the wind back before the algorithm terminates?

6.2 What is the maximum connectivity of the tree which is grown in question 6.1?

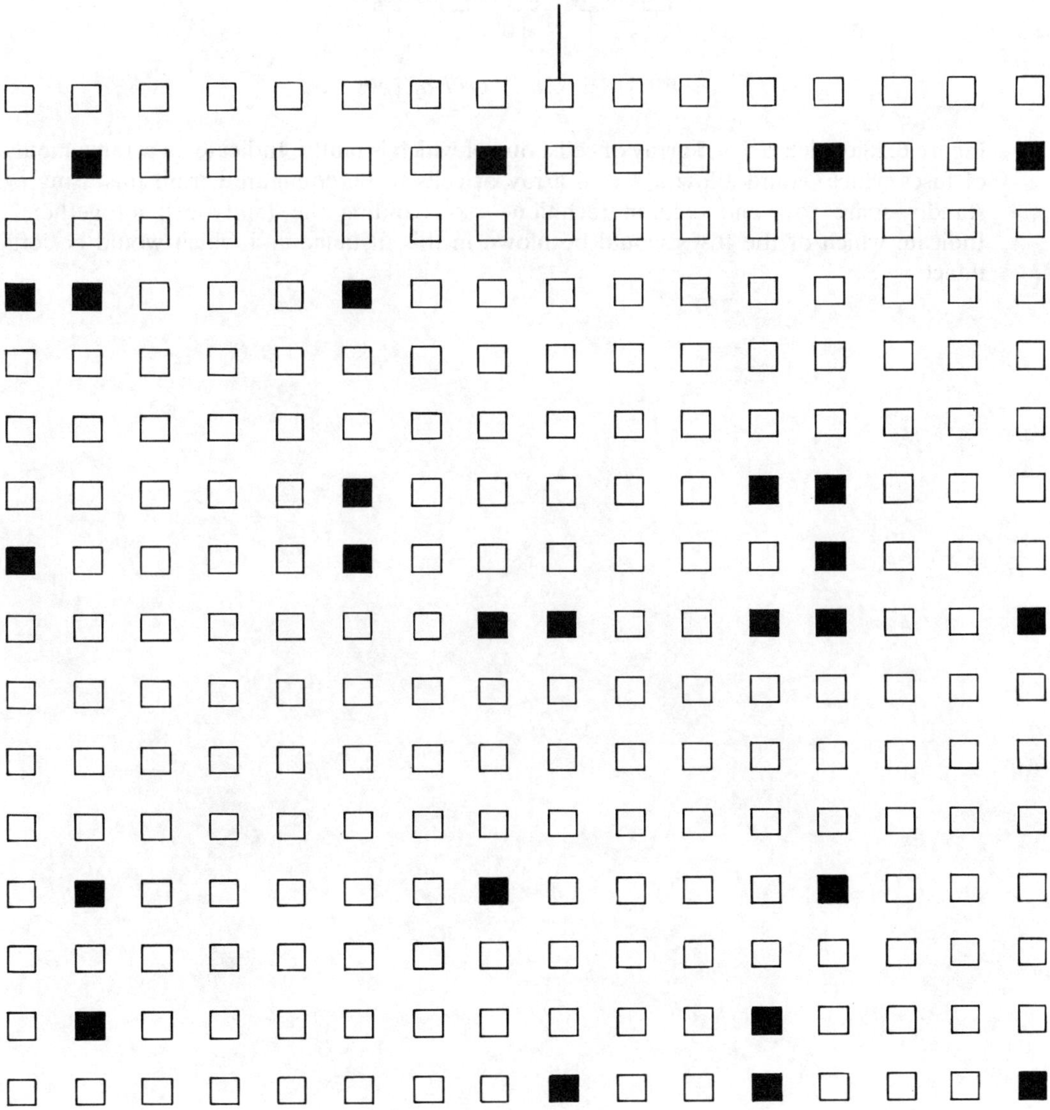

FIGURE 6.27 *Uncommitted 16 × 16 array*

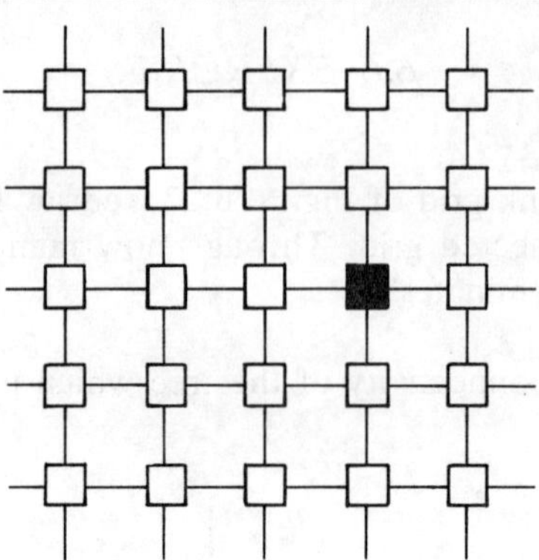

FIGURE 6.28 *A grid of cells*

6.3 Figure 6.28 depicts a 5×5 array of cells, one of which is faulty. Indicate an arrangement of fuses which would allow a 4×4 array of cells to be configured from this using a standby-spare row and column technique (so avoiding the faulty cell altogether). Indicate which of the fuses would be blown in this instance and which would be left intact.

7

PHYSICAL AND ELECTRICAL DESIGN ISSUES

Previous chapters have described the desirability of WSI and the sorts of circuits which can be fabricated using these techniques. This chapter describes why WSI has not yet become available as an option in the armoury of the microelectronics designer. It is concerned with such physical issues as clock, signal and power distribution between the cells, the problems which are caused by packaging, power dissipation and the unequal treatment experienced by different parts of the wafer during the fabrication process (Figure 7.1).

Chapter 5 showed how faulty components can be avoided, but little attention was paid to the problem of a faulty component which permanently shorts out a wire in a global bus, or worse, shorts out the power supply. Other problems exist too, even in fault-free wafers, concerning the distribution of clocks, signals and power over long distances using thin conductors. These are the subjects of the first two sections.

7.1 CLOCK AND SIGNAL DISTRIBUTION

Backus (1978) noted that the von Neumann model for computation is far from ideal from a computer science point of view; it is also far from ideal from a microelectronics point of view. If the intention were to design a large, conventional computer on a complete wafer of semiconductor, it would first be necessary to take the data, address and control buses a substantial distance across the wafer. However, aluminium tracks are not perfect electrical conductors, since they are: resistive, causing the signal to be attenuated; dispersive, causing distortion to digital signals; and capacitive, picking up noise from adjacent conductors. Most of these effects conspire to impose an extra time delay on signal transmission. The use of long distance global signals is, therefore, to be discouraged.

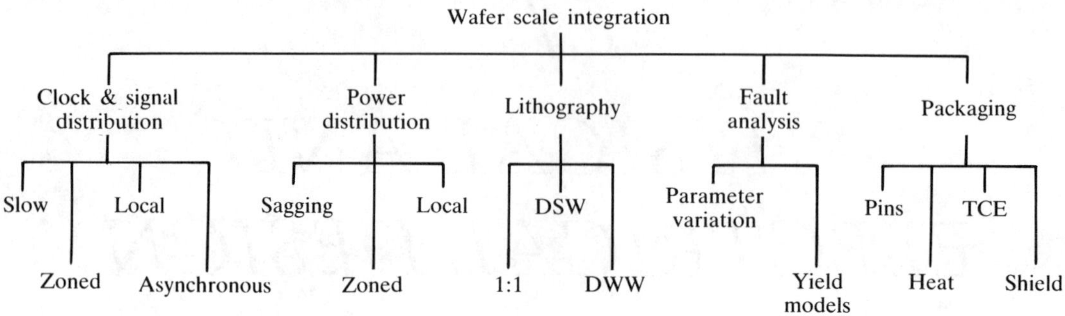

FIGURE 7.1 *Electrical and physical concerns of wafer scale integration*

Possible solutions might be to design with the worst-case clock (Section 7.1.1.), to arrange for clocks to be zoned into smaller regions across the wafer (Section 7.1.2), or to rely only on nearest-neighbour signalling (Section 7.1.3) or even completely asynchronous signalling (Section 7.1.4). The first of these is discussed in the next section.

7.1.1 Slow clock

Since a large skew is anticipated for signal edges as they travel along the longest lines across the wafer, and as the edges are expected to be eroded by dispersion, one idea is to slow the clock down to a workable speed. This has the advantage of reducing the power requirements of complementary metal oxide semiconductor (CMOS) circuits. If the device is a large, parallel computer, it might suggest that the disadvantages of a slow clock might be more than compensated for by other performance gains. However, the skew and dispersion are severe. MOS technologies are favoured for use in WSI owing to their high packing density and low power requirements. However, the high capacitance of the connections, and the time delays incurred in signal drivers, means that communication time is proportional to the square of the wire length (Mead and Conway 1980). The clock must be reduced to very slow rates, with 10 MHz suggested (Coleman and Lea 1986) for 100 mm wafers. It might be possible to increase this figure by extremely careful design of the signal lines, treating each one as a transmission line (Donlan *et al.* 1986)

7.1.2 Clock zoning

By making sure that even the longest communications paths are only local, signals can be transferred at a high clock speed. Thus, nearest-neighbour interconnection is encouraged. The technique of *clock zoning* (Coleman and Lea 1986) capitalises on this, relying on the use of a tree-structured architecture. For simplicity, the binary H-tree is illustrated in Figure 7.2, though Wasp (Lea 1986a) in fact uses the better connectivity of a higher order *n*-ary tree, but the principle is the same.

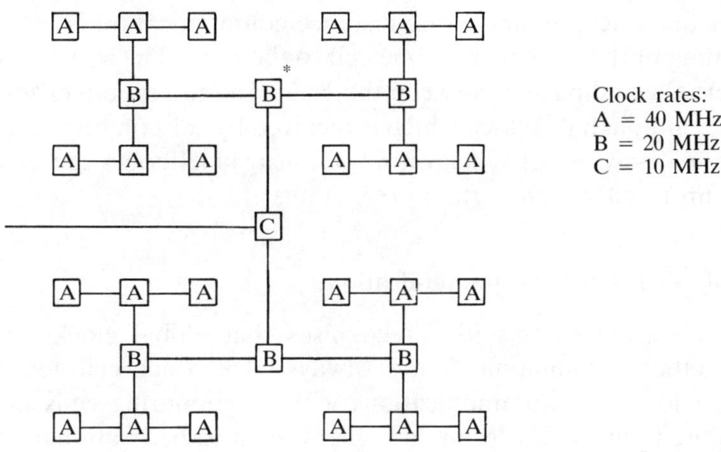

FIGURE 7.2 *Binary H-tree*

The cells which are marked 'A' in Figure 7.2 communicate with members of their local group using a high speed clock. They communicate with cells in other local groups via those cells which are marked 'B' at a slower clock rate because of the larger distances which are involved. They communicate with cells on the other side of the tree, or to the slow high current tracks of the external PCB, via cell 'C' using an even slower clock. This slowest clock can be generated externally and used to derive the faster clocks internally (Coleman and Lea 1986).

As well as the normal root-node bottleneck experienced by most tree-configured architectures, there is an extra penalty which is incurred by passing messages through any slow rate node. The execution model used on the system must therefore be one which makes maximum use of locality.

The tree-cutting reconfiguration algorithm is described in Section 5.5.1 but, to summarise, suppose that cell B* in Figure 7.2 conducts a test on its western neighbour's logic and finds it to be faulty. It can simply record the fact that this branch cannot be used, and proceed to function with one descendant. Tests for more drastic faults/failures are readily supported using this scheme. Suppose that before cell B* conducts a test of its western neighbour's logic it first tests this neighbour's power supply and other global signal lines. If any are found to be short circuited, it can isolate this branch of the system without proceeding to test it any further. Thus potentially catastrophic faults are prevented from disrupting the remainder of the system.

7.1.3 Local, equal-length communications only

Some computers, for example as described by Anderson *et al.* (1987), consist of a two-dimensional grid of identical tessellating cells communicating through a packet-switched network, able only to exchange tagged data packets (tokens) with their immediate neighbours. Long distance communication is achieved by repeated forwarding of the packet from one cell to the next. The system clock could be supplied externally and passed between the cells. The full speed 40 MHz, say, could be used since, although the clock which is received by cells on opposite sides of the wafer will be hopelessly out of synchronisation, near neighbours can be arranged to be always synchronised within certain error limits.

7.1.4 Asynchronous communication

An extension to this idea recognises that global clocks can be dispensed with altogether if communication is always local. Each cell generates its own clock at which to work. Communications with neighbouring cells must involve full handshaking (Seitz 1980). Many designers seem to be irrationally fearful of making this step but, as Stevens (1984) observes, the initial design effort is well compensated. Two major facets of circuit design are the specification of system's function and the specification of its timing. The former is equally difficult in either design style, whilst the latter is, superficially, easier with synchronous systems. Synchronous systems have the advantage of specifying timing events only within certain time windows, so allowing designers to be less than rigorous. Signal glitches and races hazards are all tolerated, so long as they are stable by the end of the clock period. However, beyond this, asynchronous systems are more amenable to making timing abstractions. Smaller, self-timed modules are used as black-box components to larger systems, the only constraints being those which are directly applicable to the current level of abstraction.

Asynchronous systems require more elaborate, time-consuming handshaking for all communications. However, this disadvantage can be offset by the fact that all modules can work at their own speed and do not have to allow for some globally determined worst case. Asynchronous systems can therefore be much faster than their synchronous counterparts.

7.2 POWER DISTRIBUTION

A very similar set of constraints, and solutions, applies to the power supply and signal network designs. These involve designing within the problem, using a degraded supply (Section 7.2.1), using zoned networks (Section 7.2.2) or using localised distribution (Section 7.2.3). The first of these is taken next.

7.2.1 Degraded supplies

Attenuation is the major concern in power supply design, with a significant lowering of the voltage of the supply towards the wafer centre compared with that nearer the edge. Current densities also pose a problem; circuits at the edge must carry the full current for the entire wafer. A wafer dissipating 100 W, which is not atypical of present designs (CMOS clocked at 10 MHz dissipates about 0.01 W/mm^2), at 5 V demands a total of 20 A. The voltage cannot be increased, since this might risk the breakdown of the thin insulating gate oxides. The power supply leads must be wide enough, and thick enough, not to degrade the voltage supply. For ULSI, this results in power leads which occupy between 50 and 90 per cent of the circuit area, so leaving little room for the clock and signal leads. One idea would be to dedicate an extra layer of metallisation to the power distribution network, involving the use of perhaps three or more layers of metal. Alternatively, the lines can be made narrower, and hence will occupy a smaller area of semiconductor, if they can be also made thicker. However, aluminium is already laid to its greatest thickness possible without the risk of it peeling away. One promising idea involves the electroplating of copper to build up the thickness of the aluminium power supply lines (Barrett *et al.* 1986). Copper also has a higher conductivity than aluminium. Silver or gold would be even better, were it not for the electron traps which would be introduced as the metal ions migrate into the silicon.

All of this is aggravated by the fact that the power supply does not supply direct current when it has to meet the fluctuating demands of millions of synchronously clocking circuits, causing significant energy surges at their clock edges. Consequently, the current carried by the power supply lines fluctuates with peak loads significantly greater than those of the mean. The use of large synchronous circuits is therefore to be discouraged.

7.2.2 Zoned power networks

Since multiple supply connections are favoured, one solution would be to supply a separate power network from each point (Warren *et al.* 1986). Any catastrophic fault then scuttles only one part of the net.

7.2.3 Local power distribution

Another idea is the inclusion of extra buffering transistors (Fried 1986c) to isolate faulty circuits (Figure 7.3). Unfortunately, this means that each node must be capable of controlling the power needs of all of its descendant networks. The transistors which are used for this purpose are enormous and dissipate large amounts of power, especially those in the nodes near to the root of the network. The inclusion of power isolation transistors increases the attenuation further, hence accentuating the power rail sag.

The asynchronous signal distribution idea can be applied to the power supplies too. The power-isolating circuits must be capable of being supplied from either direction. This requirement appears to be feasible since the isolating transistor is potentially a bidirectional device. If this can be achieved, it will be possible to supply the power from several points around the wafer's edge and not to place the burden on one cell to supply the needs of the entire system.

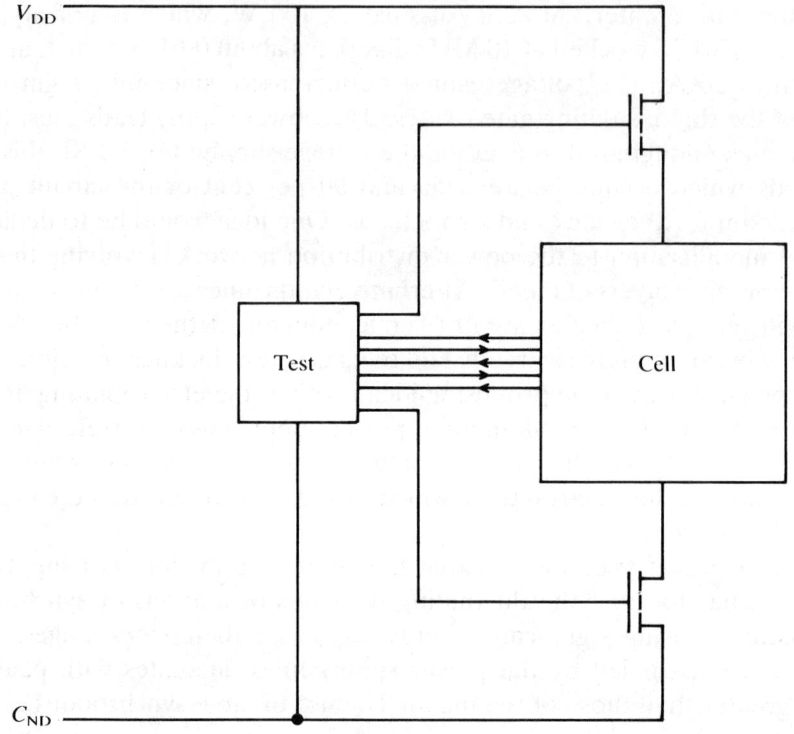

FIGURE 7.3 *Arrangement for isolating power rails*

7.2.4 Possible future techniques

Rather than routing power from the outside world through the wafer to the internal cells, photoelectric collectors, which are illuminated externally, might be able to supply enough power for each cell's needs. Similarly, clock and signal distribution might be achieved in this way, with photoelectric sensors replacing some of the bonding pads.

The use of superconductor signal and power leads has also been mooted. This would cut down on some unnecessary wastage of power. None of the ideas of this section appears to be practical yet, though.

7.3 LITHOGRAPHY

Another practical problem is that of patterning the wafer. Lithography is used in microelectronics to write patterns into the semiconductor (McGillis 1983). Conventionally, this is used to mean 'photolithography': the use of light to write a pattern in an analogous fashion to that of conventional photography. Figure 7.4 lists some of the alternative ways of exposing the photosensitive surface to the desired pattern.

The first is most like conventional photography, and uses a single, diffuse source to flood the area with light, but with an intervening opaquely patterned area to cast shadows on the photographic surface. The second method uses a single, diffuse source which is masked by an adjustable, rectangular aperture whose length, width, orientation and position can each be adjusted. The pattern is then built up by exposing the surface to a large number of abutting rectangles. The third method uses a single, focused source in much the same way to track across the surface, perhaps guided by moving mirrors, writing the pattern where it is required. The last technique also uses a single, focused source, but one which is scanned across the entire area in a zig-zag pattern, analogous to a television raster, with the light source turned off when the raster crosses regions which are not to be exposed.

Transmission exposure
Flash exposure
Vector scan exposure
Raster scan exposure

FIGURE 7.4 *The different modes of exposure*

The two main problem areas are resolution and registration. Due to interference effects, light cannot be used to write patterns whose dimensions are comparable with, or less than, the wavelength used. The use of white light has given way to the use of short wavelength monochromatic light, and thence to ultraviolet. Some research is devoted to using X-rays instead, but the problems of making suitable photomasks are great.

Registration is important since the layers must be mutually aligned over the complete area of the device to an accuracy which is smaller than the grid size, λ. When dice are small and features are large relatively little problem is experienced. When circuits covering an entire wafer aligned to an accuracy of $\pm\lambda$ (where λ is presently about 1 μm) are contemplated, the problems are great indeed.

The traditional lithographic method is briefly described next (Section 7.3.1), showing why the techniques are unlikely to be practical for WSI. Sections 7.3.2 and 7.3.3 describe two alternative techniques which were originally proposed for VLSI, and appear to offer some promise for WSI.

7.3.1 One-to-one

The traditional approach to integrated circuit lithography is to make a full scale photomask for each layer of the final wafer. Each photomask is therefore at least as big as the wafer, and bears as many repetitions of the pattern as there are to be repetitions of the cell on the wafer.

The process consists of at least three stages: reticle exposure, photomask exposure and wafer exposure. The first and second can be fairly lengthy processes, but each are conducted relatively infrequently. The second is conducted either photographically with the cells exposed one at a time using a transmission source step-by-repeat camera, or using a raster scan electron beam. Reticle exposure is usually conducted using flash exposure, with the adjustable aperture driven by a computer. By contrast, when the pattern on the photomask is transferred to the photoresist on the wafer, transmission exposure is used and is a very fast process.

Traditionally, *contact printing* is used for wafer exposure, with the disadvantage that both the wafer and the photomask can be damaged by mechanical abrasion. Photoresist can peel off when the photomask is taken away after exposure, so exposing areas of the wafer which should not have been exposed. More importantly, the photoresist which is left stuck to the photomask goes on to disrupt the pattern on many successive wafers. Projection printing is now used increasingly to circumvent this.

The main disadvantage of these techniques, though, is the need to align the photomask with previous patterns across the full length and breadth of the wafer. Due to various sources of wafer distortion, it is the edges of the wafer which are usually found to be least well aligned. Moreover, due to a problem of *runout*, pattern misalignment is accentuated at the edges of the wafer by thermal expansion of the photomasks, caused by temperature variations even of 0.1°C between one mask exposure and the next. Furthermore, with the projection systems, optical distortions are worst at the edges too.

7.3.2 Direct step on wafer

Present day VLSI technology required the development of a better technique, and this is described next. In effect, the three-stage process described above is modified with one step removed. Instead of using a step-and-repeat camera to expose a photomask, it is used directly to replicate the pattern on to the wafer, as described in below, or else a direct-write method is used on the wafer, as described in Section 7.3.3. The major problem with either of these techniques is that previously this slow operation was performed only once in order to make the photomask. Now the slow process is experienced at wafer exposure time.

Another problem with the direct step on wafer (DSW) techniques is that they are less tolerant of blemishes on the photomask. With 1:1 processing any blemish will affect one die site on every wafer, whilst with direct step on wafer any blemish will affect every die site on every wafer. However, since a projection system is employed, with a five- or ten-fold reduction, the blemishes are reduced in size too, many of them being reduced below the resolving power of the equipment.

Many of the regular topologies which are shown in Chapter 5 would seem to lend themselves to step-and-repeat exposure. Even six-connected hexagons and eight-connected, tessellating octagons have been shown to be representable as brick-shaped rectangles (Aubusson 1979) and squares (Kelly and Shute 1986b) respectively (Figure 7.5).

For ULSI, the alignment problem can be avoided if each circuit is individually aligned. With WSI though, each circuit must be aligned with its neighbours. Various

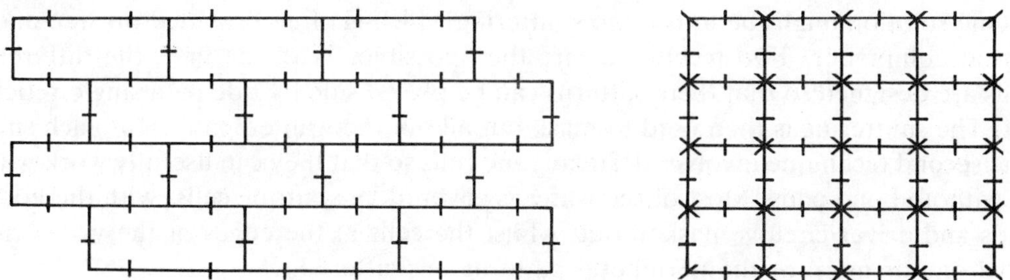

FIGURE 7.5 *Orthogonal representations of hexagons and octagons*

schemes have been proposed to tackle this problem. One involves wire bonding between adjacent circuits. Though a time-consuming task, this is consistent with the wire-bonding method which is described in Section 6.2.2. It does fail to realise some of the advantages of WSI though – that is, speed of fabrication, reduction of the area, time and power requirements of bonding pads, and avoidance of the low reliability aspects of bonding. Another technique is to lay thick interconnection tracks where adjacent cells need to communicate, thus tolerating a greater misalignment (Figure 7.6). The main objection to this idea is the capacitance, and hence time delay and power requirements, introduced by thick lines, and the limit that it creates on the number of interconnections.

One other problem remains though. Most of a wafer scale device is highly regular, in order to facilitate application of the fault/failure tolerance algorithm. However, most systems still contain a residual area of hardcore logic. Even if this has been designed out of the system, the bond pads and associated drivers, will be only required at a few cell sites – predominantly those around the edges of the wafer. If at least two different cell types are required, this might suggest the use of two complete sets of reticles and photomasks. However, this is both a very expensive solution, owing to the cost of generating reticles, and an impractical one, owing to the time-consuming, damage-inducing operation of swapping photomasks in and out of the step-and-repeat camera.

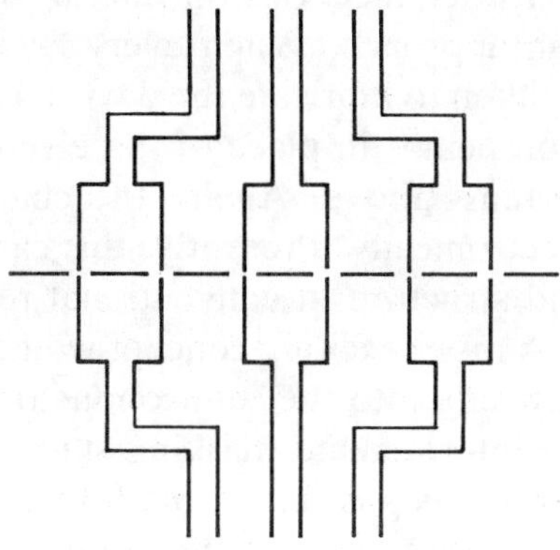

FIGURE 7.6 *Track abutting at the mask boundaries*

One solution might be to use the shuttering which is often provided on step-and-repeat equipment. Two techniques are then possible. With the first, the different cells are designed so that their patterns can be placed side by side on a single reticle set. The shuttering is then used to mask out all but the wanted pattern at each site. The second technique involves designing the cells so that they can usefully work with or without bond pads. Most of the wafer is covered by abutting cells, with the bond pads and driver circuits masked out, whilst the cells at the edges of the wafer can have one or more of the peripheral patterns unshuttered.

7.3.3 Direct write on wafer

An alternative to using electromagnetic lithography, with its limited resolution, is to use electron beam lithography, since electron beams are capable of much finer wavelengths. Most of the techniques to date tend to use the mechanical properties of a high energy beam of particles to make or break molecular bonds in a conventional, but specially chosen, resist material.

Rather than using a transmission-type electron beam, and having to create a suitable blocking material from which to construct the photomasks, a scanning beam mode of operation is used. As with a conventional television raster, the intensity of the beam is modulated electronically in order to build up the required two-dimensional pattern. Although this system is not restricted by the limitations of a mechanical stepping system, it finds even more restriction in the electrical bandwidth to the control circuitry for the electron beam. The patterning of a wafer full of circuitry represents a truly massive amount of data to be transferred over a serial link.

Electron beam direct write on wafer (DWW) could be used to solve the registration problem since it can be used to read information from the surface, like an electron microscope, whilst it is in the process of writing the pattern. Suitable computer software might be able to use this information to adapt the pattern so as to make allowances for undulations and other imperfections.

The section on discretionary wiring (Section 6.2.2) reported on laser and electron beam systems which can directly write on to the surface of the wafer. Under those systems, only the small 'extra' connections on one layer of the circuit were to be written, using a vector-scan approach. When every layer of every circuit is to be written, however, the time taken to fabricate the device becomes significantly larger.

Another idea is to use ion beams in place of the electron beams which were described in some of the systems above. Again, the charged ions can be focused, scanned and modulated electronically. Presently, this can be used as an alternative to light to modify the bond structure in conventional resist, or instead of the diffusion stage (Seidel 1983). A more exciting concept would be to use the ion beam to implant the active atoms directly into the semiconductor, literally writing the transistors without recourse to intermediate masking stages. Present ion source techniques seem unlikely to make this possible in the foreseeable future, since they are either too weak for the operation to be fast enough to be cost effective, or they are insufficiently focused to be capable of writing the intricate patterns of microelectronic circuitry.

The next section describes several aspects of defect and fault distribution, mentioning a number of origins and reasons for the problems which they cause. It shows how the choice of lithographic techniques has a direct impact on the fault density.

7.4 FAULT DENSITY AND PARAMETER VARIATION

One of the greatest stumbling blocks to WSI is the nature of the fault density, D. Chapter 5 shows that practical techniques exist for configuring circuits in the presence of faults/failures. However, the choice of an appropriate strategy from the many which are suggested there, and the initial decision as to whether WSI is an economic method for implementing a given device, depends on the ability to quantify the numbers and positions of the faults. Despite the vast amounts of research devoted to this topic, concrete answers are noticeably lacking. Theories, models and formulae exist, but most are controversial, or are challenged by counter-theories, models and formulae. Not only is it difficult to extrapolate the yield results from one fabrication line to another, but the performance of a single line is unpredictable, varying from one day to the next and from one batch or wafer to the next. It is within this uncertain, incomplete setting that this section classifies some of the alternative theories and models.

There are three major types of flaw: gross, local and random. Gross flaws are caused by process inadequacies such as bad photomask alignment, and by incorrect operating conditions such as the use of wrong chemicals or temperatures. These cause the failure of entire wafers, or complete batches. Generally, the solution is to tighten up on operational procedures.

It is more difficult, though, to deal with local flaws: the failure of one very small part of a single circuit. Photomasks are never perfect, especially if they have been used for some time, with imperfections which are introduced by impurities in the chemicals and by mechanical abrasion. Usually, therefore, imperfections are in the form of extra flecks or missing pattern on the photomask. The conducting layers, such as metal, polysilicon and diffusion, are each susceptible to unintentional open circuits where pattern is missing, and unintentional short circuits where extra pattern is included. The insulating layers are prone to unintentional connections between conducting layers (pinholes) where pattern is missing, and to badly formed *vias* where extra pattern is present. The quality of the deposited metal is also a source of flaw, particularly because the metal, being one of the top-most layers, has the roughest terrain to cover. Continuity is threatened by sharp edges which cause cracking in the metal, and by a poor coating on the steep vertical rises of the steps.

As a fabrication process matures, the occurrences of gross and local flaws can be made to tend to zero. However, the third type, the random dislocations, etc., remain, and the wafer is prone predominantly to these naturally occurring defects in the materials. Junction leakage and contact to substrate short circuits are common.

Section 7.4.2 catalogues some models which have been developed for predicting cell yield. First, though Section 7.4.1 describes some reasons why the fault density might not be constant over the water surface and why this, along with some quite unrelated phenomena, can be of major concern even to the abstract system architect.

7.4.1 Parameter variation

When a wafer is fabricated, normally in furnaces and chemical baths, not all parts receive the same degree of heating, nor the same flow of gases and other chemicals. Nor is photomask aligning perfect at every point in the circuit. As a result, conductors and transistors vary from one point to another, with variations of resistance, capacitance, gain, transit time and frequency response. Added to this, different parts of circuits receive different power supply voltages, as described above. Each circuit must be able to work with a wide variety of parameters in its components.

The problem of parametric variation can be tackled by designing the cells to work asynchronously, each generating its own high speed clock. Each cell can then work at the speed which suits it best. Each clock will be completely out of phase and frequency synchronisation with its neighbours, and full handshaking is then necessary for all intercell communication.

As well as these physical parametric variations, there are logical ones. When a device has undergone fault/failure tolerance reconfiguration, some signal paths are physically longer than others. This leads to variations in capacitance, resistance and

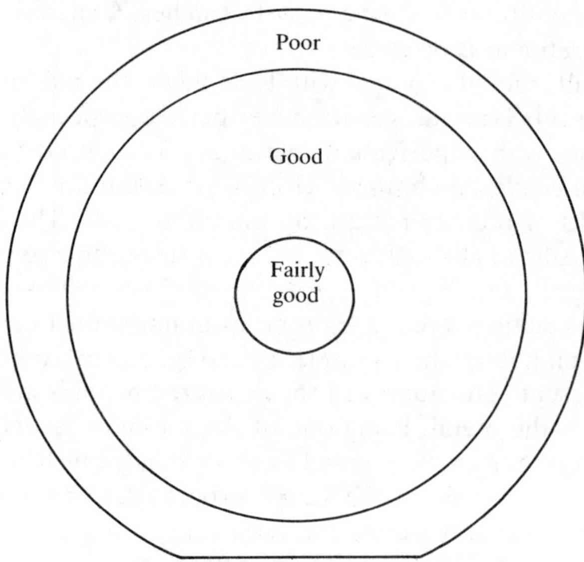

FIGURE 7.7 *Yield zones on a wafer*

most importantly in time delay. This problem is particularly troublesome in systolic array design, and has been rigorously investigated by Leighton and Leiserson (1986).

It is widely believed that defects are not generally random in their distribution (Stapper 1985), and tend to be found in clusters. The distribution is dependent on the radial distance from the centre of the wafer (Ferris-Prabhu *et al.* 1987). Cell yield is very low at the wafer edge, due to thermal warping and physical problems caused by photoresist which is not distributed uniformly by the spinner. It is also slightly lower in the centre, in the area where the photoresist is introduced. It is best in the anulus between these two areas, as depicted in Figure 7.7. However, the significance of this zoning is still highly contentious, and as yet unproved.

Some workers believe that there is possibly a small angular distribution too (Ferris-Prabhu *et al.* 1987), which is dependent on the orientation of the wafer in gas and chemical streams. In general, therefore, the fault density, D, is not constant, but is dependent on the polar coordinates of the position on the wafer, $D(r,\theta)$. Figure 7.8a plots the values of D against various values of r for a typical cross-section across the wafer. Figure 7.8b uses polar coordinates to plot D against the angle, θ, for a constant radius from the centre of the wafer.

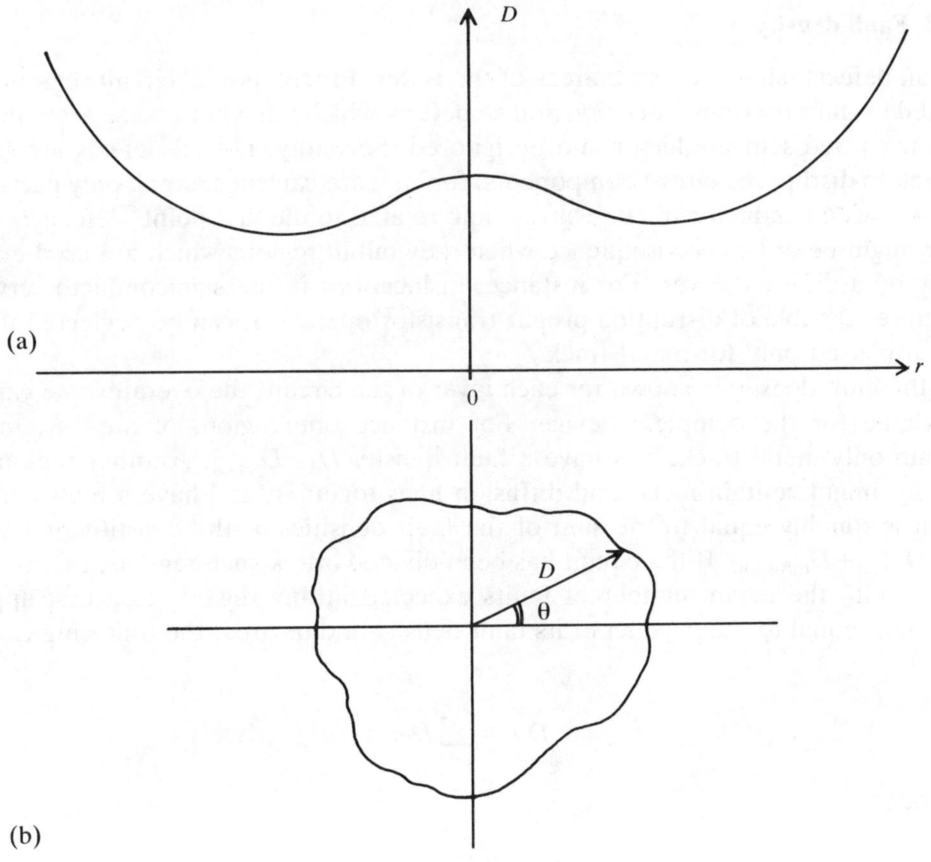

FIGURE 7.8 *Graphs of D against r and θ*

In addition, variations in mask alignment, and the occurrences of scratches and large blemishes, are manifested as macroscopic defects, each capable of affecting several adjacent circuits at a time. Even the choice of a direct write on wafer technique does not prevent the appearance of clustered defects; non-uniformities in the electron beam, for instance, cause problems which are akin to photographic misalignment.

On a more global scale, there is a wafer-to-wafer variation which could be due to their different positions in wafer boats, and planetary systems. Also, there are anisotropic effects concerned with heating, and turbulent gas and chemical flows. There is also a batch-to-batch variation in cell yield due to fluctuations in temperature, humidity, dust count and gas/chemical flow/concentration. There are not only random variations in time, but also the intentional effects of the maturing of the process.

For VLSI, mean figures can be obtained for the device yield, averaging out the effects of the above angular, radial and batch-related fluctuations. Some of these derivations are catalogued next as a starting point for future WSI calculations.

7.4.2 Fault density

Not all defects fall on sensitive areas of the wafer. Firstly, not all circuit regions are packed to their maximum density, and so defects which fall within these areas might fall on unused semiconductor and be ignored. Secondly, not all defects are large enough to disrupt the circuit components, for instance causing a break only part-way across a wide conductor track. Thirdly, and related to the first point, defects in one layer might be of little consequence when they fall in regions which are used exclusively by a different layer. For instance, dislocations in the semiconductor crystal structure, capable of disrupting proper transistor operation, can be neglected if the region is used only for metal track.

If the fault density is known for each layer of the circuit, the overall value can be calculated for the complete device. For instance one region, of area a_1, might contain only metal track, and have a fault density $D_1 = D_{metal}$. Another region, of area a_2, might contain metal and diffusion lines together, and have a fault density which is roughly equal to the sum of the fault densities of the constituent layers, $D_2 \simeq D_{metal} + D_{diffusion}$. If the circuit has been divided into k such regions, that is: $a = \Sigma_{j=1}^{k} a_j$, with the mean number of faults expected in any region (to a first approximation) equal to the product of its fault density and its area, the following can be stated:

$$Da = \sum_{j=1}^{k} D_j a_j$$

and hence:

$$D = \frac{1}{a} \sum_{j=1}^{k} D_j a_j$$

A further refinement to this treatment is to take the polar coordinates of each region into account too: $D_j(r,\theta)$. This inevitably involves dividing the circuit into a larger number of regions, whose fault densities are within a given range.

The function, ν, which was derived in Chapter 5 is applicable only when point faults are found and are distributed randomly over the wafer according to a *Poisson distribution*. According to the theoretical treatment (Stapper 1985), the chances of finding a circuit with k faults is given by:

$$P(k \text{ faults}) = e^{-Da}(Da)^k/k!$$

Thus the yield is given by the probability of finding a circuit which contains zero faults.

Alternatively, the faults can be assumed to be dispersed according to a *binomial distribution* (Stapper 1985). In this case the probability of finding k faults in a circuit placed on a wafer (whose effective area is W) becomes:

$$P(k \text{ faults}) = \frac{(DW)!}{k!(DW-k)!}(a/W)^k(1 - a/W)^{DW-k}$$

Other investigations have suggested other laws which might be tried (Figure 7.9). Each one has some grounding in theory, and a substantial basis in empirical observation. Each therefore has its own merits and weaknesses, and the choice of which one to believe really relies on a process of trial and error.

The *negative binomial model* or *inverse binomial model*, takes account of fault clustering. This is a particularly appropriate model when investigating some of the reconfiguration algorithms of Chapter 5, many of which will not work when faults are clustered, for example in adjacent cells. For this, it is assumed that $D(r,\theta)$ takes the form of a gamma function. The clustering parameter, α, is used to tune the shape of the function. Stapper observed that α starts large, indicating a high degree of clustering, and gradually reduces as the process is matured and only the completely random faults remain. The value of α has an effect on the standard deviation, σ, which was used in Section 5.4.2.

It is worth noting that for small D and a all of the models, except Seeds, predict the number of faults to be proportional to Da which is in accordance with the first naïve model which was developed in Chapter 5.

The Poisson model fits the $\nu(D,a_1+a_2)=\nu(D,a_1)\times\nu(D,a_2)$ property exactly. The binomial and inverse binomial models approximate to it when a is small. These are therefore consistent with intuition for these special cases.

With VLSI, the above models can be used to predict the expected crop from a wafer, averaging out any variation in the fault density. With WSI, this is no longer valid; the circuit must be designed to accommodate the variation in D over the wafer, perhaps placing most sensitive circuitry in areas of low fault density. Similarly, it is not possible to rely on faults, if and when they occur, being of any single predictable type since variations are large, not only from fabrication line to fabrication line, but also from day to day and from batch to batch on the same line. Techniques must therefore allow for the most general faults.

Theoretical expression	*Series expansion*
Poisson: e^{-Da}	$1 - Da + \frac{D^2a^2}{2} - \ldots$
Binomial: $\left(1 - \frac{a}{W}\right)^{DW}$	$1 - Da + \left(\frac{D^2a^2}{2} - \frac{Da^2}{2W}\right) - \ldots$
Murphy: $\left[\frac{1 - e^{-Da}}{Da}\right]^2$	$1 - Da + \frac{7D^2a^2}{12} - \ldots$
Seeds: $e^{-\sqrt{Da}}$	$1 - \sqrt{Da} + \frac{Da}{2} - \ldots$
Bose–Einstein: $\frac{1}{1 + Da}$	$1 - Da + D^2a^2$
Inverse binomial: $\left[1 + \frac{Da}{\alpha}\right]^{-\alpha}$	$1 - Da + \frac{D^2a^2}{2}\left(1 - \frac{1}{\alpha}\right) - \ldots$

FIGURE 7.9 *Theoretical yield expressions*

The device yield is, of course, highly dependent on the value of the fault density, but this only determines the yield of the fabricated devices. The next stage in the manufacturing process, namely packaging, to which all of the working devices must be subjected, also carries an attendant risk of incurring catastrophic damage. It also presents significantly new and challenging problems to the practical realisation of WSI, as discussed next (Section 7.5).

7.5 PACKAGING

Many of the traditional techniques for VLSI packaging (Steidel 1983) cease to be applicable when attempting to house a device which is as large as a complete wafer (McKirdy and Lea 1986, Val 1986). Figure 7.10 lists some of the rôles and requirements that are expected of it. In addition, packaging is a process step which adds to the risk of introducing new faults, and so the *device yield* must be multiplied by the *packaging yield* to obtain the *packaged device yield*.

The device is not useful unless it can make contact with the outside world to receive electrical power, and to receive and transmit electrical signals and clocking

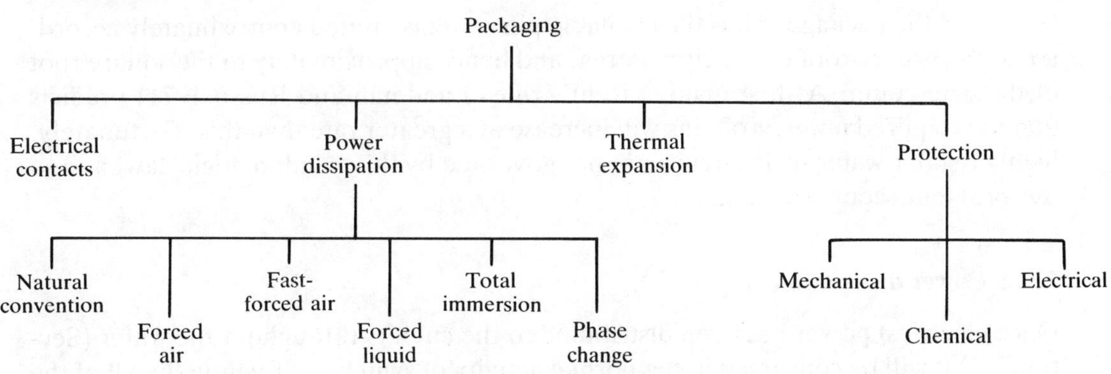

FIGURE 7.10 *Packaging concerns*

information (Section 7.5.1). The next problem, having injected electrical power into the device, is to transfer the same amount of thermal power back out again (Section 7.5.2). Since this cannot be conducted without some form of temperature change, the problems of thermal expansion must be addressed (Section 7.5.3). Lastly, the package must provide the necessary protection for the device (Section 7.5.4).

7.5.1 Electrical contacts

The first problem is the choice of a suitable connection material, which must not only be a good electrical conductor, but must also make good electrical contact to the wafer and to the pins of the package. It must also provide mechanical support for its own weight, especially if large spans are to be made, for instance in the case of an outward-grown Catt spiral.

Of the configurations which are currently used, those in Figure 7.11 can be listed. In all but the cases of pin grid arrays, the number of pins is limited by the circum-

TO5
Dual in-line integrated circuits (DILIC)
Staggered DILIC
Chip carrier (leaded)
Chip carrier (leadless)
Pin grid array (PGA)
(Periphery) tape-automated bonding (TAB)
ATAB (area TAB)
Solder bumps
Edge connector type
Unpackaged chip and wire

FIGURE 7.11 *Styles of packaging*

ference of the package. Thus the available pin count is limited approximately according to the square root of the circuit area, and hence approximately to the square root of the gate count. At first glance, Rent's rule (Landman and Russo 1971) predicts that the required number of pins will increase at a greater rate than this. Fortunately, highly regular wafer scale circuits are not governed by this 'random logic' law, and so the problem seems tractable.

7.5.2 Power dissipation

Once electrical power has been distributed to the circuits throughout the wafer (Section 7.2) it will be consumed in the normal activity of switching. Eventually, all of the supplied power is converted to heat, and must be removed if the circuits are not to overheat. A large proportion of the internally generated power is dissipated along the external leads since good electrical conductors tend also to be good thermal conductors. This is a useful bonus. The remaining power, which is not removed in this way, must then be dissipated through the packaging material since this immediately surrounds the device.

A classification scheme has emerged for thermal management systems, graded according to the degree of cooling that is needed. Three classes of system exist: less than 50 W, between 50 and 100 W, and more than 100 W.

The simplest technique involves natural convection. Passive conduction is used from the wafer to the package, and then convection from the package to the surrounding air. One improvement is to attach a large heat-sink to the package. In the most expensive embellishments of these systems, spring-loaded heat-pipes are used to make intimate contact with each part of the wafer. However, cheaper intermediate solutions are available for systems with less acute needs in heat dissipation. For instance, cooling fins can be added to the heat-sink and, further, the boards can be housed vertically so that natural convection currents are induced, with the warmed air rising, drawing in cooler air from the bottom. This process can be enhanced by use of a fan. Standard *forced air* systems generate air flows of up to 4 m s^{-1}, Stronger, *fast-forced air* systems, are available, producing air flows of up to 8 m s^{-1}, but with consequent electrical noise problems.

The next step is to provide channels near to the package, possibly even connected directly to the back of the wafer, which can be plumbed to a cooling system. Air could be pumped round the system, but more usually a liquid coolant is chosen, water being a common choice.

The wafer can be totally immersed in its coolant. Water could be used if the wafer could be protected from chemical contamination, and electrical conduction, whilst still maintaining thermal conductivity. Alternatively, especially in cases which need extremely effective cooling, some of the cryogenic liquid gases such as nitrogen or helium can be used. A final increase in the heat transfer coefficient from the immersed wafer might be possible through the use of phase change cooling. An inert liquid is again needed, of which perfluorocarbons have been suggested as an example.

7.5.3 Thermal expansion

Since heating is involved, and the packaging material is to be in intimate contact with the wafer, the two must have the same thermal coefficient of expansion (TCE). Since different materials generally have different expansion coefficients, one approach is to use electrically insulating silicon as the package material (Johnson 1986). Another alternative is to place several layers between the silicon and the final package material, each one graded with a slightly different coefficient of expansion. In this way, small mismatches in expansion can be accommodated.

The choice of adhesives is significant, not least because it forms part of the intervening structure between the wafer and the package. From the discussion in the previous paragraph, it must have a thermal coefficient of expansion which, when the adhesive has set, is intermediate to the coefficients of the two materials that it bonds. This immediately narrows down the choice of suitable adhesives. Moreover, most adhesives are poor thermal conductors. In addition, most adhesives are fluid when they are applied, and hence highly susceptible to the formation of voids. These are bubbles of gas, or even vacuum, between the two surfaces, which locally disturb the intimacy of the contact. They can be minimised, but not eradicated, and as a result some regions are better cooled than others and hot-spots can develop on the wafer.

7.5.4 Protection: mechanical, chemical and electrical

The package must protect the wafer from vibration and shock. Unfortunately, this is not completely consistent with the need for rigid thermal and electrical contacts. It must also protect against mechanical intrusion whilst the system is being assembled, and from bombardment by foreign objects which are inadvertently forced around in the cooling system.

The package must also provide chemical protection, shielding the device from the environment. Even normal air is a problem. Most circuits can be protected from attack from the water vapour in the air, but the leads and bond pads remain vulnerable. Normally, the package is hermetically sealed, often using a glass with a low melting point. The specification for military circuits, and hence the pace setter for commercial circuits, requires that remaining water vapour contained in the device cavity be no more than 5000 p.p.m.

Lastly, the package might be required to isolate the contents from external electrical noise (Val 1986). For this, a metal package can act as a Faraday cage.

7.5.5 Packaging material

Thus, in summary, the package material must be a good thermal conductor, it must make good thermal contact with the wafer, and hence must be extremely flat, and be a good electrical insulator. However, good thermal conductors tend also to be good electrical conductors.

Metal packages are popular, but they must have a dielectric layer for electrical isolation if it is not to cause shorting within the device. However, the dielectric layer must be very thin, since most electrical insulators are also very poor thermal conductors. But if the dielectric is very thin, the metal must be very flat if it is not to pierce through the insulating layer. Another popular material is ceramic. This is an electrical insulator, so does not suffer from the same problems as metal packaging. However, it is not ideal for thermal conduction. Beryllia would be extremely good if it were not for its high toxicity. Plastic packages are also popular, but these have most of the disadvantages of ceramic and few of the advantages.

7.6 CONCLUSIONS

This chapter has been concerned with the issues which affect the realisation of WSI and ULSI. It represents the bottom level of this book: the conclusion of a top-down design process. However, few things in this world are black and white, and so top-down design can work only if it is mixed with a certain amount of bottom-up design. The designer needs to know where he (or she) is heading, and what problems to anticipate there, before he is able to make progress towards his goal. Many of the problems which have been described in this chapter, particularly those of power distribution, must be addressed very early in the design, even whilst the system is being described at an abstract level.

The next chapter starts to summarise the concerns of the wafer scale designer, especially with regard to his choice of modularity, regularity and granularity. As well as having implications on the performance of the device, these issues also affect the demands which are placed on the designer and his computer-aided tools.

7.7 EXERCISES

7.1 A processor cell has an active area of 5 mm × 5 mm, and reports from the fabrication line indicate that 150 of them work out of every 500 which are fabricated over a 150 mm diameter area. What do the Poisson, binomial and Seeds models suggest as respective values for the fault density?

7.2 A modified version of the processor, from question 7.1, is proposed, with an active area of 6 mm × 6 mm. What do each of the three models from question 7.1 predict will be the new cell yield?

8
DESIGN CONSIDERATIONS

Much has been said about the virtues of modularity, and the advantages of breaking a large problem recursively into smaller subproblems so as to make some operation, such as design, easier to perform. Modularity is needed in hardware design for precisely the same reasons as those described in Chapter 2 for computer programming, namely to allow the human designer to break up large problems in a divide-and-conquer manner so that only very simple subproblems need be tackled at a time. The circuitry of a wafer scale device involves such large transistor counts that it is only tractable if the problem can be broken into modules, with many further subdivisions. However, as with computer software, there is a need to use clean interfaces throughout; it is counter-productive if modules cause side effects.

Ideally, all signals should be local, nearest-neighbour interconnections between abutting cells. This helps both at the design stage, simplifying the work of the human and the design programs, and when the floor plans of the abutting cells are designed. In general, software needs the same locality of communications: functions receive parameters from the tops of stacks, or the ends of combinator expressions; functions return values to the place in the stack, or combinator string, where they found their parameters. This suggests two things: functional programs should map readily on to large circuits which have the same properties; functional programs should find a rôle in the new generation of computer-aided design.

The act of breaking a system into modules is that of *partitioning*, and can generally be by function or by bit-slice. For instance, a large SISD computer can be divided into its individual functional modules (such as the CPU, memory, etc), or into individual columns of bit-slice processors. Large memories can be divided in this way too, for example 1M × 16 bits might be composed of 16 64K × 16-bit memories, or 16 1M-bit memory columns. This chapter is concerned with the influences that implementing fault/failure tolerance strategies (Section 8.1), designing the circuit (Section 8.2) and incorporating test logic into the system (Section 8.3) have on the choice of an appropriate partitioning. The first of these is tackled next.

8.1 PARTITIONING

This section is concerned with the fault/failure tolerance aspects of partitioning. Section 8.1.2 describes the use of fault/failure tolerance applied hierarchically to fault/failure tolerant modules, but Section 8.1.1 starts by considering the mapping of fault/failure tolerance strategies on to some commonly used module types.

8.1.1 Applicability of the fault/failure techniques

The design of computer memory can make use of most of the techniques which are listed in Chapter 5. This is precisely the reason for choosing it as the common illustration. Similarly, large, regular processor arrays can make use of many of the techniques. The other module types which hardware designers find useful are generally less able to make use of more than a few of the techniques (Figure 8.1). ROM, for instance, cannot make use of common spares since the hard-wired contents of its individual cells bear no regular relationship to one another. In common with PLA, though, there might be some scope for implementing a fault tolerant strategy which is brought into action before the array is programmed. The comments which were made in Section 6.2.4 are then applicable, though, and so this idea is not incorporated into Figure 8.1.

	RAM	*Multi-processor*	*ROM*	*PLA*	*ALU*	*Non-regular*
Patching	•	•	•	•	•	•
Device replication	•	•	•	•	•	•
Column replication	•	•	•	•	•	
Row replication	•	•	•	•		
Cell replication	•	•	•	•	•	•
Standby-spare column	•	•			•	
Standby-spare row	•	•				
Standby-spare cell (column)	•	•			•	
Standby-spare cell (row)	•	•				
Rotary (column-orientated)	•	•			•	
Rotary (row-orientated)	•	•				
Time redundancy (column)		•			•	
Time redundancy (row)		•				
NMR (device)	•	•	•	•	•	•
NMR (column)	•		•	•	•	
NMR (row)				•		
NMR (cell)	•	•	•	•	•	•
Hamming (column)	•		•	•	•	
Hamming (row)				•		
Hamming (cell)	•	•	•	•	•	

FIGURE 8.1 *Applicability of reconfiguration techniques to circuit types*

Random logic and non-regular architectures are generally the most restricted, and must probably rely on integer replication, or modular redundancy of complete blocks (Sumerling *et al.* 1986b). However, there is great scope for defining the cell boundaries. Thus the simple system of Figure 8.2a could employ: cell replication using multiple independent copies of A, B and C, device replication using multiple copies of ABC, or a hybrid replication using multiple copies of AB and C, that is treating AB as a single cell. The last of these three options is depicted in Figure 8.2b.

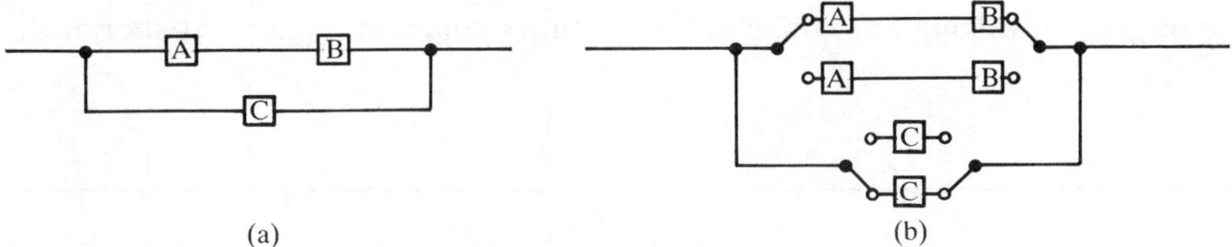

FIGURE 8.2 *An irregular architecture*

The problem of fault clustering was briefly mentioned in Section 7.4. With memory, there is a simple method for minimising its effect (Stewart and Dixon 1986). Since memory is usually shaped logically as a very elongated rectangle, for instance 1 048 576 cells × 16, it is normally fabricated with several words per row since there are many advantages in keeping the chip shape as square as possible. There is then an opportunity to interleave the bits of each word. For instance, if each row contains the bits from 256 words, then the bits of the first word can be spread out to lie in every 256th position, with the corresponding bits of the other words interspersed between them. So long as any large defect, or a cluster of defects, is smaller than the width of 256 bits, no word can contain more than one defective bit. This property is beneficial to all of the redundancy schemes, whether they be standby-spare or Hamming, and regardless of whether they are for fixed aim or graceful degradation. Unfortunately, processor architectures are usually unable to use this technique. For high communications speed, and minimum area occupied by intercell communications links, communicating modules need to be placed as close together as possible.

For all applications, there are trade-offs to be made between circuit complexity (granularity), that is the number of cells per circuit, and tolerance of low yield. Fried (1986a, b) describes a spreadsheet style program written in Prolog, in which the hardware configuration can be described and an optimal partitioning found by the automated investigation of several alternatives.

8.1.2 Hierarchical fault/failure tolerance

Section 6.5 showed that there is a considerable need to keep the cell yield as high as possible, since this can have such a dramatic effect on the cell harvest. Assuming that there is little more that can be done to reduce the fault density, D, the next approach would be minimise the cell area a. However, this limits the functionality of the cell.

Another approach is to make the cells themselves fault/failure tolerant (Fried 1986a) so that a single fault within a cell will no longer render the whole cell unusable.

First, though, consider a different use for partitioning. Supposing that a fault tolerant fixed- aim array of m rows by n columns is required; one possibility would be to select one of the approaches from Chapter 5, and to implement it directly using M rows and N columns. Another would be to treat the device as jk arrays, each containing M/j rows and N/k columns (Figure 8.3), and hence each independently fault/failure tolerant. This solution would probably be simpler to implement than the original, involving less configuration circuitry communicating over shorter dis-

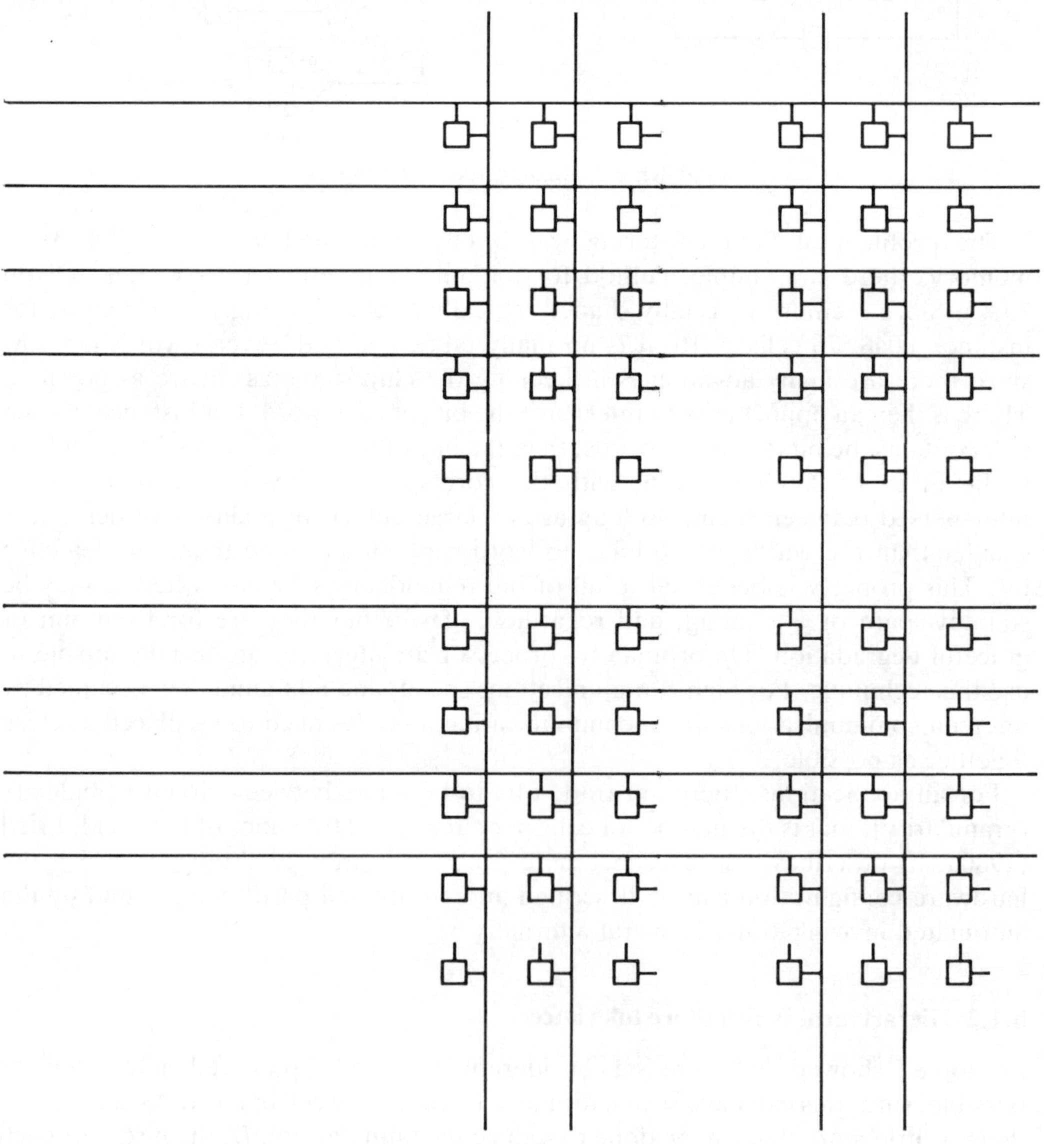

FIGURE 8.3 *An 8 × 4 array arranged as four (4 + 1) by (2 + 1) arrays*

tances, but at the cost of being less effective when the cell yield is lowered, as unused working circuits in one partition cannot be utilised to repair excessive damage in another.

The idea can be extended. For simplicity, take j=1, that is with no row-orientated partitioning. If k+1, or more, of the arrays are fabricated, there will be two levels of tolerance: one inside each subarray, and one outside (Figure 8.4). There is of course no reason why the same fault/failure tolerance approach need be adopted at the two levels. Further, the individual partitions might be themselves partitioned, so allowing three or more levels of fault/failure tolerance (Sumerling *et al.* 1986a).

It could be noted that a different fault/failure tolerant strategy could be adopted in each subarray also (Tamir and Séquin 1984). In this way, the device can tolerate limited amounts of design error (Anderson and Lee 1981) by disconnecting or overriding modules whose design causes them to operate incorrectly.

Another technique for two-dimensional arrays is to treat them hierarchically as a one-dimensional vector of one-dimensional vectors. For instance, memory consists of a vector of words which can be supplied with spare words with which to conduct

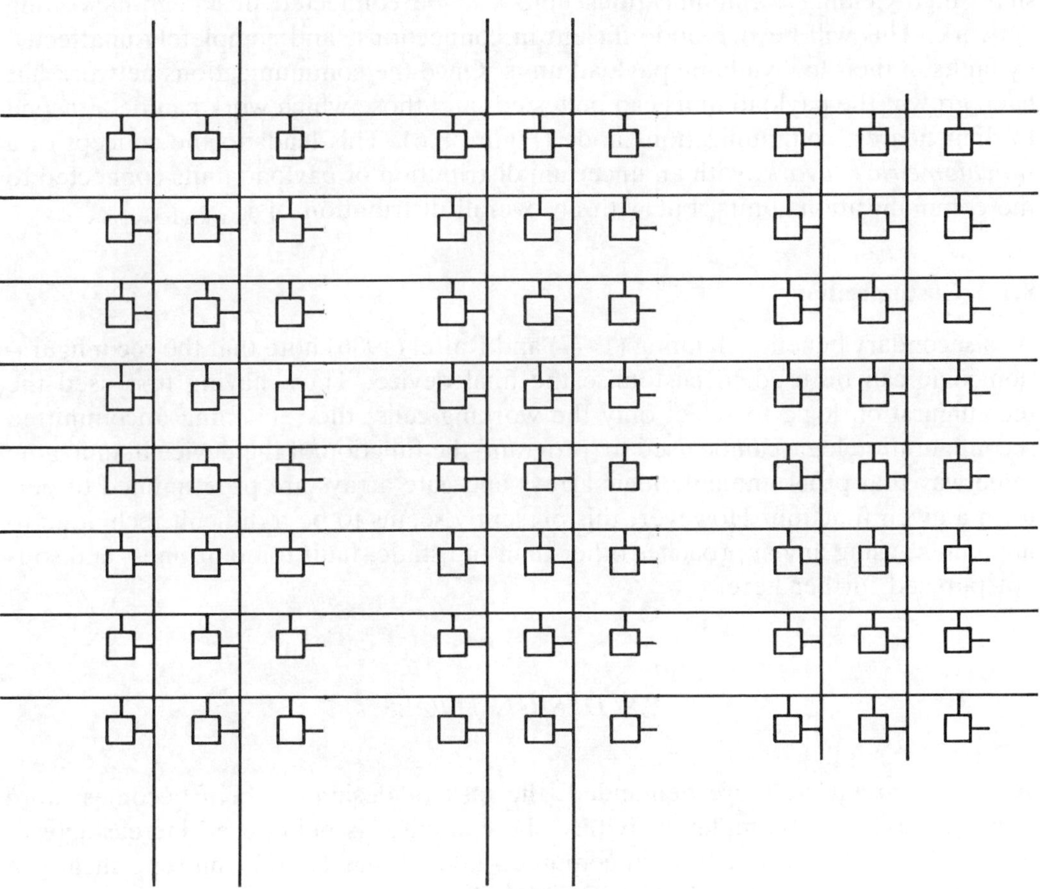

FIGURE 8.4 *An 8 × 4 array arranged as (two + one) 8 by (2 + 1) arrays*

spare-row fault tolerance. Each word is then a vector of bits, each of which can be provided with spares, thus employing local spare-column fault tolerance. The performance of the technique is derived in Figure 8.5. A coarser grain, more realistic, version of this technique (Bentley and Jesshope 1986) involves placing a block of memory within each cell.

Min working cells in row:	n from N
Row yield:	*atleast*(n,N,y)
Min working rows in device:	m from M
Device yield (Y'):	*atleast*$(\mathrm{m},M,$*atleast*$(n,N,y))$

FIGURE 8.5 *Performance of this fixed aim approach*

Another idea for increasing the cell yield, and hence the cell harvest, is to ignore the faults in all but a small part of the cell. Kelly points out (Kelly and Shute 1986b) that, by testing only the communications circuitry and ignoring the payload logic, small high-yielding communications units can be connected in a high-harvesting network. This will be rich and efficient in connections, and completely unaffected by faults in their low-yielding payload units. Once the communications network has been grown, the payload units can be tested, and those which work can be attached to their nearest communications node (Figure 8.6). This leads to the concept of a *stoichiometric network*, with an uncertain distribution of payload units connected to the communications units, but with an overall distribution of $y_{\mathrm{payload}}:y_{\mathrm{comms}}$.

8.1.3 Customisation

As a secondary benefit, Manning (1977) and Raffel (1986) note that the reconfiguration logic can be used to customise the final device. Thus, having first used the reconfiguration logic to select only the working cells, the remaining uncommitted reconfiguration logic can be used to 'program' the function of the device in much the same way that programmable logic arrays and gate arrays are programmed to perform a given function. However, this presently seems to be a difficult technique to implement using any approaches other than the static, fault tolerant ones, and so is not pursued further here.

8.2 DESIGN TOOLS

As larger circuit sizes are demanded, the task of designing them becomes more difficult. Like most complex activities, the computer is being used increasingly to help in the process, in the form of computer-aided design (CAD), and specifically in electrical computer-aided design (ECAD). The computer can perform only the more routine, mechanical activities in the design process, though, which is fortunate,

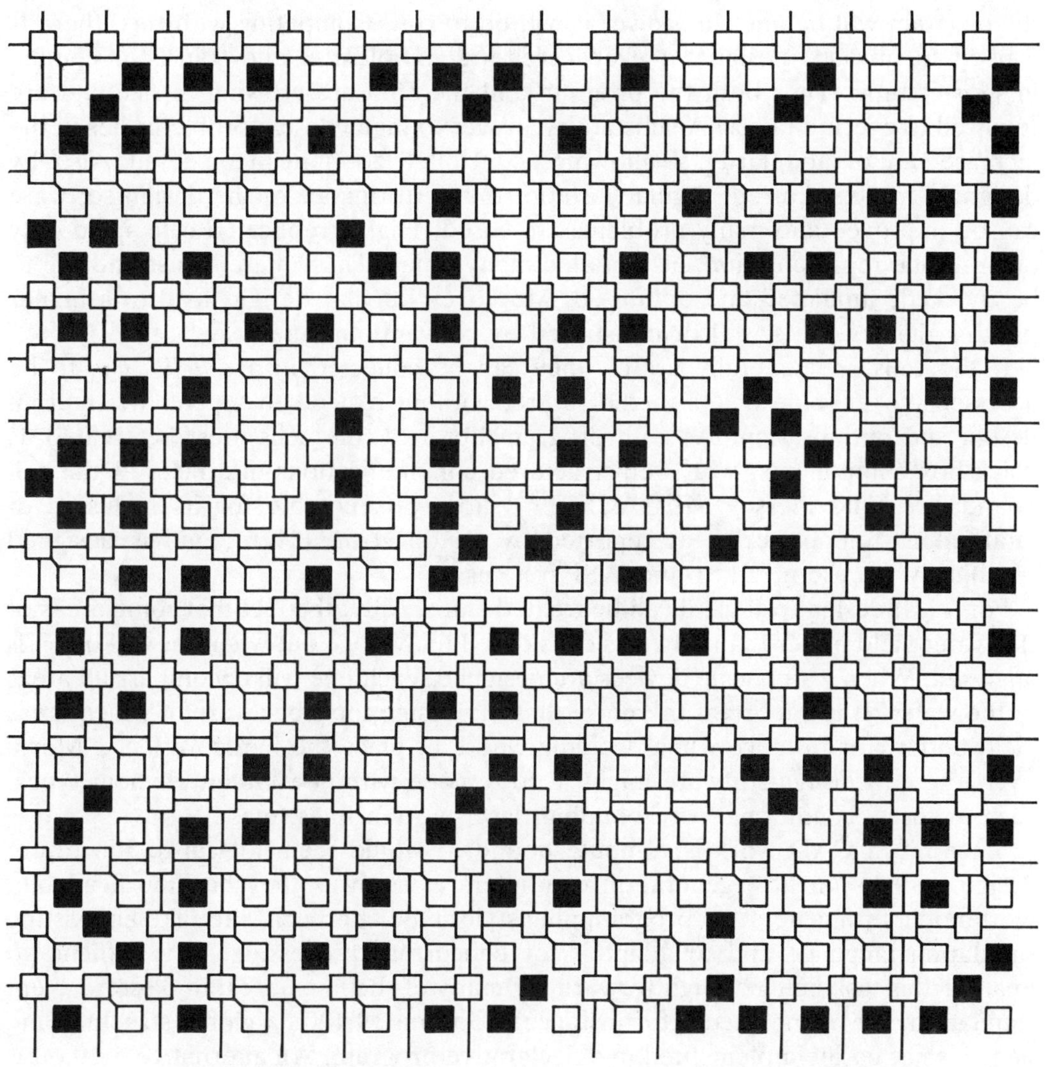

FIGURE 8.6 *Stoichiometric processor: communications array*

since these are precisely the activities from which the human operators wish to be released. As computer programs are made more capable, they are able to take over more of the work, releasing the human designer to move on to the more challenging design work. As with program compilation, silicon compilation (Werner 1982, Mavor *et al*. 1983) needs to use a language which is formal, unambiguous and able to express abstract ideas succinctly. It should be possible to specify the required circuit behaviour in the language and to simulate it at its many levels of abstraction (Breuer and Hartenstein 1981), and for the compiler to generate the necessary hardware layout.

In general, the more complex the work undertaken by the computer, the larger the program will be and the slower it will be to run. Competing with this, there is a need to produce designs of ever-increasing complexity, and transistor counts, in shorter time. Thus both the program and the data are growing in size and are required to execute faster. A substantial answer to many design problems lies in the increased use of modularity, so allowing a controlled 'zooming in' on detail. Also, by designing in a structured, regular fashion, the performance of the design software can be improved and many problems are eased. Highly replicated cells need only one internal representation, instantiated many times. Thus, there is just one cell to be checked, simulated and optimised. Moreover, regular designs lead to a higher packing density, as is well demonstrated by conventional memory.

If the cells are generally useful, they can be collected in a *cell library*, to be accessed by other designers in the future, without a need to repeat the internal design and optimisation. As with program libraries, the cells must be treated as black-box components, with well-structured communications interfaces at the cell boundaries. The Plessey MEGACELL^{TM} library is notable for its inclusion of fault/failure tolerant cells, as reported by Dixon *et al.* (1986), and is designed specifically for use in ULSI and WSI systems.

For VLSI design, cell yield can be treated statistically; the fact that some areas of the wafer yield better than others is considered to average out when the full batch is analysed. When wafer-scale devices are designed, each one will encompass all areas of the wafer. It is important therefore that the design tools be aware of which areas yield better, for instance when deciding where to place the hardcore logic. Moreover, the new design software might need to cope with new circuit element types, such as fuses, conditional wire bonding, laser-written lines, etc.

Since much CAD work is compute bound, it would seem logical to run future design systems on fifth generation computers as soon as they become available, written in a fifth generation programming style. One approach is to take an existing simulation language and to adapt it for concurrent processing. It is difficult to imagine this task being straightforward for many of the languages; in discrete event simulation, the event queue (for instance) (Gordon 1978) is a global structure and hence is not easily implemented in a declarative program. An alternative method is to tread the same route as the early single processor simulation languages, that is to take a programming language which was designed for the machine and to modify it for use in simulation, in a similar manner to Simula's evolution from Algol-60. FFP is particularly interesting because the hardware description language, μFP (Sheeran 1984, 1985), has already been derived from it.

The advantages of a declarative style were expounded by Backus (1978). In comparison to imperative languages, they are readily hierarchical and are semantically clean, with origins in mathematical logic. This in turn facilitates other advantages, such as correctness proving and automatic optimisation of the design, as described in Chapter 2. As an example of how hardware design can benefit from these, the characteristics of the language μFP (Sheeran 1984, 1985) are briefly summarised. In addition to the programming constructs, which are needed for program writing, hardware design needs some specialised primitives, for example to represent the passage of time, which is where the μ is used in μFP.

Computer hardware description languages (CHDL) generally have two aims (Barbacci 1981): to describe the structure of the circuit (Section 8.2.1) and to describe its behaviour (Section 8.2.2). The real value of a language like μFP is that the designer can concentrate on the abstract ideas of the latter, and leave the details of the former for the computer to derive (Section 8.2.3).

8.2.1 Describing circuit structure

The ability of the APL programming language to describe the regular structures which are frequently encountered in computer hardware is demonstrated by Blaauw (1976). The FFP programming language, as a distant derivative of APL, should be capable of the same descriptive power. This, then, is the starting point for the CHDL, μFP.

The series connection of two hardware modules is represented in μFP by the composition symbol '.' applied to the two functions (Figure 8.7).

The parallel connection of hardware modules is represented in μFP by the construction symbol '[,]' (Figure 8.8).

The selector function '2nd' is a module which derives its output from its second input and ignores all of its other inputs (Figure 8.9).

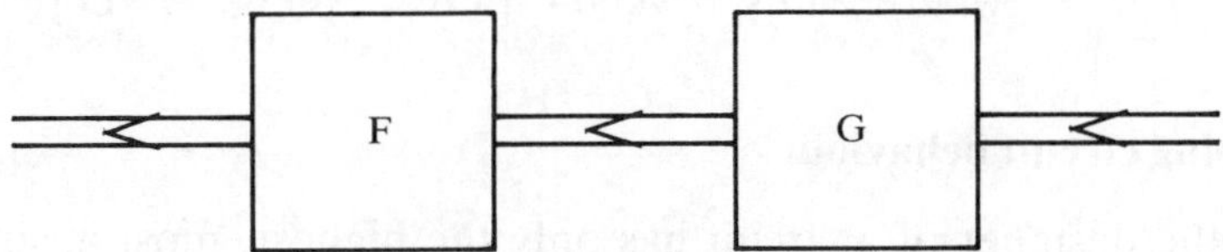

FIGURE 8.7 *The composition: F . G*

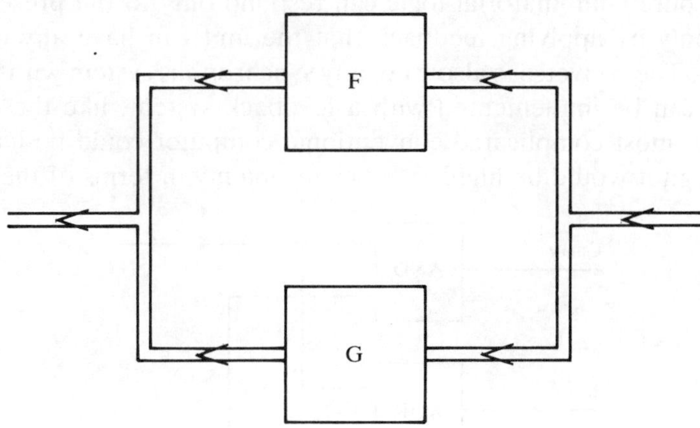

FIGURE 8.8 *The construction: [F, G]*

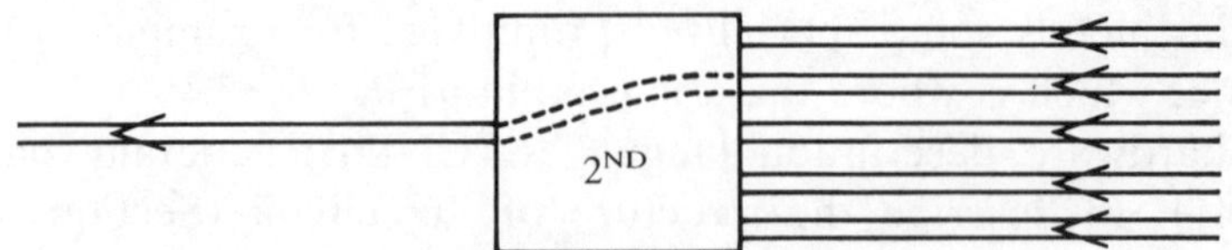

FIGURE 8.9 *The selector: 2nd*

As an example, consider the arrangement of logic gates required to form a half-adder (HA) circuit, as shown in Figure 8.10.

Step-wise refinement is a central idea in top-down design, and is related to the process of *functional decomposition* (Glaser *et al.* 1984) which is facilitated by μFP. HA is defined in terms of 'exclusive or' XOR, which is defined separately. The complete definition of HA can be obtained by refining references to the symbol XOR to its constituent AND, OR and NOT gates, thus giving the diagram which is shown in Figure 8.11.

In both the graphical and the μFP descriptions, the structure is the same in Figure 8.11 as it is in Figure 8.10. Thus:

HA = [AND , AND . [OR , NOT . AND]]

has the same meaning as:

HA = [AND , XOR]
where XOR = AND. [OR , NOT . AND]

8.2.2 Describing circuit behaviour

Fortunately, the designer of a circuit has only the highest, most abstract, specification of its behaviour from which to work. The aim is to convert the high level description into a lower, more detailed layout description of the component modules.

A block of pure combinatorial logic can respond only to the present state of its inputs. It is only by applying feedback that the unit can have any memory of its previous state. The converse is also true: any synchronous system with finite memory requirements can be implemented with a feedback system, like the one in Figure 8.12. Even the most complicated conventional computer could be implemented in this way, though it would be highly inefficient, mainly in terms of the area of semi-

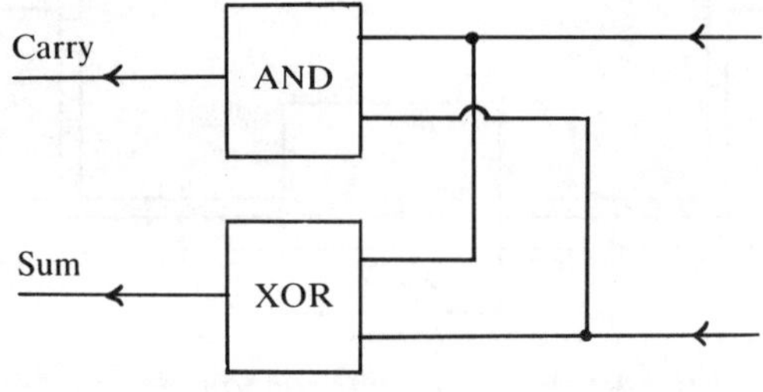

FIGURE 8.10 *HA = [AND, XOR]*

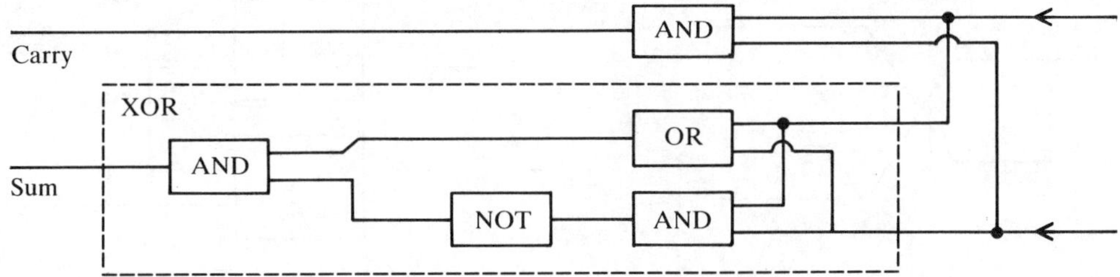

FIGURE 8.11 *HA = [AND, AND . [OR, NOT . AND]]*

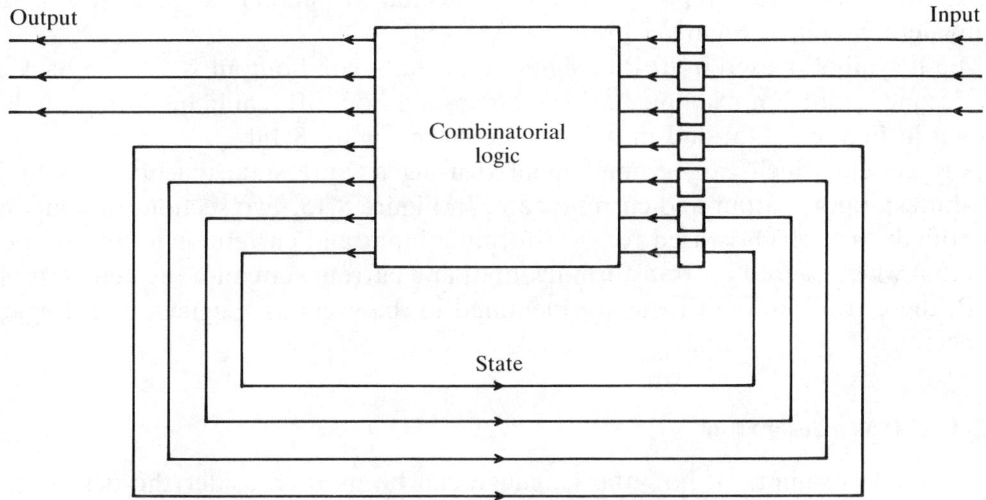

FIGURE 8.12 *A finite state machine*

conductor consumed. A computer with eight registers and 64K words of memory, each 16 bits wide, would require *at least* 1 048 704 bits of information in the feedback path.

Mead and Conway (1980) present a simple introduction to the *finite state machine* (FSM). They commence by describing a machine which consists of a block of combinatorial logic with all inputs and outputs buffered by the system clock (Figure 8.12). They describe that there are two types of output signal: those which exit to the outside world, and those which are fed back round to the input. Similarly, there are two types of input: those which arrive from the outside world, and those which are received back round from the output. The output from the system then depends not only on the states of the inputs in the current clock cycle, but also on the states of some of the outputs from the previous cycle. The two-phase clocking not only synchronises the unit with the other modules in the sytem, since Mead and Conway assume that this clocking scheme is used throughout the design, but it ensures that the feedback signals do not affect the output of the unit until the next clock cycle.

To understand how μFP is used to represent synchronous finite state machines, consider first a twisted pair of wires (Figure 8.13a). In μFP, this can be represented

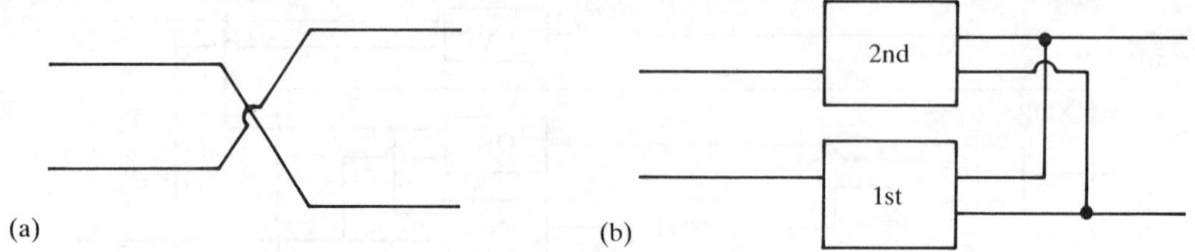

FIGURE 8.13 *Twisted signals represented by [2nd, 1st]*

using two selector functions which are connected in parallel, as indicated in the equivalent circuit of Figure 8.13b.

The μ symbol is used in μFP to signify that the second output is latched back to the second input. For example, a single binary flip-flop, SR, could be represented as shown in Figure 8.14a, and in μFP as shown in Figure 8.14b.

Any system which can be implemented using a finite state machine has three attributes: input, output and current state. In Figure 8.15, two sections of logic are identified: that which is used for transforming input and current state into output, and that which is used for transforming input and current state into the new state. In μFP, these two blocks of logic are identified in the sections 'LogicO' and 'LogicS' respectively.

8.2.3 μFP as a design tool

As a simple example of how the language can be used, consider the design of a synchronous system whose output is merely a four-cycle delay of its input. It should be apparent that, represented as a single loop finite state machine, there must be at least four signals in the feedback loop: for the most recent, the second to most recent, the third to most recent and the fourth to most recent inputs. Since these are bundled together, and treated as the multicore cable which is called 'current state', they are collectively part of the second input to the finite state machine, as in Figure 8.15, whose individual members are known respectively as: '1st.2nd', '2nd.2nd', '3rd.2nd' and '4th.2nd'.

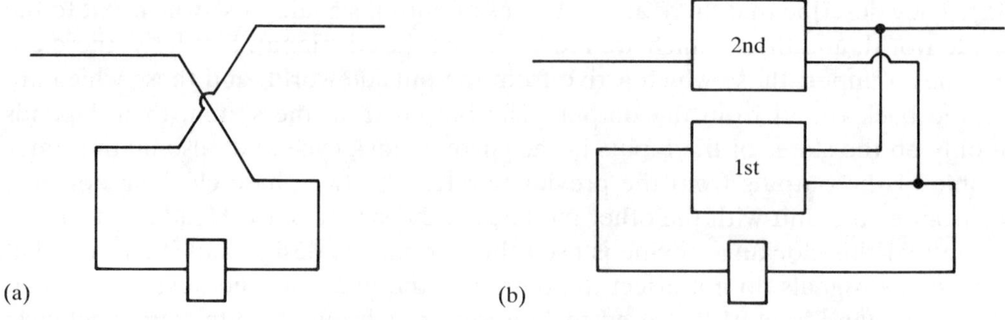

FIGURE 8.14 *A flip-flop represented as μ[2nd,1st]*

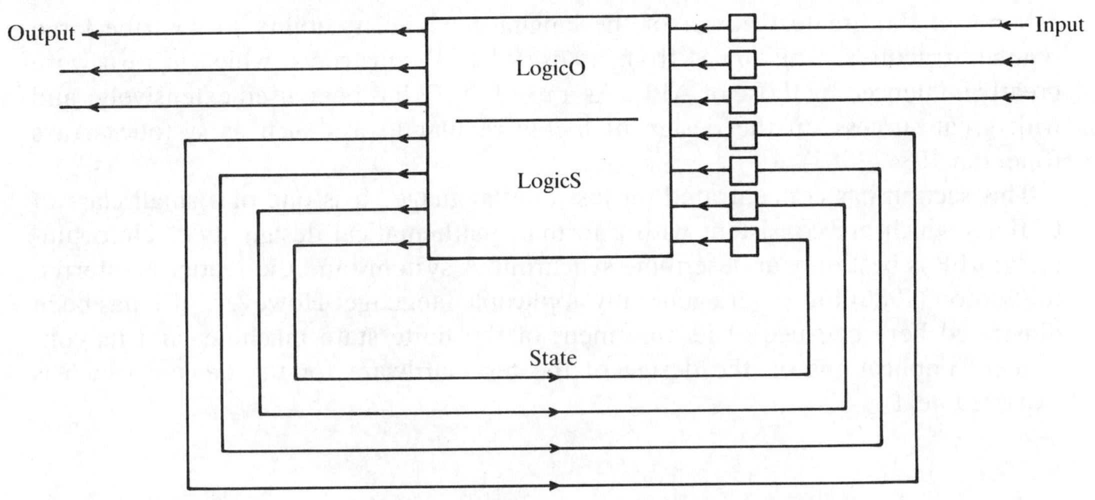

FIGURE 8.15 *A finite state machine represented as μ [LogicO, LogicS]*

In each cycle, the fourth to most recent signal is presented at the output, each of the others are moved along by one position, and the system's external input, '1st', is stored as the most recent input. Thus the system is described by:

$$\text{SR4} = \mu[\,\text{4th.2nd}\,,\,[\,\text{1st},\,[\,\text{1st, 2nd, 3rd}\,].\text{2nd}\,]\,]$$

Using various transformations, each of which yields a new *equivalent* description of the system, the following description can be obtained:

$$\begin{aligned}\text{SR4} &= \mu[\,\text{2nd}\,,\text{1st}\,]\,.\,\mu[\,\text{2nd}\,,\text{1st}\,]\,.\,\mu[\,\text{2nd}\,,\text{1st}\,]\,.\,\mu[\,\text{2nd}\,,\text{1st}\,]\\ &= \text{SR . SR . SR . SR} \qquad \text{where SR} = \mu[\,\text{2nd}\,,\text{1st}\,]\end{aligned}$$

Thus, the original behavioural description has been transformed into the traditional, structurally more efficient, description of a four-bit shift register. The behavioural description, with one large μ expression, has been transformed into the equivalent structural description with many smaller μ expressions.

A more complex example is shown by Finn (1983), involving the specification of a simple processor from Minsky (1967). The first attempt at its specification involves describing the processor in terms of a single system, with input, output and current state. Such a specification could indeed be implemented, and it would work, but the feedback loop would be enormous. Specifically, the contents of every register would be taken round the loop in every machine cycle, irrespective of whether they had been altered. Finn demonstrates, though, that the rules of μFP can be applied to transform this specification into one which is behaviourally identical but which involves the interconnection of several smaller loops, each represented by smaller μ expressions. This process is analogous to the technique which is described by Mead and Conway (1980, Section 6.2) in which various registers, that is elements which can be represented by small μ expressions, are successively removed from the main array and are connected externally.

Some of the greatest power of the language lies in its ability to describe large regular structures. This arises from its use of FFP constructs, which in turn were greatly influenced by those of APL. As a result, μFP has been used extensively, and with great success, in the design of highly regular arrays such as systolic arrays (Sheeran 1984, 1985).

This section has concentrated on just one language. It is one of a small class of CHDLs which are consistent with a formal, mathematical design style. Unfortunately, μFP is best only at describing synchronous systems and the reader is referred to Gordon (1986) for a more generally applicable language. However, μFP has been illustrated here because of its treatment of the finite state machine, and its consequent implications on the design of the test hardware for the device, which is explored next.

8.3 TESTING, SELF TESTING AND TESTABILITY

The ability to test a circuit for correctness is central to the implementation of fault/failure tolerant systems (Russell *et al.* 1985, Waters 1986). The traditional approach is to leave testing until the final stages of manufacture, selecting on the basis of whether the circuit produces the correct output for the tested inputs. VLSI circuits have too many possible internal states for the outputs to be tested exhaustively, and so tests are made for a statistically large number of cases. So large are the test sequences that they must be conducted automatically, with vast sums of money already involved in purchasing and running of fast automatic test equipment (ATE), with the capital depreciation of this contributing significantly to the price of the devices (Maunder 1985).

1. Test complexity ($\propto \varkappa!$)
2. Test access ($\propto \sqrt{\varkappa}$)
3. Test performance
4. Test cost

FIGURE 8.16 *Summary of test problems*

As the circuit which is to be tested becomes large, the amount of information required, or supplied, by the external tester increases. The pin count cannot rise at the same rate as the gate count since the gate count increases with the square of the circuit dimensions, but the pin count is limited to a linear growth in all but the pin grid array packaging styles. Even if high pin counts were available, processing such large volumes of data would become prohibitive. There is therefore a problem with test data bandwidth. Whether WSI or some other high transistor count technique is used in the future, the use of modularisation will be important – partitioning to reduce the test costs (Figure 8.16(1)) and wherever possible, test data should be obtained and control signals supplied at the natural interfaces to the system (Figure 8.16(2)).

The problem of testing the finished device can no longer be left to the final stage of manufacture (Spencer and Savir 1984), but must be considered at the initial design stage. Neither is it adequate to handcraft a testing scheme for each specialised application, and so the process must be formalised. These two aims are incorporated in what has become known as the *design for testability* (DFT) philosophy (Pradhan 1986).

Since circuits are so complex that only a statistical sample of tests can be conducted, it is advantageous to make a very quick initial test to sort out the devices which have obvious faults. With these removed, a more rigorous test can be conducted. This idea can be extended by having several stages, each one more rigorous than its predecessor, but being applied to fewer devices.

The 'rigorousness' of a test is called the *test coverage*, TC. This is another measure which runs from zero (no fault detected ever) to unity (every fault successfully detected). TC should be made as near to unity as is practically possible, so giving a high confidence level for the validity of the test.

The test coverage measures the proportion of faults which are detected per device. The *test quality*, TQ, is the proportion of faulty devices which are successfully detected per batch, and is another measure which runs from zero to unity. When the fault density, D, is assumed to be small, random and manifested in point-sized faults, the cell yield, y, is close to unity. When the test coverage, TC, is also high, Wadsack (1978) showed that:

$$TQ = 1 - (1 - y)(1 - TC)$$

Intuitively, this means that the proportion of faulty circuits which go undetected, $(1-TC)$, multiplied by the proportion of faulty devices which are fabricated, $(1-y)$, gives the proportion of faulty circuits out of total number fabricated which escape detection. The test quality is the inverse of this, namely the proportion of faulty circuits to the total number fabricated which are successfully detected.

Williams and Brown (1981) carry the analysis further, and show that the following is a better approximation over a greater range of values of TC and y:

$$TQ = y^{(1-TC)}$$

Since the aim is to make TQ approach unity, it is convenient to refer instead to its inverse. The failure level, $FL = 1 - TQ$, is so called here because it represents the number of faulty devices which are left to be discovered by the customer once they have been placed in service. Conventionally, this figure can be made low enough to be measured in parts per million.

The next section considers the implications of tesing on WSI (Section 8.3.1). This is followed by a classification of some test philosophies (Section 8.8.2), a classification of some of the strategies (Sections 8.8.3 and 8.8.4) and some ideas on highly parallel automatic testing (Section 8.8.5). The first of these is discussed in the next section.

8.3.1 Implications on wafer scale integration

Not only are there more points to probe and to control with WSI, but feedback might also be required to monitor and to control the reconfiguration logic. This is particularly significant when one of the static, hard-wired reconfiguration approaches is adopted, such as electrical or laser fuse blowing.

Catt observed (1986) that there is an irony in investing substantial sums in computer equipment to conduct the test and configuration when the wafer is already covered with processors. The need for expensive test equipment, and the bandwidth problem between it and the wafer, might both be minimised by performing more of the testing on the wafer. Even if the wafer contains devices which are less powerful than processors, special test processors can be embedded at strategic sites to oversee the testing operation. There then becomes a distinction between routine cell test, performed internally, and validity-checking device test, performed externally. With fault tolerance, the information describing the positions of the faulty cells can be gathered and sent to external test equipment in the form of a single global map. With failure tolerance, the centralised gathering of a single map is less appropriate since reconfiguration decisions must be made on a local basis if the number of extra control lines is to be minimised.

8.3.2 Classification of tests

In the most passive forms of testing, the behaviour of the system is merely monitored, looking for invariant properties, perhaps continuously, and with the system still on line and in service. More active forms of testing, though, can be conducted only when the system is off line or during idle periods. In either case the aim is the same: to check that the system never enters an invalid state.

With a digital system, the 'state' consists of a (large) pattern of binary logic values. This is most easily seen in the finite state machine to be the bits in the feedback loop. It is traditional to check merely that each observed bit in the state has the expected logic value. Faults/failures are classified according to whether a particular bit is constantly at logic level '1', or constantly at logic level '0', when it should be varying. Such *stuck-at* fault/failures can be caused by the short-circuiting of a signal line (not necessarily the one being monitored, but one on which its value depends) to one of the power supplies or to a logic gate which fails to operate, or owing to a break in a signal lead, or owing to a short-circuit to an adjacent signal. As a result of the continual push for smaller grid size, where transistors and conductors fail to operate digitally as switches and signal leads, and also as a result of using exotic circuit components such as fuses, antifuses and chemical vapour deposition tracks, certain non-digital failure modes might soon be regularly encountered where the digital system fails to generate clean logic values.

For *passive testing*, in addition to testing the system outputs, checks can be made at designated test points, thus giving access to some of the internal states of the system. For digital systems these and the other outputs can be tested not only for valid logic values, but also for valid voltage levels to represent the logic states. Inputs can be tested too, for example checking for satisfactory input impedances. Similarly, the power supply terminals can be tested for their voltages and currents being within certain limits, and for correct ranges of input impedance. In most cases, newly failed circuits should be turned off immediately, even if the system is in midcomputation. Its results can no longer be trusted, so they will be lost anyway, but it is better not to risk the possibility of the failing circuit causing any further damage.

Active testing can allow rare or critical events to be simulated. It might not be satisfactory to wait for the occurrence of these whilst the device is in service in order to judge whether it is fully functioning. Some systems provide for restricted active testing to be conducted whilst they are in operation. For instance, test programs and test data can be supplied to the system during idle periods. A multiprogrammed computer can run test programs concurrently with payload programs, for example. However, many of the active testing techniques are incapable of testing for certain timing conditions with the system running at full speed.

Thus both types of test have their relative merits. Passive tests can be unobtrusive and continuous, whilst active tests are potentially more extensive. It is wise to implement both classes of test in the system, for example actively testing the device immediately upon manufacture, and thereafter at convenient intervals, but subjecting it to continuous passive testing between these intervals. Indeed, this fits in well with the multistage, statistical testing idea – passive testing being a set of fast and simple tests which are conducted to check for obvious errors, and only if one is found is a full diagnostic test run to determine the best method for failure tolerant reconfiguration.

Anderson and Lee (1981) highlight certain important classes of test styles. *Replication checks* such as are provided by the voting systems not only provide a means of overriding faulty circuits, but a signal can be derived to warn that one of the circuits is misbehaving. If only this signal is required, replication factors using even numbers can be used. *Timing checks* often involve the use of *watch-dog circuits* which simply look out for some expected activity from the main circuits every so often, reporting suspected errors when it fails to occur. *Reversal checks* are applicable only in a few special cases and rely on the ability to reverse certain computations, reporting an error if the original data are not reconstructed. Examples of *coding check* include Hamming codes, parity checks and check-sums. In these, an error is reported if the data and its encoded forms are inconsistent. *Reasonableness checks* simply check that output data never strays into illegal values.

Diagnostic checks involve testing the components rather than the data. Unlike any of the other checks listed above, these can only be conducted actively. Test data are applied and the result, or *signature*, is compared against the expected value; if it differs in any way, the circuit is assumed to be faulty. The correct value can be derived by one of several techniques: it can be predicted by a proved correct simulation program, it can be generated by a known, working circuit, or it can be ascertained by majority vote, given that the chance of several faulty cells generating the same wrong value is very small.

The techniques for implementing these checks fall mainly into two categories: observability/controllability enhancements, and built-in self test. These are described in the next two sections (8.3.3 and 8.3.4) respectively.

8.3.3 Observability and controllability enhancements

For active testing, combinatorial circuits are fairly easily exercised, checking that the outputs are correct for each value of the provided inputs. Sequential circuits present a greater problem because they are sensitive not only to the present settings on their inputs, but also to the history of earlier settings. Since any synchronous sequential machine is a finite state machine, the number of tests must be finite. However, many of the states can be obtained only at the end of large numbers of cycles of the machine, and it could take an arbitrarily large time to reach some of the test conditions. The time might be finite, but still it might be longer than the lifetime of the universe.

The problem can be greatly eased by the provision of extra connections, test points, to enable more signals to be observed. It also helps if extra connections, control points, are provided to force parts of the circuit into required states. This is depicted in an abstract fashion in Figure 8.17.

One problem with this is that extra connections cannot always be afforded, particularly if they must be allocated to external pins on the package. Multiplexing can be used to achieve the same effect with fewer pins, but with an understandable degradation in test speed.

The *scan/set* technique is a formalised method for organising the multiplexing of this *ad hoc* approach. Figure 8.18 shows how the required test signals can be shifted into the 'scan/set' register from a single connection. When it is in position, the 'set' signal can be asserted. When the 'scan' signal is next asserted, the appropriate levels, from monitor points within the system logic, are loaded into the 'scan/set' register. The contents of the register can then be shifted out, again using just a single connection line.

The design described above involves the inclusion of possibly large amounts of extra circuitry. This of course occupies valuable area. The aim of most test techniques is to minimise the hardware overhead by (re)utilising as much payload logic

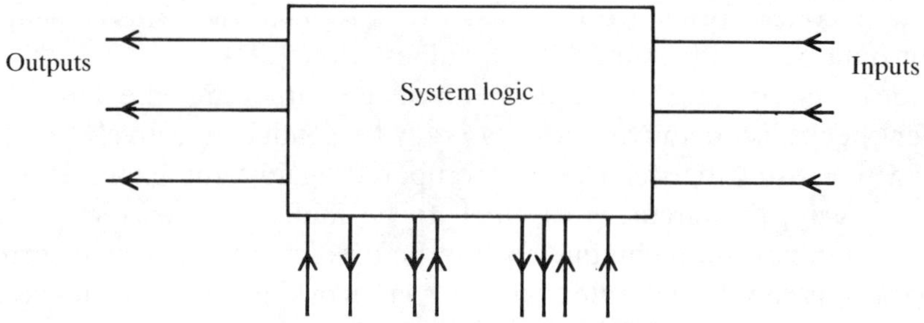

FIGURE 8.17 *Observing and controlling a system during test*

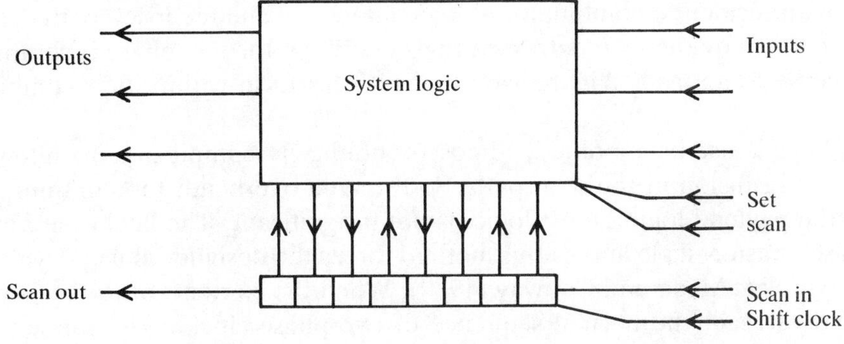

FIGURE 8.18 *Scan/set*

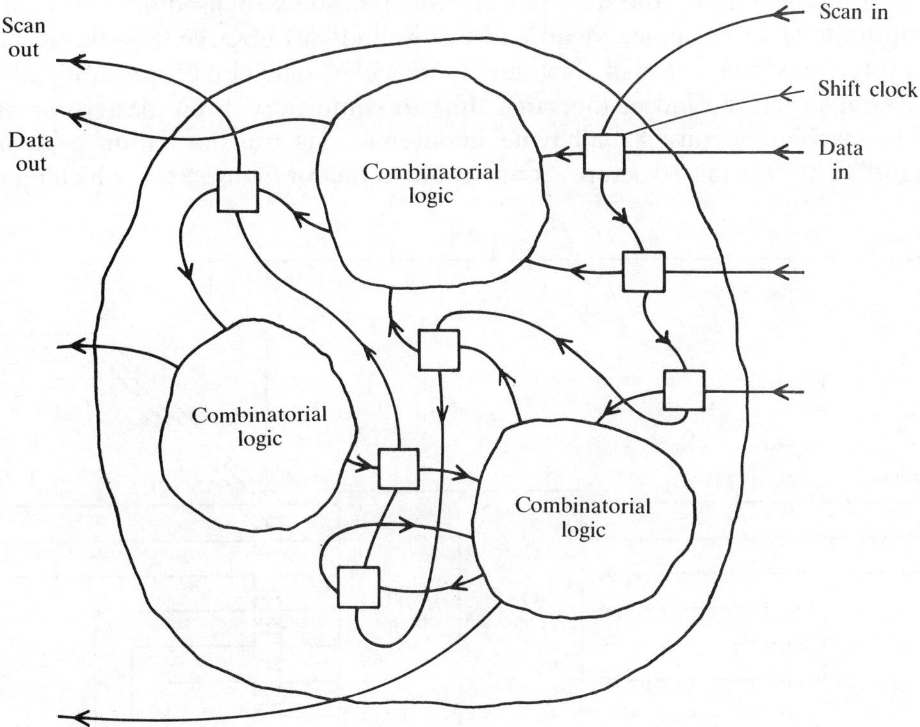

FIGURE 8.19 *Level sensitive scan design*

as possible (Commerford and Lyman 1983). One such approach is known as *level sensitive scan design* (LSSD); the usual method of depicting it is as shown in Figure 8.19. It arranges for each of the latches in the payload logic to be optionally connected as a large snake-like structure called the *scan path* (Komonytsky 1983, Russell *et al.* 1985).

Since the scan path contains all of the latches from the system, the remaining blocks must each contain only combinatorial logic. So the system looks like a shift register with incidental combinatorial logic attached. The feedback paths are therefore interrupted by the scan path shift register. When the test phase is complete, the latches cease to act as a shift register and return to use within their combinatorial circuits.

Each latch must be modified, almost doubling its complexity, to allow for its conditional inclusion in the scan path. So the area overhead, though minimised by reusing the payload logic as test logic, is not insignificant. The latches are generally two-phase, master–slave and so this method forces the designer to use a synchronous design style, *à la* Mead and Conway (1980). When the contents of the register are to be loaded or read, the normal sequence of two-phase clocking is stopped and the scan clock is used in place of one of the phases. This method is therefore intrusive, that is active.

It is interesting to note how this system could be visualised arranged as a single loop finite state machine. Mead and Conway (1980) observe how the PLA can be used to transform a design for a highly irregular logic circuit into a highly regular physical structure, and at the same time to conform with the design for the finite state machine. Figure 8.19 having undergone this transformation is depicted in Figure 8.20. It is this structure, comparable to that of Figure 8.15, which makes μFP

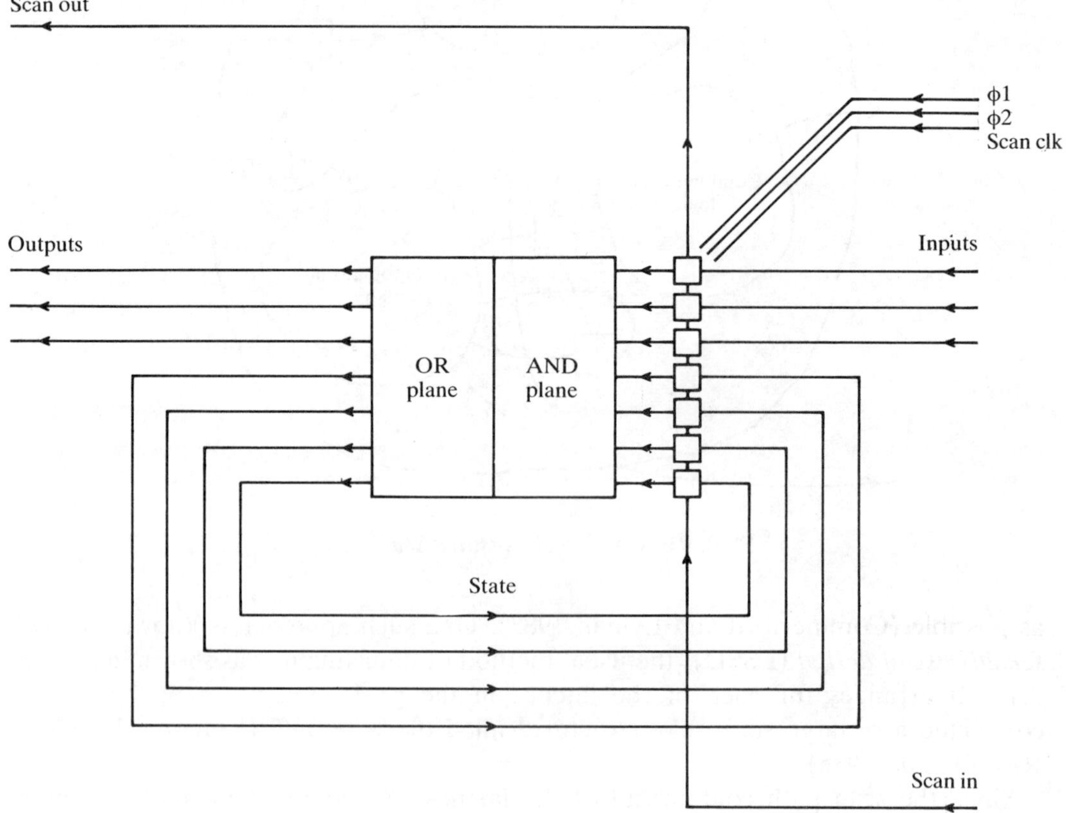

FIGURE 8.20 *LSSD on a programmable logic array*

a possible choice for a design style which is able to deal meaningfully with the test logic.

One major problem is the large volume of test data which must be supplied, and the large volume of test results which must then be analysed. In order to accelerate the process, some of the generation and analysis of the test data can be performed in the device itself. The built-in self-test (BIST) techniques which are described next (Section 8.3.4) tackle this problem.

8.3.4 Built-in self-test

The techniques which are described in the previous section involve the generation of large streams of test results. These must be somehow compressed, to be represented using fewer bits and hence to be reduced to more manageable proportions, for most practical systems. This is advantageous for so-called *manual test pattern generation* (MTPG), but it is imperative when more of the testing function is to be implemented on the chip.

The compression of data must necessarily involve the loss of information, but two points can be noted: (a) some of the information might be tautological and can be deleted safely, and (b) even if information is lost the testing process will be much faster so that, having found the obviously faulty circuits quickly, time can be afforded to test the remaining ones more thoroughly.

A simple integer can be used as a summary of the test results, using a technique which is analogous to the ones for *cyclic redundancy code* (CRC) generation (Peterson and Brown 1961). It is necessary only to compare this *signature* for equality with the expected one to determine whether the circuit is unusable. The chance of a faulty units registering as good can be arbitrarily minimised, and naïvely, is a chance of one in 2^k, where k is the number of bits in the integer.

One technique for computing the integer involves taking the string of bits from the scan path shift register and counting the number of 'ones'. Alternatively, the number of transitions from logic 'zero' to logic 'one' can be counted. If the circuit under test produces a different value to that predicted, the tested circuit must be faulty. This technique is now renowned, though, for its inability to detect certain classes of fault, and a more rigorous version called *syndrome testing* (Russell *et al.* 1985) is better, though it is not pursued further here.

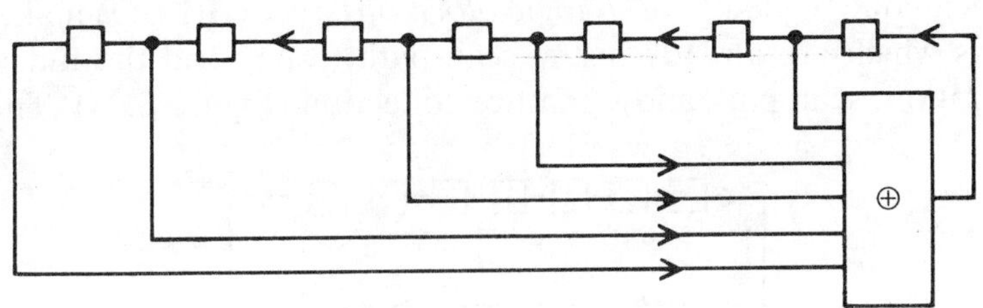

FIGURE 8.21 *An arbitrary linear feedback shift register*

A more successful technique is based around the *linear feedback shift register* (LFSR). This is the name given to any shift register whose input is fed with the modulo 2 addition of some of its outputs (Davies 1966) (Figure 8.21).

Two special cases have been investigated extensively (Davies 1966), namely: the Möbius or twisted ring counters, which use one output only fed back through an inverter, and the more general *chain code generators*, which sample two outputs and feed them back through a two-input XOR gate (Figure 8.22).

Linear feedback shift registers are frequently used as pseudo-random number generators. If the shift register is initialised with a preset, non-zero integer, it will start to produce new integers at each cycle of the shift register's clock. After 2^{k-1} clock cycles, for a carefully designed k-bit shift register, the last non-zero integer will be generated and the sequence starts again. The sequence is deterministic: after any known number of clock cycles the integer which is held in the register can be predicted with certainty. Moreover, if the circuit is initialised with the same preset integer on another occasion, the same sequence of integers will be generated again.

Linear feedback shift registers can be used to generate test patterns, as depicted in Figure 8.23. Pseudo-random test patterns are not as efficient in the task of statistically testing for faults, but this is more than compensated by the speed advantage of this *automatic test pattern generation* (ATPG) over the 'manual' method, and hence by the increased number of tests which can be conducted within the same time.

By adding an extra input to the LFSR, supplied by the system's logic, the shift register will no longer keep to the same sequence as before. However, assuming that the system and the shift register are supplied by the same clock, the final integer will still be deterministic, that is the same value will be obtained whenever the experiment is rerun with the same initial conditions and the same inputs to the system. This arrangement is depicted in Figure 8.23 using the traditional finite state machine arrangement. The reader is invited to confirm that this approach can equally well be applied to Figure 8.19.

The process can be continued, say for 100 different initial conditions; any error in the signature need not be identified any more accurately than the fact that one is present, hence indicating that the circuit should be rejected. A faulty system might feasibly generate a valid signature, but by careful design and choice of Hamming distances (Peterson and Brown 1961) the chances of this happening can be minimised.

Another technique, called *built-in logic block observer* (BILBO) makes use of the same registers which are already in the scan path to perform the functions of test pattern generation, scan path and signature collection (Figure 8.24). The test phase

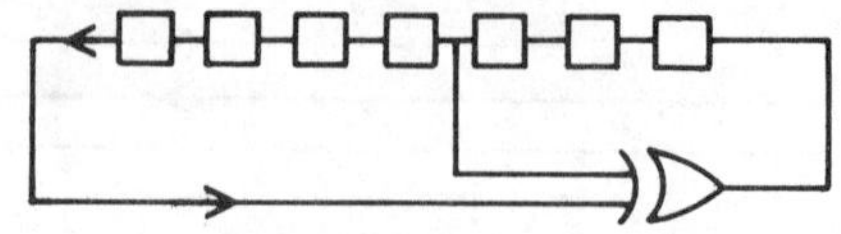

FIGURE 8.22 *A linear feedback shift register*

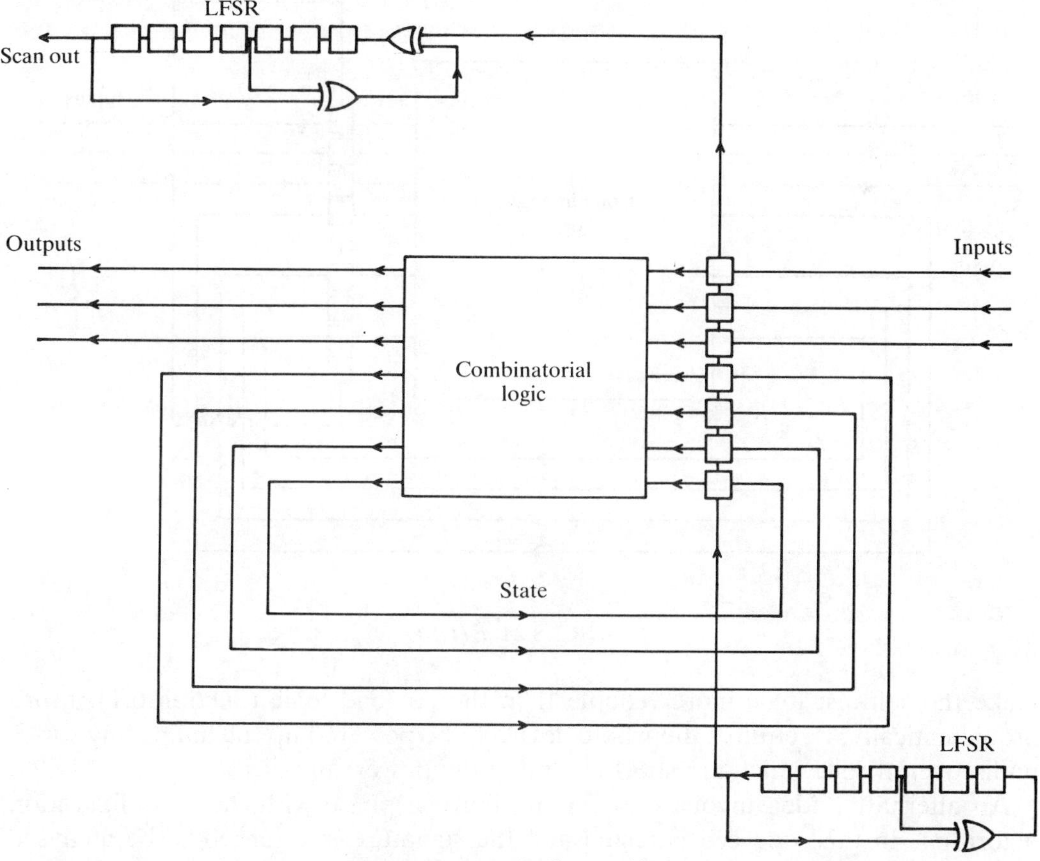

FIGURE 8.23 *Built-in self-test*

is broken into two cycles. In the first, one half of the scan path is used as the test-pattern-generator/signature-collector and the other as the scan path. In the second cycle, the rôles are reversed. At the end of this, the signature which is read out is the combined result of testing the two halves.

Many of the applications which have been suggested require configuration schemes which are automatic, such as those of Section 6.3.3. There is little question that these will need to make use of built-in self-test techniques. Some further implications of this are described in the next section.

8.3.5 Automatic configuration

Given that the device will contain a large number of identical cells, and that every one will need to be tested, it is tempting to assume that they can all be commanded to self-test concurrently, the results of which will then be available for the configuration phase. This scheme has the advantage that the test phase is highly parallel, and hence conducted very quickly. It has the disadvantage that each cell is in charge of its own diagnosis (Catt 1986) but, contrary to Catt's well-justified fears, it is possible to

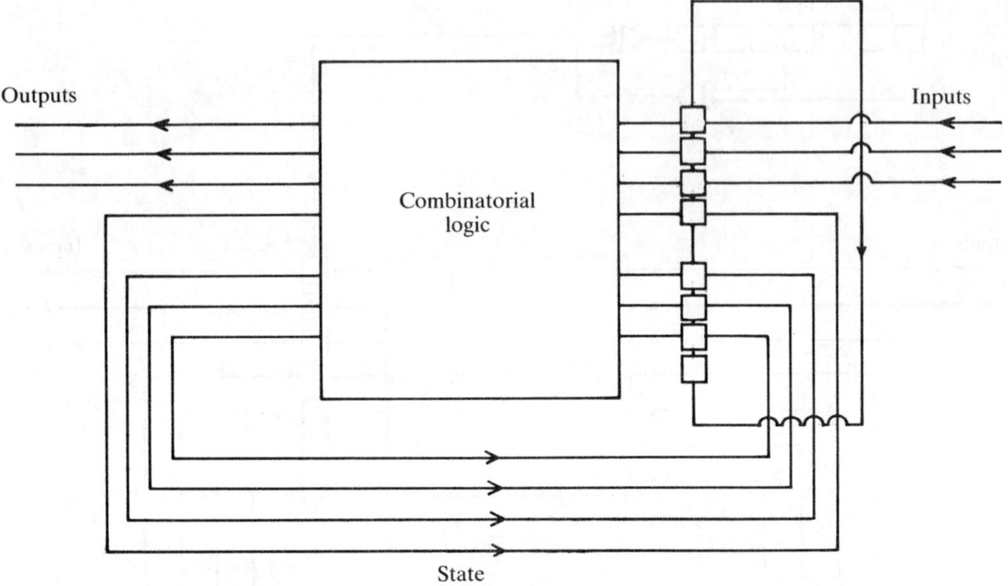

FIGURE 8.24 *BILBO*

make the self-test logic more reliable than the payload logic (Section 6.1). More problematically, it requires the whole device to be powered up, including any so-far undiscovered cells which are short-circuiting the power supplies.

An alternative idea involves combining the test phase with the reconfiguration algorithm. In this, one cell is tested and the signature is returned to be analysed externally. If the cell works, it can be trusted to act as the test equipment for its neighbour(s). In Figure 6.16, for example, the test of 'available[diro]' can be preceded by 'test(diro)' to initiate the test sequence in the neighbour and to check the validity of the returned signature. This, however, leads to a sequential operation in which cells are tested and added to the spiral in a linear fashion, and a configuration time which is of the order of minutes can be expected (Aubusson and Gledhill 1978).

Figure 8.25 indicates a workable compromise depicted almost halfway through its operation. The test sequence is conducted prior to the reconfiguration sequence, and is initiated by external test equipment in the bottom left corner of the device. If this cell works correctly, it commands all of its neighbours to initiate their own tests and then analyses each of the results. A wavefront of testing sweeps diagonally across the device. Some protocol must be included for dealing with multiple requests for testing of the same cell. Thus only processors which are known to be working are allowed to test their neighbours, having remembered their own correctly generated signature. Alternatively, each processor can compare its own signature with those of its neighbours and then take a majority decision on what the correct signature is, since the chance of two processors generating the same wrong signature can also be made negligibly small.

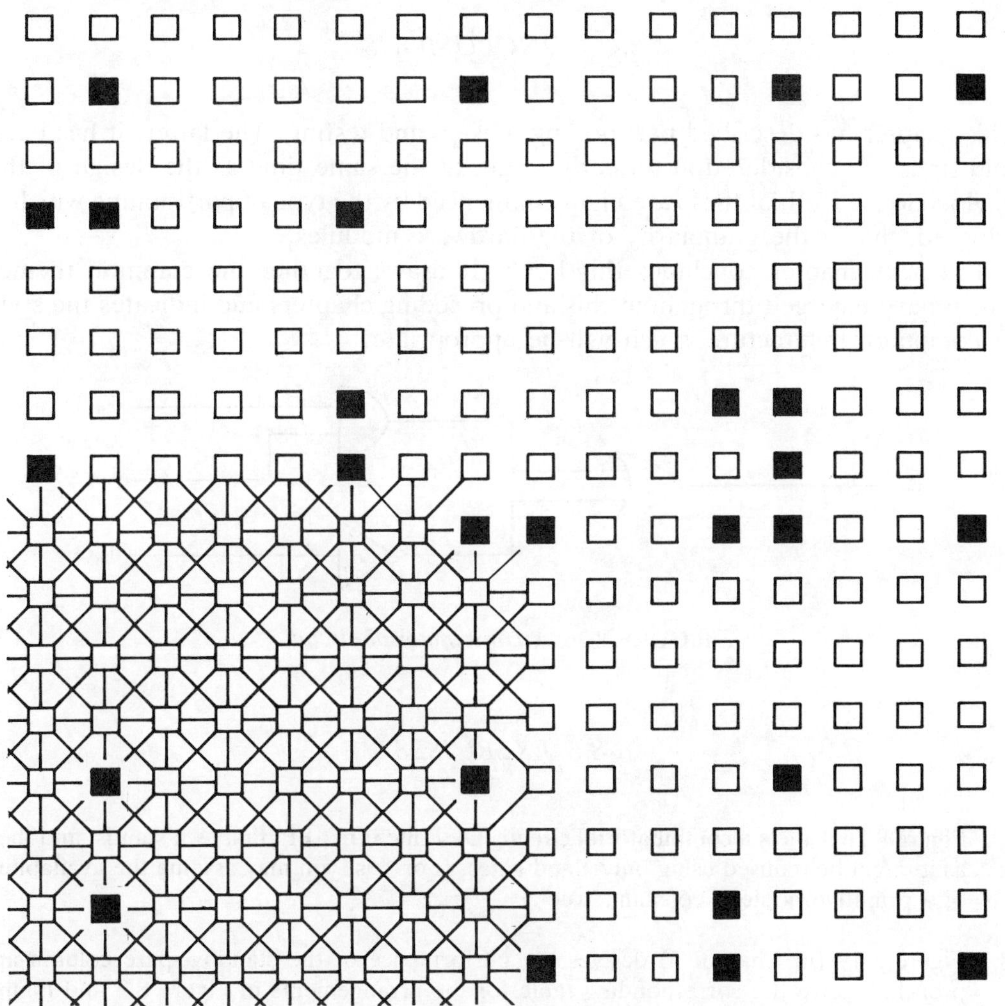

FIGURE 8.25 *Wavefront of testing*

It is worth mentioning at this stage that, for coordinate addressing architectures, it is necessary to provide each cell with an address which is not only unique but signifies the relative position within the array. It would be inconvenient to have to hard-wire the address into each cell since this would involve at least one uniquely patterned reticle for each cell in the array. One of the easiest soft-wiring, that is data latching, alternatives involves propagating a wavefront of messages in very much the same manner as that shown in Figure 8.25. The first tested cell is informed, by definition, that its address is (0, 0). From then on, all other cells are informed of their addresses recursively from their neighbours. Any cell whose address is known, (x, y), can inform its eastern neighbour that its address is $(x + 1, y)$, its northern neighbour is $(x, y + 1)$, the western one is $(x - 1, y)$, and the southern one is $(x, y - 1)$. Similarly, for eight-connected grids, the north-eastern neighbour is $(x + 1, y + 1)$, and so on.

8.4 CONCLUSIONS

This chapter has described partitioning, design and testing. The latter, it has been said, must be considered at an early stage, at the same time as the design of the payload logic. Both of these are highly influenced by the type of partitioning which is adopted, that is the granularity of the hardware modules.

The next chapter concludes this book. It draws together the common themes which have emerged throughout this and preceding chapters and indicates the style of computer architecture which will be appropriate.

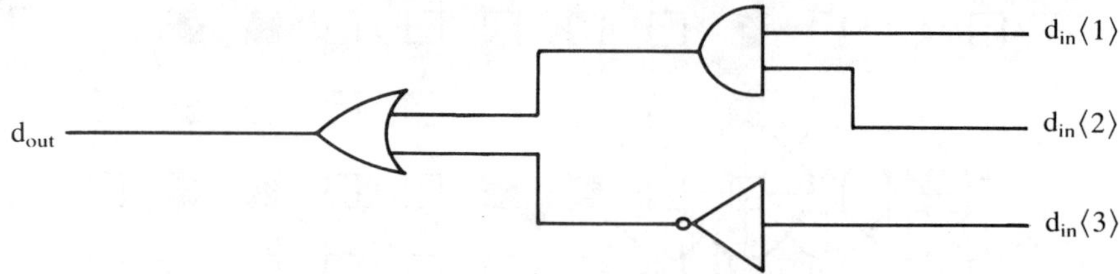

FIGURE 8.26 *A combinatorial circuit*

8.5 EXERCISES

8.1 Figure 8.26 depicts a combinatorial circuit. Describe it in μFP, first as it stands, and then as it might be realised using only Nand gates. (For this, you may assume the availability of a primitive boolean constant 'true'.)

8.2 Figure 5.19 (in Chapter 5) derives the performance of the standby-spare column approach. Derive the corresponding table for the arrangements in Figure 8.3 and Figure 8.4.

9

ECONOMICS-DRIVEN RESEARCH AND DEVELOPMENT

The major part of this book has reviewed objectively many of the alternative techniques which are available to the designer. However, it originally set out with the more specific aim of finding methods for implementing fifth generation computers. This chapter highlights those techniques whose properties could be used beneficially towards this aim.

Ultimately the driving force to find better solutions, or at least the funding for it, is one of economics. Moreover, it too works at several levels of granularity, with differing extents of recurring and non-recurring costs. Savings through reductions in program execution time, for example on a particularly fast computer, are made every time that a program is run and for every instruction execution within the program. Program development time on the other hand is a one-off event, in which savings are made only every time that a new program is written or an existing one is modified. However, it too is aided by reductions in computer execution time since program development involves the running of program development tools, and is directly influenced by the speed at which these run. Less frequently still, savings through reductions in hardware manufacture time are made for every circuit produced from the fabrication line. Finally, hardware development time is another one-off event, savings being made only on each new circuit which is designed. Again, it is partly dependent on program execution time due to the heavy reliance on CAD.

However, this overlooks two important details. The first is that technology and the market-place are moving extremely rapidly. Products have relatively short lifespans before their successors are designed. Thus the values of n_2 and n_4 in Figure 9.1 are relatively small numbers now. The second detail is that salaries are now very high, and that the cost of providing and running machines is fairly small by comparison. Thus n_1c_1 and n_3c_3 can dominate n_2c_2 and n_4c_4.

This chapter now summarises the findings of the previous ones, as applicable to fifth generation computer design, fabrication, programming and use. It highlights

	Average number	Average unit cost	Overall cost
Computers designed:	n_1	c_1	n_1c_1
Computers manufactured:	n_2 per design	c_2	$n_2n_1c_2$
Programs developed:	n_3 per computer	c_3	$n_3n_2n_1c_3$
Program runs:	n_4 per program	c_4	$n_4n_3n_2n_1c_4$
TOTAL:	$n_1(n_2(n_3(n_4c_4 + c_3) + c_2) + c_1)$		

FIGURE 9.1 *Economics of computer design and use*

the interdependencies of the various proposed solutions. This is approached in the top-down manner of studying the programming concerns (Section 9.1), followed by the hardware concerns (Section 9.2). Finally, some comments are made regarding future work and developments which might be expected (Section 9.3).

9.1 ECONOMICS OF PROGRAM DEVELOPMENT AND EXECUTION

The commercial demands of a rapidly changing market, and the high cost of salaries, necessitate the adoption of faster program development techniques (Figure 9.2). The use of declarative programming languages in preference to imperative ones has been indicated as being beneficial in this respect. However, declarative languages are executed very inefficiently on present day computers; hence there is a need to design new computers which are tailored for the declarative programming style.

Many computer programs are compute bound, and require the use of faster models for program execution (Figure 9.2). One route by which this can be achieved is the use of highly parallel arrangements of processors. However, conventional programming languages are not well suited to describing algorithms for these new arrangements, so there is a need to adopt new types of programming languages. Furthermore, if program development time is not to be impaired, the details of how to use the parallel processors should not be added to the programmer's load. Again the use of declarative languages seems to offer the greatest promise for solving these problems (Section 9.1.2).

Program execution speed is also dependent on the data communications speed. This is particularly relevant to parallel multiprocessor systems since these make notoriously heavy use of interprocessor communications (Kung 1982). In order to improve the raw speed of the communications channels, whether they be interprocessor or intraprocessor, as much circuitry as possible should be fitted on to a single piece of semiconductor. One ultimate aim is to occupy a complete wafer with a single contiguous system. As well as speeding up the communications paths, though, there is a need to choose execution strategies which minimise the amount of communication, harnessing locality within the program and limiting computation to a small cluster of processors wherever possible. This is discussed in Section 9.1.1.

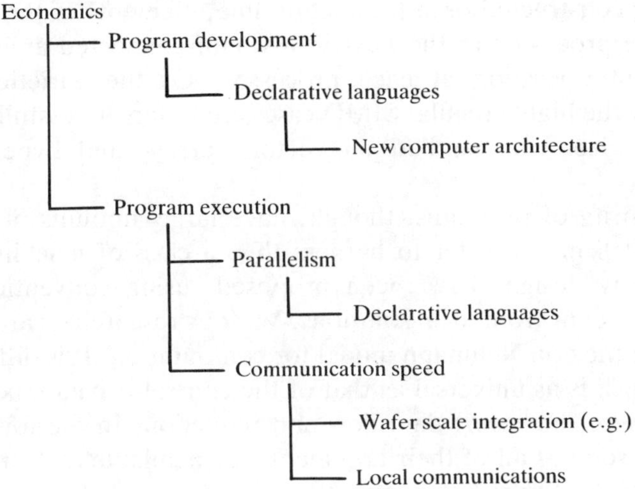

FIGURE 9.2 *Dependencies of program development and execution*

9.1.1 Parallelism

The aim is to provide many processors within the one architecture, each capable of executing a different part of the program, and hence co-operating towards the execution of the problem. Two major design decisions must be made: one concerning what each processor should contain, and the other concerning how the processors should be interconnected. For the first concern, it is tempting to use the processors which are familiar, well tested and available commercially in great numbers. For the second concern, several topologies have been proposed and investigated, each with its own compromises, making use of whatever regularity can be exploited in the application. These include the examples listed in Figure 9.3.

Unfortunately conventional SISD machines are far from ideal as components in general purpose multiprocessor systems. As a result, applications have tended to concentrate on particular special cases of parallelism. Vertical, pipelined, MISD parallelism is applicable when a vector or stream of data is to be processed, each element of which is to undergo a number of operations in sequence. Like motor cars

PSN.Shared bus	CSN.Shared bus
PSN.Cross-bar exchange	CSN.Cross-bar exchange
PSN.Vector	CSN.Vector
PSN.Ring	CSN.Ring
PSN.Grid	CSN.Grid
PSN.Star	CSN.Star
PSN.Tree	CSN.Tree
PSN.Butterfly	CSN.Butterfly
PSN.Hypercube	CSN.Hypercube

FIGURE 9.3 *Networks*

which are being constructed on a production line, elements of the data stream are passed from one processor to the next in a vector-connected architecture, undergoing a different operation at each processor. Of the varieties of horizontal parallelism, only the highly regular SIMD cases are so far successfully utilised. Large vectors and matrices are handled on vector-, array- and hypercube-connected architectures.

The vast majority of programs, though, have large amounts of very irregularly structured parallelism. In order to harness this, a class of machine called MIMD is required. Many designs have been proposed, using conventional computers. However, these are far from ideal solutions. Various researchers are working to find an alternative to the von Neumann model for computation. It is difficult, though, to find a model which is as universal as that of the control-driven model. Two models show great promise, however: data flow and reduction. In the former, all instructions execute as soon as all of their arguments are available and sufficient free processors are available. In the latter, only those instructions whose results are needed are executed. In both cases, many of the topologies listed in Figure 9.3 have been investigated.

9.1.2 Functional programming languages

The other motivation behind computer architecture design was that of programmer throughput: the rate at which human programmers can write finished, working programs. This must necessarily be tied up with programming language design.

The conventional, imperative programming languages were developed in order to program computers of the 1940s and 50s. The languages carry many of the hallmarks of those early machines: characteristics which computer scientists now identify as being unhelpful to the articulation of human programming thoughts. Instead, further change is advocated, and languages are proposed of a declarative style which obey the laws of mathematics.

It should not be considered to be discouraging that industry is slow to adopt the new languages. The same laws of economics dictate that large suites of programs, and the hard-won skills of teams of computer programmers, cannot be discarded overnight. Change is slow and must be gradual. Nonetheless change is occurring, even though it is disguised. Fortran-77 (Monro 1982), for instance, owes more to Pascal than it does to the original specification of Fortran, though it implies by its name that it is upwardly compatible from the latter. It will be interesting to await the emergence of a wholly declarative Fortran.

One major reason for wanting to imitate mathematics is the quest for *mathematical tractability*. Once a program obeys the normal laws of mathematics it can be treated as a mathematical statement, capable for instance of being subjected to formal proof (Darlington *et al.* 1982). One great ideal is to test programs before they are officially released, and to prove formally that they will always meet the specification regardless of the data which they are given. In addition, over the centuries, mathematicians have built up a vast armoury of tools to perform transformations on mathematical expressions. Thus, given a program P, which has been proved to meet its specification S, there will be transformations readily available to produce a program P' which also meets specification S. By choosing only certain appropriate transformations, program P' will be more efficient than program P. The process of optimisation is therefore one of transformation which can be applied to valid programs. However, this is a fairly recent area of study, and far from simple.

More importantly, though, mathematical logic is also very natural as a medium for human thought, and encourages the use of hierarchical modularisation. A large problem can be broken down into several subproblems, each of which might be further subdivided. Having designed one module, which might be a function or a subroutine, and then tested it, the designer can trust it. He is able to abstract away, able to forget about the detail of how it works and able to treat it as a black-box component. Having tested it in isolation, it can be trusted to work when connected to other components. This means that he is free to concentrate on writing the next part of the program. Most imperative languages provide for this, but with nothing to force the programmer to design in this way.

Despite the fact that many people shy away from anything to do with mathematics, mathematical logic comes very naturally to human beings. It is largely the burden of formal proof and complicated transformation which they fear in reality and, since the computer is charged with performing these jobs, only the expressive side of mathematics remains. This is the side in which all humans are expert. Thus the use of declarative programming languages makes programs easier to write, easier to understand and easier to modify later.

This is a powerful enough argument on its own, but it is strengthened all the more by the quest for methods to extract parallelism. To have many concurrent operations, perhaps all executing asynchronously, adds orders of magnitude of extra complexity to design of programs. Modifications to conventional languages have been tried (Bornat 1984, Wand and Wellings 1984), but it is only the semantic cleanliness of the declarative languages which can keep this complexity under control. Indeed, they can even hide from the programmer the fact that parallelism is involved at all. Not only does this mean that the programmer is not troubled by such considerations, but also that his programs will be portable: if a program does not explicitly specify the amount of parallelism at any point, then there are fewer problems in copying a program which is designed for an N-processor computer to one which has M processors.

Even having selected declarative languages for direct support in the instruction set, there are many mechanisms which can be chosen for their implementation. Figure 9.4 summarises the affinities which were observed in Sections 3.2.5 and 4.7.

The main problem is that the declarative languages are not ideally suited for execution on conventional computers. Since the imperative languages were tailored for conventional machines, they are highly efficient for execution on these computers. Given that declarative languages are so attractive, there is a need to design new types of computer which can execute efficiently any programs which are written in them.

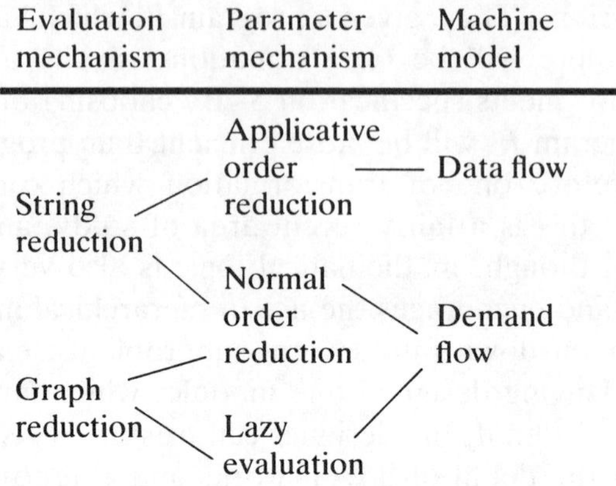

FIGURE 9.4 *Affinities of evaluation mechanisms to computer models*

One immediate advantage follows from the embodiment of declarative language semantics, wherein the instruction sets and behaviours of these new designs will have mathematical properties which are expressible using declarative notation (Durham 1986). At last hardware design too will be amenable to formal proof, confirming that it meets its specification (Gordon 1986).

9.2 ECONOMICS OF HARDWARE DEVELOPMENT AND MANUFACTURE

At the lower, hardware level the need for fast development of the system, again stemming from the economics of high salaries and a rapidly changing market, necessitates the use of better CAD (Figure 9.5). Since this involves computer programming, albeit a subset which is aimed at hardware design, the same arguments hold as for program development. Thus circuit design should become more declarative in style. The design burden is eased when the hardware consists of highly regular

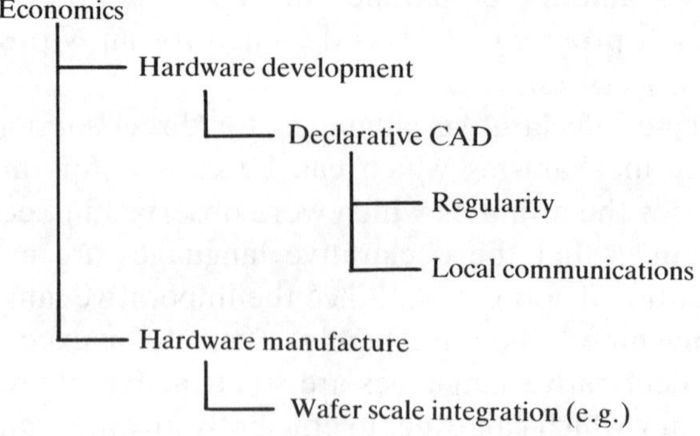

FIGURE 9.5 *Dependencies of hardware development and manufacture*

arrangements of identical cells (as summarised in Section 9.2.2), which communicate cleanly with each other without side effects, using short, simple, local connections.

In order to minimise fabrication time, a number of techniques offer promise for reducing the time taken to test devices, to package them and to assemble them as complete circuits. Although not the only answer, this book has been concerned with the use of WSI in this rôle, as summarised in Section 9.2.1.

9.2.1 Wafer scale integration

The adoption of WSI leads in turn to a whole series of new constraints (Lea 1986b) (Figure 9.6). Most significantly perhaps, the imperfect nature of materials requires that the system be tolerant of defects, faults or failures, preferably in a hierarchy of levels. Fault and failure tolerance can be achieved by designing the system to be constructed as a highly regular arrangement of identical cells, preferably with NNI (Sutherland and Mead 1977, Kung 1982); however, it also requires that the system be able to make use of an irregular final arrangement of working cells. Some

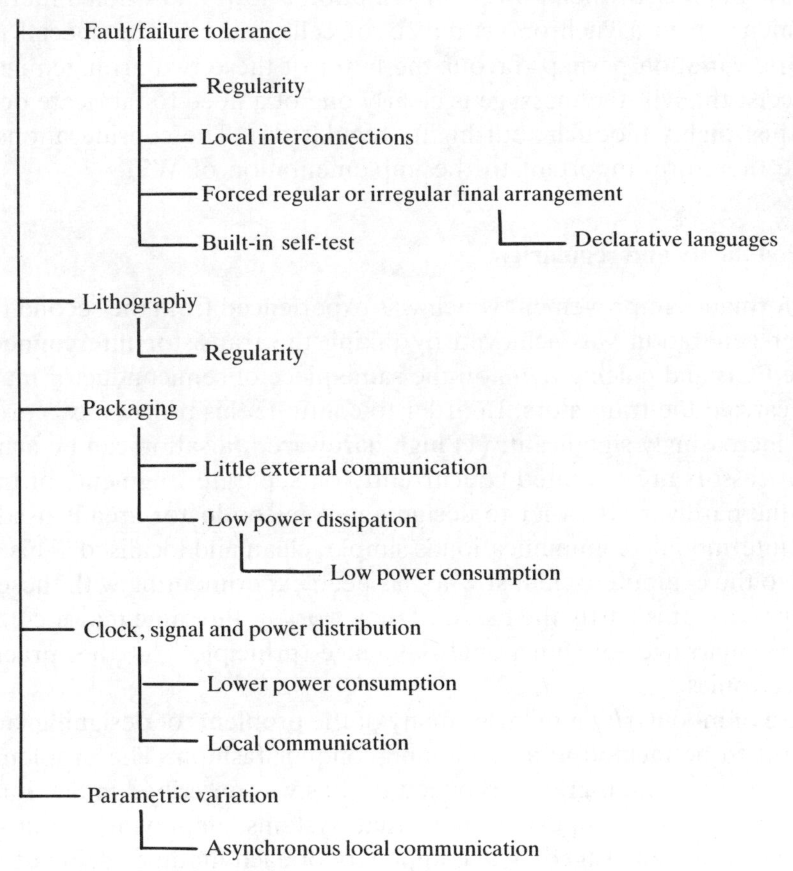

FIGURE 9.6 *Dependencies of wafer scale integration*

applications require that regularity, and possibly also a fixed size, be forced upon the irregular arrangement of working cells. This is achieved by choosing an appropriate harvesting strategy. Other applications, though, use the irregular arrangement as best they can, executing programs which, after all, are also generally irregular in nature. In these latter cases, the execution of a program should be able to adapt rapidly to whatever arrangement of processors is available. This argues in favour of the use of automatic methods for the extraction of parallelism, and hence to the adoption of declarative programming languages as indicated earlier.

Fault and failure tolerance, particularly the latter, require the use of suitable built-in self-test techniques. The results from these tests must then be used to reconfigure the system accordingly. In the case of failure tolerance, this configuration must be reversible, possibly using transistor switches which are driven by the test logic.

The use of WSI also requires the choice of suitable lithography and packaging techniques (Figure 9.6). Current lithography practice favours the use of highly regular arrangements of identical cells. Packaging requirements necessitate small numbers of external connections (i.e. few pins), low power dissipation and low power consumption. In addition, the problems of clock, signal and power distribution are minimised when power consumption is low, and when a hierarchical tree arrangement or an asynchronous matrix of cells is used. The special problems of parametric variation perhaps favour the latter of these two arrangements. In all of these facets, though, the message is clearly one of a need to fabricate devices which are not just highly modular, but highly regular too. The considerations of Section 9.2.2 are therefore important to the implementation of WSI.

9.2.2 Modularity and regularity

The performance improvement which was experienced from the second to the fourth computer generation was achieved by taking the transistor interconnections away from the PCB and placing them on the same piece of semiconductor material which already carried the transistors. In order to continue this process, two properties will become increasingly significant: (1) high hardware utilisation can be achieved when many processors are operated concurrently on separate fragments of the program, and (2) the hardware is easier to design and semiconductor area is used to greatest effect if intermodule communication is simple, clean and localised. This sounds very familiar to the computer scientist who has been experimenting with these same ideas for many years. It is partly the fact that they work to the same major constraints that helps the marriage of functional language principles to the practicalities of microelectronics.

The use of modularity minimises many of the problems of designing large systems, enabling it to be tackled in a divide-and-conquer fashion. The problems of testing the final devices is then greatly reduced too, as was described in Section 8.3. These points are especially important now that systems employing about 150 million transistors can be envisaged. The complexity of each module, being of the order of a few thousand transistors for example, is kept suitably small. The overall system complexity can then be built up by the repetition of these modules, in this example perhaps a hundred thousand times.

Regularity is a very desirable property in design, particularly in microelectronics design. It removes much of the burden on the designer, or the CAD program suite, by allowing generalisations to be made about the design. It also allows for a very dense packing of the design on to the two-dimensional surface of a semiconductor wafer.

Lastly, the only viable method which engineers have at present for coping with faults in the semiconductor involves the use of repeated module circuits. Wherever a module is found to be faulty, its job can be taken over by one of its identical neighbours. The fact that nature also uses this method, for example in the cells of biological tissue, is encouraging and might indicate that this is a good approach.

9.3 THE HISTORY AND FUTURE OF WAFER SCALE INTEGRATION

Despite the improvements in performance which have been achieved so far, there is always a requirement for more. Once WSI has been developed for one project which particularly needs its unique qualities, for example for use in space, there will be no shortage of applications. This is not a universally held view, though. Some observers doubt that there will be any economic applications in the future. They suspect that the advantages which it offers, such as cheaper construction costs and faster circuit operation, do not promise an order of magnitude improvement and so are hardly worth the effort. However, the same arguments could have been presented in the late 1950s when integrated circuits were first contemplated seriously. At that time, it was the reduction in size, weight and power consumption and the increase in system reliability, however marginal, that made them extremely attractive for use in space and on military projects. It was only later, when the technology had been developed for these projects, that commercial advantages were found for integration, and electronics design without it cannot now be imagined.

Since WSI (full slice technology) offers so much, it is beginning to attract much attention. A good historical treatment is given by Moore (1986a). The oldest quoted paper dates back to 1964, at Westinghouse with Sack *et al.* Since then, involvement has been sporadic, with seminal papers from Texas Instruments, Hughes, Honeywell, IBM, McDonnell Douglas, Trilogy, and Burroughs. Catt's patent (1974) was notable, as was Aubusson and Catt's paper (1978) in which the term 'wafer scale integration' was first coined. The British involvement is now largely centred on the Alvey project 073 (Dickson 1984).

There is little doubt that WSI is here to stay. Past projects have come and gone, but interest has now exceeded a critical mass, as witnessed by the interest which has been generated by recent dedicated conferences and workshops (Jesshope and Moore 1985, Saucier and Trilhe 1986a, Lea 1987). This is not to say, though, that an economic application, even in a specialised niche, is certain to be found. Several workers have attempted to quantify the potential cost benefits of WSI, notably Moore (1986b) and Sumerling (1986), with equations and graphs, but there is still little that is concrete to report. Most significantly, the verdict of whether WSI is economic or not depends on having a precise model for the fault distribution function, ν. Sumerling shows that placing a belief even in either of the simple models of Poisson or Murphy leads to opposite verdicts. This therefore is an area in which much research work must be concentrated before the future of the technology can be known with any certainty.

9.4 THE EMERGENCE OF THE FIFTH GENERATION COMPUTER

In conclusion, it would seem that the most profitable systems to investigate are ones which are composed of highly regular matrices of identical processors, consuming as little power as possible. They should work in a declarative fashion, completely asynchronously, and communicate locally without side effects.

There are still many problems to be solved. However, the author is confident that they are tractable, and that their solution, with or without WSI, is imminent. Maybe the nominal setting of the 1991 completion date is liable to slip a little now; nevertheless the project target to produce a working fifth generation computer will be met in the very near future.

APPENDIX 1

CIRCUIT MODULES

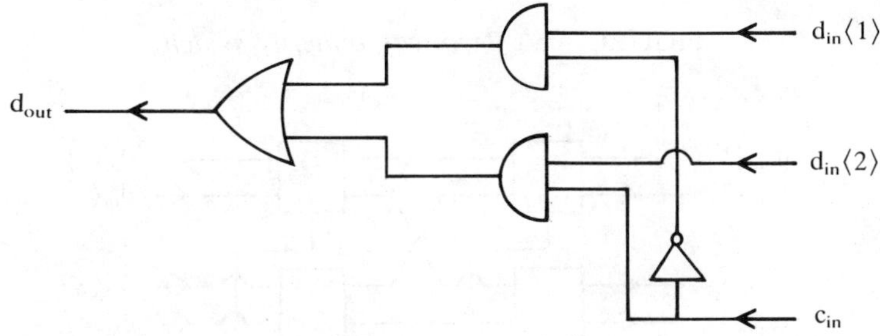

MUX2 = OR . [AND. [1.1, NOT.2], AND[2.1, 2]]

FIGURE A1.1 *Two-way multiplexer cell*

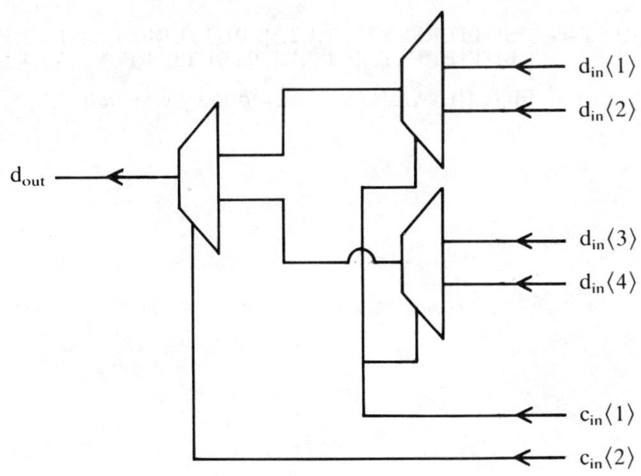

MUX4 = MUX2 . [MUX2.[1.1,2.1,1.2], MUX2.[3.1,4.1,1.2], 2.2]

FIGURE A1.2 *Four-way multiplexer cell*

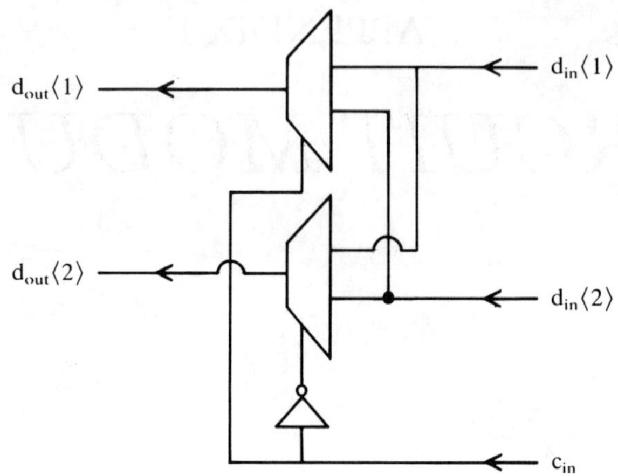

BUTTERFLY2 = [MUX2.[1.1,2.1,2], MUX2.[1.1,2.1,NOT.2]]

FIGURE A1.3 *Two-way butterfly switch*

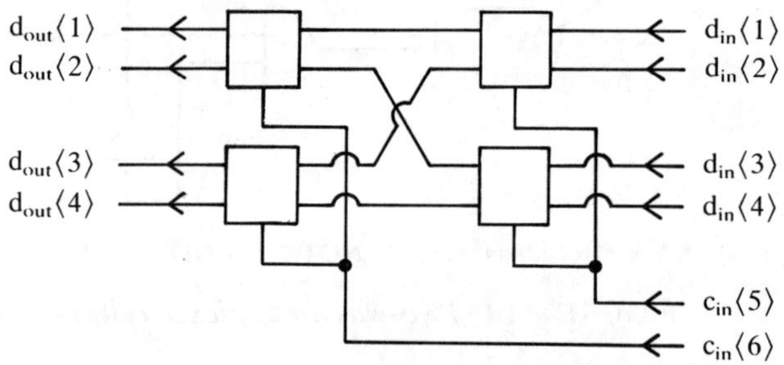

BUTTERFLY4 = [BUTTERFLY2.[1.1,1.2,3], BUTTERFLY2.[2.1,2.2,3]].
[BUTTERFLY2.[1.1,2.1,1.2], BUTTERFLY2.[3.1,4.1,1.2], 2.2]

FIGURE A1.4 *Four-way butterfly switch*

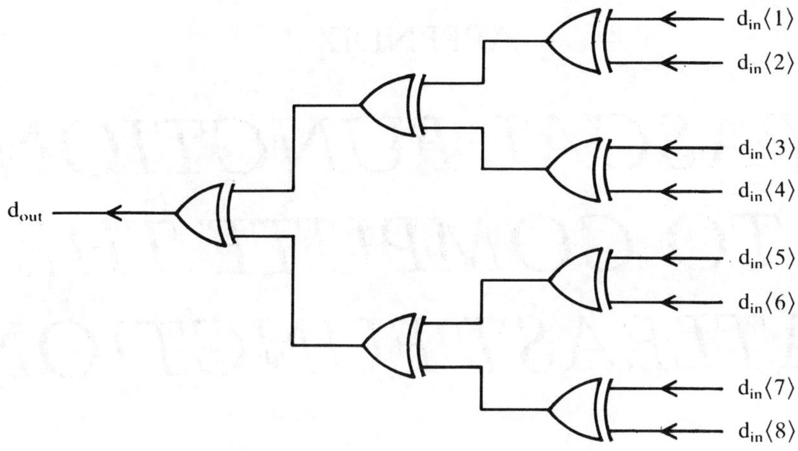

MOD2ADD8 = XOR . [MOD2ADD4.[1,2,3,4], MOD2ADD4.[5,6,7,8]]
where MOD2ADD4 = XOR . [MOD2ADD2.[1,2], MOD2ADD2.[3,4]]
where MOD2ADD2 = XOR

FIGURE A1.5 *Eight-input modulo 2 addition (parity) module*

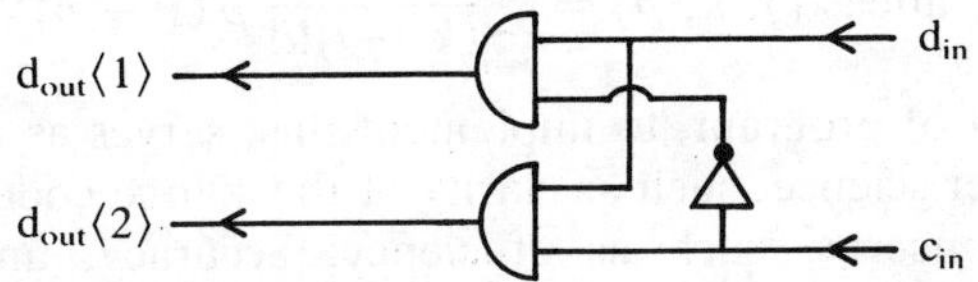

DEMUX2 = [AND. [1,NOT.2], AND]

FIGURE A1.6 *Two-way demultiplexer cell*

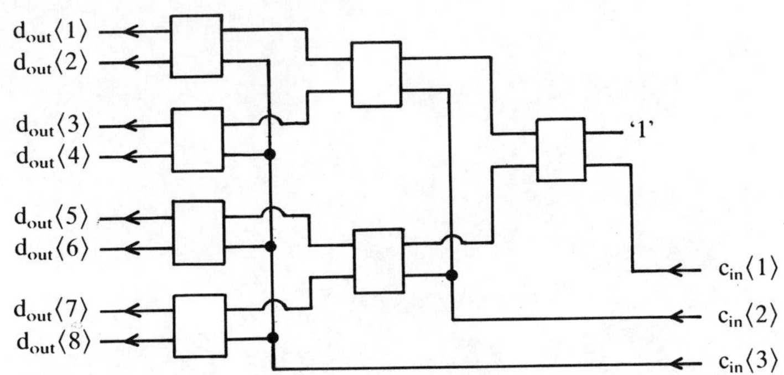

ADRSDEC8 = DEMUX8 . [true, 1]
where DEMUX8 = [DEMUX4.[1.1,[2.2,1.2]], DEMUX4.[2.1,[2.2,1.2]]] .
[DEMUX2, 1, 3.2]
where DEMUX4 = [DEMUX2.[1.1,1.2], DEMUX 2.[2.1,1.2]] .
[DEMUX2, 1, 2.2]

FIGURE A1.7 *Address decoder*

APPENDIX 2

PASCAL FUNCTION TO COMPUTE THE ATLEAST FUNCTION

The probability function, 'atleast(j,k,p)', evaluates the chance of at least j events succeeding out of a total of k tries, given that the probability of one event succeeding is p.

$$\text{atleast}(j, k, p) = \sum_{i=j}^{k} \frac{k!}{(k - i)!i!} p^i(1 - p)^{k-i}$$

The following fragment of program, to implement this, serves as an illustration of how the finest ideals of computer science, such as clarity of the source code, are still at the mercy of overriding practical concerns, such as efficiency, accuracy, and working within finite resources. The 'atleast' function makes such heavy use of the 'factorial' and 'power-of' functions that the programmer has to be very careful lest the intermediate results become too big, or too small, to be represented within the fixed size word length.

```
FUNCTION combp( n, r : integer; p : real ) : real;
VAR ans, q : real; nr, i : integer;
BEGIN
  nr := n - r;
  q := 1.0 - p;
  ans := 1.0;
  i := 1;
  WHILE ( i <= r )AND( i <= nr ) DO BEGIN
    ans := ans * (nr+i ) * p * q / i;
    i := i + 1;
  END;
  WHILE i <= r DO BEGIN
    ans := ans * (nr+i) * p / i;
    i := i + 1;
  END;
  WHILE i <= nr DO BEGIN
    ans := ans * q;
    i := i + 1;
  END;
  combp := ans;
  END;

  FUNCTION atleast ( j, k : integer; p : real ) : real;
  VAR ans, term : real; i : integer;
  BEGIN
    i := j;
    term := combp( k, i, p );
    ans := 0.0;
    WHILE i <= k DO BEGIN
      ans := ans + term;
      term := term * ( k-i ) * p / ( (i+1) * (1.0-p) );
      i := i + 1;
    END;
    at1 := ans;
  END;
```

APPENDIX 3

PASCAL PROGRAM TO BUILD A SYNTAX TREE

```
PROGRAM parse( input, output );
(* Program to read an arithmetic expression into a syntax tree *)
(* and to print the tree out in each of the three orders        *)

CONST HEADCELL = 1;
      NCELLS = 100;

TYPE lnk = HEADCELL..NCELLS;

TYPE celltype = RECORD
  data : char;
  precedence : integer;
  1ptr : lnk;
  rptr : lnk;
  inuse : boolean;
END;

VAR cell : ARRAY [lnk] OF celltype;
    brackval, level : integer;

PROCEDURE init;
(* Initiallise the cells *)
VAR i : lnk;
BEGIN
  brackval := 5;
  level := 0;

  WITH cell [HEADCELL] DO BEGIN
    precedence := 0;
    rptr := 0;
```

```
    inuse := true;
  END;
  FOR i := HEADCELL+1 TO NCELLS DO BEGIN
    cell[i].inuse := false;
  END;
END;

FUNCTION newcell : lnk;
(* Function to return a pointer to a currently unused cell *)
VAR ptr : lnk;
BEGIN
  ptr := HEADCELL;
  WHILE ( ptr <= NCELLS )AND( cell[ptr].inuse ) DO ptr := ptr + 1;
  newcell := ptr;
END;

FUNCTION lev(ch : char) : integer;
(* Function to calculate the precedence of the given char *)
BEGIN
  IF ch IN ['+', '−', '*', '/', '↑'] THEN BEGIN
    CASE ch OF
      '+': lev := level + 1;
      '−': lev := level + 1;
      '*': lev := level + 2;
      '/': lev := level + 2;
      '↑': lev := level + 3;
    END;
  END
  ELSE lev := level + 4;
END;

PROCEDURE addtotree ( ch : char; lev : integer; ptr : lnk );
(* Procedure to add a new character symbol to the syntax tree *)
VAR ptr1, ptr2, ptrnew : lnk;
      prec : integer;
BEGIN
  ptrnew := newcell;
  WITH cell[ptrnew] DO BEGIN
    data := ch;
    precedence := lev;
    lptr := 0;
    rptr := 0;
    inuse := true;
  END;

  ptr2 := ptr;
  REPEAT
    ptr1 := ptr2;
    ptr2 := cell[ptr2].rptr;
```

```
    IF ptr2 <> 0 THEN prec := cell[ptr2].precedence;
  UNTIL ( ptr 2 = 0 ) OR ( lev <= prec );
  cell[ptrnew].lptr := cell[ptr1].rptr;
  cell[ptr1].rptr := ptrnew;
END;

PROCEDURE readtree ( ptr : lnk );
(* Procedure to convert the input into a tree *)
VAR ch : char;
BEGIN
  read( ch );
  WHILE ch = ' ' DO read( ch ); (* ignore spaces *)
  WHILE ch<> ';' DO BEGIN
    IF ch = '(' THEN level := level + brackval
    ELSE IF ch = ')' THEN level := level - brackval
    ELSE addtotree ( ch, lev( ch ), ptr );
    read( ch );
    WHILE ch = ' ' DO read( ch );
  END;
END;

PROCEDURE work( ptr : lnk );
(* Procedure to do useful work on the given element of the tree *)
BEGIN
  write( cell[ptr].data, ' ' );
END;

PROCEDURE inorder ( ptr : lnk );
(* Procedure to perform an 'in-order' walk of the given tree *)
VAR leaf : boolean;
BEGIN
  leaf := ( cell[ptr].lptr = 0 ) AND ( cell[ptr].rptr = 0 );
  IF NOT leaf THEN write ( '(' );
  IF ( cell[ptr].lptr <> 0 ) THEN inorder ( cell[ptr].lptr );
  work ( ptr );
  IF ( cell[ptr].rptr <> 0 ) THEN inorder ( cell[ptr].rptr );
  IF NOT leaf THEN write ( ')' );
END;

PROCEDURE preorder( ptr : lnk );
(* Procedure to perform a 'pre-order' walk of the given tree *)
VAR leaf : boolean;
BEGIN
  leaf := ( cell[ptr].lptr = 0 )AND( cell[ptr].rptr = 0 );
  IF NOT leaf THEN write( '(' );
  work( ptr );
  IF( cell[ptr].lptr <> 0 ) THEN preorder( cell[ptr].lptr );
  IF( cell[ptr].rptr <> 0 ) THEN preorder( cell[ptr].rptr );
```

```
  IF NOT leaf THEN write( ' )' );
END;

PROCEDURE postorder( ptr : lnk );
(* Procedure to perform a 'post-order' walk of the given tree *)
VAR leaf := boolean;
BEGIN
  leaf := ( cell[ptr].1ptr = 0 )AND( cell[ptr].rptr = 0 );
  IF NOT leaf THEN write( '(' );
  IF( cell[ptr].lptr <> 0 ) THEN postorder( cell[ptr].1ptr );
  IF( cell[ptr].rptr <> 0 ) THEN postorder( cell[ptr].rptr );
  work( ptr );
  IF NOT leaf THEN write( ')' );
END;

BEGIN (* MAIN program *)
  init;
  writeln('INPUT');
  readtree( HEADCELL );
  writeln;
  writeln('IN-ORDER');
  inorder( cell[HEADCELL].rptr );
  writeln;
  writeln('PRE-ORDER');
  preorder( cell[HEADCELL].rptr );
  writeln;
  writeln('POST-ORDER');
  postorder( cell[HEADCELL].rptr );
  writeln;
END.

(* Example of a typical run of this program:
INPUT
s(x) + (1 + k)*c(x);
IN-ORDER
( ( s x )+ ( ( 1 + k ) * ( c x ) ) )
PRE-ORDER
( + ( s x ) ( * ( +1 k ) ( c x ) ) )
POST-ORDER
( ( x s ) ( ( 1 k + ) ( x c )* )+ )
*)
```

APPENDIX 4

ANSWERS TO EXERCISES

1.1 4007, 2006, 6005, 2005, 0000, 0046, 0012, 0012

1.2 20

2.1
```
FUNCTION fibonacci( n : integer ) : integer;
BEGIN
  IF ( n = 1 )OR( n = 2 ) THEN fibonacci := 1
  ELSE fibonacci := fibonacci(n − 1) + fibonacci(n − 2);
END;
```

2.2
```
FUNCTION fibonacci( n : integer ) : integer;
VAR i, prev, last, new : integer;
BEGIN
  prev := 1;
  last := 1;
  FOR i := 2 TO n DO BEGIN
    new := last + prev;
    prev := last;
    last := new;
  END;
  fibonacci := last;
END;
```

3.1
```
: quadroot C3 C3 C3 C3 C3 C3 D3 D1 C1 D1 0 O1 □ −
O3 O3 O3 C3 C3 C3 D1 D1 C1 □ O1 □ * O3 O3 O3 D2
C2 C2 D1 C1 D1 4 O1 □ * O2 O2 D2 □ * − sqrt +
O3 O3 O3 D2 D1 C1 D1 2 O1 □ * / ;
```
i.e.
```
: quadroot C3 C3 C3 C2 0 O1 − O3 O3 O3 C2 C1 *
D3 O2 O2 C2 4 * D3 * − sqrt + D3 D2 O1 2 * / ;
```

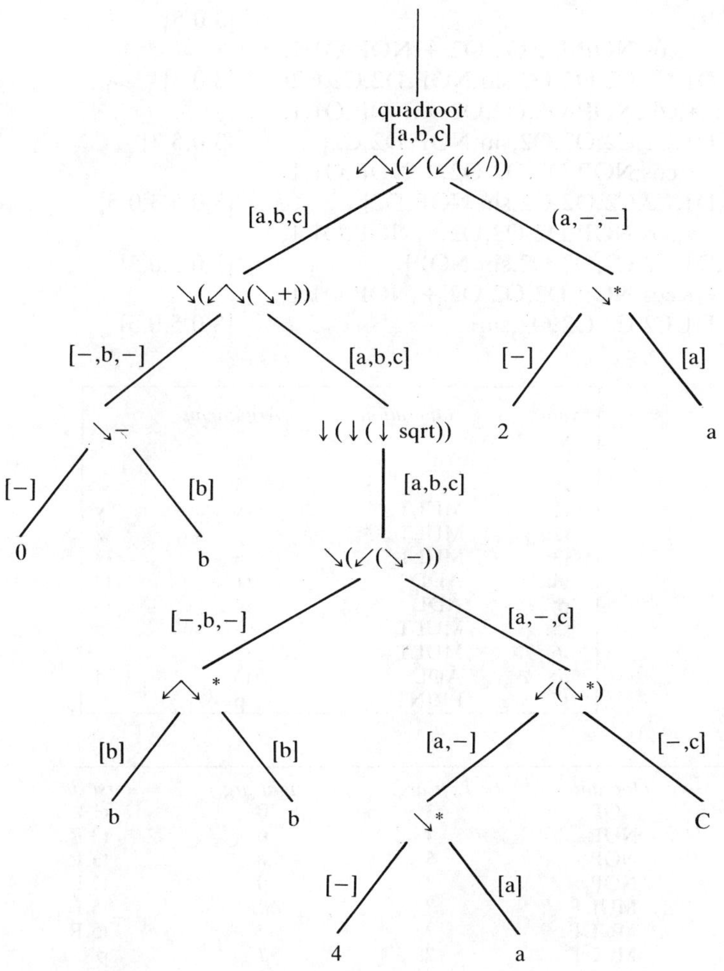


```
3.2  quadroot = (↙↘ (↙ (↙ /))
                    (↘ (↙↘ (↘ +))
                        (↘ − 0 □)
                        (↓ (↓ (↓ sqrt))
                            (↘ (↙ (↘ −))
                            (↙↘ * □ □)
                            (↙ (↘ *)
                                (↘ * 4 □)
                                □)))))
                        (↘ * 2 □))
```

i.e.
quadroot = (S′ (C′ (C′ /)) (B′ (S′ (B′ +)) (− 0) (B (B (B sqrt))
(B′ (C′ (B′ −)) (W ∗) (C′ (B′ ∗) (∗ 4) I)))) (∗ 2))

3.3	[print,filt,0.5,3]	[]
	[print,filt,0.5]	[3]

[print,filt]	[3,0.5]
[print,+,*,cos,NOP,D2,O2,O2,+,NOP,O1,1, D1,C1,D1,C2,C2,O2,O2,sin,NOP,D2,C2,C2]	[3,0.5]
[print,+,*,cos,NOP,D2,O2,O2,+,NOP,O1,1, D1,C1,D1,C2,C2,O2,O2,sin,NOP,D2,C2]	[3,0.5,3]
[print,+,*,cos,NOP,D2,O2,O2,+,NOP,O1,1, D1,C1,D1,C2,C2,O2,O2,sin,NOP,D2]	[3,0.5,3,0.5]
[print,+,*,cos,NOP,D2,O2,O2,+,NOP,O1,1, D1,C1,D1,C2,C2,O2,O2,sin,NOP]	[3,0.5,0.5]
[print,+,*,cos,NOP,D2,O2,O2,+,NOP,O1,1, D1,C1,D1,C2,C2,O2,O2,sin]	[3,0.5,0.5]

etc.

4.1

Name	*Operation*	*Arguments*	
x:		3	
y:		4	
z:		5	
t1:	MULT	x	y
t2:	MULT	y	z
t3:	MULT	z	x
t4:	ADD	t1	t2
p:	ADD	t4	t3
t5:	MULT	3	x
t6:	MULT	t5	x
q:	ADD	t6	4
t7:	PRINT	p	

4.2

Name	*Operation*	*Left arg.*	*Right arg.*	*First dest.*	*Second dest.*
x:	NOP	3	0	t1.L	t6.L
y:	NOP	4	0	t2.R	t3.L
z:	NOP	5	0	t3.R	t4.L
t1:	NOP	?	0	t2.L	t4.R
t2:	MULT	?	?	t5.L	0
t3:	MULT	?	?	t5.R	0
t4:	MULT	?	?	p.L	0
t5:	ADD	?	?	p.R	0
p:	ADD	?	?	t9.L	0
t6:	NOP	?	0	t7.R	t8.R
t7:	MULT	3	?	t8.L	0
t8:	MULT	?	?	q.L	0
q:	ADD	?	4	0	0
t9:	PRINT	?	0	0	0

5.1 82%, 61%, 90%

5.2 449

5.3 23 × 23 processors, $Y = e^{-423.2} \simeq 6.2 \times 10^{-183}$, i.e. about one in 1.6×10^{184}.

5.4 (Figure 5.5) y=97%, h=100%
(Figure 5.6) y=98%, h=51%
(Figure 5.7) y=98%, h=51%
(Figure 5.10) y=90%, h=100%
(Figure 5.12) y=90%, h=28%
(Figure 5.14) y=90%, h=58%
(Figure 5.15) y=90%, h=92%
(Figure 5.16) y=90%, h=63%
(Figure 5.17) y=98%, h=82%
(Figure 5.18) y=97%, h=91%

(Figure 5.21) y=90%, h=56%
(Figure 5.23) y=97%, h=82%
(Figure 5.24) y=96%, h=70%
(Figure 5.25) y=96%, h=70%
(Figure 5.28) y=90%, h=70%
(Figure 5.30) y=98%, h=73%
(Figure 5.31) y=98%, h=73%
(Figure 5.32) y=98%, h=82%
(Figure 5.33) y=98%, h=82%
(Figure 5.34) y=93%, h=43%
(Figure 5.35) y=91%, h=78%
(Figure 5.36) y=94%, h=90%
(Figure 5.38) y=90%, h=100%
(Figure 5.39) y=90%, h=100%
(Figure 5.40) y=90%, h=100%
(Figure 5.44) y=97%, h(spatial)=100%, h(temporal)=52%
(Figure 5.46) y=90%, h=100%
(Figure 5.48) y(switch)=91%, y(cell)=97%, h(cell)=99.6%
(Figure 5.51) y=63%, h=70%
(Figure 5.52) y=63%, h=70%
(Figure 5.57) y=90%, h=98%
(Figure 5.58) y=99%, h=34%
(Figure 5.60) y=100%, h=71%
(Figure 5.61) y=98%, h=58%

5.5 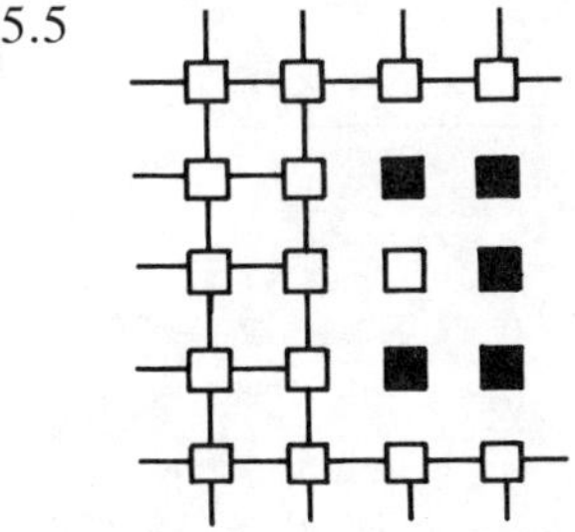

One missing link here.

(Detail from middle right-hand side of Figure 5.40.)

5.6 y=90%, h=28% (only processors which are at the intersections generally do any useful work, with the others usually acting as message forwarding stations. This is significant to systolic array applications, which can tolerate arbitrary delays, so long as they are experienced uniformly across the rows and columns)

6.1 21 positions, i.e. 945°

6.2 The quaternary tree is four-connected at its most connected points

6.3 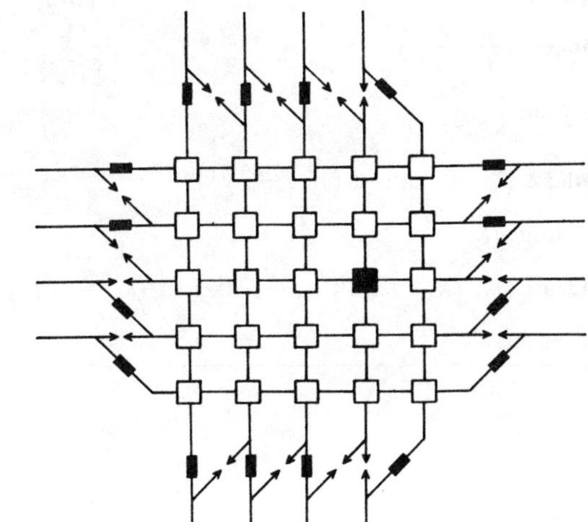

7.1 $D_{\text{Poisson}} \simeq 0.048\ \text{mm}^{-2}$, $D_{\text{binomial}} \simeq 0.048\ \text{mm}^{-2}$, $D_{\text{seeds}} \simeq 0.058\ \text{mm}^{-2}$, ($D_{\text{Murphy}} \simeq 0.054\ \text{mm}^{-2}$)

7.2 $Y_{\text{Poisson}} \simeq 18\%$, $Y_{\text{binomial}} \simeq 18\%$, $Y_{\text{seeds}} \simeq 24\%$, ($Y_{\text{Murphy}} \simeq 19\%$)

8.1 OR . [AND.[1,2], NOT.3]

NAND . [NAND.[1,true], NAND.[2,true]].
[NAND.[NAND,true].[1,2],NAND.[1,true].3]

or:

NAND . [NAND.[1,true], NAND.[2,true]].
[NAND.[NAND[1,true]].2, NAND.[3,true]]

8.2 In Figure 8.3:

Min. working cells in column:	$\frac{m}{j}$ from $\frac{M}{j}$
Column yield:	atleast $\left(\frac{m}{j}, \frac{M}{j}, y\right)$
Min. working columns in group:	$\frac{n}{k}$ from $\frac{N}{k}$
Group yield:	atleast $\left(\frac{n}{k}, \frac{N}{k}, \text{atleast}\left(\frac{m}{j}, \frac{M}{j}, y\right)\right)$
Min. working groups in device:	jk from JK
Device yield (Y'):	atleast $\left(\frac{n}{k}, \frac{N}{k}, \text{atleast}\left(\frac{m}{j}, \frac{M}{j}, y\right)\right)^{jk}$
where $j = k = 2$ in Figure 8.3	

In Figure 8.4:

Min. working cells in column:	$\frac{m}{j}$ from $\frac{M}{j}$
Column yield:	atleast $\left(\frac{m}{j}, \frac{M}{j}, y\right)$
Min. working columns in group:	$\frac{n}{k}$ from $\frac{N}{k}$
Group yield:	atleast $\left(\frac{n}{k}, \frac{N}{k}, \text{atleast}\left(\frac{m}{j}, \frac{M}{j}, y\right)\right)$
Min. working groups in device:	jk from JK
Device yield (Y'):	atleast $\left(jk, JK, \text{atleast}\left(\frac{n}{k}, \frac{N}{k}, \text{atleast}\left(\frac{m}{j}, \frac{M}{j}, y\right)\right)\right)$
where $j = J = 1$, $k = 2$ and $K = 3$ in Figure 8.4	

GLOSSARY

This is not a dictionary, but a glossary of terms as they are used in this book. Many of the words and phrases have many more general meanings, some of which are applicable in quite diverse subject areas. However, the definitions which are set beside each term here are the ones which are applicable within the context of this book.

Abstraction The ability to ignore the details of a module's internal construction, i.e. to treat it as a black-box component.

Accumulator A register attached to an arithmetic and logic unit for holding partial results and other intermediate data from computations.

Address An integer which specifies a position, for example in memory.

Address decoder The hardware which takes the address integer, and uses it to select the word which is located at that numerical position (for example in a vector of memory words).

Addressing mode The meaning of the noun part of a machine instruction. For instance, 'ADD 6, Accumulator' might variously mean: add the number 6 to the accumulator, add the contents of memory location 6 to the accumulator, or add the contents of the memory location which is addressed by the contents of memory location 6 to the accumulator.

Algorithm The method for performing a compound operation.

Algorithmic problem solving The methodical, precise solution of problems (cf. **heuristic problem solving**).

Application A (useful) project in which given technology(s) are employed. However, *see also* **function application**.

Applicative language *See* **functional language**.

Applicative order A model of function application in which the parameters are fully evaluated before being passed to the function body (cf. **normal order**).

Architecture Structure.

Argument Additional, parametric information which is received by the function at the time of its evaluation. By convention, arguments are the variables which are named in the function definition, whereas parameters are the values which are given to it by the function application.

Artificial intelligence (AI) Characteristic of a machine, for example a computer, which can be made to converse or to reason like a human.

Assembler A program which translates low level language source code into object code. Distinguished from a compiler by the fact that it produces only a few binary numbers of object program for each statement of the source program that it reads. Common varieties include: binary, octal, decimal, hexadecimal, symbolic, macro and cross assemblers.

Assignment The destructive writing of a new value to replace the previous contents of a memory location.

Atleast(*j*,*k*,*p*) The probability of at least *j* events succeeding out of a total of *k* tries, given that the probability of one event succeeding is *p*.

Automaton An automatic machine, e.g. a computer.

Best-case failure The minimum number of faults/failures which will cause the whole device to fail.

Binary The base 2 counting system.

Binary search A method of finding an item in a vector of items by splitting the vector in two and selecting one of the halves for further binary searching.

Binary tree A tree structure in which no node has more than two descendants.

Binding The act of associating parameters to the arguments of a Curryed function.

Bit A single binary digit, which can be stored in a flip-flop.

Bootstrap A method of building simple things on primitive ones, and complex things on the simple ones.

Bound variable An argument in a function definition (cf. **free variable**). *See also* **local variable**.

Bug These are more than just mistakes in the program; they are often quite subtle, fallaciously constructed parts of the program which seem, at a superficial level, to be completely correct.

Bus A series of signals which traverse the computer, so called because an arbitrary number of modules can be hooked on to it in the same manner as commuters attaching themselves to the 'bus-bar' in a crowded bus or railway carriage. Common varieties include: data bus, address bus, control bus, communications bus.

Byte Eight bits, capable of representing unsigned integers in the range 0 to 255.

Cache memory Very fast, local memory within a processor, which can be topped up from the slower main memory. Common varieties include: data cache, instruction cache.

Calculator Historically, this term was used to mean a human employee who calculates, but now it is used to mean a machine which calculates. Further, it tends to be destinguished from the word 'computer' to imply a machine which can only execute single instructions as and when they are supplied manually.

Call-by mechanism The mechanism for passing parameters to functions and procedures. Common examples are: call-by-value, call-by-reference, call-by-address, call-by-name, call-by-string.

Cell A logical partition of circuitry.

Cellular automaton Subclass of SIMD processor, with the following properties: composed of a (large) regular grid of cells, all cells are identical, cells operate synchronously within the grid, each cell has a 'state', the state is updated at every clock cycle, and the next state is calculated from the cell's own previous state and those of its neighbours.

Central processor unit (CPU) The module which controls the operation of the rest of the computer, and which performs the calculations.

Chip-z A processor on a large self-testing device which is dedicated to controlling the test sequence.

Circuit A region of a device whose failure is caused by the occurrence of just one fault. Thus for a circuit to work, it must be fault free.

Circuit-switched network (CSN) A network in which messages are transferred between the source to the destination nodes by first instructing intervening nodes to set up a 'path' along which the messages can travel. The 'path' is kept in place, even through blank periods of the message, until the intervening nodes are instructed to break the connection.

Closely coupled system A multiprocessor computer in which the processors communicate fairly fine grain data over a network, usually within a single large cabinet. *See also* **MISD, SIMD** and **MIMD** (cf. **loosely coupled system**).

Code Any string of text; or numbers, particularly those which are used to represent a computer program [a historical reference to the code-breaking computers of World War 2]. Common varieties include: assembler, executable, intermediate, interpretive, machine, object, program, pseudo, source codes.

Code generator A part of a compiler, generally one which translates an intermediate code into object code.

Combinator A function which does not use any free variables, but merely rearranges the order of its bound variables.

Command driven/flow *See* **control driven/flow.**

Compiler A program which translates high level source code into object code. Distinguished from an assembler by the fact that it can accept arbitrarily complicated expressions, and produce correspondingly large streams of binary numbers.

Compile-time The moment at which the program is compiled (cf. **run-time**).

Compute bound Activity which is restricted by a lack of processing capacity (cf. **input/ output bound**).

Computer Historically, this term was used to mean a human employee who computes, but now it is used to mean a machine which computes. Further, it tends to be distinguished from the word 'calculator' to imply a machine which can automatically execute instructions repetitively.

Control-driven A class of computer which selects instructions, during a fetch cycle, according to the demands of centralised program counter(s).

Control flow A class of computer which never examines the selected instructions, but passes them over immediately for execution.

CPU intensive *See* **compute bound**.

Crop The number of usable devices on the wafer.

Cross-assembler An assembler which accepts source code for one computer, and generates the appropriate object code for a different one.

Curryed function A function which has some, but not all, of its parameters bound to it.

Currying The act of binding parameters to a function to form a Curryed function.

Data driven A class of computer which selects all of the instructions in the program for examination.

Data flow A class of computer which only passes those instructions over for execution which have all of their data ready and available.

Decimal The base 10 counting system.

Declarative language A programming language which consists primarily of mathematically sound declarations (cf. imperative language).

Defect These are unavoidably introduced during the fabrication of semiconductor circuits, though it is possible to minimise them.

Defect density The number of defects which might be expected on average within a unit area. Some sources use this to mean fault density.

Defect level *See* **failure level**.

Defect tolerance The ability to cope with defects. This is achieved by relaxing the design rules; for instance 1 μm blemishes can be tolerated by using 5 μm design rules. The larger defects, the ones which are not tolerated so readily, manifest themselves as faults, i.e. they cause the malfunction of a part of the circuit or interconnect. Saucier and Trilhe (1986a, b) use the term to mean fault tolerance, as used in this book.

Demand-driven A class of computer which only selects instructions for examination if their results are needed.

Demand flow *See* **reduction**.

Deterministic A system whose response can be predicted with certainty, knowing its initial conditions and its inputs.

Device A packagable object (for instance a semiconductor memory chip).

Director These are annotations which indicate which branches of a syntax tree need the given argument. Related to combinators.

Disk A disc coated with magnetic material for mass storage (i.e. 'k' spelling is used to distinguish the specific from the general).

Divide-and-conquer A method of solving or evaluating a problem by splitting into two or more similar, but simpler problems.

Dynamic fault tolerance *See* **failure tolerance**.

Engine Frequently used to mean 'computer' [historical reference to the early mechanical computers].

Error correction The remedying of erroneous data.

Evaluation order The model of function evaluation. Common varieties include: normal order, applicative order, lazy evaluation. *See also* **call-by mechanism**.

Examination mechanism The model for deciding which of the selected instructions should be executed. For examples *see*: **control flow, data flow, reduction.**

Execution mechanism The part of the instruction cycle in which the accepted instruction(s) are executed with their parameters to generate results.

Expert system (ES) A computerised, interactive encyclopaedia-like system which is capable not only of looking up answers to problems, but advising on what action to take next, what the chances are of success, and what the reasons are for coming to these conclusions.

Failure A deviation of the state of the system from that required by its specification whilst it is in service.

Failure correction The overriding of failed hardware.

Failure level (FL). The number of faulty devices which go undetected. *See also* **test quality**.

Failure tolerance The ability to cope with failures which develop in the device whilst it is in service (cf. **fault tolerance**).

Fault A failure which is present from the time of the system's fabrication.

Fault density (*D*). The number of faults which might be expected on average within a unit area. *See also* **defect density**.

Fault-free processing The traditional method of discarding all devices which contain one or more faults.

Fault tolerance The ability to cope with the physical faults that are accidentally built into the device. They are detected on a statistical basis at the end-of-manufacture test stage. Any that escape this test manifest themselves as failures when the circuit is in service (cf. **defect tolerance**). Saucier and Trilhe (1986a, b) and Anderson and Lee (1981) use the term to mean failure tolerance, as used in this book.

Fetch cycle *See* **selection mechanism**.

Fifth generation The next breed of computer system after the VLSI computer on a chip.

Firmware Software, for example a computer program, which is permanently represented in hardware, such as in a read-only memory, or in a programmable logic array.

Flip-flop A bistable storage element, capable of storing an electronic representation of a binary digit. A physical implementation of a latch.

Floating-point A format for representing fractional numbers using fixed length (binary) integers.

Free variable Any variable whose value is assumed from an environment, without it being passed as an argument to the function (cf. **bound variable**). *See also* **global variable**.

Full slice technology Also known as full wafer technology, but now called wafer scale integration.

Function An object which can take a number of parameters and evaluate a result.

Functional language One based on the use of functions: their definition and their application.

Function application The act of applying a function to (some of) its arguments (cf. **function call**).

Function body The main part of the function definition, specifying what the function will do to perform its work.

Function call The imperative language equivalent of function application, in which the function is made to execute.

Function definition The specification of how the function will work, and how it will appear when used.

Function evaluation The act of applying a function to the parameters which it has been given.

Function header The part of the function definition which specifies how the function will appear when it is used, giving information about its name and its arguments.

Function invocation *See* **function application**.

Global area network A network of computer systems, communicating very coarse grain data files, over the public telephone and other national and international networks (cf. **local area network**).

Global variable A variable whose value is directly accessible to many unrelated functions (cf. **local variable**). *See also* **free variable**.

Graceful degradation The ability to work with an uncertain number of resources. When the device is in service, failures cause parts to be taken out of operation, but the overall device continues to function, albeit using its diminished resources.

Grid size The unit of length, λ, for microelectronics layout design.

Hardcore The part of the device which is not fault/failure tolerant.

Hardware Anything tangible, such as metal cabinets, magnetic tapes, line-printer paper, ink, etc. Generally used to refer to the computer's circuit boards and associated housing.

Harvest The ratio of utilised items to usable items. Common varieties include: device harvest, H, and cell harvest, h.

Heap A haphazard arrangement for using memory.

Heuristic problem solving An inprecise, rule-of-thumb method of solving problems (cf. **algorithmic problem solving**).

Hexadecimal The base 16 counting system.

High level language Distinguished from a low level language by its greater power of expression: complex ideas can be expressed more clearly, and with fewer symbols. Compiled on a compiler.

Higher order function *See* **Curryed function**.

Horizontal parallelism A generic term for SIMD and MIMD.

H-tree A physical, two-dimensional layout for a binary tree.

Hypercube A regular, orthogonal object which occupies more than three dimensions.

Imperative language One based on the issuing of commands of sequence to the computer (cf. **declarative language**).

Information Structured data.

Input/output bound Activity which is resticted by a lack of communications bandwidth (cf. compute bound).

Instantiation The mathematical act of associating a value, for the first and only time, to a variable (cf. **assignment**).

Instruction A primitive operation which is directly supported in the computer's hardware. A single, simple statement from an assembler language.

Instruction cycle The repetitive sequence of select, examination, execution which is needed by every instruction in the program.

Instruction set The menu of primitive operations which the computer directly supports in its hardware.

Integer A non-fractional, whole number.

Integrated programming systems environment (IPSE) A consistent, well-structured system of operating system, editors, compilers, text formatters and other utility programs in which new programs and documents can be developed.

Intelligent knowledge-based system (IKBS) A computer system which can represent, store, retrieve and process large quantities of information in a knowledge base. Generally one which is able to infer useful new information from old.

Interpreter A program which directly executes the user's source code, or a pseudo-code version of it.

Knowledge base A large collection of information.

Lambda calculus A mathematical calculus in which functions are treated as the principle object.

Language The medium for communicating ideas, particularly to a computer. Common varieties include: high level, low level, assembler, machine languages.

Latch A storage element for holding (i.e. storing or delaying) a representation of a binary digit (cf. **flip-flop**).

Latency The time delay between demanding a service and the service being granted (cf. **throughput**).

Lazy evaluation An evaluation mechanism in which parameters are left unevaluated until (if ever) they are needed (cf. **normal order evaluation**).

Local area network (LAN) A network of computers, and related equipment, communicating coarse grain data within a small geographical area, for instance within a single building. *See also* **loosely coupled systems** (cf. **global area network**).

Local variable A variable whose value is only directly accessible from the function in which it is defined (cf. **global variable**). *See also* **bound variable**.

Logic language One which is based on predicate calculus.

Loosely coupled system A coarse grain multicomputer system. *See also* **local area network** (cf. **closely coupled system**).

Low level language A computer programming language in which the program is described in great detail, each statement of which relates directly to the primitive operations which the computer supports in its instruction set. Assembled on an assembler (cf. **high level language**).

Macro A program module, the defining statements of which are expanded in the object code, at compile-time, once for each time that they are called (cf. **subroutine**).

Mainframe computer A large, fast, high storage capacity computer.

Man–machine interface (MMI) The means by which users and computers interact to exchange data, programs and results.

Memory A hardware module for the storage of data. Varieties include: random access memory (RAM), serial access memory (SAM), core memory, cache memory, read only memory (ROM), programmable read only memory (PROM), content addressable memory (CAM), first-in first-out queue (FIFO), last-in first-out queue (a stack) (LIFO).

Microcomputer A small computer, with a microprocessor as its major component.

Microcontroller A very simple processor, used to control the central processor unit of a larger processor.

Microprocessor A simple processor, generally implemented with only a few integrated circuits.

Mill *See* **central processor unit** [historical reference to a component of Babbage's mechanical computer].

MIMD Multiple instruction stream, multiple data stream computers.

Minicomputer A fairly simple computer, consisting of about one rack of printed circuit boards.

MISD Multiple instruction stream, single data stream computers.

Mnemonic An easy to remember name.

Module An abstraction. A black-box component.

Multicomputer A computer system which consists of a loosely coupled system of individual computers.

Multiprocessor A computer which consists of a closely coupled system of processors.

Normal order A model of function application in which literal, unevaluated parameters are passed to the function body (cf. **applicative order**).

Object code A numerical representation of a program.

Octal The base 8 counting system.

Off-line failure tolerance Failure tolerance which can only be activated when the system is temporarily out of service.

On-line failure tolerance Failure tolerance which can be exercised non-disruptively, even whilst the system is in midcomputation.

Operand address The address (in memory) at which the computer can find the data for a given instruction.

Operation code (op code) The operation which the computer is to perform on the data, as defined by the **instruction set**.

Order code *See* **operation code**.

Packet A block of data which is handled as a single unit (i.e. which cannot be broken into its component parts by modules which are not entitled to do any more than shuffle it from one place to another).

Packet-switched network (PSN) A network in which messages are transferred between the source and the destination nodes by forming it into a (small) data packet, complete with its destination address afixed to it, and passing it between successive intervening nodes.

Parameter Additional information which is given at the time of function application (cf. **argument**).

Parkinson's law The project will expand to consume the available resources. No matter how generous the deadlines and financial limits are, human nature will cause the project to slip at least up to these limits.

Parse The act of analysing the words and phrases in a piece of text, particularly in a piece of source code.

Parser A program which takes the user's source code, generally translating it into an intermediate code for use by the code generator.

Picocontroller An extremely simple processor which is used to control a microcontroller.

Pipeline A communications channel which can queue several messages along its length, or a production-line style processor system. *See also* **MISD**.

Pop The act of removing the top item from a stack (cf. **push**).

Predicate calculus A branch of mathematical logic which is based on the use of predicate or boolean functions.

Primitive A system-defined, built-in facility, usually an atomic object, i.e. one which cannot, or need not, be expressed more simply in the notation (cf. **user defined**).

Procedure *See* **subroutine**.

Program Specification of the programme of activity for a computer (i.e. spelling used to distinguish the specific from the general).

Program counter (PC) A register attached to the central processor unit to store the address of the next instruction to be fetched from memory.

Pseudo-code A type of object code which is derived from the source code, but which is not the proper object code for the host computer. Generally used by an interpreter.

Push The act of inserting a new top item on to a stack (cf. **pop**).

Real-time Computation which is conducted on the fly, on-line, processing input data at least as fast as it is being generated.

Reconfiguration The act of reconnecting a failure tolerant system, or connecting a fault tolerant one. In the latter case, the 'reconfiguration' is considered to refer to the act of finding a workable structure from the one which was originally fabricated.

Recursion The act of defining in terms of itself. Varieties include: self recursion, mutual recursion.

Reduction The act of substituting an expression by an equivalent, but simpler, one. Also a class of computer which uses this principle. Also a class of computer which passes instructions over for execution if all of their data are ready and available, and otherwise issues demands for those items of data to be evaluated. Varieties include: string reduction, graph reduction.

Redundancy Numerically equivalent to the replication overhead.

Referential transparency The ability to interchange equivalent objects.

Register A simple vector of storage elements, possibly used for storing a word of data, which can be accessed readily in the hardware of a given module.

Relational language One designed to access relational databases.

Relative area The ratio of the final area to the area of the non fault/failure tolerant equivalent. Common varieties include: relative device area, *rda*, relative processor area, *rpa*, and relative cell area, *rca*.

Relative overhead The ratio of the area of the fault/failure tolerant circuitry, plus that of any spare cells, to the area of the non-fault/failure tolerant equivalent. Common varieties include: relative device overhead, *rdo*, relative processor overhead, *rpo*, and relative cell overhead, *rco*.

Reliability The inverse of the failure rate of a large sample of units. Common varieties include: device reliability, B, and cell reliability, b.

Replication factor (*R*) The ratio of the number of items which are fabricated to the number which are needed.

Replication overhead The ratio of the number of items which are fabricated in excess to the number which are needed.

Run-time The moment at which the program is run (cf. **compile-time**).

Selection mechanism The method for deciding which of the program instructions should be examined. For examples *see*: **control driven, data driven, demand driven**.

Semantics Meaning.

Side effect An effect which is not part of the primary, 'obvious' behaviour of the unit (cf. **referential transparency**).

SIMD Single instruction stream, multiple data stream computers.

SISD Single instruction stream, single data stream computers.

Smallest replaceable unit *See* **circuit**.

Software Anything intangible, such as an idea of a circuit diagram. Generally used to mean an idea of a computer program.

Software engineering (SE) The development of the tools and environment in which programs and data files can be constructed.

Software gap The difference in the power of expression between the chosen high level language and the target assembler language.

Source code The representation of the program as written and understood by the programmer.

Stack The arrangement of memory in which new words can be stored one after another, and retrieved sequentially in the reverse order. Common varieties include: data, arithmetic, return, address, system stacks.

Statement A single command from an imperative programming language, or a single declaration from a declarative one. Common varieties include: simple statement, compound statement, statement block, instruction.

Static fault tolerance *See* **fault tolerance**.

Stoichiometric A structure, such as a molecule, which contains a massive number of atoms of a few elements in a given ratio. By analogy, a multiprocessor computer which contains processors and communications units, say, in some globally observed ratio.

Subprogram A generic term for functions and subroutines.

Subroutine A program module, the defining statements of which appear once in the object code, and are only expanded temporally at run-time.

Sugaring The act of making a program easier to understand. Syntactic sugaring involves laying the program out, using extra (superfluous) spaces and blank lines, so that it is easier for the human eye to extract information from it. Semantic sugaring involves disguising unnecessary detail, so that it appears to conform to some other general form (for instance, making data input/output look like any other data movement operation within main memory or disk memory).

Supercomputer Used variously to mean 'the best computer which is presently available', or 'the breed of computers which will soon be available'.

Supermicrocomputer A microcomputer which has the performance of a minicomputer.

Superminicomputer A minicomputer which has the performance of an earlier model of mainframe computer.

Syntax The layout, spelling and grammar, particularly of a computer programming language.

System utility A tool to help in the process of writing programs.

Systolic array A subclass of cellular automaton whose data are restricted to using fixed paths, and travelling at a constant velocity. It should be noted, though, that the definition varies considerably between sources.

Tesselate To fit together exactly without gaps, like tiles.

Testable unit An area of logic which is bounded by test registers.

Test coverage (TC) The proportion of faults/failures which are detected in a device.

Test quality (TQ) The number of faulty/failed devices which are detected. *See also* **failure level**.

Throughput The rate at which input is converted into output.

Tightly coupled system *See* **closely coupled system**.

Tractability, mathematical Capable of being subjected to formal mathematical proof and formal mathematical transformation.

Usage *See* **harvest**. Common varieties include: device usage, processor usage and cell usage.

User defined A module which is defined, and named, by the designer, (cf. **primitive**).

Utilisation *See* **harvest**. Common varieties include: device utilisation, processor utilisation and cell utilisation.

Vertical parallelism *See* **MISD**.

von Neumann A computer architect just after the Second World War who proposed the model of computer which is still in almost exclusive use today. The main characteristics of the design include: CPU, memory and input/output units communicating along bus(es); instructions selected one at a time, in sequence, by a program counter, destructive-write, non-destructive-read fixed integer memory; program and data held in the same memory vector.

Wafer A circular slice of single crystal semiconductor, normally with one, or two, flat edges cut into the circumference for reference purposes.

Wafer scale integration (WSI) The act of designing and fabricating a circuit which occupies a single entire wafer of semiconductor material.

Word A vector of bits which is handled as an atomic unit, able to represent a single binary integer of a given maximum magnitude.

Worst-case success The maximum number of faulty cells that can be tolerated.

Yield The ratio of working items to fabricated items. Often expressed as a percentage. Common varieties include: device yield, Y, and cell yield, y.

REFERENCES

Abelson, H. and G.J. Sussman, with J. Sussman (1985). *Structure and Interpretation of Computer Programs*, MIT Press, Cambridge, Mass., and McGraw-Hill, New York.

Abramsky, S. and C.L. Hankin, eds (1987). *Abstract Interpretation of Declarative Languages*, Ellis Horwood, Chichester.

Aho, A.V. and J.D. Ullman (1977). *Principles of Compiler Design*. Addison-Wesley, Reading, Mass.

Anderson, A., M. Tracey and Micromotion (1984). *Mastering Forth*, Prentice Hall Inc., Englewood Cliffs, NJ.

Anderson, P. (1987). Performance of a heavily congested two dimensional Cartesian routing communications system in the presence of faults', internal report TCU/CS/1987/18, City University, London.

Anderson, P., C.L. Hankin, P.H.J. Kelly, P.E. Osmon and M.J. Shute (1987). 'Cobweb-2: structured specification of a wafer scale supercomputer', in J.W. de Bakker, A.J. Nijman and P.C. Treleaven, eds, *Parallel Architecture and Languages Europe, Lecture Notes in Computer Science*, Vol. 258, pp. 51–67, Springer Verlag, Berlin.

Anderson, T. and P.A. Lee (1981). *Fault Tolerance: Principles and Practice*, Prentice Hall International, Hemel Hempstead.

Ansade, Y., R. Cornu-Emieux, B. Faure and G. Mazare (1986). 'WSI asynchronous cells network', in G. Saucier and J. Trilhe, eds, *Wafer Scale Integration*, pp. 77–88. North-Holland, Amsterdam.

Aspinall, D. (1984). 'Architecture', in F.B. Chambers, D.A. Duce and G.P. Jones, eds, *Distributed Computing*, pp. 219–29. Academic Press, Orlando, Florida.

Aubusson, R.C. (1979). 'Wafer scale integration of semiconductor memory', PhD thesis, Middlesex Polytechnic, London.

Aubusson, R.C. and I. Catt (1978). 'Wafer scale integration: a fault-tolerant procedure', *IEEE Journal of Solid State Circuits*, Vol. SC-13(3), 339–43.

Aubusson, R.C. and R.J. Gledhill (1978). 'Wafer scale integration: some approaches to the interconnection problem', *Microelectronics Journal*, Vol. 9(1), 5–10.

Babbage, C. (1837). 'On the mathematical powers of the calculating engine', in B. Randell, ed., *The Origins of Digital Computers*, 3rd edn. pp. 19–54. Springer Verlag, Berlin.

Backus, J. (1978). 'Can programming be liberated from the von Neumann style? A functional style and its algebra of programs', *CACM*, Vol. 21(8), 613–41.

Barbacci, M.R. (1981). 'Syntax and semantics for CHDLS', in M. Breuer and R. Hartenstein, eds, *Computer Hardware Description Languages and their Applications*, North-Holland, Amsterdam.

Barker, J.R. (1986). 'The physical limitations of integration and size reduction in semiconductors', *Microelectronics Journal*, Vol. 17(1), 15–25.

Barrett, J.J., E.M. Smits and P.L. Moran (1986). 'A copper tracking technique for wafer scale integration', in G. Saucier and J. Trilhe, eds, *Wafer Scale Integration*, pp. 291–300. North-Holland, Amsterdam.

Barron, D.W. (1977). *An Introduction to the Study of Programming Languages*, Cambridge University Press, Cambridge.

Bell, C.G. and A. Newell (1971). '*Computer Structures: readings and examples*, McGraw-Hill, New York.

Bennett, K.H. (1984a). 'Communications', in F.B. Chambers, D.A. Duce and G.P. Jones, eds, *Distributed Computing*, pp. 147–60. Academic Press, Orlando, Florida.

Bennett, K.H. (1984b). 'Distributed filestores', in F.B. Chambers, D.A. Duce and G.P. Jones, eds, *Distributed Computing*, pp. 161–78. Academic Press, Orlando, Florida.

Bentley, L. and C.R. Jesshope (1986). 'The implementation of a two dimensional redundancy scheme in a wafer scale high-speed disk memory', in C.R. Jesshope and W.R. Moore, eds, *Wafer Scale Integration*, pp. 187–97. Adam Hilger, Bristol.

Bertram, W.J. (1983). 'Yield and reliability', in S.M. Sze, ed., *VLSI Technology*, pp. 599–638. McGraw-Hill, New York.

Blaauw, G.A. (1976). *Digital System Implementation*, Prentice Hall Inc., Englewood Cliffs, NJ.

Bornat, R. (1984). 'Imperative languages in distributed computing', in D.A. Duce, ed., *Distributed Computing Systems Programme*, pp. 39–61. Peter Peregrinius, London.

Breuer, M. and R. Hartenstein, eds (1981). *Computer Hardware Description Languages and their Applications*, North-Holland, Amsterdam.

Brooks III, E.D. (1987). 'A butterfly processor-memory interconnection for a vector processing environment', in *Parallel Computing*, Vol. 4(1), 103–10. North-Holland, Amsterdam.

Burge, W.H. (1975). *Recursive Programming Techniques*, Addison-Wesley, Reading, Mass.

Burks, A.W. (1970). *Essays on Cellular Automata*, University of Illinois Press, Illinois.

Burks, A.W., H.H. Goldsteine and J. von Neumann (1947). 'A preliminary discussion of the logical design of an electronic computing instrument', in *Collected Works of von Neumann*, Vol. 5, pp. 34–79.

Burn, G.L., C.L. Hankin and S. Abramsky (1986). 'Strictness analysis for higher order functions', in *Science of Computer Programming*, Nov, North-Holland, Amsterdam.

Burns, L.L. (1986). 'Laser pantography', in G. Saucier and J. Trilhe, eds, *Wafer Scale Integration*, pp. 281–90. North-Holland, Amsterdam.

Butcher, J.B. (1984). *Wafer Scale Integration: a low cost, commonsense approach to VLSI*, VLSI-PARC, Melbourne.

Bux, W. (1981). 'Local area sub-networks: a performance comparison', *IEEE Trans. Communications*, Vol. Com-29(10), 1465–73.

Catt, I. (1974). '*Improvements Relating to Digital Integrated Circuits*, British patent specification 1377859, London.

Catt, I. (1986). '1985: the year of the first pre-production working wafers', *Silicon Design*, Vol. 3(1), 8–9.

Chambers, F.B., D.A. Duce and G.P. Jones (1984). *Distributed Computing*, Academic Press, Orlando, Florida.

Chapman, G.H. (1986). 'Laser-linking technology for RVLSI', in C.R. Jesshope and W.R. Moore, eds, *Wafer Scale Integration*, pp. 204–15. Adam Hilger, Bristol.

Chevalier, G. and G. Saucier (1986). 'A programmable switch matrix for the wafer scale integration of a processor array', in C.R. Jesshope and W.R. Moore, eds, *Wafer Scale Integration*, pp. 92–100. Adam Hilger, Bristol.

Clack, C. and S.L. Peyton Jones (1985). 'Strictness analysis: a practical approach', in J.P. Jouannaud, ed., *Functional Programming Languages and Computer Architecture, Lecture Notes in Computer Science* Vol. 201, pp. 35–49. Springer Verlag, Berlin.

Clarke, A.C. (1968). *2001: A Space Odyssey*, Hutchinson, London.

Clarke, T.J.W., P.J.S. Gladstone, C.D. MacLean and A.C. Norman (1980). *Skim: The S, K, I, Reduction Machine*, pp. 128–35. Trinity College, Cambridge University.

Codd, E.F. (1968). *Cellular Automata*, ACM monograph, Academic Press, Orlando, Florida.

Coleman, J.N. and R.M. Lea (1986). 'Clock distribution techniques for wafer scale integration', in C.R. Jesshope and W.R. Moore, eds, *Wafer Scale Integration*, pp. 46–53. Adam Hilger, Bristol.

Comerford, R.W. and J. Lyman (1983). 'Self-testing: special report', *Electronics*, Mar. p. 109.

Cousineau, G., P.L. Curien and M. Mauny (1985). 'The categorical abstract machine', in J.P. Jouannaud, ed., *Functional Programming Languages and Computer Architecture, Lecture Notes in Computer Science* Vol. 201, pp. 50–64. Springer-Verlag, Berlin.

Cripps, M.D., A.J. Field and M.J. Reeve (1986). 'The design and implementation of Alice: a parallel graph reduction machine', in S. Eisenbach, ed., *Functional Programming: Languages, Tools and Architectures*, pp. 111–27. Ellis Horwood, Chichester.

Curry, H.B. and R. Feys (1958). *Combinatory Logic* Vol. 1, North-Holland, Amsterdam.

Darlington, J., P. Henderson and D.A. Turner (1982). *Functional Programming and its Applications*, Cambridge University Press, Cambridge.

Davies, W.D.T. (1966). 'Generation and properties of maximum-length sequences', *Control*, pp. 302–4, 364–5; 431–3.

Day, A.C. (1974). *A London Fortran Course*, Athlone Press, University of London.

de Jong, M.D. and C.L. Hankin (1982). 'Structured data flow programming', *ACM Signplan Notices*, Vol. 17(8), pp. 18–27.

Dettmer, R. (1985). 'Chip architectures for parallel processing', *Electronics and Power*, Vol. 31(3), pp. 227–31. IEE, London.

Dettmer, R. (1986a). 'Flagship: a fifth generation machine', *Electronics and Power*, Vol. 32(3), pp. 203–8. IEE, London.

Dettmer, R. (1986b). 'Brighter prospects for wafer scale integration', *Electronics and Power*, Vol. 32(4), pp. 283–8. IEE, London.

Dickson, J.F. (1984). *A Fault-tolerant Design Methodology for WSI*, Alvey Proposal (VLSI), Plessey (Caswell) Research Ltd, Northampton.

Digital Equipment Corporation (1974). *PDP11/45 Processor Handbook*, Digital Equipment Corporation, Maynard, Mass.

Dixon, G.E., J.F. Dickson, J. Fox, A.K.J. Stewart and G.W. Sumerling (1986). 'A test methodology for a parameterised cell design approach to fault-tolerant VLSI and wafer scale integration', in C.R. Jesshope and W.R. Moore, eds, *Wafer Scale Integration*, pp. 237–45. Adam Hilger, Bristol.

Donlan, B.J., G.F. Taylor, R.H. Steinvorth, A.S. Bergendahl and J.F. McDonald (1986). 'Wafer scale integration using discretionary microtransmission line interconnections', in C.R. Jesshope and W.R. Moore, eds, *Wafer Scale Integration*, pp. 31–45. Adam Hilger, Bristol.

Durham, A. (1986). 'Strict commands for busy system', Over the Horizon, *Computing Magazine*, 13 Mar. London.

Economist (1986). 'The future belongs to the photon', Oct. pp. 101–4.

Edwards, J. (1985). 'Commercial memory designs', in C.R. Jesshope and W.R. Moore, eds,

UNIVERSITY COLLEGE LIBRARY CARDIFF

Proc. 1st International Workshop on Wafer Scale Integration, University of Southampton.

Evans, R.A., J.V. McCanny and K.W. Wood (1986). 'Wafer scale integration based on self-organisation', in C.R. Jesshope and W.R. Moore, eds, *Wafer Scale Integration*, pp. 101–12. Adam Hilger, Bristol.

Ferris-Prabhu, A.V., L.D. Smith, H.A. Bonges and J.K. Paulsen (1987). 'Radial yield variations in semiconductor wafers', *IEEE Circuits and Devices Magazine*, Mar. pp. 42–7.

Finn, S. (1983). 'Lvis: a VLSI transformation system', MSc thesis, Oxford University.

Finnila, C.A. and H.H. Love (1977). 'The associative linear array processor', *IEEE Trans. Computers*, Vol. C-26(2), 112–25.

Fisher, A.L., H.T. Kung and K. Sarocky (1985). 'Experience with the CMU programmable systolic chip', in P. Antognetti, F. Anceau and J. Vuillemin, eds, *Microarchitecture of VLSI Computers*, pp. 209–22. Dordrecht Publishers.

Flynn, M.J. (1972). 'Some computer organisations and their effectiveness', *IEEE Trans. Comp.*, Vol. C-21(9), 948–60.

Foster, C.C. (1976). *Content Addressable Parallel Processors*, Van Nostrand Reinhold, New York.

French, E.F. and H.W. Glaser (1983). 'Tuki, a data flow processor', *Computer Architecture News*, Vol. 11(1), 12–18.

Fried, J. (1986a). 'Automatic partitioning for yield enhancement', in C.R. Jesshope and W.R. Moore, eds, *Wafer Scale Integration*, pp. 125–36. Adam Hilger, Bristol.

Fried, J. (1986b). 'Status of a rule-based partitioning tool', in G. Saucier and J. Trilhe, eds, *Wafer Scale Integration*, pp. 223–36. North-Holland, Amsterdam.

Fried, J. (1986c). 'An analysis of power and clock distribution for WSI systems', in G. Saucier and J. Trilhe, eds, *Wafer Scale Integration*, pp. 127–42. North-Holland, Amsterdam.

Gachet, P., P. Quinton and P. Frison (1986). 'Diastol: a systolic design tool with multiple hardware design style capabilities', in G. Saucier and J. Trilhe, eds, *Wafer Scale Integration*, pp. 237–52. North-Holland, Amsterdam.

Genestier, P., C. Jay and G. Saucier (1986). 'A reconfigurable microprocessor for wafer scale integration', in G. Saucier and J. Trilhe, eds, *Wafer Scale Integration*, pp. 13–30. North-Holland, Amsterdam.

Gilman, L. and A.J. Rose (1984). *APL: an interactive approach*, 2nd edn. John Wiley, New York.

Girard, P., F.M. Roche and B. Pistoulet (1986). 'Electron beam effects on VLSI MOS: conditions for testing and reconfiguration', in G. Saucier and J. Trilhe, eds, *Wafer Scale Integration*, pp. 301–10. North-Holland, Amsterdam.

Glaser, H.W., C.L. Hankin and D.R. Till (1984). *Principles of Functional Programming*, Prentice Hall International, Hemel Hempstead.

Goldberg, B. and P. Hudak (1985). 'Serial combinators: optimal grains of parallelism', in J.P. Jouannaud, ed., *Functional Programming Languages and Computer Architecture*, *Lecture Notes in Computer Science* Vol. 201, pp. 382–99. Springer Verlag, Berlin.

Gordon, G. (1978). *System Simulation*, 2nd edn., Prentice Hall, Inc., Englewood Cliffs, NJ.

Gordon, M.J.C. (1986). 'Why higher-order logic is a good formalism for specifying and verifying hardware', in G.A. Milne and P.A. Subrahmanyam, eds, *Formal Methods for VLSI Design*, pp. 153–77. North-Holland, Amsterdam.

Grimsdale, R.L. (1984). 'Run-time support', in F.B. Chambers, D.A. Duce and G.P. Jones, eds, *Distributed Computing*, pp. 239–50. Academic Press, Orlando, Florida.

Gurd, J.R., I. Watson and C.C. Kirkham (1984). 'The Manchester dataflow project', in D.A. Duce, ed., *Distributed Computing Systems Programme*, pp. 270–89. Peter Peregrinius, London.

Hamacher, V.C, Z.G. Vranesic and S.G. Zaky (1984). *Computer Organisation*, 2nd edn,, McGraw-Hill, New York.

Hedge, S.J. and R.M. Lea (1986). 'Intra-module fault-tolerant strategies for the Wasp device', in G. Saucier and J. Trilhe, eds, *Proc. Workshop on Wafer Scale Integration*, LCS-IMAG, Grenoble, France.

Hedlund, K.S., (1986). 'The design of a prototype Wasp machine', in G. Saucier and J. Trilhe, eds, *Wafer Scale Integration*, pp. 89–98. North-Holland, Amsterdam.

Hellyer, H.W. (1971). 'Transistor circuitry for beginners, Part 1', *Practical Wireless*, Vol. 47(6), 507–12.

Higgs, M.J. (1983). 'The implementation of a functional programming language on innovative computer architectures', PhD thesis, University of London.

Hillis, W.D. (1985). *The Connection Machine*, MIT Press, Cambridge, Mass.

Hockney, R.W. and C.R. Jesshope (1981). *Parallel Computers*, Adam Hilger, Bristol.

Hofstadter, D.R. (1980). *Gödel, Esher, Bach: the eternal golden braid*, Penguin, Middlesex.

Hughes, R.J.M. (1982). 'Super-combinatiors: a new implementation method for applicative languages', in *Symp. on Lisp and Functional Prog., ACM*, Aug. pp. 1–10.

Hughes, R.J.M. (1984). *The Design and Implementation of Programming Languages*, Technical Monograph PRG-40, Programming Research Group, Oxford University Computing Laboratory.

Hwang, K. and F.A. Briggs (1985). *Computer Architecture and Parallel Processing*, McGraw-Hill, New York.

IBM (1986). *A Guide to the IBM 4381 Processor*, 3rd edn. ref. GC20-2021-2, IBM, White Plains, New York.

Inmos (1985). *Transputer: Reference Manual*, Inmos, Bristol.

Intel (1979). *MCS 80/85 Family User's Manual*, Intel, Santa Clara.

Jensen, K. and N. Wirth (1975). *Pascal: user manual and report*, Springer Verlag, Berlin.

Jesshope, C.R. and L. Bentley (1986a). 'A low-cost restructuring technique for WSI', in J. Fox, ed., *Proc. Colloquium on Fault Tolerant ICs/Wafer Scale Integration*, pp. 5/1–5/6. Institution of Electrical Engineers, Groups E10 and E3, London.

Jesshope, C.R. and L. Bentley (1986b). 'Techniques for a wafer scale RPA', in G. Saucier and J. Trilhe, eds, *Proc. Workshop on Wafer Scale Integration*, LCS-IMAG, Grenoble, France.

Jesshope, C.R. and W.R. Moore, eds (1985). *Proc. First International Workshop on Wafer Scale Integration*, University of Southampton.

Jesshope, C.R. and W.R. Moore, eds (1986). *Wafer Scale Integration*, Adam Hilger, Bristol.

Johnson, R.R. (1984). 'The significance of wafer scale integration in computer design', *Proc. IEEE ICCD'84: VLSI in Computers*, pp. 101–5.

Johnson, R.R. (1986). 'A cost-effective step towards WSI: M-chips and whip', in A.P. Ambler, ed., *Proc. 3rd Silicon Design Conference*, pp. 477–84. Electronic Design Automation, London.

Johnson, R.W., J.L. Davidson and R.C. Jaeger (1986). 'Silicon-based hybrid wafer scale packaging', in G. Saucier, and J. Trilhe, eds, *Proc. Workshop on Wafer Scale Integration*, session k.1, LCS-IMAG, Grenoble, France.

Johnstone, K.K., P.H.J. Kelly and M.J. Shute (1987). 'Fault and failure tolerance using cellular automata', to be published.

Jones, G. (1985). '*Programming in occam*', Technical Monograph PRG-43, Programming Research Group, Oxford University Computing Laboratory.

Jones, S.R. and R.M. Lea (1986a). 'Interconnection strategies for the Wasp device', in C.R.

Jesshope and W.R. Moore, eds, *Wafer Scale Integration*, pp. 85–91. Adam Hilger, Bristol.

Jones, S.R. and R.M. Lea (1986b). 'Content-addressable memories for WSI associative string processor (Wasp) devices', in G. Saucier, and J. Trilhe, eds, *Wafer Scale Integration*, pp. 115–26. North-Holland, Amsterdam.

Kapp, O., (1957). *The Presentation of Technical Information*, Constable, London.

Katevenis, M.G.H. and M.G. Blatt (1986). 'Switch design for soft-configurable WSI systems', in G. Saucier and J. Trilhe, eds, *Wafer Scale Integration*, pp. 255–70. North-Holland, Amsterdam.

Kelly, P.H.J and M.J. Shute (1986a). 'Cobweb-2: reconfiguration and routing algorithms for a computer architecture implemented in WSI', in J. Fox, ed., *Proc. Colloquium on Fault Tolerant ICs/Wafer Scale Integration*, pp. 7/1–7/4. Institution of Electrical Engineers, Groups E10 and E3, London.

Kelly, P.H.J. and M.J. Shute (1986b). 'Cartesian routing and fault tolerance in a wafer scale multi-computer', in G. Saucier and J. Trilhe, eds, *Proc. Workshop on Wafer Scale Integration*, pp. 291–312. LCS-IMAG, Grenoble, France.

Kennaway, J.R. and M.R. Sleep (1984a). 'The "language first" approach', in F.B. Chambers, D.A. Duce and G.P. Jones, eds, *Distributed Computing*, pp. 111–24. Academic Press, Orlando, Florida.

Kennaway, J.R. and M.R. Sleep (1984b). 'Towards a successor to von Neumann', in F.B. Chambers, D.A. Duce, and G.P. Jones, eds, *Distributed Computing*, pp. 125–38. Academic Press, Orlando, Florida.

Kernighan, B.W., and D.M. Ritchie (1978). *The C Programming Language*, Prentice Hall Inc., Englewood Cliffs, NJ.

Komonytsky, D. (1983). 'Synthesis of techniques creates complete system self-test', *Electronics*, Mar. pp. 110–15.

Kreyszig, E. (1972). *Advanced Engineering Mathematics*, 3rd edn., John Wiley, New York.

Kung, H.T. (1982). 'Why systolic architectures?' *IEEE Computer*, Jan, pp. 37–46.

Kung, H.T. and C.E. Leiserson (1980). 'Algorithms for VLSI processor arrays', in C. Mead and L. Conway, eds, *Introduction to VLSI Systems*, pp. 271–92. Addison-Wesley, Reading, Mass.

Kung, S.Y. (1987). 'VLSI array processors', in Moore, W.R., A.P.H. McCabe and R. Urquhart, eds, *Systolic Arrays*, pp. 7–24. Adam Hilger, Bristol.

Landin, P.J. (1964). 'The mechanical evaluation of expressions', *Computer Journal*, Vol. 6(4), 308–20.

Landman, B.S. and R.L. Russo (1971). 'On a pin versus block relationship for partitions of logic graphs', *IEEE Trans. Computers*, Vol. C-20(12), 1469–79.

Lea, R.M. (1986a). 'WASP: a WSI associative string processor for structured data processing', in C.R. Jesshope and W.R. Moore, eds, *Wafer Scale Integration*, pp. 140–7. Adam Hilger, Bristol.

Lea, R.M. (1986b). 'WSI: what a stimulating idea!', in A.P. Ambler, ed., *Proc. 3rd Silicon Design Conference*, pp. 135–48. Electronic Design Automation, London.

Lea, R.M. (1987). '*Proc. Workshop on Wafer Scale Integration*', Brunel University, Middlesex.

Lea, R.M. and M. Streetharan, (1979). 'WSI distributed logic memories', in *Caltech Conference on VLSI*, Jan. pp. 187–97.

Leighton T. and C.E. Leiserson (1986). 'A survey of algorithms for integrating wafer scale systolic arrays', in G. Saucier and J. Trilhe, eds, *Wafer Scale Integration*, pp. 177–96. North-Holland, Amsterdam.

Lewin, D. (1985). *Design of Logic Systems*, Van Nostrand Reinhold, New York.

Magó, G.A. (1980). 'A cellular computer architecture for functional programming', *Compcon*, Spring, pp. 179–87.

Manning, F.B. (1977). 'An approach to highly integrated, computer-maintained cellular arrays', *IEEE Trans. Computers*, Vol. C-26(6).

Maunder, C. (1985). 'Built-in test', *Eclectronics and Power*, Vol. 31(3), 204–8. IEE, London.

Mavor, J., M.A. Jack and P.B. Denyer (1983). *Introduction to MOS LSI Design*, Addison-Wesley, Reading, Mass.

McBurney, D. and M.R. Sleep (1986). 'Transputer-based experiments with the Zapp architecture', internal report, SYS-C86-10, University of East Anglia.

McGillis, (1983). 'Lithography', in S.M. Sze, ed., *VLSI Technology*, pp. 267–302. McGraw-Hill, New York.

McKirdy, R.D. and R.M. Lea (1986). 'Physical design issues for WSI', in G. Saucier and J. Trilhe, eds, *Wafer Scale Integration*, pp. 311–20. North-Holland, Amsterdam.

Mead, C. and L. Conway (1980). *Introduction to VLSI Systems*, Addison-Wesley, Reading, Mass.

Minsky, M.L. (1967). *Computation: Finite and Infinite Machines*, Prentice Hall Inc., Englewood Cliffs, NJ.

Monro, D.M. (1982). *Fortran 77*, Edward Arnold, London.

Moore, W.R. (1986a). 'A critical review of fault-tolerant chips and WSI', in C.R. Jesshope and W.R. Moore, eds, *Wafer Scale Integration*, pp. 1–8. Adam Hilger, Bristol.

Moore, W.R. (1986b). 'Comparison of techniques for configuring 2-D arrays on WSI circuits', in G. Saucier and J. Trilhe, eds, *Proc. Workshop on Wafer Scale Integration*, LCS-IMAG, Grenoble, France.

Moore, W.R. (1986c). 'A review of fault tolerant techniques for the enhancement of integrated circuit yield', *Proc. IEEE*, Vol. 74(5), 684–98.

Moore, W.R., A.P.H. McCabe and V. Bawa (1986). 'Fault-tolerance in a large bit-level systolic array', in C.R. Jesshope and W.R. Moore, eds, *Wafer Scale Integration*, pp. 259–72. Adam Hilger, Bristol.

Moore, W.R., A.P.H. McCabe and R. Urquhart, eds, (1987). *Systolic Arrays*, Adam Hilger, Bristol.

Myers, G.J. (1982). *Advances in Computer Architecture*, 2nd edn. John Wiley, New York.

Negrini, R. and R. Stefanelli (1986). 'Comparative evaluation of space and time redundancy approaches', in G. Saucier and J. Trilhe, eds, *Wafer Scale Integration*, pp. 207–22. North-Holland, Amsterdam.

Nicolas, G. (1986). 'Technical and economical aspect of laser repair for WSI memory', in G. Saucier and J. Trilhe, eds, *Wafer Scale Integration*, pp. 271–80. North-Holland, Amsterdam.

Oppenheim, A.V. and R.W. Schafer (1975). *Digital Signal Processing*, Prentice-Hall Inc, Englewood Cliffs, NJ.

Osmon, P.E. (1978). 'The clean architecture computer', internal paper, Westfield College, University of London.

Parkin, A. (1982). *Cobol for Students*, 2nd edn, Edward Arnold, Baltimore, Maryland.

Peterson, W.W. and D.T. Brown (1961). 'Cyclic codes for error detection, *Proc. IRE*, Jan. pp. 228–35.

Peyton Jones, S.L. (1984). 'Directions in functional programming research', in D.A. Duce, ed., *Distributed Computing Systems Programme*, pp. 220–49. Peter Peregrinius, London.

Peyton Jones, S.L. (1987). *The Implementation of Functional Programming Languages*, Prentice Hall International, Hemel Hempstead.

Peyton Jones, S.L., C. Clack, J. Salkild and M. Hardie (1987). 'Grip: a high performance architecture for parallel graph reduction', submitted to *3rd International Conference on Functional Programming and Computer Architecture*, Portland, Oregon.

Pradhan, D.K., ed. (1986). *Fault Tolerant Computing: theory, and techniques*, (2 Vols.), Prentice Hall Inc., Englewood Cliffs, NJ.

Raffel, J.I. (1986). 'The RVLSI approach to wafer scale integration', in C.R. Jesshope and W.R. Moore, eds, *Wafer Scale Integration*, pp. 199–203. Adam Hilger, Bristol.

Ramacher, U. (1987). 'A cost orientated redundancy model for defect-tolerant VLSI/WSI systems', in *Proc. Workshop on Designing for Yield*, Oxford University.

Randell, B. (1982). *The Origins of Digital Computers*, 3rd edn. Springer Verlag, Berlin.

Rosenberg, A.L. (1986). 'Graph-theoretic approaches to fault-tolerant WSI processor arrays', in C.R. Jesshope and W.R. Moore, eds, *Wafer Scale Integration*, pp. 10–23. Adam Hilger, Bristol.

Russell, G., D.J. Kinniment, E.G. Chester and M.R. McLauchlan (1985). *CAD for VLSI*, Van Nostrand Reinhold, New York.

Sack, K.A., R.C. Lyman, and G.T. Chang (1964). 'Evolution of the concept of a computer on a slice', *Proc. IEEE*, Vol. 52, 1713–20.

Saucier, G. and J. Trilhe, eds (1986a). *Proc. IFIP Workshop on Wafer Scale Integration*, LCS-IMAG, Grenoble, France.

Saucier, G. and J. Trilhe, eds (1986b). *Wafer Scale Integration*, North-Holland, Amsterdam.

Seidel, T.E. (1983). 'Ion implantation', in S.M. Sze, ed., *VLSI Technology*, pp. 219–66. McGraw-Hill, New York.

Seitz, C.L. (1980). 'System timing', in C. Mead and L. Conway, eds, *Introduction to VLSI Systems*, pp. 218–62. Addison-Wesley, Reading, Mass.

Sheeran, M. (1984). *μFP, An Algebraic VLSI Design Language*, Technical Monograph PRG-39, Programming Research Group, Oxford University Computing Laboratory.

Sheeran, M. (1985). 'Designing regular array architectures using higher order functions', in J.P. Jouannaud, ed., *Functional Programming Languages and Computer Architecture, Lecture Notes in Computer Science* Vol. 201, pp. 220–37. Springer-Verlag, Berlin.

Shute, M.J. and P.E. Osmon (1986). 'Cobweb: a reduction architecture', in C.R. Jesshope, and W.R. Moore, eds, *Wafer Scale Integration*, pp. 169–78. Adam Hilger, Bristol.

Simons, G.L. (1983). *Towards Fifth-generation Computers*, National Computing Centre, Manchester.

Sleep, M.R. and F.W. Burton (1981). 'Towards a zero assignment parallel processor', *Proc. IEEE*, pp. 80–5.

Sleep, M.R. and J.R. Kennaway (1984). 'The zero assignment parallel processor (Zapp) project', in D.A. Duce, ed., *Distributed Computing Systems Programme*, pp. 250–69. Peter Peregrinius, London.

Spencer, T.H. and J. Savir (1984). 'Layout influences testability', *Proc. IEEE ICCD'84: VLSI in computers*, pp. 291–5.

Stapper, C.H. (1985). 'The effects of wafer to wafer defect density variations on integrated circuit defect and fault distributions', *IBM J. Res. Develop*, Vol. 29(1), 87–97.

Stapper, C.H. and R.J. Rosner (1982). 'A simple method for modeling VLSI yields', *Solid State Electronics*, Vol. 25(6), 487–9.

Steele Jr, G.L. and G.J. Sussman (1980). 'Design of a Lisp-based microprocessor', *CACM*, Vol. 23(11), 628–45.

Steidel, C.A. (1983). 'Assembly techniques and packaging', in S.M. Sze, ed., *VLSI Technology*, pp. 551–98. McGraw-Hill, New York.

Stevens, K. (1984). 'Re: self timed vs synchronous, let's discuss', *UUCP Network News*, net.1si, Message-ID: <3019@utah-cs.UUCP>, 06 Sep.

Stewart, A.K.J. and G.E. Dixon (1986). 'Fault tolerant parameterised memory', in J. Fox, ed., *Proc. Colloquium on Fault Tolerant ICs/Wafer Scale Integration*, pp. 3/1–3/2. Institution of Electrical Engineers, Groups E10 and E3, London.

Straubs, R.V. (1980). *N.mPc: ISP' User's Manual*, Case Western Reserve University, Cleveland, Ohio.

Sumerling, G.W. (1986). 'Cost models for ULSI and WSI', unpublished paper.

Sumerling, G.W., G.E. Dixon and A.K.J. Stewart (1986a). 'An assessment of non-regular cell based architecture for ULSI and WSI', in G. Saucier and J. Trilhe, eds, *Wafer Scale Integration*, pp. 3–12. North-Holland, Amsterdam.

Sumerling, G.W., G.E. Dixon and A.K.J. Stewart (1986b). 'Achieving high complexity ULSI and WSI application specific integrated circuits', in A.P. Ambler, ed., *Proc. 3rd Silicon Design Conference*, pp. 149–56. Electronic Design Automation, London.

Sutherland, I.E. and C.A. Mead (1977). 'Microelectronics and computer science', *Scientific American*, Vol. 237(3), 210–28.

Sze, S.M., ed. (1983). *VLSI Technology*, McGraw-Hill, New York.

Tamir, Y. and C.H. Séquin (1984). 'Reducing common mode failures in duplicate modules', *Proc. IEEE ICCD'84: VLSI in computers*, pp. 302–12.

Thurber, K.J. (1976). '*Large Scale Computer Architecture*', Hayden, Rochelle Park, NJ.

Touretzky, D.S. (1984). *Lisp: A Gentle Introduction to Symbolic Computation*, Harper & Row, New York.

Treleaven, P.C., D.R. Brownbridge and R.P. Hopkins (1982). 'Data-driven and demand-driven computer architectures', *Computer Surveys*, Vol. 14(1), 93–143.

Turner, D.A. (1979). 'A new implementation technique for applicative languages', *Software Practice and Experience*, Vol. 9, 31–49.

Turner, D.A. (1985). 'Miranda: a non-strict functional language with polymorphic types', in J.P. Jouannaud, ed., *Functional Programming Languages and Computer Architecture*, *Lecture Notes in Computer Science* Vol. 201, pp. 1–16. Springer Verlag, Berlin.

Ullman, J.D. (1984). *Computational Aspects of VLSI*, Computer Science Press, Rockville, Maryland.

Val, C. (1986). 'Wafer scale integration (WSI) packaging', in G. Saucier and J. Trilhe, eds, *Wafer Scale Integration*, pp. 321–44. North-Holland, Amsterdam.

Vladimirescu, A., A.R. Newton and D.O. Pederson (1980). *Spice Version 2G.0 User's Guide*, University of California, Berkeley.

Wadsack, R.L. (1978). 'Fault coverage in digital integrated circuits', *Bell Sys. Tech. J.*, Vol. 57(5), 1475–88.

Wand, I.C. and A.J. Wellings (1984). 'Programming languages', in F.B. Chambers, D.A. Duce and G.P. Jones, eds, *Distributed Computing*, pp. 201–15. Academic Press, Orlando, Florida.

Warren, K.D., M.B.E. Abdelrazik, R.D. McKirdy and R.M. Lea (1986). 'A power distribution strategy for WSI', in C.R. Jesshope and W.R. Moore, eds, *Wafer Scale Integration*, pp. 54–61. Adam Hilger, Bristol.

Waters, D.G.P. (1986). 'Test planning for reconfigurable circuits', in G. Saucier and J. Trilhe, eds, *Wafer Scale Integration*, pp. 157–68. North-Holland, Amsterdam.

Watson, I. and J. Gurd (1982). 'A practical data flow computer', *IEEE Computer*, Feb., pp. 51–7.

Welcome, M.L. and S.K. Skedzielewski (1985). 'Dataflow graph optimisation in IF1', in J.P. Jouannaud, ed., *Functional Programming Languages and Computer Architecture*, *Lecture Notes in Computer Science* Vol. 201, pp. 17–34. Springer Verlag, Berlin.

Welsh, J. and A. Hay (1986). *A Model Implementation of Standard Pascal*, Prentice Hall International, Hemel Hempstead.

Werner, J. (1982). 'The silicon compiler: panacea, wishful thinking, or old hat?', *VLSI Design*, Oct., pp. 46–52.

Williams, T.W. and N.C. Brown (1981). 'Defect level as a function of fault coverage', *IEEE Trans. Computers*. Vol. C-30(12), 987–8.

Wilson, I.R. and A.M. Addyman (1982). *A Practical Introduction to Pascal: with BS6192*, 2nd edn. Macmillan, London.

Winston, P.H. and B.K.P. Horn (1981). *Lisp*, Addison-Wesley, Reading, Mass.

Yassaie, H. (1986). *IMS A100*, Notes 1 to 4. Inmos, Bristol.

Yuba, T. and H. Kashiwagi (1987). 'The Japanese national project for new generation supercomputing systems', in *Parallel Computing*, Vol. 4(1), 1–16. North-Holland, Amsterdam.

INDEX

UNIVERSITY COLLEGE LIBRARY CARDIFF